TRANSGENDER:
one shade of grey

The legal consequences for man & woman,
schools, sport, politics, democracy

Patrick J Byrne

Guest chapters by
Professor John Whitehall &
Lane Anderson (a pseudonym)

Published by Wilkinson Publishing Pty Ltd
ACN 006 042 173
Level 4, 2 Collins Street
Melbourne, Vic 3000
Ph: 03 9654 5446

www.wilkinsonpublishing.com.au

Copyright © 2018 Patrick J Byrne

All rights reserved. No part of this publication may be reproduced, stored in a retrieval system or transmitted in any form by any means without the prior permission of the copyright owner. Enquiries should be made to the publisher.

Every effort has been made to ensure that this book is free from error or omissions. However, the Publisher, the Author, the Editor or their respective employees or agents, shall not accept responsibility for injury, loss or damage occasioned to any person acting or refraining from action as a result of material in this book whether or not such injury, loss or damage is in any way due to any negligent act or omission, breach of duty or default on the part of the Publisher, the Author, the Editor, or their respective employees or agents.

A catalogue record for this book is available from the National Library of Australia

Planned date of publication: 09-2018
Title: Transgender: one shade of grey.
The legal consequences for man & woman, schools, sport, politics, democracy.
ISBN(s): 978192564254 : Printed - Paperback

Printed by Brougham Press.
Designed by Film Shot Graphics

ACKNOWLEDGEMENTS

I would like to thank the numerous lawyers, politicians, medical professionals, journalists, students, parents, friends and reviewers whose pertinent questions helped shape this book.

Recently, a friend commented that writing a book is a "solitary and selfish affair". I would particularly like to thank my colleagues and family who have shown great patience over the course of this project.

Finally, my special thanks to the proofreaders without whom this book would not have eventuated.

ABOUT THE AUTHORS

Patrick J Byrne BA, BTheol, is a National President of the National Civic Council. He has been a long-time writer and written on social, political, economic and cultural issues for the NCC magazine, News Weekly. He has researched transgenderism in relation to current identity politics. His organisation, the National Civic Council, was formed, and led for many years, by the late BA Santamaria (1915-1998).

Dr John Whitehall is Professor of Paediatrics at Western Sydney University. His 50-year career began at Sydney University, continued through developing countries and western Sydney as a general paediatrician, then focused on neonatology before coming to WSU. For 15 years, he was Director of Neonatal Intensive Care in Townsville, North Queensland, which included antenatal diagnosis, resuscitation, and management and transportation of premature, dysmorphic and sick neonates, many of whom were Indigenous. In Townsville, he was deeply involved in the establishment of the medical school at James Cook University and, for 20 years, taught modules of Tropical Paediatrics in the Masters program in the School of Public Health. In recent years, he has also worked as a consultant physician in PNG, Sri Lanka and Madagascar. Currently, he teaches, leads research and has duties in general paediatrics. He has spent recent years researching the medical and psychological aspects of gender transitioning, particularly in children.

Lane Anderson (a pseudonym) is a practising psychotherapist in North America who has worked extensively with "trans teens" and their families. She shares her clinical insights into her clients, adolescent psychology, and the impact of the transgender phenomenon on society.

CONTENTS

Acknowledgements	iii
About the authors	iv
Prologue	1
Two world views: overview of this book	7

    1.1   Stories

    1.2   The transgender world view: one shade of grey

    1.3   Confusion over the meaningof transgender

    1.4   The purpose of this book

    1.5   The structure of this book

Part A	23
Transgender world view in language, social sciences and philosophy	23
Transgender world view: the new language of human identity	25

    2.1   Ideologies have their own language

    2.2   The language of individual gender identities

            2.2.1   Australian sex survey

            2.2.2   Facebook's 58 gender identities

            2.2.3   Safe Schools' list of gender identities and sexual orientations

    2.3   Gender identity in laws redefining the human person

    2.4   From diversity to gender-neutral language

    2.5   The transgender language paradox

The biological world view: sex matters	33

    3.1   Sex creates life

    3.2   Defining sex: biological differences between male and female

    3.3   Sex is political

    3.4   The state's interest in sex, marriage and family

    3.5   Sex defines rights, responsibilities, privileges, protections and access to services

    3.6   Conclusion

Transgender: from theory to ideology	41

    4.1   Introduction

Contents

- 4.2 Transgender: a social construct redefining sex
- 4.3 Defining transgender and queer theories
- 4.4 Preliminary critique of transgenderism
- 4.5 Australia – a case study in transgender laws
- 4.6 Conclusion

Transgenderism: conflating intersex and transsexuals into non-binary gender   53

- 5.1 Introduction
- 5.2 Intersex or disorder of sexual development (DSD)
  - 5.2.1 Defining intersex
  - 5.2.2 How intersex people identify
  - 5.2.3 Wrongly conflating DSD/Intersex with transgender
  - 5.2.4 Recognition of intersex/DSD in law
- 5.3 Laws and courts redefining men as women and women as men
  - 5.3.1 Medical transitioning to change sex on birth certificates
  - 5.3.2 Social transitioning to change sex on birth certificates
  - 5.3.3 Anti-discrimination and equal opportunity laws recognising transsexuals
  - 5.3.4 Discussion of social transitioning
- 5.4 Conclusion

The ambiguity of gender identity and gender orientation   75

- 6.1 Introduction
- 6.2 The fluidity of gender identity
  - 6.2.1 Defining gender identity
  - 6.2.2 The ambiguity of gender identity
  - 6.2.3 Are transsexual and intersex people evidence of a third sex or of non-binary gender identities?
  - 6.2.4 Are gender identities really personality traits?
  - 6.2.5 Does gender identity make sex meaningless?
  - 6.2.6 The transgender conundrum
  - 6.2.7 Does transgender confuse the fictional with the real?
  - 6.2.8 The failure to coherently define gender identity
  - 6.2.9 Subjective gender identity versus objective biological sex
  - 6.2.10 How many people identify as transgender?
  - 6.2.11 Young people transitioning, desisting and detransitioning
  - 6.2.12 Summarising gender identity

6.3 Sexual orientation and "gender orientation"
    6.3.1 Defining sexual orientation and "gender orientation"
    6.3.2 What's ascertainable and what's ambiguous?

6.4 Conclusion: Writing "personality traits" into law

Transgenderism: body-self dualism versus dynamic unity view of the mind and body   103

7.1 Introduction

7.2 Body-self dualism

7.3 Dynamic unity

7.4 The consequences of body-self dualism
    7.4.1 Body dysmorphic disorder (BDD)
    7.4.2 Body integrity identity disorder (BIID)
    7.4.3 Anorexia nervosa
    7.4.4 Gender dysphoria

7.5 Confusion over conversion versus affirmation therapies

7.6 Conclusion

Part B   113

Australia: writing the transgender world view into laws   113

Transgendering the federal *Sex Discrimination Act 1984*   117

8.1 Introduction

8.2 The Sex Discrimination Act 1984
    8.2.1 Redefining objects of the Sex Discrimination Act
    8.2.2 Redefining men and women as fluid gender

8.3 Guidelines implementing the SDA amendments

8.4 Further evidence of the SDA and Guidelines dissolving biological sex, man and woman

8.5 Cases where "gender identity" makes "sex" and "equality" ambiguous

8.6 Creating wide conflicts

8.7 Does gender identity make heterosexual, gay, lesbian and bisexual ambiguous?

8.8 AHRC and Law Council of Australia supports these changes

8.9 Legal paradox

8.10 State and territory anti-discrimination laws and identity documents

8.11 Conclusion

Contents

Transgendering birth certificates — 145

- 9.1 Introduction
- 9.2 Key sex identifiers of the human person
- 9.3 Australian Human Rights Commission advocates transgender recognition on birth certificates
- 9.4 ACT recognises non-binary on birth certificates
- 9.5 South Australia legalises transgender recognition on birth certificates
- 9.6 Are Male and Female only cisgender terms on SA and ACT birth registration forms?
- 9.7 Failed attempt to change birth certificates in Victoria
- 9.8 Tasmanian Equal Opportunity Commission options paper for transgender birth certificates
- 9.9 Conclusion

Legalising transgender marriage — 165

- 10.1 No debate over transgender marriage
- 10.2 The ABS survey on transgender marriage
- 10.3 Recognising transgenders on marriage forms
- 10.4 The ambiguity of unlimited forms of transgender marriage
- 10.5 Anti-discrimination laws protecting transgender marriage
- 10.6 Conclusion: Legal uncertainty and conflicts

The road ahead — 182

- 11.1 Introduction
- 11.2 The AHRC's "Road map for Inclusion"
- 11.3 Labor Party transgender policy commitments
- 11.4 Conclusion

PART C — 187

Consequences of the transgender world view changing the culture — 187

Transgendersim: from theory to law to education — 189

- 12.1 Introduction
- 12.2 New policies on access to school toilets, showers, change rooms
- 12.3 Applying the transgender world view to schools
- 12.4 How many children are transgender, experiencing gender dysphoria?
- 12.5 Conflict of rights

Contents

- 12.6 Child agency: blurring the lines between child and adult
- 12.7 What happened to sex?
- 12.8 Issues for educators
- 12.9 Conclusion

Safe Schools Coalition Victoria: a case study of transgenderism in schools 203

- 13.1 Introduction
- 13.2 Focus on transgenderism and sexuality
- 13.3 Connecting students with LGBTQ organisations
- 13.4 Opposing the "heteronormative"
- 13.5 Safe Schools and child agency
- 13.6 Concern at children transitioning
- 13.7 Other transgenderism school programs
- 13.8 Conclusion

Children transitioning: childhood gender dysphoria 219

- 14.1 Introduction
- 14.2 How common is childhood gender dysphoria?
- 14.3 Are there any other clinical problems associated with gender dysphoria?
- 14.4 Is there an inherent risk of self-harm and suicide?
- 14.5 What are the personality characteristics of parents bringing children to gender dysphoria clinics?
- 14.6 What options are there for treatment of children with gender dysphoria?
- 14.7 What does the Dutch Protocol involve?
- 14.8 What problems may a child encounter on the Dutch pathway?
- 14.9 Is there evidence the Dutch Protocol is beneficial?
- 14.10 Is anything else at risk?
  - 14.10.1 What does the law have to say in North America?
  - 14.10.2 What does the law have to say in Australia?
- 14.11 What does the future hold?

Exiles in their own flesh: a psychotherapist speaks 261

Abolishing women's safe spaces 268

- 16.1 Introduction
- 16.2 US midwives replace "pregnant woman" with "pregnant person"

Contents

    16.3   Australian midwives reject "person-centred" care

    16.4   US restroom and change room privacy conflicts

    16.5   Australian toilet controversies

    16.6   Medical trials and treatments according to sex-based biology

    16.7   Women's prisons

    16.8   Women's services, safe spaces, affirmative action

    16.9   Erasing female, feminism, gay, lesbian

    16.10 Conclusion

Transgendering women's sports   288

    17.1   Transgender male-to-females in female sports

    17.2   How do male and female bodies differ?

    17.3   Evolving IAAF and Olympic policies on eligibility for women's competitions

    17.4   Significance of testosterone

    17.5   Australian sporting policies

    17.6   Wider female-transgender conflicts

    17.7   Conclusion

Can conflicted biological versus transgender rights be resolved?   306

    18.1   Conflicted world views, conflicted solutions

    18.2   Three forms of conflicts

    18.3   Other areas of conflict

    18.4   Solution: write definitions of "man", "woman" and "sex" into law and tolerate transgenderism in culture

    18.5   Transgenderism's objections to recognising the biological world view in law

    18.6   Conclusion

Transgenderism laws undermining a tolerant democracy   327

    19.1   Evolution of tolerant democracies

    19.2   Man, woman and beliefs recognised in the UDHR and ICCPR

    19.3   Gender identity as a new state-established "belief"

    19.4   Conclusion

Conclusion: two protections for rights, liberties and freedoms   333

    20.1   Introduction

    20.2   Living with different views of marriage

20.3	Alleviating conflicts between the biological and transgender world views	
20.4	Conclusion	

Postscript 339

21.1	Universal Declaration of Human Rights	
21.2	Foucault dissents	
21.3	Rights: only for the most powerful?	
21.4	Conclusion	

Definitions and terms 345

PROLOGUE

This textbook and commentary is on the political ideology of transgenderism. It explains *how* transgender laws impact on society, many people have asked me *why* this phenomenon is happening? This prologue offers some thoughts and insights.

Laws protecting a person's gender identity sit alongside other laws protecting other aspects of human identity – age, ethnicity, sex, sexual orientation, race, disability and membership of a minority, political affiliation, economic status, religion, etc. These are some of the intersecting components of identity politics, the attributes by which some people regard themselves as disadvantaged. Whereas human attributes like age, sex and race are objectively determined, others like gender identity and religion are personal and thus subjective.

Some people have suggested that identity politics represents the search for meaning in an atomised society where many fundamental family, economic and social relationships that once offered them a purpose to their existence are gradually imploding. It is an attempt to fill a void; an attempt to find one's identity through attributes like race, ethnicity or other forms of minority status.

A way to think about how we define our own identity is to consider you are at a party and meet someone for the first time. Typically, conversations start and progress around questions like: What's your name? What do you do, that is, what is your work? Where did you go to school/university? What do your parents do? What about your brothers and sisters? Are you married? Do you have kids? Where did you go to school? Where do you live? Are you a secular or religious person?

Such conversations revolve around the people and things that connect us and that shape people's lives – their families, friends, work and other meaningful relationships and activities.

For many XYZ and millennial people, the answers to these questions are difficult, if not painful.

"Painful" refers, in part, to the high rates of depression, particularly among young people. About 30 years ago, a university psychology lecturer described to me how the life-time incidence of depression and anxiety was very low for people in the 1950s but, for those born since 1970, the rates were far higher. Today, the Black Dog Institute estimates that one-in-seven Australians will experience depression in their life-time, 40 per cent will experience mental illness in their lifetime and, in any one year, 20 per cent of the population has a mental illness.[1]

I asked this psychologist, "But people in the 1950s had been through two brutal world wars and the Great Depression, how can it be that mental illness and depression is far higher for later generations who live in an era of peace and rising prosperity?" He replied, saying that, for earlier generations, supporting social structures were far stronger. Families were larger and, in the times before modern transportation made people mobile, communities were more cohesive. In those times, there were more supports available for a person who was "down". Family (parents and multiple siblings), extended family (grandparents, aunts, uncles, and numerous cousins) and friends helped prevent a person spiralling into depression, anxiety and other forms of mental illness.

Today, for many, this social fabric has unravelled. Social structures, that once would have supported them in times of stress, are no longer available. I know of psychiatrists who say, "For many patients, I can only treat them medically. They have no one to support them, no one".

The undoing of this community fabric has many causes. Some elements include the great destabilisation of societies by two world wars and rapid economic and technological change such as has never been seen before in history, the '60s cultural revolution and the sexualisation of society.

Consider the world wars. War economies mobilised whole populations. Killing was on an industrial scale and a significant proportion of the world's population became victims. Men went to war for many years. Millions of girlfriends and wives either lost their loved ones, or came to the conclusion that they would never see them again. For tens of millions, their families were torn apart.

Consider changes to the structure of families over the past three or four generations. Only a few generations ago it was common for parents to have four children. If those four children married and had four children, and these marriages were into families of four children, then a third-generation child would have, from the mother and father bloodlines, three siblings, 12 aunts/uncles and 24 cousins.

If these families were all stable, which was common, and, given that many extended families lived in local communities, this extensive family network formed strong concentric rings of relationships that helped to profoundly define a person's identity and provided an extensive psychological and economic support network to help any family member in need. A child with many siblings and relatives can define their place in the world, find self-worth and learn resilience from many close role models and from the rough and tumble of such close relationships. Close blood relationships, tight and stable local communities and long-term friendships gave meaning and identity to a person.

In contrast, today, if a young person is a third generation only child, then this person has no siblings, cousins, aunts or uncles, and only two parents and four grandparents to draw on if they need support in times of psychological or material needs. If their parent and/or grandparent were sole parents, their support network is even smaller. If their identity is no longer the product of such close relationships, then how do they find, define, and construct their identity? If it is not from the normal human experience, is it so surprising that they turn to identity politics to fill the void?

Economic changes have altered the nature of work, at least for many people. The problem of unemployment and part-time and intermittent contract work plagues a large number of young people. Australia's McCrindle research shows that the average 18 year old leaving school and working until 75 will have five changes of career and 17 different employers.[2] The uncertainty this creates to having a reliable income stream compounds the problem of finding a partner and buying a home.

Having five changes of career is daunting for many young people. Having 17 changes of job makes it difficult to form long-term work friendships, especially if this involves living away from the local community where a person spent their childhood, and far from family.

Sexualisation of society by advertising, movies, television programs and, more recently, the tsunami of pornography on the internet and social media, is not only confronting to many young people but disrupts normal sexual relationships and, for some, sexual identity.

Transgenderism, the idea that a person's "gender identity" may differ from their birth/biological sex and that a person can change their gender accordingly, is being taught to children and young people in kindergartens and schools through picture books such as *The Gender Fairy* for kindergarten and lower primary and the Safe Schools Coalition resources (see Chapter 13). The "normalisation" of transgender has distorted the reality of biological sex for many young people to the point that transgender is a new "norm".

Then there are the ideologues campaigning for transgender ideology to be written into law. They have gone largely unchallenged in the universities, (where society's elites are trained), in human rights and trans lobby organisations. A few years ago, *Spiked* editor Brendan O'Neill wrote about how these "post-traditional, relativistic elites" have adopted the LGBTIQ agenda to "both subtly denigrate older values and also impose a set of whole new values" on society.[3]

While O'Neill called it the weaponisation of homosexuality and same-sex marriage, I argue in this book that his description fittingly describes the weaponisation of transgender ideology by political, professional and academic elites. Appropriating his words to transgenderism, this ideology is "fundamentally about eradicating old moral values and enforcing new ones … [I]t constantly verges on being coercive, expressing a hostility towards its opponents that tends to treat them, not simply as wrong or pesky, but as actual blocks, as 'ideological enemies', to the elite's attempted enforcement of a new moral outlook".

O'Neill says they are hostile "to the straight world – which means not just people who are sexually straight, but also so-called straight culture and straight values, straightlacedness itself, ways of life that are based on commitment, privacy, familial sovereignty, things that tend to be viewed by the modern cultural clerisy as outdated or, worse, dangerous and destructive".

He says the speedy and strikingly authoritarian way governments have adopted transgenderism is because many elites "recognise in it the opportunity to push further their instinctive hostility towards traditional communal and familial ideals that to a large extent exist outside of the purview of the state".

Understanding this impulse behind the feverish adoption of this ideology and laws is key to understanding what makes this new movement so "illiberal and intolerant". It makes "criminals" of those who criticise and resist laws imposing the transgender world view on society.[4]

For these elites, their ultimate purpose is to impose the revolutionary transgender world view of human sexuality on the entire society, civil and religious.

Then there is the money being invested in, and made from, the new transgender medical and lifestyle market. As environmental activist and writer Jennifer Bilek[5] has recently revealed, in the United States, "exceedingly rich" billionaires are funding the transgender lobby and various transgender organisations. Pharmaceutical giants and tech companies are backing the project.

Bilek says, "The first gender clinic for children opened in Boston in 2007. In the past ten years, more than 30 clinics for children with purported gender dysphoria have arisen in the United States alone, the largest serving 725 patients.

"Over the past decade, there has been an explosion in transgender medical infrastructure across the United States and the world to 'treat' transgender people. In addition to gender clinics proliferating across the United States, hospital wings are being built for specialized surgeries, and many medical institutions are clamoring to get on board with the new developments …

"Puberty blockers are another growing market. The plastic surgery arm of medicine is staged for an infusion of cash as well as organ transplants … With the medical infrastructure being built, doctors being trained for various surgeries, clinics [are] opening at warp speed…"[6].

Against this powerful array of institutions, against these financial and political forces, how are the vulnerable, particularly children, to resist the transgender push on society? In atomised modern societies, where traditional social support structures have been weakened, how are children struggling with their identity to find direction? How are those who are on the autism spectrum, or psychologically distressed, or suffering psychological illness, or isolated, or bullied at school, or trying to come to grips with their body changes in puberty, to work out sexual identity when the transgender world view is pushed on them from kindergarten to university, by the health professions, by the media and on addictive social media forums?

For a significant proportion of young people in modern societies, the great social disruption over the past century has upended normal expectations about sexuality, relationships, family, friends and work. The things that gave meaning and identity have been denied to many.

Mary Eberstadt asks: "'Who am I?' An illiterate peasant of the Middle Ages was better equipped to answer that question than many people in advanced societies in this century …". Her observations about identity politics provide some explanation for the transgender phenomenon. If we understand that "many people, no matter how well-off or privileged, have been deprived of the most elementary of human connections – we can grasp why 'identity politics' is the headline that just won't go away"[7].

* * * * * * *

Endnotes

1. "Facts & figures about mental health", Black Dog Institute. https://www.blackdoginstitute.org.au/docs/default-source/factsheets/facts_figures.pdf?sfvrsn=8 Accessed 14 July 2018

2. "Job Mobility in Australia", McCrindle research group, 18 June 2014. https://mccrindle.com.au/insights/blog/job-mobility-australia/ Accessed 21 July 2018.

3. Appropriating Brendan O'Neill, "Same-sex marriage: coercion dolled up as civil rights", *Spiked*, 30 April 2014. http://www.spiked-online.com/newsite/article/same-sex-marriage-coercion-dolled-up-as-civil-rights/14967#.VdlqXb4xZjw Accessed 21 July 2018.

4. Ibid.

5. Jennifer Bilek, "Trans ideology awash with big money from big biomed and big pharma", *News Weekly*, 7 April 2018. http://www.newsweekly.com.au/article.php?id=58023&s=SISJhE Accessed 20 July 2018.

6. Ibid. Accessed 21 July 2018.

7. Mary Eberstadt, "The Zealous Faith of Secularism: how the sexual revolution became a dogma", *First Things*, January 2018. https://www.firstthings.com/article/2018/01/the-zealous-faith-of-secularism Accessed 21 July 2018.

CHAPTER 1

TWO WORLD VIEWS: OVERVIEW OF THIS BOOK

1.1 STORIES

In December 2017, a female friend was in the women's change room at a Melbourne swimming pool. The change room is used by women and girls of all ages. A male-to-female transsexual, who had not undergone sex-change surgery, entered the change rooms in the presence of biological women in various stages of undress. My friend said it was a moment of consternation as the biological women present felt their privacy violated. They felt acute embarrassment and loss of a sense of safety. She said, "There were women from various ethnicities in the room – and most of them were changing very modestly and carefully – so it was doubly shocking for them as this person was being rather defiant. In the end, the ladies kind of stared this person out and he lost his nerve". Her concerns were that "if a transsexual person is free to enter women's safe spaces, why can't a voyeuristic man who pretends to be transsexual also enter this space? Why can't a man with a grudge against women enter this space to deliberately embarrass and intimidate women? This encounter was particularly confronting to the women from ethnic backgrounds. This encounter was particularly confronting to the women from ethnic backgrounds. It was a scary experience".

Around the same time, I was at a Sydney Returned Services League (RSL) club for dinner with several friends, including a woman who encountered a male-to-female transsexual in the women's toilets. Startled, my friend called out, "Not happy". She said, "What upset me was the sight of somebody who didn't appear female being in the women's toilet. I'm not talking about the different sort of appearances women may have; rather, someone who doesn't look like a genuine female. It made me instinctively uncomfortable". Her considered response was similar to that of the women at the public swimming pool change rooms – this person may be a transsexual, but what if a vexatious male simply wanted to antagonise and embarrass women by entering female safe spaces, posing as a transsexual?

In 2014, the Midwives Alliance of North America (MANA) replaced the term "pregnant woman" with "pregnant person" and "birthing parent". This was to avoid offending transgenders, particularly female-to-males who become pregnant, and biological men who identify as women.[1]

Women athletes have expressed concern that male-to-female athletes are being permitted to play in female sporting competitions that until now have been restricted to biological women. Males-to-females have been allowed to compete in the Olympics without sex-change surgery.[2]

In 2011, the Tasmanian Education Department called for calm among concerned parents over shared unisex toilets at Burnie Primary School, claiming it was an "anti-bullying" measure. Parents said they had not been consulted.[3] Since then, there have been calls for unisex toilets in all public buildings.[4]

Early in 2017, US President Trump overturned an Obama administration transgender edict. A joint letter from top officials from the Trump Administration's Justice Department and Education Department rejected the Obama administration's order to allow transgender students to use the washrooms of their choice.[5]

Over the last few years, the education departments of New South Wales, Queensland, Victoria and South Australia have issued transgender school policies that require school authorities to allow boys who identify as girls to use the girls' toilets, showers and change rooms, and to play in girls' sports. Similarly, girls identifying as boys are able to choose which facilities they use and the sports in which they play (see Chapter 12.2).

In 2016, the federal government announced it would not extend any further funding to the controversial Safe Schools Coalition Australia program, following a speech in Federal parliament exposing how the program was advocating transgenderism and providing links to explicit webpages. The government had provided $8 million to the program (see Chapter 13.1).

1.2 THE TRANSGENDER WORLD VIEW: ONE SHADE OF GREY

Each of these cases confronts what most people would regard as the normal experience of people being recognised and respected according to their biology, as male or female, men or women, mothers or fathers, grandfathers or grandmothers, as boys or girls. These cases are not one-off events.

Indeed, the world is witnessing an extraordinary contest of ideas over the nature of human sexual identity. The biological understanding of men and women is being challenged by the revolutionary transgender idea that a person can have a gender identity separate from, or in place of, his or her biological sex as recorded at birth.

The biological world view recognises that a person's sex is part of their inherent, immutable, biological hardware. Historically, sex is defined by the binary (two complementary) reproductive functions of men and women. Historically, the terms *man*, *woman* and *sex* have been taken to be self-evident facts that did not require definitions in law.

In the biological world view, sex means *binary* male and female. Binaries are heterosexuals, gays, lesbians, medically transitioned transsexuals (who identify as the opposite to their birth sex) and most intersex people. These people recognise their birth sex as inherent or, in the case of transsexuals and some intersex people, as opposite to their birth sex. All recognise biological sex.

In contrast, the transgender world view is based on a belief that a person can have a gender identity separate from and other than their sex at birth. A person's gender identity is their cultural and social software, based on their feelings about their identity, as manifest by their "outward social markers, including their name, outward appearance, mannerism and dress"[6]. This world view says laws, regulations and codes should recognise and protect a person by their self-defined gender identity, not by their biological sex.

One meaning of gender identity is that a biological man can identify as a woman, and a biological woman can identify as a man. Another meaning is that a person can identify as being on a spectrum of somewhere between 100 per cent male and 100 per cent female. A third meaning is that people can go beyond the idea of male and female altogether and identify with a term like androgynous, or gender queer, or any of a host of other non-binary terms. A fourth meaning is that a person can identify as having no gender; that is, as being genderless. As these characteristics are subjective and individual to each person, they are better categorised as personality traits than as descriptions of sexual identity.

The transgender world view represents *non-binary* persons who self-identify with a gender identity other than their sex at birth; that is, those who don't identify as male or female. This includes people who do not undergo sex-change surgery but who socially identify as transsexuals.

This belief, that a person can have a gender identity other than their biological sex, is based on just one aspect of what it is to be human, a person's sexual identity. This new description of human beings has been given extraordinary emphasis and extensive protections in laws affecting wide areas of society.

The transgender belief confronts and deeply conflicts with the biological world view, which says human sexuality is biologically self-evident and immutably male or female, and binary.

The idea that people are male or female has been taken as self-evident throughout history. Consequently, definitions of man, woman and sex have only occasionally been found in law. More often, definitions have been considered unnecessary.

A wide array of rights, protections, privileges and access to services – found in a rule matrix of laws, regulations, policies and codes – is bestowed on people, depending on whether they are male or female. Sometimes, they are automatically assumed in customs, mores and culture. Little research has been done to document comprehensively the many areas of law and culture where such rights, protections, privileges and access to services are found: perhaps it has been so self-evident and obvious that such research and documentation has not been considered, or deemed unnecessary.

Today, however, documentation and clarity are required because the transgender world view creates new rights that conflict with the rights of those who recognise their biological sex as immutable.

For example, transgenderism claims that schools should teach children that people can change their sex or gender. This conflicts with the rights of parents who do not want this taught to their children.

As another example, consider how a person records their sex on official documents. Once, official documents recorded only Male or Female. The meaning was clear: a person was either a biological man or biological woman, according to the accepted biological world view of the human person.

However, today, when filling out a Federal Government form – such as a Medicare or Notice of Intended Marriage form – a person is asked to identify as any of Male, Female, X (Indeterminate, Unspecified, Intersex). On these forms, Indeterminate means any fluid gender identity and Unspecified means no specific sex or gender.

These forms reflect new federal laws that allow a Male to change his sex to Unspecified; or a Female to change her sex to Indeterminate. The forms treat Male and Female as assigned terms, like a name is optionally assigned at birth. What is assigned at one time can be reassigned at another time. A biological man can *choose* to self-identify as a Female; or a biological man can *choose* to self-identify as a Male, in which case "Male" is a cisgender term, not a statement of biological fact. This is like saying, "I am cishuman, I *choose* to identify as human", as opposed to saying, "I don't choose to be human, I *am* human. I was born human and I am fixed in my immutable, biological nature as human".

All terms on such forms are fluid, changeable, mutable. A person is only required to have an appropriate form signed by an approved health professional to register their preferred gender identity.

Arguably, biological sex has been replaced by cisgender terms on many official forms.

There are other knock-on effects of defining a person by their gender identity in law and culture. Some institutions, like the Victorian Public Service, are implementing guidelines requiring that, in everyday language, pronouns like he/she, him/her be replaced with gender neutral language like zie/hir. The International Olympic Committee has ruled that men who identify as women can play in female competitions if their testosterone level is below a certain concentration.

So, in the name of diversity, transgenderism insists on the uniformity of gender-neutral language. What is said to be a spectrum of colourful different genders becomes same-same, one shade of grey.

Effectively, laws overriding biological reality and giving legal status to the transgender world view constitute an experiment in social and, in some cases, medical, re-engineering of the sexual nature of human beings. This is despite Australians having no clear understanding of what it is to be transgender, let alone the deep legal and cultural conflicts being created when people are recognised in law by their gender identity in place of their biological sex.

Table 1.1 provides a non-exhaustive list of areas where there are conflicts between the biological and transgender world views. The table also indicates areas of common ground and areas of conflict between heterosexuals, on the one hand, and gays, lesbians and bisexuals on the other.

1.3 CONFUSION OVER THE MEANING OF TRANSGENDER

In 2016, this author commissioned polling to determine what Australians understood about the transgender world view. In December 2016, the Sexton Marketing Group polled 2,500 adult respondents (18+ years), randomly selected to be proportionately representative of the national population on age and sex profiles, state by state population size and capital city versus non-capital populations.

In part, the polling explored what Australians thought the term *transgender* meant. While transgender refers to a person choosing a gender identity other than their sex recorded at birth, 72 per cent thought it only involved a person identifying as opposite to their birth sex. When asked if transgender included "a person who does not identify themselves as being either male or female, but who identifies themselves as something else or having no fixed gender", only 39 per cent agreed with this definition, 38 per cent disagreed and 22 per cent didn't know.

This indicates that there is no agreement in the broad community about what transgender means. Arguably, this is because the transgender belief that a person can change their gender identity is an alien idea to most people, beyond their normal experience of binary human sexuality. Also, this may account for the significant proportion who were "undecided".

The transgender world view of the human person may have stayed in the ivory towers of university sociology departments but for the fact that it has been given legal status in a variety of Australia's federal, state and territory laws without debate. It was written into the *Marriage Act 1961* (see Chapter 10) after the 2017 national survey on same-sex marriage, despite there being no public or parliamentary debate over expanding the definition of marriage to include transgender (or gender-fluid) marriage. It has been written into many anti-discrimination laws without major public debate and with little awareness of the consequences by most policy makers.

1.4   THE PURPOSE OF THIS BOOK

An open and free society allows each person the liberty to identify as they please. Some people choose to be known by their nickname or pseudonym instead of their name assigned at birth. Some people choose to identify themselves according to their self-defined gender identity, which may be other than their sex objectively recorded at birth. In a tolerant democracy, a person has the liberty to make these choices. Such personal matters are not the concern of this book.

Rather, this book has three main concerns.

First, gender identity is a narrow, ambiguous, uncertain and contested descriptor of the human person. Arguably, it is better categorised as a personality trait, each such trait being unique to each human person on earth. Part A examines and critiques the transgenderism claim that a person's gender identity is separate from, or replaces, their biological sex. The ambiguous nature of gender identity is highlighted by the fact that transgender terms are invariably defined against a person's sex at birth in the first place. Further, there is no agreed definition of gender identity.

Second, this sets the stage for understanding the significance of writing gender identity, an ambiguous term, into law. It creates uncertainty in law. It provides grounds for legal prosecutions, professional sanctions and other punishments for non-compliance with laws that cannot be reasonably observed because the meaning of gender identity is uncertain.

Part B examines where transgenderism has been incorporated into Australian laws.

Writing gender identity into anti-discrimination and marriage laws imposes on the whole of society the idea that humans have a fluid gender identity, at the expense of the rights of the vast majority of people who take biological sex as self-evident, fixed and immutable. For example, it forces state schools to allow boys who identify as girls to access girls' facilities.

Consequently, imposing the transgender world view on society creates deep conflicts for individuals, workers and professional people, children, families and communities who take it as self-evident that humans are binary, biological male and female. These conflicts are across wide areas of culture, as listed in Table 1.1. Part C examines the many areas of conflicts, citing numerous case studies.

Third, this book is concerned with the consequences for freedom of speech, thought, belief, conscience and religion, and for democracy based on tolerance, when the state adopts as law the transgenderism belief that human sexual identity is fluid. Chapters 18-21 examine this in detail.

Analogous to writing gender identity into law would be the state making Catholic belief a protected attribute in anti-discrimination law. This would mean that state schools would be required to teach the Catholic faith, atheist organisations could be forced to employ Catholics and employers could face discrimination charges for treating Catholics less favourably in the workplace. Effectively, the government would be making Catholicism a state religion that is intolerant of people who hold other beliefs. When a government adopts and imposes a state belief, it is automatically at the expense of all other beliefs.

A foundational principle of modern democracies has been tolerance of all beliefs. A tolerant democracy does not protect or favour any one belief, but remains neutral. It ensures all people are free to express their views, opinions and beliefs, no matter how contested, conflicted or contrary they may be to science and reason.

This book explains how transgenderism does not have any solid scientific or theoretical foundation. It a belief in the idea that a person can have a gender identity separate from, or in place of, their biological sex.

In contrast, this book recognises that human beings are male or female because it is a scientific, biological fact. That some people are intersex, or that some people identify as other than their birth sex, doesn't invalidate the reality of humans being biologically, immutably male or female.

By imposing a state belief on society, the state is violating the right of citizens to freedoms of thought, conscience, belief and religion, as set out in the UN *International Covenant on Civil and Political Rights* (1966). It endangers freedom of speech and association. These are the freedoms necessary for a tolerant, open and free democracy. A tolerant democracy is the custodian of these freedoms.

If these freedoms are severely constrained or lost, then a liberal, tolerant democracy devolves into an authoritarian state. Writing gender identity into anti-discrimination law, overriding the biological reality of human sexuality, risks our system of government shifting from a tolerant democracy to an authoritarian state.

New social movements are often controversial and contested. Transgenderism is not only a social movement: it holds to a political program for writing the transgender world view into law and, in various ways, imposing that world view over the biological world view. In the end, this book is a political commentary on transgenderism, an ideological movement that aims to create a transnormative society.

1.5 THE STRUCTURE OF THIS BOOK

This book is in three parts.

Part A examines transgender language and why transgenderism is an ideological belief. It critiques the assumption that sex cannot be defined and describes the ambiguity of gender identity. It also examines the philosophical assumptions of transgenderism and raises questions about what these assumptions mean for the treatment of a range of psychological disorders.

Part B examines how transgender political advocacy has led to the concept of gender identity being written into law in place of the recognition of people by their biological sex. The major changes have been to some anti-discrimination laws, some births, deaths and marriages registration acts and to the Federal *Marriage Act 1961*. Part B also describes the agenda for further recognition of transgenderism in laws, regulations and services widely across the culture.

Part C examines the application of transgender theory to educational institutions and the curriculum, with the controversial Safe Schools Coalition program as a case study. It draws attention to medical concerns about children transitioning, and has a psychologist tell her story of working inside a gender clinic. Part C also details how transgenderism is undermining women's rights in many areas of the culture.

Finally, Part C examines how transgender laws undermine liberties and freedoms that are the foundation of a tolerant democracy.

Endnotes

1 *Midwives Alliance Core Competencies*, Midwives Alliance of North America. https://mana.org/resources/core-competencies Accessed 7 May 2017

2 "Transgender athletes to be allowed to compete as the other sex in the Olympics WITHOUT having gender reassignment surgery", *Daily Mail,* 24 January 2016. http://www.dailymail.co.uk/news/article-3412969/Olympics-change-policies-allow-transgender-athletes-compete-without-having-gender-reassignment-surgery.html Accessed 25 February 2018

3 "Call for calm over unisex school toilets", *ABC News,* 21 June 2011. http://www.abc.net.au/news/2011-06-10/call-for-calm-over-unisex-school-toilets/2753582 Accessed 25 February 2018

4 "Politically correct loo-nacy! LGBT campaigners push for gender-neutral toilets in ALL public and commercial buildings nationwide", *Daily Mail,* 17 December 2017. http://www.dailymail.co.uk/news/article-5186091/LGBT-push-gender-neutral-toilets-Australia.html Accessed 25 February 2018

5 "Trump Rescinds Rules on Bathrooms for Transgender Students", *New York Times,* 22 February 2017. https://www.nytimes.com/2017/02/22/us/politics/devos-sessions-transgender-students-rights.html Accessed 25 February 2018

6 *Australian Government Guidelines on the Recognition of Sex and Gender* (July 2013, Updated November 2015), Attorney General's Department, pg. 9. https://www.ag.gov.au/Publications/Documents/AustralianGovernmentGuidelinesontheRecognitionofSexandGender/AustralianGovernmentGuidelinesontheRecognitionofSexandGender.PDF

TABLE 1.1:
CONFLICT BETWEEN THE BIOLOGICAL WORLD VIEW AND THE TRANSGENDER WORLD VIEW OVER RIGHTS, PRIVILEGES, PROTECTIONS AND ACCESS TO SERVICES

Biological world view: Heterosexual, Lesbian, Gay, Bisexual (HLGB)
Biological sex = Male, Female
Sexual orientations

Transgender/queer (TQ) world view: people identify by their gender Identity
Gender identity = (Cis)Male, (Cis)Female, Indeterminate, Unspecified, Intersex†
Gender identity

	Access to services and spaces, employment and identity documents	Heterosexual	Gay, Lesbian, Bisexual (GLB)	People identify by gender identity Sexual/gender orientation is between persons according to their respective gender identities
1	Birth certificate sex identifier	Male, Female		Male, Female, X (Indeterminate, Unspecified, Intersex) Indeterminate covers non-binary
2	Sex identifier on official documents	Male, Female		Male, Female, X (Indeterminate, Unspecified, Intersex); or Male, Female, Other
3	Access to toilets, showers, change rooms	Person uses male or female facility according to their biological sex at birth		Person uses facility according to their self-defined gender identity. Options include a biological man who identifies as a woman using female facilities, or a third unisex facility; or all facilities become unisex facilities.

	Access to services and spaces, employment and identity documents	Heterosexual	Gay, Lesbian, Bisexual (GLB)	People identify by gender identity Sexual/gender orientation is between persons according to their respective gender identities
4	Access to sex-specific schools	Boys attend boys' schools. Girls attend girls' schools.		A child attends a school according to their self-defined gender identity. A boy who identifies as a girl can attend a girls' school.
5	School sex education	Teach male and female biology, reproduction and aspects of heterosexual sexual expression	Teach male and female biology, reproduction and aspects of gay, lesbian, bisexual sexual expression. Refusal to teach this constitutes discrimination against LGBs	Teach that gender identity can be other than sex at birth and be on a spectrum of 100% male to 100% female, or non-binary (e.g. pangender, gender queer, androgynous, etc.) or genderless. Teach that medical intervention can change a body to the opposite of a person's birth sex. Teach wide range of sexual expressions. Refusal to teach this constitutes discrimination against transgenders.
6	School dormitories and camps	Boys and girls use sex-specific dormitories and camp facilities.		A child accesses dormitories and camp facilities according to their self-defined gender identity.
7	Marriage application form	Groom, Bride	Groom, Bride, Partner	Groom, Bride, Partner Each can identify as Male, Female, Indeterminate, Unspecified or Intersex.
8	Services to weddings	Some people choose to service only man+woman weddings as a matter of thought, belief, conscience or religion.	People choosing not to service same-sex weddings as a matter of thought, belief, conscience or religion accused of discrimination against same-sex couples	People choosing not to service transgender weddings as a matter of thought, belief, conscience or religion accused of discrimination against transgenders

Table 1.1:

	Access to services and spaces, employment and identity documents	Heterosexual	Gay, Lesbian, Bisexual (GLB)	People identify by gender identity Sexual/gender orientation is between persons according to their respective gender identities
9	Marriage counselling	Cultural, conscience and religious convictions of marriage counsellors mean they choose to counsel only heterosexual couples.	Counsellors choosing to counsel only heterosexual couples as a matter of thought, belief, conscience or religion accused of discrimination against same-sex couples and bisexual couples	Counsellors choosing not to counsel transgender couples as a matter of thought, belief, conscience or religion can be accused of discrimination against transgender couples.
10	Language of sex and gender	Descriptions of persons based on their biological sex and sexual orientation: male, female, sex-specific pronouns (him, her, mother, father, son, daughter), heterosexual, gay, lesbian, bisexual		As there can be as many gender identities as there are people on earth, addressing people by their individual gender identity is not possible. Governments and other organisations require the use of gender-neutral pronouns, e.g. they, them, zi, hir, partner. Failure to comply risks loss of employment or no renewal of contracts.
11	Access to sex-specific sports, women-only clubs and organisations	A person plays in male or female sport, or becomes a member of men's or women's clubs, according to their sex at birth.		A person plays in male or female sport according to their self-defined gender identity. A biological man who identifies as a woman plays in female-only sport.
12	Provision of health services such as female pap smear test	Women can ask for female health providers to take pap smears and carry out other intimate examinations and treatments.		Women can be accused of discrimination against transsexual male-to-females if they ask for biological females to carry out intimate medical examinations and treatments.

	Access to services and spaces, employment and identity documents	Heterosexual	Gay, Lesbian, Bisexual (GLB)	People identify by gender identity Sexual/gender orientation is between persons according to their respective gender identities
13	Medical treatments, referrals, provision of pharmaceuticals	Men and women receive treatments according to their biological sex, given that men and women have different physiologies requiring sex-specific treatments.		Due to problems identifying a transgender's underlying sex, medical professionals can be accused of (a) medical negligence for failure to provide biological sex-specific treatments, or (b) discrimination for asking a transsexual/transgender person to identify their birth sex in order to provide sex-specific treatments. For example, how does a doctor identify the biological sex of a female-to-male person who potentially needs treatment for ovarian cancer?
14	Medical research	The new scientific field of sex-based biology says it is important to conduct diagnosis, pharmaceutical trials and other medical treatments separately on biological men and women as diagnosis and treatments can be different for men and women.		Researchers doing sex-based medical research – which includes conducting diagnosis, pharmaceutical trials and other medical treatments of persons according to their biological sex at birth – could be accused of discrimination for (a) asking a transsexual/transgender to identify by their birth sex, or (b) excluding a person who refuses to identify their birth sex for a medical study or trial.

Table 1.1:

	Access to services and spaces, employment and identity documents	Heterosexual Gay, Lesbian, Bisexual (GLB)		People identify by gender identity Sexual/gender orientation is between persons according to their respective gender identities
		Heterosexual	Gay, Lesbian, Bisexual (GLB)	
15	Psychological counselling of, doctors' referrals for, pharmacies' provision of pharmaceuticals for, people (including children) transitioning to the opposite sex	Gender dysphoria is listed in the DSM-5, a manual of psychological disorders, along with anorexia and body identity disorder. Counselling treatments push back against the condition.		Gender dysphoria is resolved by supporting a person to transition to a gender identity other than their birth sex. Counselling that pushes back against transitioning is considered discrimination against transgenders. Discouraging a child from transition is considered as domestic violence against the child. Doctors refusing to prescribe, and pharmacists refusing to supply, puberty blockers and sex-change drugs are at risk of discrimination charges and face loss of professional qualifications.
16	Female beauty salon services, like waxing	Biological women can choose to have a biological female provide some intimate salon services, like waxing.		Women can be accused of discrimination against transsexual male-to-females if they ask for biological females to provide intimate salon services, like waxing.
17	Access to female-only safe spaces; for example, female gyms, domestic violence shelters	Women access female-only spaces, e.g. gyms, female-only domestic violence shelters that provide female-only showers, change rooms, toilets and other facilities.		A biological man who identifies as a woman has right to access female-only spaces, e.g. female-only gyms, homeless and domestic violence shelters. They could be accused of discrimination for failing to provide services to transgenders.
18	Affirmative action, e.g. women's scholarships, jobs, pre-selection for parliament	Biological males not eligible to apply		A biological man who identifies as a woman has the right to apply for biological women's-only scholarships, jobs, positions, pre-selection for parliament. Refusal on grounds of their birth sex could constitute discrimination against transgenders.

Access to services and spaces, employment and identity documents	Heterosexual	Gay, Lesbian, Bisexual (GLB)	People identify by gender identity Sexual/gender orientation is between persons according to their respective gender identities
19 Accommodation in prison	Prisoners housed in prison according to their biological sex. Prisons provide sex-specific showers and toilets.		A biological male prisoner who identifies as a woman has the right to be accommodated in a prison for biological females and access the same cells, showers, toilets as provided for biological females. With transgender marriage legalised, a man who identifies as female could marry a biological female prisoner, be recognised as being in a lesbian marriage and have children in prison.
20 Access to lesbian-only organisations, spaces, events	Not apply	Biological female lesbians have exclusive access.	A biological man who identifies as a woman and as a lesbian has the right to access lesbian-only organisations, spaces, events. Refusal of access could be regarded as discrimination against transsexual male-to-females.
21 Employment	Biological males can face charges for discriminating in employment against biological women, on the basis of their sex, across many areas of employment.	Heterosexuals can face charges for discriminating against gays, lesbians and bisexuals, on the basis of their sexual orientation. Charges could lead to loss of employment or professional qualifications: 5, 8, 9 above.	Employers may face charges for discriminating against transgenders on the basis of their fluid gender identity. Employees can face workplace discipline, or loss of professional accreditation, e.g. in the areas above: 3, 4, 5, 6, 8, 9, 10, 11, 12, 13, 14, 15, 16, 17, 18, 19, 20.

† Note: Intersex is a disorder of sexual development and, as will be argued in Chapter 5.2.3, should not be included on sex identifiers with non-binary transgenders. Intersex is listed here because it appears on federal government forms in the non-binary category – Male, Female, X (Indeterminate, Unspecified, Intersex).

PART A

TRANSGENDER WORLD VIEW IN LANGUAGE, SOCIAL SCIENCES AND PHILOSOPHY

Transgenderism advocates legal and cultural recognition of people by their gender identity, which can be separate from, or in place of, their biological sex.

Part A of this book examines transgender theory, the ambiguity of transgender language, and the highly contested sociological, psychological and philosophical arguments for transgenderism.

Transgender theory has its own language and terminology, which is novel to most people (see Definitions and Terms). Some words have been invented to explain how a person can be other than their sex at birth. Other words have taken on conflicted meanings, depending on their context. An old English word like "gender" means man and woman to most people, who think in terms of a person's biological sex but, in transgender theory, "gender identity" can mean non-binary, that is, not associated with being a biological man or woman. Chapter 2 outlines the differences in language between the biological and transgender world views.

Does biological sex matter? Obviously, sex matters because sexual reproduction from male and female gametes is how human beings come into existence. Chapter 3 defines sex, examines why sex matters and begins explaining how the biological world view stands juxtaposed to the transgender world view of the human person.

Chapter 4 examines transgender theory, its morphing into the political ideology of transgenderism, the questions it asks but does not answer, some of its theoretical contradictions and overviews and some of the conflicts it creates with the biological world view.

Chapter 5 contests the starting point of transgenderism, that biological sex cannot be defined because some people are intersex or are transsexual. It explains that intersex conditions (disorders of sexual development) and transsexuality have become the thin edge of a wedge to recognise people in law by their fluid gender identity in place of their biological sex. It also examines where the terms intersex and transsexual are found in law.

Chapter 6 examines how gender identity and sexual/gender orientation are ambiguous terms. The more closely they are examined in the social sciences, the more slippery these terms become. The question is raised: if laws demand clarity of terms to deliver justice, why are terms that lack clarity, that are uncertain and ambiguous, being written into law?

Chapter 7 examines the common philosophical understanding of a person by their biological sex. This is called dynamic unity, which describes how the mind and biological body work together as an integrated whole. In contrast, body self-dualism, the philosophical principle of transgender theory, says the mind can dominate over the body. It can reshape the human body to conform with the mind's image of the body. When the mind is conflicted with the body and causes psychological stress, it is called gender dysphoria, a psychological disorder. The question is asked: what would be the consequences of applying the body-self dualism concept of the human person to other psychological disorders like anorexia nervosa?

CHAPTER 2

TRANSGENDER WORLD VIEW: THE NEW LANGUAGE OF HUMAN IDENTITY

Gender identity is said to be each person's unique, self-defined identity based on appearance or mannerism or other characteristics, irrespective of their sex at birth, and regardless of whether the person has undergone medical intervention.

2.1 IDEOLOGIES HAVE THEIR OWN LANGUAGE

Every ideology has its own language. Transgenderism has its own language to describe the idea of every person on earth having their own individual gender identity and gender orientation.

Paradoxically, while new forms of individual gender identity are being found, at the same time there is a push by governments and other institutions for gender-neutral language.

2.2 THE LANGUAGE OF INDIVIDUAL GENDER IDENTITIES

2.2.1 Australian sex survey

In a voluntary 2016 online sex survey, some Australians said they identified with a gender identity other than biological male and female.

The sex survey was conducted by researchers at the Queensland University of Technology (QUT). Partner sponsors included the Australian Sex Party, the Eros Association, the Adult Matchmaker, Gay Matchmaker, Lesbian Matchmaker, the Love Club, and Max Black.[1] Incentives, donated by the adult sex industry, were offered to participate in the survey.[2]

Of the participants in the voluntary study, about 7.6 per cent identify variously with one of up to 33 gender identities.[3] News.com and the Gender Centre Inc. added definitions for these terms. The following is a slightly edited list.

Transgender Man: A person who was assigned female at birth, but now identifies as male.

Transgender Woman: A person who was assigned male at birth, but now identifies as female.

Trans person: This can mean transsexual or transgender.

Trans Man: A trans male is someone who was assigned female at birth, but now identifies as male.

Trans Woman: A person who was assigned male at birth, but now identifies as female.

Female to Male: This term is often abbreviated to 'FTM' and refers to a transsexual or transgender male.

Male to Female: This term is often abbreviated to 'MTF' and refers to a transsexual or transgender female.

Transsexual: A person who emotionally and psychologically feels that they belong to the opposite sex.

Cisgender: A person who identifies with the gender in which they were born; for example, if someone is born as a female and identifies as female.

Cis Female: Cis is short for cisgender. So, a cisgender female is a female who identifies as female.

Cis Male: Cis is short for cisgender. A cisgender male is a male who identifies as male.

Gender Non-conforming: A person who does not identify with either the male or female genders.

None Gender: A person who does not identify with any gender in particular.

Non-binary: A person who does not identify entirely with either the female or male genders. They may identify somewhere on a spectrum between male and female.

Gender Identity Spectrum

100% Male   100% Female

Neutrois: A person with a non-binary gender identity which is considered to be a neutral or null gender.

Genderfluid: A person who does not identify entirely with either the female or male genders.

Genderqueer: An overarching term used to describe people who do not identify exclusively as either male or female.

Demigender: This term (demi, meaning 'half') is an umbrella term for non-binary gender identities that have a partial connection to a certain gender.

Demigirl: A person (can also be called a demiwoman or a demifemale) who identifies partially with being female or has feminine characteristics. They may have been assigned female at birth, but they could also have been born as a male.

Demiboy: A person (can also be called a demiman or demimale) who identifies partially with being male or has masculine characteristics. They may have been assigned male at birth, but they could also have been born as a female.

Agender: This literally means 'without gender', so a person who doesn't identify with any gender.

Intergender: Intergender people have a gender identity that is in the middle between the binary genders of female and male, and may be a mix of both.

Intersex: A person who is born with a disorder of sexual development.

Pangender: A person who identifies as more than one gender.

Poligender: Translates to 'many genders'.

Omnigender: Translates to 'all genders'.

Bigender: Translates to 'two genders'. A person who identifies as both male and female genders. Some bigender people have two distinct male and female personas.

Androgyne: A person who doesn't identify with either gender. They are both feminine and masculine.

Androgyny: The combination of masculine and feminine characteristics. Androgyny can apply to many things – someone's gender identity, sexual identity, and even fashion.

Third Gender: People who identify as neither male nor female. Some cultures refer to some of their people by a third gender.

For example, in Samoa, *fa'afafines* are male at birth but, if a family had more boys than girls and needed more women to help with housework, a male child could be raised as a *fa'afafine*.

Trigender: Translates to three genders. A person who shifts between the male, female and third genders.

Woman: A person born as a female, and who identifies as female.

Man: A person born as a male, and who identifies as a male.

2.2.2 Facebook's 58 gender identities

In 2014, America's *ABC News* provided a list of 58 Facebook gender identities, saying:

> Previously, users had to identify themselves as male or female. They were also given the option of not answering or keeping their gender private.
>
> Users can now select a "custom" gender option.
>
> 'There's going to be a lot of people for whom this is going to mean nothing, but for the few it does impact, it means the world,' Facebook software engineer Brielle Harrison told the Associated Press. Harrison, who worked on the project, is in the process of gender transition, from male to female...[4]

In addition to the Australian sex survey list of 33 gender identities, the *ABC News* added other gender identities, including Androgynous, Bigender, Gender Questioning, Gender Variant, Neither, Other and Two-Spirit.

2.2.3 Safe Schools' list of gender identities and sexual orientations

The controversial Safe Schools Coalition program has introduced its version of transgender forms of identity into many schools.

All of Us: Health and Physical Education Resource – Understanding Gender Diversity, Sexual Diversity and Intersex Topics for years 7 and 8 was produced by the Safe Schools Coalition and Minus18 GLBTIQ youth organisation. Both are funded by the Victorian Government.[5] *All of Us* states:

> There are three [things] in particular that help us build our identity; the sex we were assigned at birth, our gender identity, and our sexual identity. Gender isn't quite as simple as whether you're 'male' or 'female'.
>
> Everyone has their own gender identity in relation to masculinity and femininity. Some identify with both, and some don't identify with either; it's up to the individual to describe what gender identity fits them best. There are a whole range of different words people use to describe their gender identity.[6]

The *All of Us* resource lists six sexual orientations (or sexual identities): lesbian, gay, bisexual, queer, pansexual, and straight (heterosexual).[7]

All of Us lists 13 gender identities: feminine (trans girl, woman, sister girl, female), gender neutral (androgynous, genderqueer, non-binary, agender, all genders) and masculine (trans guy, man, brother boy, male).[8]

2.3 GENDER IDENTITY IN LAWS REDEFINING THE HUMAN PERSON

Historically, "man" and "woman" have been regarded as self-evident (axiomatic) terms in law, language and culture. Only in a few Australian laws have man and woman been defined as being persons of the male and female sex, respectively.

In the absence of the legal definitions, transgender political advocacy has succeeded in changing key laws to redefine the human person according to their gender identity; that is, redefining the human person by their social software in place of their biological hardware.

These laws have led to a new form of sex identifier that says a person can choose to be recognised as M (male), F (female) or X (Indeterminate/Intersex/Unspecified). The gender identities described above are categorised as Indeterminate.

The Indeterminate category is indicative of the difficulty in attempting to have individual gender identities recorded on official forms like passports, and ATO and Medicare forms.

Similarly, gender pronouns cannot cover an unlimited number of gender identities. The alternative is to use gender-neutral pronouns.

2.4 FROM DIVERSITY TO GENDER-NEUTRAL LANGUAGE

The English language has a grammatical system of gender-specific pronouns, particularly third-person personal pronouns that distinguish between men and women; for example, he, she, his, hers, him and her. Third-person plural pronouns are gender neutral: they, them and their, and cover both male and female.

The array of gender-identity descriptors listed above not only challenges the age-old acceptance of man and woman as self-evident biological terms, it challenges the use of gender-specific grammar.

The Victorian Government has introduced an *Inclusive Language Guide* (2016), described by the state Commissioner for Gender and Sexuality as "a vital resource to help break down prejudices and stereotypes … developed for the Victorian Public Sector"[9].

The *Guide* recommends pronouns that refer to people who are queer, the "term used by some people to describe non-conforming gender identities and sexual orientations"; for people who are transgender (trans), which "refers to a person whose gender identity, gender expression or behaviour does not align with their sex assigned at birth"; and for people who are gender diverse and non-binary "people who do not identify as a woman or a man"[10].

The *Guide* advises that gender diverse and non-binary persons may identify with terms like agender (having no gender), bigender (both a woman and a man) or non-binary (neither male or female). It states that some Aboriginal and Torres Strait Islander persons may identify as brotherboys, "masculine spirited people who are born female", or sistergirls, "feminine spirited people who are born male"[11].

The *Guide* urges public sector employees to use gender-neutral terminology, stating that a married person should be referred to as "partner ... where the gender, sexual orientation or relationship status of a person is unknown". Sexual orientation refers to relationships based on biological sex (heterosexual, gay, lesbian and bisexual) but partner is a gender-neutral term that erases public recognition of sexual relations not only of heterosexual, but also of gay, lesbian and bisexual relationships.

In place of the gender-specific pronouns he/she and him/her, the *Guide* calls for the use of the gender-neutral pronouns zie/hir. For example, instead of "he/she went out for lunch", "zie went out for lunch", and, instead of "his/her boy plays football", "hir child plays football".

The *Guide* also states that Other should be a third alternative option to male and female on government databases, in line with the Australian Bureau of Statistics' new *Standard for Sex and Gender Variables*.[12]

2.5 THE TRANSGENDER LANGUAGE PARADOX

On the one hand, transgenderism says there is an unlimited, diverse array of possible ways that people can identify as a member of the opposite sex or as neither male nor female.

On the other hand, the impossibility of recognising and acknowledging every individual gender identity has resulted in government agencies and other institutions requiring, if not imposing, uniform gender-neutral language that distinguishes neither male nor female nor any gender identity. This would appear to be the opposite of diversity.

Some may dismiss as fanciful or whimsical the gender identities, and associated gender orientations, above. However, federal, as well as some state and territory, anti-discrimination laws protect a person by their self-defined gender identity and, in some cases, by their gender orientation. These subjective, self-determined terms have legal status.

The more transgender identity terms are adopted in law, the more language is being changed to identify people in ways said to be unrelated to, and independent of, their biological sex. In some jurisdictions, and in many institutions, gender-neutral pronouns are replacing the English language system of grammatical gender.

The absence of legal definitions for what were once regarded as self-evident biological terms, like sex, man, and woman, has left the way open for governments to adopt the transgender world view into law.

Endnotes

1. Australian Sex Survey Partners.
   http://www.australiansexsurvey.com.au/partners/ Accessed 4 December 2017.

2. Ibid.

3. "This question about gender identity has 33 possible answers", News.com.au, 29 July 2016.
   http://www.news.com.au/lifestyle/relationships/sex/thisquestionabout-gender-identity-has-33-possible-answers/news-story/66b72adfbc566d29453581cc71279d6b Accessed 25 October 2017.

4. Russell Goldman, "Here's a List of 58 Gender Options for Facebook Users", American ABC News, 13 February 2014.
   http://abcnews.go.com/blogs/headlines/2014/02/heres-a-list-of-58-gender-options-for-facebook-users/ Accessed 21 July 2015.

5. *All of Us: Health and Physical Education Resource – Understanding Gender diversity, Sexual diversity and intersex topics for years 7 and 8, Safe Schools Coalition and Minus18*, pg. 2. Minus18, pg. 2.
   http://www.education.vic.gov.au/Documents/about/programs/health/AllOfUs_UnitGuide.pdf Accessed 24 September 2016.

6. Ibid., pg. 34.

7. Ibid., pg. 24.

8. Ibid., pg. 34.

9. "Inclusive Language Guide", Victorian Government, 11 August 2016, pg. 1.
   http://www.vic.gov.au/equality/inclusive-language-guide.html Accessed 9 July 2017.

10. Ibid., pg. 3.

11. Ibid., pg. 3.

12. Ibid., pgs. 5-6.

CHAPTER 3

THE BIOLOGICAL WORLD VIEW: SEX MATTERS

The only variable that serves as the fundamental and reliable basis for biologists to distinguish the sexes of animals is their role in reproduction, not some other behavioural or biological trait.

Lawrence Mayer, Paul McHugh[1]

3.1 SEX CREATES LIFE

Sex refers to male and female, as defined by their reproductive functions. Human life is created by the union of a sperm from one man and an ovum from one woman. This is usually achieved through sexual intercourse, although reproduction has also been made possible through artificial insemination, IVF and surrogacy in recent times. Sex is a life force, the source of life itself.

Two people of the opposite sex create and embrace new life. Sexual intimacy brings into play deep and meaningful relationships, different loves, emotions, charms, passions, beauty. The intimacy of a man and a woman, and the familial love between parents and children, creates deep and abiding, lifelong bonds.

The family is also a social and economic unit. It fulfills the functions of procreation, birth, rearing, education, maintenance, psychological support, and care in old age.

The bonds are natural and needed, in part because of the dependence of children on parents and the dependence of the elderly on their children. As Harari (2011) admits in *Sapiens*, among most mammals, the newborn is soon independent of the mother. However, human children are

> born prematurely, when many of their vital systems are still underdeveloped ... [They] are helpless, dependent for many years on their elders for sustenance, protection and education.[2]

Sex, love and family relationships make infinitely fertile subjects in the theatre, music, poetry, literature, movies, and health and social sciences. The "book of life" is written around biological sex and love.

While English has one word for love, ancient Greek had four terms: *eros*, sexual love; *storge*, familial, reciprocal love and affection between parents and children; *philia*, affectionate regard, friendship between equals; *agápe*, the highest form of love in the form of charity. *Eros* and *storge* directly relate to biological sex, but all four forms of love depend on sex, because it is through sex that a person is created and able to experience all forms of love.

Through sexual intercourse leading to procreation, biological relationships stretch across generations, forming concentric rings of relationships that bind family and extended family together and, more widely, that hold civil society together.

These relationships determine our identity by telling us where we came from, and how we fit into our family, extended family and society. All these relationships, made possible by life-giving sex, shaped our own lives and the lives of generations past and future.

Sex animates language. Many names, in all languages, have male and female variations; for example, Michael and Michelle, Joseph and Josephine, Stephen and Stephanie.

While the sexual revolution has changed how some people regard sex and procreation – with about a quarter of all children living in single-parent or step-parent families – procreation and marriage remain strongly linked. Hollywood, television's sitcoms, dramas and reality shows may give the impression that the biological family is an outdated institution, but reality tells a different story.

Australian Bureau of Statistics data reveal that intact families – those with at least one child and in which all children are the natural or adopted children of both partners in the couple, but no step-children[3] – remain the typical family in Australia. Intact families made up 72 per cent of all families in 1997[4] and 74 per cent of all families in 2012-13.[5]

3.2 DEFINING SEX: BIOLOGICAL DIFFERENCES BETWEEN MALE AND FEMALE

Sex is defined as either of the two categories (male and female) into which humans are divided based upon their respective male and female reproductive functions. While a very small number of people are born with chromosomal and/or other biological anomalies, the World Health Organisation says that

> chromosome complements, hormone balances, and phenotypic variations … determine sex.[6]

However, Meyer and McHugh (2016) state that

> [I]n mammals such as humans, the female gestates offspring and the male impregnates the female. More universally, the male of the species fertilises the egg cells provided by the female of the species. This conceptual basis for sex roles is binary and stable, and allows us to distinguish males from females on the grounds of their reproductive systems, even when these individuals exhibit behaviours that are not typical of males or females.[8]

> The only variable that serves as the fundamental and reliable basis for biologists to distinguish the sexes of animals is their role in reproduction, not some other behavioral or biological trait.[9]

"Birth sex declares itself anatomically in utero and is clearly evident and acknowledged at birth," says Dr Michelle Cretella (2017), president of the American College of Pediatricians. For this reason, barring one of the rare intersex cases, also called disorders of sex development, no infant is "assigned" a sex or a gender at birth; rather their sex is recorded as self-evident.[10]

Nearly all males have 46 XY chromosomes and nearly all females have 46 XX chromosomes. Over 99 per cent of human beings are XX female or XY male.

This binary genetic differentiation underlies the biology of males and females.

The extent of these biological differences is profound. From 550 adult donors, Gershoni and Pietrokovski (2017)[11] at the Weizmann Institute "looked closely at around 20,000 protein-coding genes, sorting them by sex and searching for differences in expression in each tissue. They eventually identified around 6,500 genes with activity that was biased toward one sex or the other in at least one tissue", said a Weizmann Institute of Science summary of the study.[12] Humans have 19,000 to 20,000 genes.[13]

The Weizmann Institute summary said that some genes related to the growth of body hair were more highly expressed in the skin of men than in that of women. "Gene expression for muscle building was higher in men; that for fat storage was higher in women."

Aside from the sexual organs, the researchers discovered sex-linked genes in the mammary glands, about half of which were expressed in men. "Because men have fully fitted but basically non-functional mammary equipment, the scientists believe that some of these genes might suppress lactation."

Genes expressed only in the left ventricle of the heart in women are related to calcium uptake. These genes "showed very high expression levels in younger women that sharply decreased with age; the scientists think that they are active in women up to menopause, protecting their hearts, but leading to heart disease and osteoporosis in later years when the gene expression is shut down".

Another "gene expression in the liver in women that regulates drug metabolism, provid[es] molecular evidence for the known difference in drug processing between women and men".

The study indicates that the biological hardware differences between men and women are far more extensive than previously understood. It also emphasises "the need for a better understanding of the differences between men and women in the genes that cause disease or respond to treatments", the Weizmann Institute report concluded.

The biological hardware differences between men and women should be distinguished from masculine and feminine gender software.

A person's gender software is partly a product of biological factors. For example, women are usually the primary carers of children by virtue of their biological hardware – notably, their ability to bear and breastfeed a child. Gender software is also a product of social factors peculiar to the person's family, race and culture. For example, women's and men's dress and fashions are cultural characteristics that vary between cultures.

3.3   SEX IS POLITICAL

Sex is a political issue. In Homer's epic poem, *The Iliad* (c. 1260–1180 BC), the Trojan wars were fought over the desire of Spartan prince, Paris, for Helen of Troy. In 16th-century England, King Henry VIII had two of his six wives executed; others were compensated and pensioned off. Successive wives were disposed of or set aside for his next infatuation. His Chancellor, Thomas More, paid the ultimate price for not publicly condoning Henry's serial monogamy. He was tried and beheaded in 1535.

Sex can be such a powerful driver of human behaviour that it is grounds for an old saying: if power, money or sex aren't a person's primary motivator, then look for altruistic motivations.

Today, sex is a political issue. Governments worldwide have passed legislation aimed at overcoming unjust discrimination against the female sex, particularly in the workplace.

3.4 THE STATE'S INTEREST IN SEX, MARRIAGE AND FAMILY

The state, an organised community living in a defined locality under a system of government, has an interest in the complementary, binary, sexual nature of humans as the means of ensuring its own continuation.

Social and political stability is closely linked to stable families. If families fracture, the costs for the caring and rearing of children can shift onto the state.

Consequently, while the state has no interest in many forms of human relationships (e.g. friendships), it does have an interest in relationships that involve children. It has an interest in marriage providing a stable basis for families and children. Hence, laws protect human identity and define marital and de facto relationships and legal parentage of children.

The *Marriage Act 1961* provides a legal framework for couples to marry.[14] The marriage contract recognises parents' automatic custodial rights over their biological children and, in so doing, acknowledges that parents have responsibilities for the rearing and caring of their children. For this reason, it requires a couple to present their birth certificates as proof of their identity and kinship. The registration numbers of their respective birth certificates have been recorded on the marriage registration form.[15]

Birth certificates provide crucial evidence that a couple are not of kin, in order to avoid problems of consanguinity.

State and territory births, deaths and marriages registration laws require that all newborn children be issued an accurate birth certificate. It is a legal identity document that forms part of a chain of documents that a person will use over the course of their life to establish their identity, relationships, rights and responsibilities.

It identifies a child's sex, and parental and sibling relationships. This protects a child's right to know their biological identity. It also records their country of origin and confers their citizenship. It protects their right to be raised by their parents, wherever possible. It determines their inheritance rights and is a primary source for knowing family lineage and medical history. Hence, a birth certificate is a cardinal identifier of the human person.

Because families and their offspring are the foundation of society and the state, it is commonly understood that the first responsibility of the state is the protection of children. Children's rights are protected by state and territory births, deaths and marriages registration laws, the federal *Marriage Act 1961* and other laws that recognise the need to protect children as minors from exploitation and abuse. The state also nurtures families, providing economic assistance and benefits to families in the form of education, health and welfare services.

This is part of the state's social contract with its citizens, whereby the state provides a legal and economic framework to assist families and children, thus aiding social stability.

3.5 SEX DEFINES RIGHTS, RESPONSIBILITIES, PRIVILEGES, PROTECTIONS AND ACCESS TO SERVICES

Sex, binary male and female, is the foundation of the biological world view of the human person.

This has been so obvious that most people take for granted laws, regulations, codes, and economic and cultural frameworks, that define an extensive array of rights, responsibilities, privileges, services and benefits, depending on whether a person is male or female.

Theodore Bennett (2014), who broadly supports the transgender world view of the human person, says that the state nevertheless has a major "interest in having children registered as either biological male or female at the time of birth and continuing to identify them through these sex categories for the rest of their lives"[16].

Bennett says that a person's sex identification "is still extremely important" for numerous reasons. These include: determining which school a child attends; accessing sex-specific sports, bathrooms, toilets, change rooms, homeless shelters, and school and university dormitories; insurance; employment and placement in sectors such as the military. Sex is important for determining who can enter safe spaces, particularly safe spaces for women against rape; for affirmative action and to counter forms of discrimination based on sex; for national security; for protection against fraud; for medical research; for government planning and provision of services; for accurate monitoring of the sexes in public activities. Identification of biological sex is important for promoting procreation, particularly in relation to marriage.[17]

Bennett also suggests that the transgender and biological world views can co-exist without legal and cultural conflicts. This book examines this suggestion and outlines fundamental conflicts across the culture when the transgender world view is written into law.

3.6 CONCLUSION

Sex matters. It is part of an important part of the biological essence of the human person. In humans and all mammals, sex is defined by reproductive function.

It is natural and inherent to human identity. It defines our most important relationships – between couples, between parents and children, between generations current, past and future. It defines legal and cultural rights and responsibilities, and who has access to particular privileges and services.

Whereas the biological world view recognises a person's sex as biological and immutable, transgenderism is based on a claim that sex cannot be defined and a belief that a person can be defined by their gender identity without reference to any sexual essence.

Endnotes

1. Lawrence S. Mayer, M.B., M.S., Ph.D. Paul R. McHugh, M.D., "Sexuality and Gender: Findings from the Biological, Psychological, and Social Sciences", *The New Atlantis*, Number 50, Fall 2016, pg. 90. http://www.thenewatlantis.com/docLib/20160819_TNA50SexualityandGender.pdf Accessed 25 August 2016.

2. Yuval Noah Harari, *Sapiens: A Brief History of Humankind*, Vintage Books, 2011, pg. 11.

3. *Family Blending*, ABS, 20 September 2016. http://www.abs.gov.au/websitedbs/censushome.nsf/home/factsheetsfb?opendocument&navpos=450 Accessed 13 May 2018.

4. 20092010 *Family Characteristics Survey: Summary of Results, 2009–10*, ABS 44420DO010_20092010, 27 May 2011. http://www.abs.gov.au/AUSSTATS/abs@.nsf/DetailsPage/4442.02009-10?OpenDocument

5. *Family Characteristics and Transitions, Australia, 2012-13*, ABS, 44420DO008_20122013, 26 February 2015. http://www.abs.gov.au/AUSSTATS/abs@.nsf/DetailsPage/4442.02012-13?OpenDocument

6. *Genetic Components of Sex and Gender,* World Health Organisation (WHO). http://www.who.int/genomics/gender/en/index1.html Accessed 5 October 2017.

7. Lawrence S. Mayer, Paul R. McHugh, *Sexuality and Gender: Findings from the Biological, Psychological, and Social Sciences,* Op. cit., pg. 90.

8. Ibid., pg. 89.

9. Ibid., pg. 90.

10. Dr Michelle Cretella, M.D., "Gender Dysphoria in Children", *Homiletic and Pastoral Review,* 30 January 2017. http://www.hprweb.com/2017/01/gender-dysphoria-in-children/#fnref-18179-25 Accessed 2 April 2017.

11. Moran Gershoni, Shmuel Pietrokovski, "The landscape of sex-differential transcriptome and its consequent selection in human adults", *BMC Biology* (2017) 15:7 DOI 10.1186/s12915-017-0352-z Accessed 14 December 2017.

12. "6,500 genes expressed differently in men and women", Weizmann Institute of Science, 7 May 2017. https://weizmann.org.au/2017/05/6500-genes-expressed-differently-in-men-and-women/

13. Ezkurdia I, Juan D, Rodriguez JM, Frankish A, Diekhans M, Harrow J, Vazquez J, Valencia A, Tress ML (November 2014). "Multiple evidence strands suggest that there may be as few as 19,000 human protein-coding genes". *Human Molecular Genetics.* 23 (22): 5866–78. doi:10.1093/hmg/ddu309

14. *Marriage Act 1961*, Part 1 – Preliminary, Section 5 (1). https://www.legislation.gov.au/Details/C2013C00164 Accessed 5 May 2017

15. "Notice of Intended Marriage, Commonwealth of Australia" in accordance with the federal *Marriage Act 1961* and *Marriage Regulations 1963*, regulation 38.

16. Theodore Bennett, "No Man's Land: non-binary sex identification in Australian Law and Policy", *UNSW Law Journal Volume* 37(3), 2014, pgs. 863-64. http://www.unswlawjournal.unsw.edu.au/wp-content/uploads/2017/09/37-3-14.pdf Accessed 30 May 2017.

17. Ibid., pg. 864.

CHAPTER 4

TRANSGENDER: FROM THEORY TO IDEOLOGY

[T]here is no 'natural' sexuality; all sexual understandings are constructed within and mediated by cultural understandings.

Stanford Encyclopedia of Philosophy (2015)[1]

[W]hat is being critiqued ... is the very notion of the natural, the obvious, the taken-for-granted.

Annamarie Jagose (1996)[2]

4.1   INTRODUCTION

While the biological world view is based on biological sex – a self-evident, fixed, immutable reality – the transgender world view glosses over sex and asserts that a person's gender identity, or software, is what matters and that it is entirely separate from, or replaces, a person's biological hardware.

Gender identity is replacing biological sex in many laws, regulations and government guidelines so that, more and more, citizens are being recognised by their gender identity in place of their biological sex.

This chapter examines the basic elements of transgender theory and how its emphasis on political activism morphs this theory into a revolutionary ideology.

4.2   TRANSGENDER: A SOCIAL CONSTRUCT REDEFINING SEX

Transgender theory says that a person's gender identity, or software, is wholly a fluid social construct based on social, rather than inherent, biological, characteristics; that gender identity is a personal choice.

Some theorists claim that a person's gender identity is separate from, and coexists beside, their sex. In this case, cisfemale and cismale refer to a person aligning their gender identity with, or alongside, their biological hardware.

Others theorists claim that sex, like gender identity, is a social construct, not an immutable reality. In this case, gender identity replaces a person's sex. Gender identity replaces what most people would regard as the reality of biological male and female.

Either way, transgender theory defines gender identity against immutable sex at birth and alternates between treating sex as a separate reality from gender identity and sex as purely a social construct that is replaced by self-defined gender identity.

Variously, the Australian Human Rights Commission (AHRC) makes both claims. On the one hand, the AHRC's *Resilient Individuals* (2015) says gender identity is a social construct that can be different from a person's sex at birth, implying that sex is biologically fixed at birth:

> ['G]ender identity' refers to a person's deeply held internal and individual sense of gender... [how] a person identifies or expresses their masculine or feminine characteristics. A person's gender identity or gender expression is not always exclusively male or female and may or may not correspond to their sex[3] [recorded at birth].

On the other hand, the AHRC claims in its *Sex Files* report that sex and gender are both "socially constructed", collapsing any distinctions between sex and gender identity:

> [S]ex ... based on *social and cultural* factors ... collapses the distinction between sex and gender by arguing that sex is historically and politically specific. This perspective sees sex as a variable concept and gender diversity is built into the very nature of sex[4] (author emphasis).

Chapter 6.2.1 gives further examples of how transgender theorists alternate between treating sex as a fixed reality and a social construct.

Since initiating its sex and gender diversity project in 2008,[5] the AHRC has been one of the leading advocates for changing laws to recognise people by their fluid gender identity, either in place of their biological sex or by redefining sex as gender identity.

4.3   DEFINING TRANSGENDER AND QUEER THEORIES

The term queer theory was introduced in 1990. Some of its key influences have been Eve Kosofsky Sedgwick, Judith Butler, Adrienne Rich, Diana Fuss, Lauren Berlant, Leo Bersani, Lee Edelman and Jack Halberstam, all largely following the grandfather of queer theory, Michel Foucault.

Queer and transgender theory is based on the philosophical assumption that human beings have no common human nature, as proposed by Michel Foucault. He asserted that human nature is just a cultural construction, and man must be recognised as the product of his social and cultural circumstances. Foucault says,

> nothing in man – not even his body – is sufficiently stable to serve as the basis for self-recognition or for understanding other men[6].

He says human nature is a term that has been constructed in "terms … borrowed from our society"[7]. Human nature is a construct formed by social, political, economic and other forms of power. It does not reflect any common innate biological, metaphysical or spiritual essence between humans (see Chapter 21).

Foucault's argument opens a pathway for sex and gender also to be considered social constructs, open to redefinition and reconstruction.

The term transgenderism was first used by Virginia Prince, a former transvestite, who used it as

> an umbrella term for transvestites, transsexuals, and … transgenderists who moved between the sexes and genders and did not necessarily insist on specific medical treatment…[8].

The American Psychological Association says that transgender refers to what is not typical,

> an umbrella term for persons whose gender identity, gender expression or behaviour does not conform to that typically associated with the sex to which they were assigned at birth … The ways that transgender people are talked about in popular culture, academia and science are constantly changing, particularly as individuals' awareness, knowledge and openness about transgender people and their experiences grow.[9]

Similarly, queer theory loosely refers to opposing what is "normal", being "outside the bounds of normal society" and can be construed as "breaking the rules for sex and gender"[10] in terms of gender identity, sexual orientation and sexual expression.

Queer theory is critical of, and stands in opposition to, normal sexuality, where "normal" means "that which functions in accordance with its design".[11] It involves opposition to laws, regulations and cultural practices that distinguish between normal male and female, to paraphrase Diederik Janssen (2015)[12].

The Stanford Encyclopedia of Philosophy[13] says queer theory argues that gender identity is socially constructed and that there is...

> no 'natural' sexuality; all sexual understandings are constructed within and mediated by cultural understandings.
>
> In contrast to gay or lesbian, 'queer' ... does not refer to an essence, whether of a sexual nature or not. Instead it is purely relational, standing as an undefined term that gets its meaning precisely by being that which is outside of the norm, however that norm itself may be defined.
>
> As one of the most articulate queer theorists, puts it: 'Queer is ... *whatever* is at odds with the normal, the legitimate, the dominant. *There is nothing in particular to which it necessarily refers*. It is an identity without an essence' (David M Halperin, 1995, original emphasis)[14].

Or, as Annamarie Jagose (1996) says,

> what is being critiqued ... is the very notion of the natural, the obvious, the taken-for-granted[15].

Queer describes all that is not based on biology, not on male and female. In not referring to any sexual essence, arguably, queer is at odds not only with the heterosexual, but also the gay, lesbian and bisexual, as these are defined as orientations between people based on their fixed biological sex.

It is a broad, loose and confused (and conflicted) theory, with its main concepts differently valued in different contexts by diverse theorists and advocates.[16] As Jagose says:

> Clearly, there is no generally acceptable definition of queer; indeed, many of the common understandings of the term contradict each other irresolvably. Nevertheless, the inflection of queer that has proved most disruptive to received understandings of identity, community and politics is the one that problematises normative consolidations of sex, gender and sexuality – and that, consequently, is critical of all those versions of identity, community and politics that are believed to evolve 'naturally'... By refusing to crystallise in any specific form, queer maintains a relation of resistance to whatever constitutes the normal.[17]

Transgenderism has come to be "emblematic" of queer theory and queer politics, argues Sheila Jeffreys.[18]

The two theories have inseparably blended and fused. As Susan Stryker (2008) agues:

> By the early 1990s, primarily through the influence of Leslie Feinberg's 1992 pamphlet, *Transgender Liberation: A Movement Whose Time Has Come,* transgender was beginning to refer to something else – an imagined political alliance of all possible forms of gender antinormativity. It was in this latter sense that transgender became articulated with queer.[19]

Stryker (2004) concluded that transgender theory and politics emerged as the twin of queer theory studies and politics in the 1990s.[20]

This book uses the term transgender theory as broadly synonymous with queer theory. This is justified given that, although neither is entirely coherent or consistent in its content, they have become intertwined theories opposing the biological world view.

The *Stanford Encyclopedia of Philosophy*[21] and *Oxford Bibliographies*[22] are useful summaries of queer/transgender theory. The theory has several core concepts: (i) gender identity is fluid; (ii) opposition to "heteronormativity", in the transgender meaning of the word; (iii) advocating for child agency; (iv) advocacy for political change to recognise transnormativity in law and culture, which morphs it from a theory into an ideology.

(i) **Gender identity is fluid:** A person's gender identity is either separate from, or in place of, their biological sex at birth. It is self-defined and, since it is based on feelings and emotions that can change over time, a person's gender identity can also change; that is, it is said to be fluid.

A person can be on a spectrum between 100 per cent male and 100 per cent female, or can be non-binary (for example, agender, gender queer, androgynous, gender non-conforming, etc.), or be genderless and have no sex or gender identity, as described in Chapter 2.

This broad concept of gender identity as being self-defined and fluid is captured in the federal *Sex Discrimination Act 1984*[23], as examined in Chapter 8.

(ii) **Political opposition to "heteronormativity" and advocacy for transgenderism:** Transgender theory is politically opposed to heteronormativity, a term that has two fundamentally different meanings, depending on whether it is used in the context of the biological or transgender world view. The difference is understood by contrasting the (essentialist) feminist and transgender versions of heteronormativity.

Feminist theory says heteronormativity refers to laws, regulations and culture that emphasise stereotyped sex roles that promote the superiority of men over women, or the dominance of men over women, and that promote heterosexuality as the preferred sexual orientation, over gay, lesbian or bisexual.

Discrimination is based on the imbalance of power between the biological sexes, or an imbalance of power between the heterosexual versus the gay, lesbian and bisexual.

In **transgender theory**, heteronormativity refers to claims of discrimination against people who identify as transgender, not as male or female.

It opposes laws that grant certain legal rights to men and women based on their biological birth sex, but not to a person who identifies with a self-defined gender identity (see Table 1.1).

Discrimination is said to be based on the dominance of those who recognise sex as biologically fixed over those who choose a self-defined gender identity other than their birth sex; that is, the dominance of the biological world view over the transgender world view.

As this heteronormative world view discriminates against transgenders, heteronormativity is intrinsically transphobic.

Advocacy for transnormativity: Instead, transgender theory promotes what can be called transnormativity, political advocacy for changing laws and the culture to recognise people by their fluid gender identity, not by their biological sex.

This means legal recognition of people by their gender identity on official birth, death and marriage forms, in anti-discrimination law and in the definition of marriage. This creates a wide array of new rights for people who identify with a fluid gender. Many of these gender identity rights conflict with the inherent rights of those who recognise their biological sex as fixed.

(iii) **Transgender theory morphs into an ideology:** Transgender theory says that heteronormativity is a politically imposed form of oppression, where people are conditioned by laws and customs from birth into believing they are male or female. This conditioning restricts their freedom to choose their own gender identity. Heteronormativity must be politically resisted and replaced with transnormative laws, regulations and culture.

It is a tendentious view but one that is common to activists who believe that the transnormative world view should be the new norm.

When a theory becomes politicised, it morphs into an ideology, "a form of social or political philosophy in which practical elements are as prominent as theoretical ones. It is a system of ideas that aspires both to explain the world and to change it"[24].

Transgender theory is a social theory aimed at politically changing laws and the culture. Political advocacy morphs transgender theory from an academic theory into the political ideology of transgenderism.

(iv) **Child agency**: A core issue in transgenderism is the concept of child agency.

In transgender theory, "'child' loosely coincides with the period before or early in 'adolescence'", says Diederik Janssen (2015)[25]. Agency refers to the capacity of individuals to act independently and to make their own free choices.[26] Child agency entails holding that a child is capable of acting independently and making their decisions around issues such as gender identity and sexual orientation. Transgenderism treats children just as small adults, capable of making their own decisions.

Transgender theory says that neoliberal laws have conditioned children into stereotyped roles as males and females from the time they are born. This conditioning includes: recording only male and female on birth certificates; dressing boys and girls differently; providing separate male and female toilets and change rooms; holding sex-segregated sporting competitions; imposing male and female school dress codes; and restricting marriage only to people of the opposite sex. This conditioning is regarded as forcing children into sex-roles for the sake of heterosexual marriage and family.

In contrast, transnormative laws, regulations and customs are considered necessary to liberate children from heteronormative conditioning. In a transgender world, laws and culture would allow children to be their own agents, making their own decisions about how they identify, their gender orientations and which schools, services, sports, etc. they access.

Janssen (2015) argues that childhood (child agency) is

> a central queer concern: an arguable crucible, or ground zero, of all sexual politics[27].

4.4 PRELIMINARY CRITIQUE OF TRANSGENDERISM

Transgenderism is a highly contested theory, as discussed comprehensively in Chapter 6.

The gender identity conundrum: Transgender theory is logically inconsistent.

First, transgender language is focused on a person's gender identity which, in every case, is defined against a person being biological male or female; that is, against their sex at birth.

- A person can be on a spectrum of male-to-female, that is, somewhere *between* 100 per cent male and 100 per cent female;
- or, a person can be non-binary (for example, agender, gender queer), which means they can be *other than* "binary", other than male or female;
- or, a person can be genderless, which means *not* male or female or anything else.

Even the word transgender includes the prefix "trans" which means to *change* fundamentally from one state to another; that is, from a person's birth sex to something else.

Second, just as the ARHC's *Resilient Individuals* attempts to separate sex from gender identity, the *Australian Government Guidelines on the Recognition of Sex and Gender* (which sets out how a person is identified on all Australian government official documents) also says that sex and gender identity are "conceptually distinct" and "may not necessarily be the same"[28].

In which case, what does it mean for a person's biological sex to be male (meaning, opposite to female, binary) and their gender identity to be non-binary (not male or female)? What does it mean for a person's biological sex to be female and their gender identity to be genderless, neither male or female? How can a person's biological sex be male (opposite to female), while at the same time his gender identity is on a spectrum of male-to-female? Aren't these contradictions?

Or third, does gender identity replace a person's sex? Does sex collapse into gender identity, as argued also by the AHRC (see Chapter 4.2 above), and as suggested in the Australian government's *Guidelines*, which also says the two are used "interchangeably" in law?[29]

Either way, this leads to a conundrum. Rebecca Reilly-Cooper (2016), a political philosopher at the UK University of Warwick, says:

> [i]f gender is a spectrum [between male and female], not a binary, then everyone is trans. Or alternatively, there are no trans people [as we are all just male or female]. Either way, this a profoundly unsatisfactory conclusion ...[30].

Transgenderism has no framework – no scientific evidence or persuasive theoretical foundation – to escape this "unsatisfactory conclusion", or to overcome its inconsistencies and contradictions, other than to assert that the theory is true. The theory is based on Foucault's premise that there is no universal, common human nature.

Foucault's assumption begs a further question over the nature of human rights. If there is no common human nature, how can there be universal human rights (see Chapter 21)?

How far does child agency extend: As transgender/queer theory rejects any essence or reference to normality, it lacks the framework to make crucial evaluations and distinctions.

For example, at what age does a child have the capacity to decide permanently to change their sex or gender? Should children have agency on such matters at age five, nine, 13 or 16? Or, given that most would not have experienced sexual intimacy or seriously considered the possibility of having their own children as adults, should a decision to change their sex be restricted to adults only? Should the idea that children can change their sex or gender be taught in schools, and at what age: Year 12, Year 6, in kindergarten?

It is an open question as to whether the theory has the framework to answer yes or no to such questions.

Furthermore, if children are considered to have the maturity to be given agency over such questions, logically, should children be given agency to make other important life decisions? Should child labour laws be abolished so that children can choose to leave school at an early age and join the paid workforce? Should children be allowed to obtain a driver's licence, drink alcohol or join the armed forces?

The ambiguity of gender identity: Gender identity is an ambiguous term, so broad that it risks making sex and gender meaningless, as described in Chapter 6.

Erasing man and woman: If sex, and, therefore, man and woman, cannot be defined, how can laws defend women against discrimination?

Philosophically contested: Transgender theory rests on the philosophical notion of body-self dualism (roughly, the notion of a mind occupying and dominating over a body in an uneasy and loose relationship), which is contested by the dynamic unity (the mind seamlessly integrated with the body) understanding of the human person (see Chapter 7).

4.5   AUSTRALIA – A CASE STUDY IN TRANSGENDER LAWS

Across federal, state and territory jurisdictions, transgender laws have been implemented in Australia. These changes have included:

- redefining the *identity* of the human person by making fluid gender identity and sexual/gender orientation-protected attributes in federal, and some state and territory, anti-discrimination laws,
- which led to government regulations and guidelines that require official *sex identifiers* to recognise Male, Female, Indeterminate, Unspecified and Intersex etc. on official federal government forms and on some birth registration forms; and
- redefining marriage to allow two people to marry and be recognised by their fluid gender identity instead of their sex.

The most significant changes have been the 2013 changes to the *Sex Discrimination Act 1984* and the *Marriage Amendment (Definition and Religious Freedoms) Act 2017* (see Chapters 8, 9, 10).

These changes to recognise Australians by their gender identity in place of their biological sex have gone almost unnoticed and uncontested.

4.6   CONCLUSION

Transgender and queer theories have blended and virtually become synonymous. Transgender theory aims to redefine the human person by fluid gender identity in place of biological sex. It is an ideology with a political strategy to change the law to create a transnormative culture.

These legal changes are creating conflicts between those who claim newly created rights based on their fluid gender identity, and those who claim inherent rights based on their immutable, biological sex.

The starting point for transgenderism is the claim that sex cannot be defined, because some people are born intersex and some undergo sex-reassignment surgery. The next chapter explores and challenges this claim.

Endnotes

1. "Homosexuality", *Stanford Encyclopedia of Philosophy*, 5 July 2015. https://plato.stanford.edu/entries/homosexuality/#QueTheSocConSex Accessed 16 June 2017.

2. Annamarie Jagose, *Queer Theory: An Introduction*, New York: New York University Press, 1996, pg. 102.

3. *Resilient Individuals: Sexual Orientation, Gender Identity & Intersex Rights: National Consultation Report 2015*, Australian Human Rights Commission, 2015, pg. 5. https://www.humanrights.gov.au/our-work/sexual-orientation-sex-gender-identity/publications/resilient-individuals-sexual Accessed 6 June 2017.

4. *Sex Files: the legal recognition of sex in documents and government records*, Australian Human Rights Commission, 2009, pgs. 13-14. https://www.humanrights.gov.au/our-work/sexualorientation-sex-gender-identity/publications/sex-files-legal-recognition-sex Accessed 5 June 2017.

5. *Sex and gender diversity Issues paper*, Human Rights and Equal Opportunity Commission (now the Australian Human Rights Commission), May 2008, pg. 2. https://www.humanrights.gov.au/our-work/projects/sex-and-gender-diversity-issues-paper Accessed 5 June 2017.

6. Michel Foucault, "Nietzsche, Genealogy, History", first appeared in *Hommage a Jean Hyppolite* (Paris: Presses Universitaires de France, 1971), pgs. 145-72. Sourced at https://noehernandezcortez.files.wordpress.com/2011/04/nietzsche-genealogy-history.pdf pg. 87.

7. *Review of Noam Chomsky and Michel Foucault, Human Nature: Justice vs Power. The Chomsky-Foucault Debate*, edited by Fons Elders (London: Souvenir Press, 2011), by Asger Sørensen, Foucault Studies, No. 16, pgs. 201-207, September 2013. https://www.google.com.au/url?sa=t&rct=j&q=&esrc=s&source=web&cd=1&ved=0ahUKEwitweD-kPbbAhVEkZQKHW59AzwQFggpMAA&url=https%3A%2F%2Frauli.cbs.dk%2Findex.php%2Ffoucault-studies%2Farticle%2Fdownload%2F4132%2F4539&usg=AOvVaw39tclM43BHhl0v2K1wOgfv

8. Friedemann Pfäfflin, "Medical/Psychological Views", in *The Legal Status of Transsexual and Transgender Persons*, Ed Jens M. Sharpe, (Editor), Intersentia Ltd, Cambridge, 2015; pg.19.

9. "Transgender", American Psychological Association. http://www.apa.org/topics/lgbt/transgender.aspx Accessed 16 June 2017.

10. "Queer", Wikipedia. https://en.wikipedia.org/wiki/Queer

11. CD King, "The meaning of normal", *Yale Journal of Biological Medicine* 1945;18:493501, pgs. 493-494. https://www.ncbi.nlm.nih.gov/pmc/articles/PMC2601549/pdf/yjbm00493-0064.pdf Accessed 15 December 2017.

12. Diederik Janssen, "Queer theory and childhood", *Oxford Bibliographies*, last modified 13 May 2015. http://www.oxfordbibliographies.com/view/document/obo-9780199791231/obo-9780199791231-0022.xml?rskey=cd46Xp&result=121 Accessed 26 May 2016.

13. "Homosexuality", *Stanford Encyclopedia of Philosophy*, 5 July 2015, Op. cit.

14. David M. Halperin, *Saint Foucault: Towards a Gay Hagiography*, New York: Oxford University Press, 1995; pg. 62, original emphasis, cited in "Homosexuality", *Stanford Encyclopedia of Philosophy*, Ibid.

15 Annamarie Jagose, 1996, *Queer Theory: An Introduction*, Ibid., pg. 102.

16 Ibid., pg. 97.

17 Ibid., pg. 99.

18 Sheila Jeffreys, *Gender Hurts: A feminist analysis of the politics of transgenderism*, Routledge, New York, 2014, pg. 42.

19 Susan Stryker, "Transgender History, Homonormativity, and Disciplinarity", *Radical History Review*, Vol. 100, 2008, pg. 146.

20 Susan Stryker, "Transgender studies: Queer theory's evil twin", GLQ: A journal of lesbian and gay studies, 10(2): 212–215. Cited in "Feminist Perspectives on Trans Issues", *Stanford Encyclopedia of Philosophy*, 2014, https://plato.stanford.edu/entries/feminism-trans/ Accessed 15 December 2017.

21 "Homosexuality", *Stanford Encyclopedia of Philosophy*, Op. cit.

22 Diederik Janssen, "Queer Theory and Childhood", *Oxford Bibliographies*, Op. cit.

23 *Sex Discrimination Act*, 1984, Section 4. http://www.austlii.edu.au/au/legis/cth/consol_act/sda1984209/

24 "Ideology", *Encyclopedia Britannica*. https://www.britannica.com/topic/ideology-society Accessed 17 June 2017.

25 Diederik Janssen, "Queer theory and childhood", Op. cit.

26 Chris Barker, *Cultural Studies: Theory and Practice*, Sage, London, 2005; pg. 448.

27 Ibid.

28 *Australian Government Guidelines on the Recognition of Sex and Gender* (July 2013, Updated November 2015), Attorney-General's Department, Australian Government, pg. 4. https://www.ag.gov.au/Publications/Documents/AustralianGovernmentGuidelinesontheRecognitionofSexandGender/AustralianGovernmentGuidelinesontheRecognitionofSexandGender.PDF Accessed 19 June 2017.

29 Ibid.

30 Rebecca Reilly-Cooper, "Gender is not a spectrum", *Aeon*, 28 June 2016. https://aeon.co/essays/the-idea-that-gender-is-a-spectrum-is-a-new-gender-prison Accessed 24 April 2017.

CHAPTER 5

TRANSGENDERISM: CONFLATING INTERSEX AND TRANSSEXUALS INTO NON-BINARY GENDER

*The fact that some huma*ns are born intersex does not negate binary sex, any more than a person born without eyes negates the reality that humans are sighted beings.

Transsexuals have been recognised in law and culture as changing their sex, but a person cannot change *their sex biologically.*

5.1 INTRODUCTION

The Australian Human Rights Commission (AHRC) says that sex can't be defined. It claims "there are … no fixed legal, social or medical views about sex and gender diversity" because "there are also people who are born not exclusively male or female and are intersex". Consequently, the term "sex and gender diversity" is used as a term that recognises "the complete spectrum of sex identity"[1].

Transgender/queer theorist Judith Butler says that intersex[2] and transsexual[3] people are evidence that sex is not a fixed essence and cites both to leverage the concept of gender identity being self-defined and separate from biological sex.

Theodore Bennett (2014) says that "any legal approach to identifying and categorising people on the basis of [biological] sex is thoroughly artificial"[4].

The transgender world view is founded on the claim that the intersex condition means people can be other than either male or female, and that transsexual people are evidence that people can change their sex. These two assertions are then conflated into the claim that people can have non-binary, fluid gender identities other than their sex at birth.

This chapter examines the intersex condition, which is better described as a disorder of sexual development (DSD). Management guidelines for DSD people describe how DSD people identify and challenge the conflation of intersex people as evidence of transgenderism.

It also examines the legal and biological issues surrounding both medically transitioned transsexuals and persons who socially identify as transsexual. It distinguishes between the legal recognition of the transsexual person and the immutable nature of a person's sex.

Finally, this chapter looks at the logical contradiction involved in transgender theory's claim that sex is wholly a social construct, while at the same time arguing that DSD and transsexual people provide biological evidence that a person can be other than their birth sex.

5.2   INTERSEX OR DISORDER OF SEXUAL DEVELOPMENT (DSD)

5.2.1   Defining intersex

A small number of people are born with disorders of sexual development (DSD), also called intersex.

The Intersex Society of North America (ISNA) states that one in 1,666 people is different from XX female and XY male, and roughly one in 100 people have anomalies that make their bodies differ in some biological way from standard male or female.[5]

ISNA states that its *Clinical Guidelines for the Management of Disorders of Sex Development in Childhood* (2006)[6] [the *Clinical Guidelines*] was the product of "an extraordinary collaboration among clinicians who care for people with disorders of sex development (DSDs), parents of children with DSDs, adults with DSDs, and other patient advocates". It involved 26 specialist pediatricians, psychiatrists, medical specialists and ISNA leaders.

The *Clinical Guidelines* define DSDs as including "anomalies of the sex chromosomes, the gonads, the reproductive ducts, and the genitalia"[7]. Causes of DSD "include chromosomal and genetic anomalies, *in utero* exposure to sex hormones ingested or produced by the mother, and random developmental variation"[8].

ISNA prefers the term DSD, saying the term "intersex" is imprecise.[9] Some intersex people prefer the term "difference in sexual development".

The *Clinical Guidelines* outlined the following as some elements of DSD:

- congenital development of ambiguous genitalia, e.g. 46,X virilising congenital adrenal hyperplasia, clitoromegaly, micropenis;
- congenital disjunction of internal and external sex anatomy, e.g. Complete Androgen Insensitivity Syndrome, 5-alpha reductase deficiency;

- incomplete development of sex anatomy, e.g. vaginal agenesis (incomplete development), gonadal agenesis (incomplete development);
- sex chromosome anomalies, e.g. Turner Syndrome, Klinefelter Syndrome, sex chromosome mosaicism;
- disorders of gonadal development, e.g. ovotestes.[10]

The *Clinical Guidelines* lists 21 forms of DSD.[11] The list is not exhaustive and some DSDs overlap. In many cases, DSDs are only diagnosed later than the newborn period, sometimes only in adulthood.[12]

ISNA says that the gender identity of people with DSD derives from

> a complex interaction between genes and environment.[13] [Consequently,] it is impossible to predict with complete confidence what gender any child will eventually come to identify with.[14]

5.2.2 How intersex people identify

Many transgender theorists argue that intersex is evidence that people can be other than male or female; that in cases where intersex people adopt a sex identifier opposite to their birth sex, this is evidence of transgenderism, or that intersex is evidence of a third sex other than male or female.

However, the ISNA *Clinical Guidelines* state otherwise. It says that "[i]n a small number of cases", multidisciplinary teams of specialists working with DSD people and their families "will find that the child's initial gender assignment may not accord with the self-identity of the child"[15]. The *Clinical Guidelines* refer to two representative studies to make it clear that most DSD people identify with their sex at birth.

Dessens et al. (2005) found that of 250 people with congenital adrenal hyperplasia [CHA] who were raised female, 94.8% later still identified as female, while 13 (5.3%) experienced gender dysphoria. Among 33 raised male, 29 later identified as male while 3 (12.1%) suffered serious gender dysphoria. While in both sets of patients this was higher than the occurrence of female-to-male transsexuals in the general population of chromosomal females, the researchers conclude that "assignment to the female gender as a general policy for 46, XX patients with CAH appears justified, even in severely masculinized 46, XX newborns with CAH (Prader stage IV or V)".[16]

Mazur (2005), in a review article of the medical management and care of individuals born with several DSD conditions, found that there were no documented cases of gender change in any of 156 individuals with CAIS [Complete Androgen Insensitivity Syndrome], or 79 males and 10 females with micropenis, while nine out of 99 individuals with PAIS [Partial Androgen Insensitivity Syndrome] changed gender. The study concluded that "self-initiated gender reassignment was rare. Gender dysphoria also appears to be a rare occurrence. The best predictor of adult gender identity in CAIS, PAIS, and micropenis is initial gender assignment"[17]. Of 334, 2.4 per cent changed their gender.

These studies indicate that most intersex people identify with their sex at birth. A small number identify later in life with the opposite sex to their sex assigned at birth.

Those who later identify with the opposite to their sex at birth are "correcting" their sex assigned at birth. They are not "changing" their sex. There is an important distinction between those with DSD – who have an "innate biological condition" for whom sex "is complex and dependent on a variety of genetic, hormonal, and physical factors",[18] on account of which some "correct" their sex identifier later in life – and individuals with a "normal genotype and hormonal axis" who identify as transsexual, with some undergoing sex reassignment surgery.

5.2.3   Wrongly conflating DSD/Intersex with transgender

In summary, studies found that a sizeable majority of DSD/intersex people identify as male or female, as assigned at birth, or as the opposite to their sex at birth, but not as transgender or as a third sex.

Many intersex people reject claims by transgender advocates that DSD/intersex conditions and treatments are evidence of transgenderism. For example, an intersex person, who also happens to identify as a trans woman, has described the "mounting frustration[s]" among intersex people over transgender advocates using "intersex people as leverage" for their "gender identity" politics:

> The kind of rhetoric I'm talking about looks like this: a dyadic [non-intersex] trans person will be arguing against transphobia, and somewhere in their defence, they say, 'Gender can be a spectrum because sex is too, look at intersex people, they exist'. Or, 'Because there are more than just male and female, there can obviously be more than two genders'. Often these will be attached with statistics about various 'conditions', fun factoids about how our genitals are arranged, how interesting our hormones are, or how often people like us occur in the general population. These comments contribute to the feeling of being on display at the freak show; the ongoing story of my life.[19]

Despite the frustrations of DSD/intersex people, in 2013, the federal Attorney General's Department issued the *Australian Government Guidelines on the Recognition of Sex and Gender*, which lumped together "intersex" people, who are said to have "diversity of bodies and identities"[20], with "transgender and/or gender diverse communities"[21], implying that intersex is a form of transgender. The *Guidelines* require federal government documents to provide choices for individuals to self-identify as Male, Female, X(Indeterminate, Intersex, Unspecified), where the X marker places intersex alongside the non-binary categories of Indeterminate and Unspecified (see Chapter 8.3).

The AHRC has also conflated intersex with gender diversity, claiming that "[s]ome common terms for people who are sex and gender diverse include transgender, transsexual or intersex"[22].

Others, such as legal academics Beth Gaze and Belinda Smith (2017), have claimed that intersex is evidence of "at least three sexes"[23]. What does it mean to say there is a third sex?

ISNA answers the question, "[d]oes ISNA think children with intersex should be raised without a gender, or in a third gender?" ISNA says:

> No, and for the record, we've never advocated this. We certainly would like to see people become less freaked-out by people who don't fit sex and gender cultural norms. But there are at least two problems with trying to raise kids in a "third gender".
>
> First, how would we decide who would count in the "third gender"? How would we decide where to cut off the category of male and begin the category of intersex, or, on the other side of the spectrum, where to cut off the category of intersex to begin the category of female? …
>
> Second, and much more importantly, we are trying to make the world a safe place for intersex kids, and we don't think labelling them with a gender category that in essence doesn't exist would help them.[24]

Further, claims by transgender advocates that the intersex condition provides biological evidence for transgenderism, or a third sex, causes further distress to many DSD/intersex persons, particularly as most intersex persons identify with their sex as recorded/assigned at birth.

What's more, it is a contradiction for transgender advocates to argue that socially constructed, fluid gender identities are independent of biological sex, while also claiming that the anomalies of the DSD/intersex condition provide biological grounds for non-binary gender identities. Either transgenderism is based on biological evidence or it's wholly a social construct, but it can't be both.

Further, the fact that some humans are born DSD/intersex does not negate the biological fact that human sexuality is binary, any more than a person born without eyes negates the truth that humans are sighted beings.

5.2.4 Recognition of intersex/DSD in law

Laws use the term intersex, not DSD. Recognition of intersex is a sensitive and complex issue. Intersex people have personal, medical, identity and social issues that can cause considerable distress to themselves and their families. The ISNA *Clinical Guidelines* state that children born with DSDs, as well as their families, require appropriate multi-disciplinary teams of specialists committed to their health and welfare.[25]

In most Australian jurisdictions, legal recognition is offered to intersex people, should they wish to be recognised. Table 5.1 outlines the forms of recognition in federal, state and territory laws.

Intersex is broadly described in anti-discrimination laws as neither wholly/fully male or female, or neither male nor female (federal, South Australia, ACT, Tasmania), or as "indeterminate sex" (NSW), or said to be an "indeterminate" gender identity (Queensland) or "indeterminate" form of transgender (Victoria) (see Table 5.1).

Intersex conditions should be recognised appropriately in law. This is a matter for intersex persons to decide with governments. Possibly, an intersex annotation should be optional on a birth registration form alongside, but separate from, the Male and Female sex identifier.

Table 5.2 also summarises transsexual recognition in births, deaths and marriages laws, anti-discrimination and equal opportunity laws.

5.3 LAWS AND COURTS REDEFINING MEN AS WOMEN AND WOMEN AS MEN

Transgenderism also claims that transsexual persons are evidence that a person can change their sex to be other than their sex as recorded at birth. A transsexual is a biological male who identifies as a woman, or a biological woman who identifies as a man.

5.3.1 Medical transitioning to change sex on birth certificates

Medical transitioning treatments are required to register a change of sex on a birth certificate in NSW, Victoria, Queensland, Tasmania and the Northern Territory. While medical transitioning is required in Western Australia, removal of internal organs is not required[26] (see Table 5.2).

In 1979, 300 medical and legal professionals founded the World Professional Association for Transgender Health (WPATH), "devoted to the understanding and treatment of individuals with gender identity disorders". The *WPATH Clarification on Medical Necessity of Treatment, Sex Reassignment, and Insurance Coverage in the U.S.A.* (2008) said that, for a transsexual, sex-reassignment surgery was a "medical necessity".

> Medically necessary sex-reassignment procedures ... include complete hysterectomy, bilateral mastectomy, chest reconstruction or augmentation as appropriate to each patient (including breast prostheses if necessary), genital reconstruction (by various techniques which must be appropriate to each patient, including, for example, skin flap hair removal, penile and testicular prostheses, as necessary), facial hair removal and certain facial plastic reconstruction as appropriate to the patient.[27]

> Non-genital surgical procedures are routinely performed ... notably, subcutaneous mastectomy in female-to-male transsexuals, and facial feminization surgery, and/or breast augmentation in male-to-female transsexuals. These surgical interventions are often of greater practical significance in the patient's daily life than reconstruction of the genitals.[28]

WPATH says:

> [T]hese reconstructive procedures are not optional in any meaningful sense, but are understood to be medically necessary for the treatment of the diagnosed condition.[29]

Medical procedures allow for the *legal* recognition of a person as the opposite sex to their sex at birth. While these medical treatments can permanently disable a person's reproductive functions and feminise or masculinise their appearances, they cannot *biologically* change a person's reproductive function, or their inherited genetics, to that opposite to their birth sex. Biological sex is immutable. It is expressed differently in thousands of ways in cells and tissues throughout the bodies of biological males and females (see Chapter 3.2, 16.6).

5.3.2   Social transitioning to change sex on birth certificates

The transgender world view argues for legal recognition of both medically and socially transitioned transsexuals. Social transitioning means adopting the clothes, mannerism, hair styles and other external characteristics of the sex with which the person identifies. Arguably, socially transitioned transsexuals – for example, men who socially identify as women – are gender fluid. They can socially change their gender again at any time. In contrast, the medically transitioned transsexual is binary, having taken medical treatments to permanently identify only with the opposite sex to their sex recorded at birth.

The AHRC's *Sex Files* (2009)[30] and *Resilient Individuals* (2015) have argued that a person should be able to register a change of sex on their birth certificate by socially identifying as the opposite to their birth sex, without the requirement for sex-reassignment surgery. *Resilient Individuals* (2015) argues that

> [s]elf-identification removes the need for medical confirmation and can be achieved cheaply and efficiently through a form of legal declaration such as a statutory declaration.[31]

Recent changes to births, deaths and marriages registration laws in the ACT and South Australia allow a person to register a *legal* change of sex on their birth certificate by socially identifying as a member of the opposite of their birth sex, without sex-change surgery. As of 2018, Queensland is considering similar recognition on birth registration forms.

Similar recognition was granted in Western Australia by a High Court ruling in *AH & AB v the State of Western Australia* (2003).[32] The Court overruled the West Australian Gender Reassignment Board so as to recognise as males two biological females who "had their breasts surgically removed and underwent male hormone therapy, but retain some female sex organs"[33], thereby allowing both persons to receive a recognition certificate of their new gender identity.

The High Court ruled that the only "gender reassignment procedure" required was alteration of external physical characteristics that are socially recognisable. Removal of internal reproductive organs was not required.

The AHRC was granted leave by the High Court to intervene on behalf of the appellants. Following the case, the AHRC argued:

> The decision supports the view that surgery to fully remove and construct genitalia is not required in order for community members to identify a person as a man or woman in their daily lives. This view contrasts with the dictionary definitions of the male and female gender and perceived community standards, which focus upon genitalia and reproductive organs.
>
> Indeed, statutory gender or sex recognition regimes in all other Australian states (other than South Australia) and territories only enable legal recognition of a person's gender after they have undergone surgery to alter their reproductive organs. These states and territories should seek to amend their legislation so that risky surgery, not performed in Australia, is no longer a prerequisite to legal recognition of gender or sex in Australia.[34]

In the case of *NSW Registrar of Births, Deaths and Marriages v Norrie* (2014), the High Court of Australia ruled that a person who has undergone a sex-affirmation procedure, and identifies as neither male nor female, may be recognised as being of "non-specific sex" on NSW birth certificates.[35]

The case concerned Norrie May-Welby, a biological man who underwent removal of his genitals to transition to identify as a woman, but discontinued further medical intervention, claiming the sex-affirmation procedure had not eliminated the ambiguities relating to his sex. Norrie then sought to be recognised as sex "non-specific" on his birth certificate. Arguably, "non-specific" sex means "genderless". The High Court said that the *NSW Births, Deaths and Marriages Act* already recognises that a person may be other than male or female, effectively creating a third form of sex identifier.[36]

Subsequently, when Norrie May-Welby and partner then sought to obtain a marriage licence, they were refused by the Registrar of Births, Deaths and Marriages. They could not legally marry because Norrie May-Welby is legally neither a man nor a woman and, at that time, Australian marriage law stated that marriage is the union of a man and a woman.[37] Since the *Marriage Act 1961* was amended in 2017, any "two people" can now marry, regardless of their sex or gender identity.

5.3.3 Anti-discrimination and equal opportunity laws recognising transsexuals

Social transitioning – self-identifying as opposite to biological sex at birth without medical intervention – is the threshold for protected attribute status in all federal, state and territory anti-discrimination laws.

The federal *Sex Discrimination Act 1984* (SDA) is an example of a law recognising social transitioning. It says that a person can assume a self-defined gender identity, including being recognised as opposite to their birth sex, "whether by way of medical intervention or not"[38]. Based on the amended *SDA*, the *Australian Government Guidelines on the Recognition of Sex and Gender* (2013, updated 2015) (the *Guidelines*) say that secondary identification documents like passports can recognise a change of sex without medical intervention.

To this end, the *Guidelines*[39] and the Australian Government Department of Human Services[40] say that sex-reassignment surgery and/or hormone therapy are not prerequisites for the recognition of a change of gender in Australian government records. Both state that notification of a change of gender only requires one of the following documents:

- a statement from a registered medical practitioner or psychologist
- a valid Australian government travel document, such as a passport, that specifies gender
- an amended state or territory birth certificate that specifies gender
- a state or territory Gender Recognition Certificate or Recognised Details Certificate showing a state or territory.[41,42]

Inconsistencies have developed within and across jurisdictions. Some laws recognise only a medically transitioned person as a member of the opposite sex on their birth certificate, while other laws allow the issuing of secondary identification documents based on social transitioning.

Recognition of social and medical transitioning in anti-discrimination laws and in the definition of marriage, via amendments to the *Marriage Act 1961* in 2017, have become grounds for advocacy to amend births, deaths and marriages registration laws to uniformly recognise social transitioning on birth certificates.

5.3.4 Discussion of social transitioning

Transsexuals campaigned for many years to win legal recognition if they medically transitioned. Generally, there is respect for people making this choice, particularly given the hormonal and surgical treatments they undertake. However, for many feminists and lesbians, there are concerns over ongoing conflicts between some transsexual male-to-females and lesbians and lesbian organisations (see Chapters 16, 17).

For those who socially transition, there is a low threshold for transitioning. A man could socially identify as a woman and benefit from the same rights, protections and privileges granted to biological women.

Advocates for legal recognition of persons who have socially transitioned argue that the legal requirement for sex reassignment surgery should be abandoned as surgery is highly intrusive, irreversible and expensive. Further, the permanent need for taking hormonal and other drugs is expensive and carries known, and possibly unknown, long-term health consequences.

> As discussed above, the AHRC has argued for legal recognition of socially transitioned persons.

The argument for legal recognition of social transitioning appears to be at odds with the WPATH argument that sex-change surgery is "essential" for the transsexual person's wellbeing (see 5.3.1 above).

It appears that transgender advocates want the legal recognition of two separate groups: socially transitioned and surgically transitioned transsexuals.

5.4 CONCLUSION

The advocates for transgenderism conflate the intersex/DSD condition with non-binary, fluid gender identities. They do so despite most DSD/intersex persons identifying with their sex as assigned at birth and expressing resentment at their condition being used as leverage to claim that they are evidence that people can be transgender or evidence of a third sex.

Medical procedures may allow for transsexuals to have *legal* recognition as persons of the opposite sex to their sex at birth, for them to be feminised or masculinised in appearance, and to socially present as opposite to their birth sex. However, medical procedures cannot biologically change a person's reproductive functions to that of the opposite sex. Nor can medical procedures change their chromosomes or their reproductive functions. Consequently, transsexualism does not provide grounds for claiming that people can *biologically* change their sex.

It is a contradiction for transgender advocates to argue that socially constructed gender identities are independent of biological sex, while also claiming that the anomalies of DSD/intersex persons and transsexualism provide biological grounds for non-binary gender identities. Either fluid gender identities are independent of biological sex, or they are not; they can't be both. The one assertion logically excludes the other.

Further, the more the social sciences investigate fluid gender identity and related gender orientation, the more elusive these terms become, as examined in the next chapter.

Endnotes

1. *Sex Files: the legal recognition of sex in documents and government records,* Australian Human Rights Commission 2009, pgs. 13, 14. https://www.humanrights.gov.au/our-work/sexual-orientation-sex-gender-identity/publications/sex-files-legal-recognition-sex Accessed 5 June 2017.

2. Judith Butler, *Gender Trouble: Feminism and the Subversion of Identity,* London, Routledge, 1990, pg. 122.

3. Ibid., pg. xi.

4. Theodore Bennett, "No Man's Land: non-binary sex identification in Australian Law and Policy", *UNSW Law Journal,* Volume 37(3), 2014, pg. 867. http://www.unswlawjournal.unsw.edu.au/sites/default/files/g2_bennett.pdf Accessed 30 May 2017.

5. "How common is intersex?" Intersex Society of North America. http://www.isna.org/faq/frequency Accessed, 17 March 2017.

6. *Clinical Guidelines for the Management of Disorders of Sex Development in Childhood,* Consortium on the Management of Disorders of Sex Development, Intersex Society of North America, 2006. http://www.dsdguidelines.org/files/clinical.pdf Accessed 25 April 2017.

7. Ibid., pg. 2.

8. Ibid., pg. 4.

9. Ibid., pg. 3.

10. Ibid., pg. 2.

11. Ibid., pgs. 5-6.

12. Ibid., pg. 22.

13. Ibid., pg. 25, with references to:

    R Dittmann, M Kappes, et al., "Congenital adrenal hyperplasia. I: Gender-related behavior and attitudes in female patients and sisters," *Psychoneuroendocrinology* 1990;15(5-6):401-20.

    P Cohen-Kettenis, "Gender change in 46,XY persons with 5alpha-reductase-2 deficiency and 17beta-hydroxysteroid dehydrogenase-3 deficiency", *Archive of Sexual Behaviour,* 2005;34(4):399-410.

    W Reiner, J Gearhart, "Discordant sexual identity in some genetic males with cloacal exstrophy assigned to female sex at birth", *New England Journal of Medicine,* 2004;350(4):333-41. Available online (with free subscription) at content.nejm.org/cgi/content/full/350/4/333

    H Meyer-Bahlburg, "Gender identity outcome in female-raised 46, XY persons with penile agenesis, cloacal exstrophy of the bladder, or penile ablation", *Archive of Sexual Behaviour,* 2005;34(4):423-38.

    W Reiner, "Assignment of sex in neonates with ambiguous genitalia", *Current Opinion in Pediatrics,* 1999;11(4):363-5.

    W Byne, C Sekaer, "The question of psychosexual neutrality at birth", in M Legato, editor, *Principles of Gender Specific Medicine.* San Diego: Academic Press, Incorporated; 2004:155-66.

    S Coates, S Wolfe, "Assessment of gender and sex in children", in J Noshpitz, editor, *Handbook of Child and Adolescent Psychiatry: Clinical Assessment/Intervention,* New York: John Wiley and Sons; 2004:242-52.

14 Ibid., pg. 25, with references to:

   S Berenbaum, J Bailey, "Effects on gender identity of prenatal androgens and genital appearance: Evidence from girls with congenital adrenal hyperplasia", *Journal of Clinical Endocrinology Metabolism*, 2003;88(3):1102-6

   C Cohen-Bendahan, C van de Beek, S Berenbaum, "Prenatal sex hormone effects on child and adult sex-typed behavior: methods and findings", *Neuroscience & Biobehavioural Review*, 2005;29(2) 353-84..

15 Ibid., pg. 23.

16 Arianne B. Dessens, Froukje M. E. Slijper, Stenvert L. S. Drop, "Gender Dysphoria and Gender Change in Chromosomal Females with Congenital Adrenal Hyperplasia", *Archives of Sexual Behaviour*, 2005;4: 389. https://link.springer.com/article/10.1007%2Fs10508-005-4338-5?LI=true Accessed 5 May 2017.

17 Tom Mazur, "Gender Dysphoria and Gender Change in Androgen Insensitivity or Micropenis", *Archive of Sexual Behaviour*, 2005;34: 411. https://link.springer.com/article/10.1007%2Fs10508-005-4341-x?LI=true Accessed 5 May 2017.

18 Dr Michelle Cretella, "Gender Dysphoria in Children", *Homiletic and Pastoral Review*, 30 January 2017. http://www.hprweb.com/2017/01/gender-dysphoria-in-children/ Accessed 4 April 2017.

19 "The Rift Between Us – Intersex and Trans Discourse", Intersex, Trans Woman, 22, *Artist*, 18 November 2015. https://medium.com/gender-2-0/the-rift-between-us-intersex-and-trans-discourse-62dee7f7a73#.bmwk3px0r

20 *Australian Government Guidelines on the Recognition of Sex and Gender* (July 2013, Updated November 2015), Attorney General's Department, pgs. 4, 9. https://www.ag.gov.au/Publications/Documents/AustralianGovernmentGuidelinesontheRecognitionofSexandGender/AustralianGovernmentGuidelinesontheRecognitionofSexandGender.PDFIbid., pgs. 4, 9.

21 Ibid., pg. 9.

22 *Sex and gender diversity Issues paper*, Australian Human Rights Commission, May 2008. https://www.humanrights.gov.au/our-work/projects/sex-and-gender-diversity-issues-paper Accessed, 5 May 2017

23 Beth Gaze and Belinda Smith, *Equality and Discrimination Law in Australia: An Introduction*, Cambridge University Press, 2017. pg. 92.

24 "Does ISNA think children with intersex should be raised without a gender, or in a third gender?," ISNA. http://www.isna.org/faq/third-gender Accessed 4 May 2018.

25 *Clinical Guidelines for the Management of Disorders of Sex Development in Childhood*, Op. cit., pg. 9.

26 Note: In the criminal codes of all Australian states and territories, female-to-male sex-reassignment surgery is an exemption to female genital mutilation; otherwise, it would be illegal.

27 "WPATH Clarification on Medical Necessity of Treatment, Sex Reassignment, and Insurance Coverage in the U.S.", World Professional Association for Transgender Health, Inc., 17 June 2008, pg. 2, retrieved from web archive: https://web.archive.org/web/20110930040306/http://www.wpath.org/documents/Med%20Nec%20on%202008%20Letterhead.pdf Accessed 6 October 2017.

28 Monstrey S, De Cuypere G, Ettner R, "Surgery: General Principles", In Ettner R et al (eds) *Principles of Transgender Medicine and Surgery*, Haworth Press, New York, 2007, pg. 90, cited in "WPATH Clarification on Medical Necessity of Treatment, Sex Reassignment, and Insurance Coverage in the U.S.", Ibid., pg. 3.

29 "WPATH Clarification on Medical Necessity of Treatment, Sex Reassignment, and Insurance Coverage in the U.S.", Op. cit., pg. 3.

30 *Sex Files*, Op. Cit. Recommendations 2 and 3, pg. 3.

31 *Resilient Individuals*, Op. cit., pg. 53.

32 *AB v State of Western Australia & Anor* (2011) P15; *AH v State of Western Australia & Anor* P 16 HCA 42.

33 "Transgender Australians win landmark court case", *The Guardian*, 6 October 2011. https://www.theguardian.com/world/2011/oct/06/transgender-australians-win-court-case Accessed 8 May 2017.

34 *Resilient Individuals*, Op. cit., pg. 52.

35 *NSW Registrar of Births, Deaths and Marriages v Norrie* ([2014] HCA 11) Case Summary [2014] HCA Sum 10 (2 April 2014), High Court of Australia - Case Summaries. http://www3.austlii.edu.au/au/other/HCASum/2014/10.html Accessed 5 June 2017.

36 *NSW Registrar of Births, Deaths and Marriages v Norrie*, HCA 11 (2 April 2014). http://www.austlii.edu.au/cgi-bin/sinodisp/au/cases/cth/HCA/2014/11.html?stem=0&synonyms=0&query=title(Norrie%20and%20NSW%20Registrar%20of%20Births,%20Deaths%20and%20Marriages%20)#disp3 Accessed 20 June 2017.

37 "Norrie's battle to get married despite being neither man nor woman", *Daily Telegraph*, 11 February. http://www.dailytelegraph.com.au/lifestyle/relationships/norries-battle-to-get-married-despite-being-neither-man-nor-woman/news-story/74364f555980703ff29105037045edb6 Accessed 18 March 2017.

38 *Federal Sex Discrimination Act 1984*, Section 4, as amended 2013. http://www.austlii.edu.au/au/legis/cth/consol_act/sda1984209/

39 *Australian Government Guidelines on the Recognition of Sex and Gender*, Attorney General's Department, Australian Government, (July 2013, Updated November 2015), Attorney-General's Department, Australian Government, pg. 7. https://www.ag.gov.au/Publications/Documents/AustralianGovernmentGuidelinesontheRecognitionofSexandGender/AustralianGovernmentGuidelinesontheRecognitionofSexandGender.PDF

40 "Update your personal details on a Medicare card", The Australian Government Department of Human Services. https://www.humanservices.gov.au/customer/enablers/updating-your-personal-details-medicare-card Accessed 18 March 2017.

41 Ibid.

42 *Australian Government Guidelines on the Recognition of Sex and Gender* (July 2013, Updated November 2015), Op. cit., pg. 5.

TABLE 5.1
INTERSEX (DISORDER OF SEXUAL DEVELOPMENT) RECOGNITION IN LAW

Jurisdiction	Anti-discrimination, equal opportunity and other laws	Births, deaths and marriages registration Acts (BDMRA), regulations and guidelines
Federal	"Intersex status means the status of having physical, hormonal or genetic features that are: (a) neither wholly female nor wholly male; or (b) a combination of female and male; or (c) neither female nor male."[1]	Does not apply.
New South Wales	Discrimination on transgender grounds includes a person "who, being of indeterminate sex, identifies as a member of a particular sex by living as a member of that sex."[2] "Indeterminate sex"[†] appears to mean an intersex person living as a member of a particular sex.	Unclear whether covered in BDMRA. The High Court of Australia ruled in re Norrie that NSW BDMRA allowed for registration of "non-specific" sex. It is unclear if intersex people are considered "non-specific" sex.
Victoria	Discrimination on transgender grounds includes a person "who, being of indeterminate sex, identifies as a member of a particular sex by living as a member of that sex".[3] "Indeterminate sex"[†] appears to mean an intersex person living as a member of a particular sex.	Not covered in BDMRA, regulations; not on birth registration forms
Queensland	Gender identity, in relation to a person, means that the person is "of indeterminate sex and seeks to live as a member of a particular sex".[4] "Indeterminate sex"[†] appears to mean an intersex person living as a member of a particular sex.	Not covered in BDMRA, regulations or birth registration forms

Jurisdiction	Anti-discrimination, equal opportunity and other laws	Births, deaths and marriages registration Acts (BDMRA), regulations and guidelines
South Australia	Intersex status is a protected attribute.[5] Would appear to come within the definition of "gender identity" in Section 5 of the Equal Opportunity Act 1984 Acts Interpretation Act 1915 defines gender identity to cover intersex and defines "intersex status means the status of having physical, hormonal or genetic features that are: (a) neither wholly female nor wholly male; or (b) a combination of female and male; or (c) neither female nor male."[6]	BDMRA Regulations 2011 includes "Intersex" on birth registration forms.[7]
Western Australia	Not covered.[8]	Not covered in BDMRA, regulations or birth registration forms
Tasmania	"Intersex means the status of having physical, hormonal or genetic features that are: (a) neither wholly female nor wholly male; or (b) a combination of female and male; or (c) neither female nor male."[9]	Not covered in BDMRA, regulations or birth registration forms
Australian Capital Territory	Intersex status is a protected attribute in the *Discrimination Act 1991*[10] *Legislation Act 2001* says "An *intersex person* is a person who has physical, hormonal or genetic features that are: (a) not fully female or fully male; or (b) a combination of male or female; or (c) not female or male.[11]	BDMRA: "An *intersex person* is a person who has physical, hormonal or genetic features that are: (a) not fully female or fully male; or (b) a combination of male or female; or (c) not female or male."[12] Birth registration form sex identifier recognises "Intersex".[13]

Table 5.1

Jurisdiction	Anti-discrimination, equal opportunity and other laws	Births, deaths and marriages registration Acts (BDMRA), regulations and guidelines
Northern Territory	Not specifically covered Question: Is "intersex" covered by "transsexuality", which is a protected attribute though not defined?[14]	Not covered in BDMRA, regulations or birth registration forms

†Note: "indeterminate" is a term that has had three different meanings. First, historically in some jurisdictions, birth certificates allowed for "indeterminate sex" in cases where the sex of a still-born child, or premature miscarried child, cannot be determined.[15] Second, more recently in the above anti-discrimination laws, "indeterminate" appears to mean an intersex person whose sex has not been determined but who seeks to live as a person of a particular sex. Third, in the *Australian Government Guidelines on the Recognition of Sex and Gender* (2013), "indeterminate" covers any self-defined, fluid gender identity.[16]

Endnotes

1. Federal *Sex Discrimination Act 1984*, Section 4.
   https://www.legislation.gov.au/Details/C2016C00880
2. NSW *Anti-Discrimination Act 1977*, Section 38A.
   https://www.legislation.nsw.gov.au/inforce/f38c7dc7-ba45-ee6e-d61f-9c8e3cbd52cf/1977-48.pdf
3. Victorian, *Equal Opportunity Act 2010*, Section 4.
   http://www6.austlii.edu.au/cgi-bin/viewdoc/au/legis/vic/consol_act/eoa2010250/s4.html
4. Queensland *Anti-Discrimination Act 1991*, Dictionary.
   https://www.legislation.qld.gov.au/LEGISLTN/CURRENT/A/AntiDiscrimA91.pdf
5. South Australian *Equal Opportunity Act 1984*, Sections 29-45.
   https://www.legislation.sa.gov.au/LZ/C/A/EQUAL%20OPPORTUNITY%20ACT%201984/CURRENT/1984.95.UN.PDF
6. South Australian *Acts Interpretation Act 1915*, Section 4.https://www.legislation.sa.gov.au/LZ/C/A/ACTS%20INTERPRETATION%20ACT%201915/CURRENT/1915.1215.UN.PDF
7. South Australian *Births, Deaths and Marriages Registration Regulations 2011*, Section 7A, under the *Births, Deaths and Marriages Registration Act 1996*.
   https://www.legislation.sa.gov.au/LZ/C/R/BIRTHS%20DEATHS%20AND%20MARRIAGES%20REGISTRATION%20REGULATIONS%202011/CURRENT/2011.205.AUTH.PDF
8. WA *Equal Opportunity Act 1984*.
   https://www.slp.wa.gov.au/legislation/statutes.nsf/main_mrtitle_305_homepage.htmlAccessed 4 August, 2017.
9. Tasmanian *Anti-Discrimination Act*, 1998, Section 3.
   http://www.austlii.edu.au/au/legis/tas/consol_act/aa1998204/
10. ACT *Discrimination Act 1991*, Section 7.
    http://www.legislation.act.gov.au/a/1991-81/current/pdf/1991-81.pdf
11. ACT Legislation Act 2001, 169B.
    http://www.legislation.act.gov.au/a/2001-14/default.asp
12. ACT *Births Deaths and Marriages Act*, Sections 24, 25, 29A, 29B, Dictionary.
    http://www.legislation.act.gov.au/a/1997-112/current/pdf/1997-112.pdf
13. "Birth Registration Statement," Australian Capital Territory.
    https://www.accesscanberra.act.gov.au/app/answers/detail/a_id/2214/~/births%2C-deaths-and-marriages-forms-and-fees Accessed 6 June, 2017
14. Northern Territory *Anti-Discrimination Act*.
    http://www.austlii.edu.au/au/legis/nt/consol_act/aa204/ Accessed 4 August, 2017.
15. *Sex Files: the legal recognition of sex in documents and government records*, Australian Human Rights Commission 2009, pg. 23.https://www.humanrights.gov.au/our-work/sexual-orientation-sex-gender-identity/publications/sex-files-legal-recognition-sex Accessed 5 June, 2017.
16. *Australian Government Guidelines on the Recognition of Sex and Gender* (July 2013, Updated Nov 2015), pg. 9.
    https://www.ag.gov.au/Publications/Documents/AustralianGovernmentGuidelinesontheRecognitionofSexandGender/AustralianGovernmentGuidelinesontheRecognitionofSexandGender.PDF

TABLE 5.2
TRANSSEXUAL RECOGNITION ON BIRTH REGISTERS AND IN ANTI-DISCRIMINATION AND CRIMINAL LAW

Jurisdiction	Recognition of medical/social transitioning in Births, Deaths and Marriages Registration Acts (BDMRA)	Medical/social transitioning as a protected attribute in anti-discrimination and equal opportunity laws
Federal	Federal law does not cover birth certificates.	Social and medical transitioning recognised Recognised as a form of "gender identity ... whether by way of medical intervention or not" in the *Sex Discrimination Act 1984*.[1]
New South Wales	Medical transitioning required[2] However, in *re Norrie*, the High Court of Australia ruled that "non-specific" sex can be recorded on NSW birth certificates.[3]	Social and medical transitioning recognised[4]
Victoria	Medical transitioning required[5] A BDMRA amendment bill to allow social transitioning as grounds for recognising a change of sex on a birth certificate was defeated in the Victorian Parliament in 2016.	Social and medical transitioning recognised[6]
Queensland	Medical transitioning required[7]	Social and medical transitioning recognised[8]
South Australia	Social and medical transitioning recognised[9] A child under 18 years can apply by themselves to a court for a change of sex or gender.[10] No age requirement is specified for the child applicant.	Social and medical transitioning recognised[11]

TABLE 5.2
TRANSSEXUAL RECOGNITION ON BIRTH REGISTERS AND IN ANTI-DISCRIMINATION AND CRIMINAL LAW

Jurisdiction	Recognition of medical/social transitioning in Births, Deaths and Marriages Registration Acts (BDMRA)	Medical/social transitioning as a protected attribute in anti-discrimination and equal opportunity laws
Western Australia	Limited medical transitioning recognised[12]	Social and medical transitioning recognised[17]
	The Gender Reassignment Act 2000 requires sex reassignment surgery,[13] after which a gender recognition certificate is issued and presented to the Registrar of Births to amend the sex noted on the birth certificate.[14]	
	However, in *AB & AH v the State of Western Australia* (2011)[15], the High Court of Australia ruled that, under the Gender Reassignment Act 2000, the only "gender reassignment procedure" required is the altering of the external physical characteristics that are socially recognisable. Removal of internal reproductive organs is not required.[16]	
Tasmania	Medical transitioning required[18]	Social and medical transitioning recognised[19]
Australian Capital Territory†	Social and medical transitioning recognised[20]	Social and medical transitioning recognised[22]
	Parents or guardians of a child under 18 years can apply to the Registrar-General for alteration of the sex of their child.[21]	
Northern Territory	Medical transitioning required[23]	Social and medical transitioning recognised[24]

Table 5.2

Endnotes

1. Federal, *Sex Discrimination Act 1984*, Section 4.
   http://www.austlii.edu.au/au/legis/cth/consol_act/sda1984209/

2. NSW, Births Deaths and Marriages Registration Act 1995, Section 32A, 32B.
   http://www.austlii.edu.au/au/legis/nsw/consol_act/bdamra1995383/

3. NSW, *Registrar of Births, Deaths and Marriages v Norrie* [2014] HCA 11, 2 April 2014.
   http://www.hcourt.gov.au/assets/publications/judgment-summaries/2014/hca-11-2014-04-02.pdf

4. NSW, *Anti-Discrimination Act 1977*, Section 38A.
   http://www.austlii.edu.au/au/legis/nsw/consol_act/aa1977204/

5. Victorian *Births, Deaths, and Marriages Registration Act 1996*, S. 4(1) def. of sex affirmation surgery.
   http://www.austlii.edu.au/au/legis/vic/consol_act/bdamra1996383/

6. Victoria, *Equal Opportunity Act 2010*, Sections 4 Definitions, 6 (d).
   http://www.austlii.edu.au/au/legis/vic/consol_act/eoa2010250/

7. Queensland, *Births, Deaths and Marriages Registration Act 2003*, Schedule 2 Dictionary, Sections 22-24.
   http://www.austlii.edu.au/au/legis/qld/consol_act/bdamra2003383/

8. Queensland Anti-Discrimination Act 1991, Dictionary in the Schedule.
   http://www.austlii.edu.au/au/legis/qld/consol_act/aa1991204/

9. South Australian *Births Deaths and Marriages Registration Act 1996*, Sections 29H–29U.
   http://www.austlii.edu.au/au/legis/sa/consol_act/bdamra1996383/

10. Ibid., Section 29J (7).

11. South Australia, *Equal Opportunity Act 1984*, Section 5.
    http://www.austlii.edu.au/au/legis/sa/consol_act/eoa1984250/

12. West Australia, *Gender Reassignment Act 2000*, Sections 3, 14–16.
    http://www.austlii.edu.au/au/legis/wa/consol_act/gra2000200/

13. West Australia, *Gender Reassignment Act 2000*, Sections 3, 14–16.
    http://www.austlii.edu.au/au/legis/wa/consol_act/gra2000200/

14. West Australia, *Gender Reassignment Regulations 2001*, Regulations 4, 5.
    https://www.slp.wa.gov.au/pco/prod/filestore.nsf/FileURL/mrdoc_35859.pdf/$FILE/Gender%20Reassignment%20Regulations%202001%20-%20%5B00-00-00%5D.pdf?OpenElement

15. *AB & AH v the State of Western Australia* (2011) High Court of Australia 42.
    http://eresources.hcourt.gov.au/downloadPdf/2011/HCA/42

16. *AB & AH v State of Western Australia* & ANOR P15/2011; *AB & AH v State of Western Australia* & ANOR P16/2011 [2011] High Court of Australia 42, 6 October 2011.
    http://www.hcourt.gov.au/assets/publications/judgment-summaries/2011/hca42-2011-10-06.pdf

17. West Australia, *Equal Opportunity Act 1984*, Sections 35AA, 35AB.
    http://www.austlii.edu.au/au/legis/wa/consol_act/eoa1984250/

18. Tasmanian, *Births, Deaths and Marriages Registration Act 1999*, Section 3 and Part 4.
    http://www.austlii.edu.au/au/legis/tas/consol_act/bdamra1999383/

19 Tasmania, *Anti-Discrimination Act 1998*, Section 3.
    http://www.austlii.edu.au/au/legis/tas/consol_act/aa1998204/

20 Australian Capital Territory, *Births, Deaths and Marriages Registration Act 1997*, Sections 24 (1) (c), 25 (1).
    http://www.austlii.edu.au/au/legis/act/consol_act/bdamra1997383/

21 Ibid., Sections 24 (2)– (4), 25 (2).

22 Australian Capital Territory, *Discrimination Act 1991*, Section 7 and definition of "gender identity" in the Dictionary.
    http://www.austlii.edu.au/au/legis/act/consol_act/da1991164/

23 Northern Territory, Births, *Deaths and Marriages Registration Act*, Part 4.
    http://www.austlii.edu.au/au/legis/nt/consol_act/bdamra383/

24 The Northern Territory, *Anti-Discrimination Act*, Section 4 definition of "sexuality."
    http://www.austlii.edu.au/au/legis/nt/consol_act/aa204/

CHAPTER 6

THE AMBIGUITY OF GENDER IDENTITY AND GENDER ORIENTATION

Gender identity and gender orientation are subjective, ambiguous and fluid. Consequently, they can only be established by individual self-assessment at a point in time.

We risk being the first people in history to have been able to make their illusion's so vivid, so persuasive, so 'realistic' that they can live in them.[1]

Appropriating Daniel J Boorstin

6.1   INTRODUCTION

Transgenderism claims that gender identity and gender orientation are fundamental attributes of the human person that should be protected in law even though there is no agreed definition of these terms.

For example, the Australian Human Rights Commission (AHRC) says that gender identity is "a person's *deeply* held internal and individual *sense* of gender"[2] (author emphasis).

At the same time, the AHRC says that there is no consensus on a definition. It says:

> Debate exists over what are appropriate terms to refer to people who are sex and gender diverse. Much discussion on the [AHRC] *Sex Files* blog related to the specific terms and definitions used to describe sex and gender diversity. Some definitions and words are contested and draw strong views from some members of the sex and gender diverse community.
>
> The lack of consensus is partly due to the fact that there are also no fixed legal, social or medical views about sex and gender diversity.[3]

While the AHRC bases its advocacy for gender identity on the claim that sex is not, or cannot be, defined, biological science refutes this claim and says that sex is inherent and self-evident (see Chapter 3.2).

This chapter points out that gender identity suffers from conflicted, ambiguous definitions. It asks the question, why should laws recognise ambiguous, subjective gender identity that has inconsistent, conflicted definitions over what objective science has established as the reality of biological sex?

This chapter also examines what is meant by sexual orientation and gender orientation.

As the transgender world view originates from psychology (the study of the human mind and its functions)[4] and sociology (the study of the development, structure, and functioning of human society),[5] it is appropriate to turn to the extensive psychological and sociological research on gender identity and gender orientation, as well as sexual orientation.

6.2   THE FLUIDITY OF GENDER IDENTITY

6.2.1   Defining gender identity

Friedmann Pfäfflin, in *The Legal Status of Transsexual and Transgender Persons* (2015),[6] cites sociologists Richard King and Dave King as defining fluid gender identity in four ways.

One is the traditional transsexual, "who exclusively desires to be transitioned from male-to-female, or vice versa, in terms of role behaviour, bodily outfit and legal recognition". Here, Pfäfflin could have distinguished between medically transitioned and socially transitioned transsexuals.

A second type oscillates between "phases of living a male or female social life".

A third type "fundamentally negates the gender dichotomy and wants to belong to neither category". They want to be identified as neither male nor female, but as being an alternative third sex or gender.

A fourth type wants to "escape sex and gender categories". They define their attitude as "transcending". They want to overcome/bypass the sex and gender identity issue altogether. They don't want to be identified as male or female, transsexual or transgender, but only "trans" or "per".[7]

Variously, these different forms of gender identity are found in definitions and in principle statements of different organisations.

The AHRC says gender identity refers to "a person's deeply held internal and individual *sense* of gender..."[8] (author emphasis).

The Yogyakarta Principles were developed at a 2006 meeting of the International Commission of Jurists, the International Service for Human Rights and human rights advocacy groups from around the world, at Gadjah Mada University, Yogyakarta, Indonesia. These Principles say:

> Gender identity is understood to refer to each person's deeply *felt* internal and individual experience of gender, which may or may not correspond with the sex assigned at birth, including the personal *sense* of the body (which may involve, if freely chosen, modification of bodily appearance or function by medical, surgical or other means) and other expressions of gender, including dress, speech and mannerisms[9] (author emphasis).

The American Psychological Association distinguishes sex from gender identity, saying:

> Sex is assigned at birth, refers to one's biological status as either male or female, and is associated primarily with physical attributes such as chromosomes, hormone prevalence, and external and internal anatomy. Gender refers to the *socially constructed* roles, behaviours, activities, and attributes that a given society considers appropriate for boys and men or girls and women. These influence the ways that people act, interact, and *feel* about themselves. While aspects of biological sex are similar across different cultures, aspects of gender may differ[10] (author emphasis).

The Safe Schools Coalition Victoria *All of Us: Student Handout*[11] says gender is

> how you *feel* ... There are three [things] in particular that help us build our identity; the sex we were assigned at birth, our gender identity, and our sexual identity. Gender isn't quite as simple as whether you're 'male' or 'female'.

> Everyone has their own gender identity in relation to masculinity and femininity. Some identify with both, and some don't identify with either; it's up to the individual to describe what gender identity fits them best. There are a whole range of different words people use to describe their gender identity (author emphasis).

The federal *Sex Discrimination Act 1984*, as amended in 2013, gives protected attribute status to a person by their g*ender identity,* which is defined as

> the *gender-related identity*, appearance or mannerisms or other gender-related characteristics of a person (whether by way of medical intervention or not), with or without regard to the person's designated sex at birth.[12]

The Australian Government Guidelines on the Recognition of Sex and Gender (2013 and 2015), based on the *Sex Discrimination Act 1984* definition of gender identity, distinguishes sex from gender.

> [S]ex refers to the chromosomal, gonadal and anatomical characteristics associated with biological sex.[13]

> Gender is part of a person's personal and social identity. It refers to the way a person *feels*, presents and is recognised within the community. A person's gender may be reflected in outward social markers, including their name, outward appearance, mannerisms and dress …[14].

> Many terms are used to recognise people who do not fall within the traditional binary notions of sex and gender (male and female), including non-binary, gender diverse, gender queer, pan-gendered, androgynous and inter-gender[15] (author emphasis).

The Law Council of Australia, which represents its constituent bodies on national issues, has made two submissions to federal government inquiries endorsing the Yogyakarta Principles' claim that "a person's gender/sex reflect the person's profound self-defined gender identity" and endorsing the definition of gender identity inserted into the *Sex Discrimination Act* in 2013.[16] Yet it has offered no clear definition of gender identity to either inquiry.[17] The Council appears to have avoided profound definitional problems that leave these terms ambiguous (open to many interpretations) and uncertain in law.

Summary: The first argument of transgender theory is that a person's socially constructed gender is fundamental to their identity, separate from, or in place of, their biological sex. Gender identity is a subjective, emotional self-identification. It is said to include cisgender people, a socially or medically transitioned transsexual; or a person on a spectrum of male to female; or as having a non-binary identity unrelated to biological terms, or as escaping all sex and gender categories to be genderless; that is, "trans" or "per". It can be a specific identity that is fluid and changeable, or it can be a "blurred identification"[18].

Second, all definitions of "gender identity" are based on subjective "*feelings*"; that is, a person's choice of appearance, mannerisms, etc. Even the AHRC definition refers to a "person's deeply held internal and individual *sense*", where sense means "a *feeling* that something is the case"[19]. Whereas "sex" is immutable and scientifically verifiable, "feelings" refer to "an emotional state or reaction"[20]. Emotions are fluid, changeable and mutable.

Third, many definitions are circular, like in the Yogyakarta Principles and the *Sex Discrimination Act 1984*. Both define "gender identity" in terms of "gender" characteristics, but without first defining what is "gender". It is like saying that sex means sex characteristics, without defining sex as the distinguishing reproductive functions of male and female, from which sex characterises are derived. Again, this is like defining a table as an object with table-like characteristics, without explaining that a table is a flat surface with three or four legs that keep the surface level, for eating meals or doing work. Such circular definitions define neither "table" nor "gender".

Fourth, ironically, all these definitions implicitly recognise the inherent nature of biological sex by defining gender identity against a person's biological sex as recorded at birth.

Not surprisingly, the AHRC concludes that there is a "lack of consensus over the exact meaning and definition" of gender identity.[21]

The difficulty of defining gender identity based on feelings stands in contrast to sex as defined objectively by physical reproductive functions associated with physical attributes such as chromosomes, hormone prevalence, and external and internal anatomy.

6.2.2 The ambiguity of gender identity

In 2016, Paul McHugh and Lawrence Mayer produced a landmark research paper, *Sexuality and Gender: Findings from the Biological, Psychological, and Social Sciences.*[22] It presents a comprehensive summary and explanation of research – from the biological, psychological, and social sciences – related to gender identity and sexual orientation.

Indicating that the issues being considered bear on some of the most intimate and personal aspects of human life, the authors dedicated their report "to the LGBT community, which bears a disproportionate rate of mental health problems compared [with] the population as a whole".

McHugh is a professor of psychiatry and behavioural sciences at the Johns Hopkins University School of Medicine and was, for 25 years, the psychiatrist-in-chief at the Johns Hopkins Hospital. Johns Hopkins has a long history of involvement with the transgender and transsexual issue, as it pioneered sex-reassignment surgery in the 1960s.[23]

However, it discontinued transitioning surgery in the 1970s after it was demonstrated that the practice brought no important benefits.[24] Mayer is a scholar in residence in the Department of Psychiatry at the Johns Hopkins University School of Medicine and a professor of statistics and biostatistics at Arizona State University.

Mayer and McHugh state that definitions of gender identity, like those above, make it clear that "gender is *wholly* 'socially constructed' – that it is *detached* from biological sex" (author emphasis).

They refer to the works of influential queer/transgender theorist Judith Butler as representative of the transgender world view.

Butler argues that because the same personal, social and cultural attributes can apply to men or women, sex plays no significant role in determining gender identity and relationships. She rejects and deconstructs the idea that biological sex, chromosomes and reproductive function define a biologically fixed essence of men and women.

She points to transsexuals as evidence that sex is not a fixed essence, but can be changed by medical treatments.[25] She also claims that intersex people provide nature's evidence to "refute … sexual categorisation" as male or female.[26] Transsexuals and intersex people are used as a fulcrum to leverage an expansive variety of gender possibilities, and an infinite variety of self-defined gender identities.

In *Gender Trouble: Feminism and the Subversion of Identity* (1990), Butler says that "gender [identity] is neither the causal result of sex nor as seemingly fixed as sex. The distinction allows for "a multiple interpretation of sex"[27]. Rather, she says that a person's gender is

> a free floating artifice, with the consequence that *man* and *masculine* might just as easily signify a female body as a male one, and *woman* and *feminine* a male body as easily as a female one[28].

By regarding a person as a "free floating artifice", Butler says a person can be liberated from society's strictures that confine a person to being of the male or female sex, with associated male or female stereotypes.

She advances what she labels "performative theory", according to which being a woman or man is not something that one *is* but something that one *does*. The repetition of what one *does* is the process by which a person is *constituted*.

How this is achieved is analogous to a person writing and performing in a play that demonstrates how political and social structures shape a person's behaviours and identity. Over repeated performances, the person comes to understand that the ways in which their gendered behaviours are entirely the result of social conditioning, wholly the product of their society's political structures that determine the complex of laws, customs and social norms that shape a person's notion of sexuality and behaviour. The more the person rehearses and performs, the more they become aware of how their behaviours are entirely unrelated to their own biological sex. The more consciously aware the person becomes of this process, the more they can reshape their own identity independent of the social and political system.[29]

In the end, it is the person's performance that defines their gender identity, not their sex. Butler says:

> If the "reality" of gender is constituted by the performance itself, then there is no recourse to an essential … "sex"or "gender" …[30].

Further, Butler goes beyond arguing that all social roles of males and females are wholly socially constructed. She argues that the very idea of binary, biological sex is itself a "fictive" construction. Fictive is an academic and literary term for "fiction", something that is invented by the imagination,[31] like characters or events in poetry, theatre and novels.[32]

What forms of identity this leads to is not made clear. But it does mean that a person's mind can determine the body's gender identity according to any criteria it chooses; for example, according to self-chosen stylised mannerisms, actions, dress, and other personal characteristics based on their feelings. These constitute a person's "performance" and its "repetition" as a cultural ritual forms a person's gender identity. As a person's performance can change with their emotional state, their gender identity is "free floating," fluid and changeable, not permanently fixed.

Butler's claim that a person's gender identity is defined according to what the person *does*, stands in contrast to the biological world view in which an individual's sex is defined by what one *is*, a biological man or woman.

The theory has fundamental flaws.

6.2.3   Are transsexual and intersex people evidence of a third sex or of non-binary gender identities?

As described in Chapter 5.3, transsexuality involves medical or social changes for *legal* recognition of a person as the opposite sex to their sex at birth. However, medical treatments cannot change a person's reproductive functions or *biologically* change a person's sex. Biological sex is immutable.

As described in Chapter 5.2, the intersex condition is a disorder of sexual development (DSD), a biological condition, not evidence of a third sex or of gender identities other than male and female. Mostly, DSD/intersex people identify with their sex assigned at birth. Of those who don't identify with their sex at birth, most identify with the opposite binary sex.

It is contradictory for Butler to claim that gender identity is wholly socially constructed and, at the same time, claim that DSD/intersex people and transsexual people are "biological" evidence that a person can be other than male or female.

6.2.4 Are gender identities really personality traits?

Mayer and McHugh challenge Butler's argument that, because some people can have atypical behaviours for their sex, this is evidence of sex being fictive (fictional) and grounds for gender identity being regarded as free floating. They say that a person's

> gender identity could be defined in terms of sex-typical traits and behaviours, so that being a boy means behaving in the ways boys typically behave – such as engaging in rough-and-tumble play and expressing an interest in sports and liking toy guns more than dolls. But this would imply that a boy who plays with dolls, hates guns, and refrains from sports or rough-and-tumble play might be considered to be a girl, rather than simply a boy who represents an exception to the typical patterns of male behaviour.[33]

Such a "combination of characteristics or qualities that form an individual's distinctive character" is how *the Oxford Living Dictionaries* defines an individual's "personality"[34]. An individual's personality is partly based on their biological sex and is partly social, based on culture, customs and mores.

To extend the Mayer and McHugh example, most women like shopping more than men, but if a man enjoys shopping it doesn't make him a woman. Men may be louder and more assertive than most women, but because a man is quiet and retiring doesn't mean he is a woman; and because a woman is loud and assertive doesn't mean she is a man.

Arguably, Butler's "performative theory" of human identity is just describing one aspect of the unique personality of each and every human person on earth.

Furthermore, Mayer and McHugh point out that the idea of sex-typical behaviour is based on the reality of biological sex. How can there be sex-typical behaviour without biological sex in the first place? They say:

> The ability to recognise exceptions to sex-typical behaviour relies on an understanding of maleness and femaleness that is independent of these stereotypical sex-appropriate behaviours[35].

Also, they could have asked: if sex is fictive, is pregnancy also to be considered a fictive social construct?

6.2.5 Does gender identity make sex meaningless?

Mayer and McHugh contend that definitions of gender identity, like those above, dissolve the meaning of both sex and gender identity. It is an argument that ends in absurdity and is consequently meaningless. They say:

> As these terms multiply and their meanings become more individualised, we lose any common set of criteria for defining what gender distinctions mean. If gender is entirely detached from the binary of biological sex, gender could come to refer to any distinctions in behaviour, biological attributes, or psychological traits, and each person could have a gender defined by the unique combination of characteristics the person possesses.
>
> This *reductio ad absurdum* is offered to present the possibility that defining gender too broadly could lead to a definition that has little meaning.[36]

If gender identity is *wholly* a socially construct, then sex becomes irrelevant. In the cause of gender diversity, the meaning and significance of sex is lost.

6.2.6 The transgender conundrum

The claim that a person should be recognised by their gender identity in place of their sex creates a transgender dilemma. In all definitions of gender identity above, it is defined against the reality of biological sex.

To be on a spectrum of male to female, or to be non-binary, or to be genderless, one first has to be male or female, otherwise transgender terms have no meaning.

Even the word "trans" means to fundamentally change from one state to another – from a person's biological sex to something other than the person's biological sex.

Consider this question: if person A identifies as androgynous and person B as gender queer, and if person A impregnates person B who then bears a child, isn't person A male and person B female regardless of fluid gender identity?

In transgender theory, either we are all fluid gender, something other than biological male or female, or we are all just biological male and female. Either we are all trans, or nobody is trans.

However, the theory has no scientific or theoretical foundation to resolve this conundrum other than to assert that the theory is true.

This raises other questions. If a person's sex/gender identity is fluid, are other biological aspects of a person also fluid? Can a person also change their age, or their race, or identify as physically paralysed when they are not? If a person born biologically male self-identifies as a woman, can this person self-identify as being pregnant?

6.2.7 Does transgender confuse the fictional with the real?

The terminology of transgender theory uses theatrical and literary language, with terms such as fictive[37], meaning fictional; performance of gender[38]; performativity[39]; the production of gender[40].

Transvestism – the practice of dressing and acting in a manner and style traditionally associated with the opposite sex – has long been a staple of theatre, literature and, sometimes, ceremonial and religious rites. Such characters are said to cross over from their biological sex to the opposite sex.

In ancient Athenian tragedy and in Elizabethan theatre, performances were done exclusively by men, with some adopting female roles and dressing as females. Shakespeare's *Twelfth Night, All's Well that Ends Well, The Merchant of Venice* and *Cymbeline* all have female characters who disguise themselves as males. As the roles of young women required the boy actors to assume male disguises, the paradoxical situation of boys pretending to be girls pretending to be boys created boundless comedy.

English literature has many instances of members of both sexes cross-dressing.

In Charlotte Brontë's *Villette* (1853), the protagonist, a repressed Victorian governess teaching at a French boarding school, finds a kind of liberation, ecstasy and empowerment in being forced to play a male role in the school play. Acting in the role of another provides her with an outlet for the passion that she conceals beneath her everyday *persona*.

In Charlotte Brontë's *Jane Eyre*, a love story between a downtrodden young governess and a mysterious gentleman with a dark past, the gentleman disguises himself as a gypsy woman in an impertinent attempt to draw out his governess' interior self.

In Baroness Orczy's *The Scarlet Pimpernel*, the Pimpernel disguises himself as an old woman driving a cart in one of his many escapades to rescue nobility from the guillotine during the French Revolution.

Many female authors, such as the Brontë sisters or Ethel Florence Lindesay Richardson (Henry Handel Richardson), took male pseudonyms to disguise the fact that they were women, in order to be published and accepted.

Daniel Defoe's *Moll Flanders* (1722), commonly considered to be one of the first novels in the English language, is an intimate, first-hand memoir of a woman's life, written by a man.

Throughout history, humans have played with gender, transgenderism and transvestitism in literature, theatre and art. Humans have always played make-believe, imagining things that are not, or cannot be, in the real world.

These cultures, authors, actors and traditions have always known that what is represented on the page, and on the stage, is fiction. Elizabethan poet Sir Philip Sidney said, in his *Defence of Poetry,*

> The poet, he nothing affirmeth, and therefore he never lieth.[41]

Shakespeare makes this explicit in *A Midsummer Night's Dream*. He presents a "play within a play", in which a group of unintelligent tradespeople put on a play for the duke's wedding. It is a tragedy that is so badly performed it becomes farcical, because the actors think their audience cannot distinguish between theatre and reality: the man who plays a lion announces upon his entrance that he is not a real lion, but merely "Snug the joiner" so that he won't "fright[en] the ladies" in the audience.

Here, Shakespeare illustrates the folly of conflating theatricality with reality. Are transgender theorists, in appropriating the language of the theatre and literary criticism by invoking such terms as performativity[42], using them to replace real-life biological identity? Does this conflate theatricality with reality? Is transgender theory literalising literature and theatre? Is it confusing fiction and reality, representation and biology?

If so, trangenderism is treating fictional personas, or personality traits, as real persons and then insisting governments give privileged and protected status to these fictive personas in place of the protections and privileges granted to people according to their biological sex.

Across history, we have understood that instances of play-acting and appropriating another identity, name, gender, age, nationality, and so on are only acts of the imagination and belong only in the imagination, whereas transgender theory appears to fail to make this distinction and treats them as realities, confusing the acting we *do* that is *fictive* (fictional) with the acting that is what we *do* in our real (non-fictional) daily lives. To put it another way, it confuses "to perform" (imitate) with "to perform" (do).

If society accepts on a wide basis that self-defined fluid gender identity be the norm for how people identify and are recognised in law, then, to appropriate the former Librarian of the United States Congress, Daniel J Boorstin,

> We risk being the first people in history to have been able to make their illusions so vivid, so persuasive, so 'realistic' that they can live in them.[43]

6.2.8 The failure to coherently define gender identity

Is gender identity fluid and free floating, as Butler argues? Is it socially constructed, and so capable of being reconstructed, as the American Psychological Association suggests?

Or, is gender identity a stable, coherent and abiding sense of self, a "*deeply held* internal and individual sense of gender", as claimed by the AHRC? Is it, "each person's *deeply felt* internal and individual experience of gender", as claimed by the Yogyakarta Principles (author emphasis).

The former definitions claim gender identity is fluid and changeable while latter definitions claim gender identity is always biologically determined. How can what is deep and abiding be free floating and fluid?

These almost polar-opposite definitions indicate the ambiguity of self-defined gender identity. As Jagose says (1996), transgender theory, and identity politics, are "eviscerated not only by the array of different gender identities *between* subjects", that is, between people, "but also by the irresolvable difficulty *within* of each subject", that is, of each person's gender being fluid and changeable[44].

This makes transgender theory of its nature "always ambiguous", says Jagose.[45]

Again, as the AHRC admits, there is a "lack of consensus over the exact meaning and definition" of gender identity.[46]

6.2.9 Subjective gender identity versus objective biological sex

Mayer and McHugh (2016) conclude that biological sex, recognised by reproductive function, is the only objective way of recognising a person's sexual identity. It is useful to quote them again:

The underlying basis of maleness and femaleness is the distinction between the reproductive roles of the sexes; in mammals such as humans, the female gestates offspring and the male impregnates the female. More universally, the male of the species fertilises the egg cells provided by the female of the species.

This conceptual basis for sex roles is binary and stable, and allows us to distinguish males from females on the grounds of their reproductive systems, even when these individuals exhibit behaviours that are not typical of males or females.[47]

Throughout the animal kingdom, mammal reproductive function alone determines sex, regardless of social behaviour. The fact that the male Emperor penguin plays a strong maternal role looking after eggs does not cause scientists to redefine him as the female of the species. His sex is not determined by his social role in providing more care for the egg than his female partner does, but by the fact that he impregnates the female to produce an egg and thereby reproduce the species.

Even when a person is infertile due to age, medical condition or biological disorder, biological sex is still recognisable. Just as a table with a broken leg remains a table, although not a useful one, so does a blind person's eye remain an eye, even when it does not fulfill its function because of disease or genetic anomaly.

6.2.10 How many people identify as transgender?

The Williams Institute on Sexual Orientation and Gender Identity Law and Public Policy is a research institute based at the University of California Los Angeles' School of Law. It focuses on sexual orientation and gender identity research. In 2016, it conducted an extensive study to estimate how many Americans identified as transgender.[48] It asked:

> Do you consider yourself to be transgender? Yes/No [If Yes] Do you consider yourself to be male-to-female, female-to-male, or gender non-conforming?
>
> If the interviewer is asked for a definition of transgender, they respond:
>
> Some people describe themselves as transgender when they *experience* a different gender identity from their sex at birth. For example, a person born into a male body, but who *feels* female or lives as a woman, would be transgender. Some transgender people *change their physical appearance* so that it matches their internal gender identity. Some transgender people take hormones and some have surgery. A transgender person may

be of any sexual orientation – straight, gay, lesbian, or bisexual (author emphasis).

While the study found that 0.6 per cent of adults identify as transgender, its broad definition of transgender has serious definitional problems similar to the problems of defining gender identity, as discussed above.

What does it mean to *experience* a different gender identity, or to *feel* you are a different person, or to *change physical appearance*? Experience and feelings (emotions) are subjective. They can be deep and profound, vague and subject to moods, permanent or fleeting, past or present, different in the future. Changing one's appearance can involve a total change of appearance to identify as a different gender, or partial change, or minimal change. Appearance changes can be permanent, temporary or only for social occasions. They can be a fashion statement of "the new black", or an identity politics statement in opposition to the heteronormative; that is, to the state recognising only the male and female sexual identities.

Does identifying as male-to-female mean having had sex reassignment surgery, or mean wholly, partly or vaguely socially identifying as a woman? Or, does it mean a biological man's occasional feelings from his "feminine side"? Similar questions can be asked of a person identifying as female-to-male.

The Williams Institute questions did not include any psychological profiling of the respondents. There was no test for any associated psychological conditions such as autism, trauma, depression.

As the survey set no threshold for determining what it means to be transgender and did not psychologically profile respondents, the validity of the survey was compromised from being open to idiosyncratic interpretations. Nor did the survey consider how many people have detransitioned and now identify only with their birth sex.

A better insight is gained from examining how many people have gender dysphoria, and the prevalence of trans people who then detransition.

6.2.11 Young people transitioning, desisting and detransitioning

According to the American Psychiatric Association's *DSM 5* (*the 5*[th] *Diagnostic and Statistical Manual of Mental Disorders – 2013*),[49] the prevalence of gender dysphoria in males of all ages is between five and 14 in every 100,000 males and two to three in every 100,000 females.[50]

A subset of those with gender dysphoria includes children and adolescents. How many of these children identify as transgender in adulthood and how many desist from transitioning to the opposite sex?

Korte et al (2008)[51] found that

> Multiple longitudinal studies provide evidence that gender-atypical behaviour in childhood often leads to a homosexual orientation in adulthood, but only in 2.5% to 20% of cases to a persistent gender identity disorder[52]. Even among children who manifest a major degree of discomfort with their own sex, including an aversion to their own genitalia (GID in the strict sense), only a minority go on to an irreversible development of transsexualism.[53]

Korte et al also found that there were no

> valid diagnostic parameters to be identified with which one could reliably predict ... whether transsexualism will develop with ... a high degree of probability.[54]

Transgender literature emphasises the risks transgender students face if they are not allowed to socially and medically transition. Is the answer to support transitioning or to counsel them to wait until they are adults, given that a high proportion is likely to desist and not require intrusive medical intervention?

Further evidence for encouraging desistance in young people comes from those who detransition; that is, they return to identifying with their biological sex. There have been no formal studies on detransitioning. Rather, when James Caspian, a psychotherapist working with transgender people, became concerned at the numbers detransitioning and proposed a research project on detransitioning, the UK Bath Spa University initially approved the application. Caspian is a trustee of the Beaumont Trust charity, which provides support to transgender, transsexual and cross-dressing people.

His preliminary findings indicated growing numbers of young people, particularly women, regretting gender reassignment. The university ethics committee rejected his research proposal. On a BBC Radio 4 interview, he said

> [t]he fundamental reason given was that it might cause criticism of the research on social media, and criticism of the research would be criticism of the university. They also added it's better not to offend people.[55]

Nevertheless, an informal survey of female-to-males who detransitioned was conducted by Cari Stella, who describes herself as a detransitioned lesbian.[56] In 2017, she conducted a two-week survey on Survey Monkey and received 203 responses. These are women who transitioned, whether socially and/or medically, and subsequently detransitioned, as well as individuals who still identify as non-binary or gender fluid, but have desisted from medical or social transition. The survey was shared on Tumblr, Facebook, and by the blog, 4thWaveNow.

Stella said she was surprised at the sheer number of respondents in two weeks, and suggested that "detransitioners are not quite as rare as some would like to have us think". The key findings were that the average age of transitioning was 17.09 years and, of detransitioning, 21.09 years, making the average transgender duration of this group four years.

Of the 13 options to indicate why they detransitioned, the most common were

> shifting political/ideological beliefs, at almost 63%, and finding alternative coping mechanisms for dysphoria, at 59%.[57]

Stella was criticised on the Transgender Health Facebook page, which is a page for the World Professional Association for Transgender Health (WPATH) members and others involved in trans health. She was asked: "Show me a study of 12,000 trans men followed for 20 years, please?" The question cannot be answered if universities are refusing proposals for such studies?

Stella responded, saying:

> I created this because there is almost NO data on detransitioned women, or research being done into alternative treatments, other than what basically amounts to conversion therapy. We don't need conversion therapy, we need trauma-informed care. The women surveyed did not receive that. Only 6% of the women surveyed felt they received adequate counselling or information about transition, and 75% said their dysphoria had improved since detransition. 60% said that they had completely negative feelings towards their transition, and only 17% felt positive or even neutral about it. That is unacceptable. We deserve to have options presented for the treatment of dysphoria.[58]

The ambiguity of gender identity is underscored by the fact that most children with gender dysphoria do not transition to the opposite sex in adulthood and there is a sizeable, but unknown and unstudied group, who detransition.

So, why the recent spike in the number of young people wanting to transition?

In Australia, the number of children referred to Melbourne's Royal Children's Hospital for gender dysphoria increased from one in 2003[59], with 300 referrals expected in 2017.[60]

In the UK, the number of children and adolescents transitioning has risen from 51 in 2009 to 1,766 in 2016. Over this period, the average year-on-year increase in referrals for children under age 12 was 48.6 per cent for boys and 92.7 per cent for girls; in adolescents, the corresponding rates were 54.9 per cent and 88.6 per cent.[61]

Has the push for transgenderism in law, schools and culture created a transgender cultural phenomenon? Has transgender become the new black?

6.2.12 Summarising gender identity

The works of Butler – for example, *Gender Trouble: Feminism and the Subversion of Identity* (1990)[62] and *Undoing Gender* (2004)[63] – and other queer/transgender theorists have expanded into a world-wide sociological, literary and identity politics phenomenon, and laid the grounds for redefining the human person in law and culture.

Gender identity is a wholly socially constructed term. This has three consequences.

First, since each person on earth has their own unique, fluid gender identity, it can only be established by individual self-assessment at a point in time.

Second, there is no objective, consistent, agreed definition of gender identity because it is personal and unique to each person. It is an ambiguous term; that is, it is "open to more than one interpretation"[64].

Third, as gender identity is an ambiguous term that cannot be objectively defined or reasonably ascertained, legal uncertainty is created when it is written into law, with penalties for those who fail to comply with what they cannot understand with certainty. Attempting to recognise in law every idiosyncratic form of gender identity risks descending into legal and cultural incoherence.

In contrast, legally identifying a person by their biological sex provides grounds for certainty and fairness in law and culture. "Sex," "man" and "woman" can be clearly defined. Each person's sex can be biologically ascertained in almost all cases, providing grounds for sex-based rights and defences against discrimination based on a person's sex.

Based on what criteria should the theory of fluid gender identity, wholly a social construct, be written into law over objective, scientifically verifiable, biological sex?

6.3 SEXUAL ORIENTATION AND "GENDER ORIENTATION"

6.3.1 Defining sexual orientation and "gender orientation"

Historically, sexual orientation has described sexual attractions based on the biology of male and female – heterosexual, gay, lesbian and bisexual. A heterosexual person is sexually attracted to persons of the opposite biological sex. Gays and lesbians are sexually attracted to persons of the same sex, and bisexuals are sexually attracted to both sexes.

However, when the law defines a person by their fluid gender identity over biological sex, then *sexual* orientation becomes *gender* orientation. A man sexually attracted to a woman is said to have a heterosexual orientation in the biological world view. But, if the same man identifies as androgynous and the same woman identifies as gender queer, then their gender orientation is androgynous-to-gender queer in the transgender world view. If gender identity is always fluid, then gender orientation is always fluid.

The following are said to be definitions of sexual orientation but, in reality, they are definitions of gender orientation. They emphasise orientations based on gender identity, not biological sex.

The Yogyakarta Principles regard "gender" as including self-defined, non-binary *gender identities.* They go on to state:

> Sexual orientation is understood to refer to each person's capacity for profound emotional, affectional and sexual attraction to, and intimate and sexual relations with, individuals of a different *gender* or the same *gender* or more than one gender"[65] (author emphasis).

The Law Council of Australia endorses the Yogyakarta Principles[66], as does AHRC.[67] The AHRC describes sexual orientation in terms that include sexual attractions between both binary and non-binary people, saying it is

> a person's emotional or sexual attraction to another person, including, amongst others, the following identities: heterosexual, gay, lesbian, bisexual, *pansexual, asexual* or same-sex attracted[68] (author emphasis).

Similarly, the Safe Schools Coalition Victoria's *All of Us* resource says that sexual identity (that is, sexual orientation and gender orientation) involves sexual attractions between people who are non-binary. It's about

> [w]ho you love, like and hook-up with. There are lots of different components that make up your sexuality. You can be attracted to a *whole spectrum* of masculinity, femininity, both or even *none*[69] (author emphasis).

The federal *Sex Discrimination Act 1984* defines sexual and gender orientation as meaning "a person's sexual orientation towards: (a) persons of the same sex; or (b) persons of a *different sex*; or (c) persons of the same sex and persons of a *different sex*"[70], where "different sex", not opposite sex, refers to a person's fluid gender identity[71] (author emphasis) (see Chapter 8.2).

In contrast, the American Psychological Association bases sexual attractions between persons on their biological sex. It says in a public education document:

> Sexual orientation refers to an enduring pattern of emotional, romantic and/or sexual attractions to men, women or both sexes. Sexual orientation also refers to a person's *sense* of identity based on those attractions, related behaviours, and membership in a community of others who share those attractions. Research over several decades has demonstrated that sexual orientation ranges along a *continuum*, from exclusive attraction to the other sex to exclusive attraction to the same sex[72] (author emphasis).

To summarise, some organisations, like the American Psychological Association, recognise only sexual orientation, which they define as sexual attractions between persons:

- of the opposite sex; or
- of the same sex;
- or both sexes.

However, in many cases, what laws and organisations define as sexual orientation is logically gender orientation. Gender orientation is based on affections and attractions between persons:

- along a continuum between male and female; or
- with a non-binary gender identity unrelated to biological sex; or
- who identify as genderless.

6.3.2   What's ascertainable and what's ambiguous?

Most adults take their sex as self-evident, have matured in their sexual relationships and are set in their sexual attractions as heterosexual, gay or lesbian. However, there is a significant cohort for whom sexual orientation is less defined and more fluid, particularly in their younger years.

Australian surveys by Roy Morgan Research indicate that, for some heterosexuals, gays and lesbians, their sexual orientations can change over time. Three surveys involving 180,000 Australians have asked if people identify as gay or lesbian. The latest survey in 2012-14 found 3.4 per cent identifying as gay or lesbian. However, sexual orientation varies with age. In their 20s, 6.5 per cent identified as gay or lesbian, steadily falling to 1.7 per cent for people 50 plus. All three surveys since 2006-08 followed this pattern.[73]

Mayer and McHugh examined the problem of defining sexual orientation, particularly among this cohort, in *Sexuality and Gender: Findings from the Biological, Psychological, and Social Sciences* (2016).[74] The problems they find in defining sexual orientation are magnified in the case of gender orientation, if transgenderism regards each person on earth as having their own gender identity.

Mayer and McHugh argue that sexual orientation can mean patterns of desires, attractions, arousals, and behaviours, or identity. These definitional problems, discussed below, apply as much to heterosexuality, as to gay, lesbian and bisexuality.

Desires: The word "desire" can mean a feeling (emotion) to want something. These can be concrete: I feel hungry; or I want the job being offered to me. Or, desires can be a longing: I would like to be a rock star; or I want to fly to Mars. As Mayer and McHugh say,

> the language of desire is meant to include things that are less clear: indefinite *longings* for a life that is, in some unspecified sense, different or better; an inchoate sense of something being missing or lacking in oneself or one's world; or, in psychoanalytic literature, unconscious dynamic forces that shape one's cognitive, emotional, and social behaviours, but that are separate from one's ordinary, conscious sense of self.[75]

A common view is that sexual desires are the sum of the forces that incline us towards sexual behaviour. But it is not clear what constitutes the sum of desires. It can involve poverty driving a person into prostitution; alcohol-fuelled reckless sexual behaviour; pornography, creating sexual arousal; or, commonly, a desire for intimacy leading to pregnancy, a family. Sexual desires are slippery concepts.

Mayer and McHugh consider the ways in which sexual desires and orientations are considered in the social sciences. They can be:

- states of physical arousal that may or may not be linked to a specific physical activity and may or may not be objects of conscious awareness; or

- conscious erotic interest in response to finding others attractive (in perception, memory, or fantasy), which may or may not involve any of the bodily processes associated with measurable states of physical arousal; or

- strong interest in finding a companion or establishing a durable relationship; or

- the romantic aspirations and feelings associated with infatuation or falling in love with a specific individual; or

- inclination towards attachment to specific individuals; or

- the general motivation to seek intimacy with a member of some specific group; or

- an aesthetic measure that latches onto perceived beauty in others.[76]

Attractions: Sexual attraction has many meanings. Mayer and McHugh cite philosopher Alexander Pruss:

> What does it mean to be "sexually attracted" to someone? Does it mean to have a tendency to be aroused in their presence? But surely it is possible to find someone sexually attractive without being aroused.
>
> Does it mean to form the belief that someone is sexually attractive to one? Surely not, since a belief about who is sexually attractive to one might be wrong – for instance, one might confuse admiration of form with sexual attraction ...
>
> [S]imilar questions suggest that there is a cluster of related concepts under the heading of "sexual attraction", and any precise definition is likely to be an undesirable shoehorning. But if the concept of sexual attraction is a cluster of concepts, neither are there simply univocal concepts of heterosexuality, homosexuality, and bisexuality.[77]

Attractions could refer to arousal patterns, or to romantic feelings, or to desires for company, or other things; and

> each of these things can be present either sporadically and temporarily or pervasively and long term, either exclusively or not, either in a deep or shallow way, and so forth.[78]

Behaviours may or may not define how a person identifies. A person may have had gay or lesbian sexual encounters but may or may not identify as gay or lesbian. A predominantly heterosexual person may have had gay or lesbian encounters, but identify their sexual orientation as only heterosexual.

Identity: Sexual orientation can mean identifying with, and belonging to, a particular community; fantasies (as distinct in some respects from attractions and behaviours), longings, strivings, feeling the need for certain forms of companionship, and many other things.

Psychologists Lisa M. Diamond and Ritch C. Savin-Williams point out:

> The more carefully researchers map these constellations – differentiating, for example, between *gender identity* and *sexual identity, desire* and *behaviour, sexual* versus *affectionate* feelings, early-appearing versus late-appearing *attractions* and *fantasies*, or social *identifications* and sexual *profiles* – the more complicated the picture becomes because few individuals report uniform inter-correlations among these domains[79] (author emphasis).

Finally, to paraphrase sociologist Edward O. Laumann et al (1994), sexual orientation (and, by implication, gender orientation) "is fundamentally a multi-dimensional phenomenon that has manifold meanings and interpretations, depending on context and purpose."[80]

In summary, and, while many people, particularly mature adults, regard themselves as heterosexual, gay, lesbian or bisexual and stable in the sexual orientation, there is a cohort for which sexual/gender attractions are fluid and changeable and can only be established by self-assessment at a point in time.

6.4   CONCLUSION: WRITING "PERSONALITY TRAITS" INTO LAW

In a tolerant democracy and society, every person has the liberty to choose a gender identity other than their sex at birth, if they choose, and to choose their desired sexual or gender orientation.

However, this book is concerned only with the writing of these concepts into law. Whereas Mayer and McHugh point out that biological sex is immutable, "unchanging over time or unable to be changed"[81], sexual (and gender) orientation and gender identity are mutable, that is, changeable.[82]

Regardless, sexual orientations are based on the biology of male and female. Consequently, they are generally ascertainable in law.

It is a different matter when it comes to the subjective, ambiguous, fluid concepts of gender identity and gender orientation. These are personal and individual to each person and should be regarded as effectively being personality traits.

It is a legal principle that the law should have certainty and be ascertainable. Conversely, uncertainty should not be written into law. Writing subjective, ambiguous definitions or personality traits into legislation creates uncertainty in law. Uncertainty leads to injustices when people fail to comply, and face penalties on matters they cannot know with certainty.

Calls for objective, agreed, consistent definitions of gender identity and gender orientation – whether in psychology, sociology or law – cannot be achieved because these terms are fluid and subjective. Transgender advocates admit to the ambiguity of these terms.

Hence, it is curious that the Law Council of Australia, a leading advocate for recognising transgender terms in laws, has not sought to clarify the meaning of "gender identity" and "gender orientation".

In contrast, the biological sex of a person can be scientifically and objectively determined. Arguably, biological sex is the only objective sex identifier of human persons that should be recognised and protected in laws and regulations.

Endnotes

1. Daniel J Boorstin, *The Image: A Guide to Pseudo-Events in America* (1961), cited in "For America, a painful reawakening", *New York Times Magazine*, 17 May 1981.
   http://www.nytimes.com/1981/05/17/magazine/for-america-a-painful-reawakening.html?pagewanted=all Accessed 15 December 2017.

2. *Resilient Individuals: Sexual Orientation, Gender Identity & Intersex Rights: National Consultation Report 2015,* Australian Human Rights Commission, 2015, pg. 5.
   https://www.humanrights.gov.au/our-work/sexual-orientation-sex-gender-identity/publications/resilient-individuals-sexual Accessed 6 June 2017.

3. *Sex Files: the legal recognition of sex in documents and government records,* Australian Human Rights Commission 2009, pg. 14.
   https://www.humanrights.gov.au/our-work/sexual-orientation-sex-gender-identity/publications/sex-files-legal-recognition-sex Accessed 5 June 2017.

4. "psychology", *Oxford Living Dictionary.*
   https://en.oxforddictionaries.com/definition/psychology

5. "sociology", *Oxford Living Dictionary.*
   https://en.oxforddictionaries.com/definition/sociology

6. Friedmann Pfäfflin, "Medical/Psychological Views", in *The Legal Status of Transsexual and Transgender Persons,* Ed. Jens M. Sharpe, (Editor), Intersentia Ltd, Cambridge, 2015.

7. Ibid., pgs. 19-20

8. *Resilient Individuals: Sexual Orientation, Gender Identity & Intersex Rights: National Consultation Report 2015,* Australian Human Rights Commission, 2015, Op. cit., pg. 5.

9. "Introduction to the Yogyakarta Principles", Yogyakarta Principles, 2006.
   http://www.yogyakartaprinciples.org/ Accessed 13 July 2017.

10. "Answers to Your Questions About Transgender People, Gender Identity and Gender Expression", American Psychological Association, (pamphlet), http://www.apa.org/topics/lgbt/transgender.pdf Accessed 1 April 2017.

11. *All of Us: Student Hand Outs,* Minus18 resource for Safe Schools Coalition Victoria, pg. 34.
    https://www.studentwellbeinghub.edu.au/docs/default-source/all-of-us-student-version-may-2016-v4-pdf380012c4f7a6497397396f5b38789d44.pdf?sfvrsn=0 Accessed 1 April 2017.

12. *Sex Discrimination Act, 1984,* Section 4.
    http://www.austlii.edu.au/au/legis/cth/consol_act/sda1984209/

13. *Australian Government Guidelines on the Recognition of Sex and Gender* (July 2013, Updated November 2015), Attorney General's Department, Australian Government, pg. 4.
    https://www.ag.gov.au/Publications/Documents/AustralianGovernmentGuidelinesontheRecognitionofSexandGender/AustralianGovernmentGuidelinesontheRecognitionofSexandGender.PDF Accessed 19 June 2017.

14. Ibid., pg. 4.

15. Ibid., Key Terms, pg. 9.

16 Law Council of Australia, submission to the Senate Committee on Legal and Constitutional Affairs inquiry into the *Sex Discrimination Amendment (Sexual Orientation, Gender Identity and Intersex Status) Bill 2013,* 26 April 2013, pgs. 15, 16. Submission 17 available at http://www.aph.gov.au/Parliamentary_Business/Committees/Senate/Legal_and_Constitutional_Affairs/Completed_inquiries/2010-13/sexdiscrimsexualorientation/submissions Accessed 18 August 2017.

17 Law Council of Australia, submission to the Attorney General's Department inquiry into the "*Australian Government Guidelines on the Recognition of Sex and Gender*", 24 April 2013, pg. 6. Accessed 10 June 2017.

18 Matthew Waites, "Critique of 'sexual orientation' and 'gender identity' in human rights discourse: global queer politics beyond the Yogyakarta Principles", *Contemporary Politics,* 15:1 (2009), pg. 147. DOI: http://dx.doi.org/10.1080/13569770802709604

19 "sense", *Oxford Living Dictionaries.* https://en.oxforddictionaries.com/definition/sense Accessed 4 April 2018.

20 "feeling", *Oxford Living Dictionaries.* https://en.oxforddictionaries.com/definition/feeling Accessed 4 April 2018.

21 *Sex Files: the legal recognition of sex in documents and government records,* Op. cit., pg. 14.

22 Lawrence S. Mayer, M.B., M.S., Ph.D., Paul R. McHugh, M.D., "Sexuality and Gender: Findings from the Biological, Psychological, and Social Sciences", *The New Atlantis,* Number 50, Fall 2016, pg. 87. http://www.thenewatlantis.com/docLib/20160819_TNA50SexualityandGender.pdf Accessed 25 August 2016.

23 Paul McHugh, "Transgender Surgery Isn't the Solution", *Wall Street Journal,* 12 June 2015. http://www.wsj.com/articles/paul-mchugh-transgender-surgery-isnt-the-solution-1402615120 Accessed 4 September 2015.

24 Paul McHugh, "Transgenderism: A Pathogenic Meme", *The Public Discourse,* 10 June 2015, http://www.thepublicdiscourse.com/2015/06/15145/ Accessed 12 March 2016.

25 Judith Butler, *Gender Trouble: Feminism and the Subversion of Identity,* London, Routledge, 1990, pg. xi.

26 Ibid., pg. 122.

27 Ibid., pg. 9-10.

28 Ibid., pg. 10.

29 Judith Butler, "Performative acts and gender constitution: An essay in phenomenology and feminist theory", *Theatre Journal,* 1998, 40 (4), pgs. 519–531. https://www.amherst.edu/system/files/media/1650/butler_performative_acts.pdf Accessed 8 October 2017.

30 Ibid, pg. 527.

31 "fiction", *Oxford Living Dictionaries.* https://en.oxforddictionaries.com/definition/fiction Accessed 8 October 2017.

32 "fictive", *Oxford Living Dictionaries.* https://en.oxforddictionaries.com/definition/fictive. Accessed 8 October 2017.

33 Mayer and McHugh, "Sexuality and Gender", Op. cit., pg. 89.

34 "personality", *Oxford Living Dictionaries.* https://en.oxforddictionaries.com/definition/personality Accessed 8 October 2017.

35 Mayer and McHugh, "Sexuality and Gender", Op. cit., pg. 89.

36 Ibid., pg. 88.

37 Judith Butler, *Gender Trouble,* Op. cit., pgs. 141-163.

38 Ibid., pg. xiv.

39 Ibid., pgs. 161-183.

40 Ibid., pg. xii.

41 Philip Sidney, *The Defence of Poesy* or *An Apology for Poetry* (approximately 1579).

42 Notably, one of Butler's key essays on "performativity" was in the *Theatre Journal*, 1998, 40 (4): 519–531. It was titled, "Performative acts and gender constitution: An essay in phenomenology and feminist theory". Available at https://www.amherst.edu/system/files/media/1650/butler_performative_acts.pdf Accessed 4 May 2018.

43 Daniel J Boorstin, *The Image: A Guide to Pseudo-Events in America* (1961), Op. cit. Note: Boorstin was describing how television news was distorting reality in the 1960s. However, his quote appropriately describes how transgenderism aims to create a transnormative world in which the rights, privileges, protections and access to services for biological men and women are being compromised.

44 Annamarie Jagose, *Queer Theory: An Introduction*, New York: New York University Press, 1996, pg. 83.

45 Ibid., pg. 96.

46 *Sex Files: the legal recognition of sex in documents and government records,* Op. cit., pg. 14.

47 Mayer and McHugh, "Sexuality and Gender", Op. cit., pg. 89.

48 Andrew R. Flores et al, *How Many Adults Identify as Transgender in the United States?*, (white paper), Williams Institute, UCLA School of Law, 30 June 2016. http://williamsinstitute.law.ucla.edu/wp-content/uploads/How-Many-Adults-Identify-as-Transgender-in-the-United-States.pdf Accessed 7 February 2018.

49 *Diagnostic and Statistical Manual of Mental Disorders (DSM-5)*, 2013, American Psychiatric Association, https://psicovalero.files.wordpress.com/2014/06/dsm-v-manual-diagnc3b3stico-y-estadc3adstico-de-los-trastornos-mentales.pdf Accessed 14 July 2017.

50 Ibid.

51 Korte, A., Goecker, D., Krude, H., Lehmkuhl, U., Grüters-Kieslich, A., & Beier, K. M., "Gender Identity Disorders in Childhood and Adolescence: Currently Debated Concepts and Treatment Strategies". *Deutsches Ärzteblatt International*, November 2008, *105*(48), 834–841. http://doi.org/10.3238/arztebl.2008.0834 Accessed 17 April 2017.

52   Green R, Roberts CW, Williams K, Goodman M, Mixon A. Specific cross-gender behaviour in boyhood and later homosexual orientation. *Br J Psychiatry.* 1987; 151:84–88.
     https://www.ncbi.nlm.nih.gov/pubmed/3676630
     Zucker KJ. Gender identity disorders in children and adolescents. *Annu Rev Clin Psychol.* 2005; 1:467–492.
     https://www.ncbi.nlm.nih.gov/pubmed/17716096
     Cohen-Kettenis PT, van Goozen SH. Pubertal delay as an aid in diagnosis and treatment of a transsexual adolescent. *Eur Child Adolesc Psychiatry.* 1998; 7:246–248.
     https://www.ncbi.nlm.nih.gov/pubmed/3676630 All cited in Alexander Korte, et al, Ibid.

53   Korte, A., et al, "Gender Identity Disorders in Childhood and Adolescence: Currently Debated Concepts and Treatment Strategies", Op. cit.

54   Ibid.

55   "University 'turned down politically incorrect transgender research'", *The Guardian,* 26 September 2017.
     https://www.theguardian.com/education/2017/sep/25/bath-spa-university-transgender-gender-reassignment-reversal-research Accessed 28 April 2018.

56   Cari Stella, *Female detransition and reidentification: Survey results and interpretation,* 3 September 2017.
     http://guideonragingstars.tumblr.com/post/149877706175/female-detransition-and-reidentification-survey Accessed 8 May 2018.

57   Ibid.

58   Cari Stella, response on Transgender Health, Facebook page for WPATH members and others involved in trans health.
     https://www.facebook.com/groups/WPATH/permalink/1294043013973455/?comment_id=1295521843825572&comment_tracking=%7B%22tn%22%3A%22R%22%7D Accessed 8 May 2018.

59   "Transgender children: what's behind the spike in numbers?", *The Australian,* 18 July 2015, pgs. 12-16.
     https://www.theaustralian.com.au/life/weekend-australian-magazine/transgender-children-whats-behind-the-spike-in-numbers/news-story/10ccc515ef67b73a76e4e01aad92e54a Accessed 12 July2017.

60   "First regional gender clinic opens at Gateway Health Wodonga", *The Border Mail,* 21 April 2017,
     http://www.bordermail.com.au/story/4611243/first-regional-gender-service-clinic-opens-on-the-border/ Accessed 14 July 2017.

61   Nastasja M. de Graaf, Guido Giovanardi, Claudia Zitz, Polly Carmichael, "Sex Ratio in Children and Adolescents Referred to the Gender Identity Development Service in the UK (2009–2016)", *Archives of Sexual Behaviour,* 25 April 2018. https://doi.org/10.1007/s10508-018-1204-9 Accessed 8 May 2018.

62   Judith Butler, *Gender Trouble: Feminism and the Subversion of Identity*, London, Routledge, 1990.

63   Judith Butler, *Undoing Gender,* New York Routledge, 2004.

64   "ambiguity", definition in *English Oxford Living Dictionaries.*
     https://en.oxforddictionaries.com/definition/ambiguity

65   "Introduction to the Yogyakarta Principles", Yogyakarta Principles.
     http://www.yogyakartaprinciples.org/ Accessed 4 December 2016.

66 Law Council of Australia, submission to the Attorney General's Department inquiry into the draft *"Australian Government Guidelines on the Recognition of Sex and Gender"*, 24 April 2013. https://www.lawcouncil.asn.au/docs/72c29396-e502-e711-80d2-005056be66b1/130424-Submission-2712-Australian-Government-Guidelines-Recognition-Sex-Gender.PDF Accessed 12 June 2017.

67 *Resilient Individuals,* Australian Human Rights Commission, 2015, Op. cit., pgs. 52, 82.

68 Ibid., pg. 5.

69 *All of Us: Student Hand Outs,* Op. cit., pg. 24.

70 *Federal Sex Discrimination Act, 1984,* Section 4. http://www.austlii.edu.au/au/legis/cth/consol_act/sda1984209/

71 Ibid., definition of "gender identity".

72 "Answers to Your Questions for a Better Understanding of Sexual Orientation & Homosexuality", American Psychological Association, 2008. http://www.apa.org/topics/lgbt/orientation.pdf

73 "Is Australia getting gayer – and how gay will we get?" Roy Morgan Research, 2 June 2015. http://www.roymorgan.com/findings/6263-exactly-how-many-australians-are-gay-december-2014-201506020136 Accessed 5 May 2017.

74 Mayer and McHugh, "Sexuality and Gender", Op. cit., pg. 13-58.

75 Ibid., pg. 16.

76 Ibid., pgs. 17-18.

77 R. Pruss, *One Body: An Essay in Christian Sexual Ethics* (Notre Dame, Ind.: University of Notre Dame Press, 2012), 360, cited in. Mayer and McHugh, "Sexuality and Gender", Op. cit., pg. 18

78 Mayer and McHugh, "Sexuality and Gender", Op. cit., pg. 58.

79 Lisa M. Diamond and Ritch C. Savin-Williams, "Gender and Sexual Identity", in *Handbook of Applied Development Science*, eds. Richard M. Lerner, Francine Jacobs, and Donald Wertlieb (Thousand Oaks, Calif.: SAGE Publications, 2002), 101. See also A. Elfin Moses and Robert O. Hawkins, *Counseling Lesbian Women and Gay Men: A Life-Issues Approach* (Saint Louis, Mo.: Mosby, 1982). Cited in Mayer and McHugh, *Sexuality and Gender,* Op. cit., pg. 24.

80 Edward O. Laumann et al, *The Social Organization of Sexuality: Sexual Practices in the United States,* Chicago: University of Chicago Press, 1994; pgs. 300-301. Cited in Mayer and McHugh, *Sexuality and Gender,* Op. cit., pg. 24.

81 "immutable", *Oxford Living Dictionaries.* https://en.oxforddictionaries.com/definition/immutable Accessed 25 October 2017.

82 "mutable", *Oxford Living Dictionaries.* https://en.oxforddictionaries.com/definition/mutable Accessed 25 October 2017.

CHAPTER 7

TRANSGENDERISM: BODY-SELF DUALISM VERSUS DYNAMIC UNITY VIEW OF THE MIND AND BODY

7.1 INTRODUCTION

The transgender view of the human person is based on the contested philosophical concept of body-self dualism, which stands juxtaposed to the understanding of the human mind and body operating in "dynamic unity", technically called "hylomorphism"[1].

Human beings have a mind and a body. We may conceptualise them as separate things, but philosophers ask: do they operate separately, or in an integrated, dynamic union that comprises the human person?

7.2 BODY-SELF DUALISM

Body-self dualism theory says that the mind operates separately from the body such that the mind can prioritise, or dominate, over the body. It is the immaterial, the mental, the affective, that ultimately matters, while the material body is something subservient, inferior. The body is an instrument of the mind, to be used to satisfy subjective goals or produce desirable feelings in a person-as-a-conscious-subject.

Friedmann Pfäfflin, in his contribution to the book, *The Legal Status of Transsexual and Transgender Persons* (2015),[2] says that the dualist account of the mind-body relationship stresses the distinction between the body and the mind, and prioritises the mind over the body. This indicates that a person's identity resides exclusively in the mind and can be independent of the body. This extensive text is devoted to the global development of transgender law.

The mind taking priority and dominating over the body is the philosophical basis for a person claiming they can define their own fluid gender identity independent of the body's biological sex.

This allows queer/transgender theorist, Judith Butler, to describe gender as a "free-floating artifice" (see Chapter 6.2.2). In cases where the person identifies as the opposite sex, the person should have access to sex-reassignment surgery and hormonal treatments to make the body conform to the mind's wish to be the opposite sex.

A parallel influence that echoes body-self dualism is "transhumanism," a post-modern theory espoused by an iconoclastic movement popular among people in the high-tech industrial sciences. It advocates using science and technology to artificially enhance mental and/or physical abilities beyond what is considered normal for the human person. Augmenting the human body with advanced bionics and brain enhancement to go beyond human limits is a concept in cinematic dramas, such as *The Matrix, Transcendence, Ghost in the Shell, Lucy, Avatar,* etc. More popular examples include *The Six Million Dollar Man, RoboCop, Captain America, Iron Man,* series like *Dr Who* and *Star Trek* (the Borg), and the animation series, *Futurama*. Variously, these portray ghost-in-the-machine characters: body-machine beings in which the mind resides and in which the mind controls the body.

Body building has been a major driver of transhumanism. Body building drugs – anabolic steroids and growth hormones – became prevalent in sports as a result of government-sponsored doping programs by the states of the old Soviet Union beginning in the 1960s.[3] After the collapse of Soviet communism, these doping substances spread widely into sports of other nations. Despite their damaging effects on human health, these drugs are now promoted as part of the transhumanism project.

Some of these drugs, or their derivatives, are also used as part of transitioning programs of those changing to the opposite sex.

At the same time, the development and expansion of cosmetic surgery has also advanced both the transhumanist and transgender causes. Aside from its many therapeutic uses, cosmetic surgery also has the ability to re-shape a person's body to their preferred image.

Dr Kenneth Zucker (2015), in his capacity as former Chair of the Work Group on Sexual and Gender Identity Disorders for the fifth edition of *The Diagnostic and Statistical Manual of Mental Disorders* (2013), alludes to body-self dualism as being at the heart of the debate over transgenderism. He says that, in some respects,

> Gender Dysphoria is a good example of something that truly borders the mind-body division.[4]

7.3   DYNAMIC UNITY

Opposed to body-self dualism, the dynamic unity understanding of the human person says that the mind and the body interact together, informing each other in a rational being. It says that we are neither gendered minds inhabiting a separate, detached male/female body, nor purely biological beings that happen to be occupied by a mind, but a unity of body and mind. The body is no mere extrinsic instrument of our personal reality or self, but is an integral part of the personal reality of the human being.[5]

To explain, consider what you are doing now, reading this book. First, you are *perceiving* (becoming conscious of) words as your eyes see text on this page. Simultaneously, your mind is *understanding* what you are perceiving. You understand that you are reading words – not numbers, or viewing pictures, animals or a sunset.

Simultaneously, as you see with your eyes (part of your biological body), your mind (integrated with your body's senses) is understanding abstract letters forming words individually and as a sentence. A person can hold both parts together in a single judgement – the sensory image and the abstract concept – only because of the integrated operation, the dynamic unity, of the body's sensory organs and the mind's intellectual capacity.

Just as the eye sees words and the mind understands, so, too, the mind also perceives the reality of the bodily self as male or female.

The integrated mind and body, the lived reality of rational human beings throughout history, was recognised and described by Greek philosopher Aristotle (384–322 BC). Aristotle identified the mind as a faculty of the soul, of which he said:

> It is not necessary to ask whether soul and body are one, just as it is not necessary to ask whether the wax [of a candle] and its shape are one, nor generally whether the matter of each thing and that of which it is the matter are one. For even if one and being are spoken of in several ways, what is properly so spoken of is the actuality.[6]

Aristotle observed that the normal relationship between soul and body was uncomplicated, as uncomplicated as saying that a cubical shape is a property of a toy building block. For him, the mind is an integrated property of the human person.

Here, normal …

> is objectively, and properly, to be defined as that which functions in accordance with its design. Design and function are inseparably correlated in nature – even when one or the other factor happens to be unknown to us – and the term, normal, was originally invented and employed in recognition of that relationship.[7]

This dynamic unity of the mind and body is the normal lived experience of the vast majority of people across history. Their minds and bodies have lived in harmony. They have not found their mind and body in conflict and have not sought to change sex or gender. Their experience is not of two separate entities. Their bodies are not extrinsic instruments of the mind. Their sex is part of their basic biological organisation such that changing their sex is a metaphysical impossibility, because it is a biological impossibility.

Put commonly, their minds have accepted and loved the body they're in.

Whereas "normal" refers to the common human nature of human beings, Michel Foucault theorised that there is no human nature paving the way for a view that the mind can dominate over the body and embrace what is not normal (see Chapter 4.3).

Certainly, a person reading this book can say, "no, what I'm doing is looking at a sunset", just as a person can say, "no, I'm not a girl, I'm a boy in a girl's body". For some people, their mind *is* in conflict with their body. Their experience is of being exiles in their own flesh.

Perceptions that conflict with material or biological reality – particularly when the conflict involves highly sensitive and emotional issues such as one's own sexuality – can cause distress and social impairment. In these cases, "conflict between matter and mind can be as destructive as any other confusional state and deserves our compassion" and help, as understood by Australian paediatrician, Professor John Whitehall (2017).[8]

7.4 THE CONSEQUENCES OF BODY-SELF DUALISM

Based on the contested body-self dualist view of the human person, the transgender concepts of socially defined gender identity and gender orientation have been written into law, replacing public recognition of male and female across the culture.

Advocacy for such extensive legal recognition of transgenderism raises a question: if the person's mind can dictate that their healthy body can be medically transitioned to make the body conform to the mind's perception of wanting to be in a different body, then what else should the mind be able to do with the body should the two experience other forms of conflict? Consider these other body-mind conflicts.

7.4.1 Body dysmorphic disorder (BDD)

A person with body dysmorphic disorder (BDD) is constantly distressed with the erroneous conviction that, real or perceived, physical flaws make them unattractive/unsightly. As the Anxiety and Depression Association of America explains, people with BDD

> can't control their negative thoughts and don't believe people who tell them that they look fine. Their thoughts may cause severe emotional distress and interfere with their daily functioning. They may miss work or school, avoid social

situations and isolate themselves, even from family and friends, because they fear others will notice their flaws.[9]

They may even undergo unnecessary plastic surgeries to correct perceived imperfections, never finding satisfaction with the results.

The logic of the body-self dualism view of the human person, the view that forms the foundation of transgenderism, is that a psychologist should respect the deeply held feelings of the BDD patient who prioritises the mind over the body. Psychiatrists and psychologists should not regard BDD as a disorder and respect the patient's wish to undertake endless plastic surgeries in a fruitless attempt to resolve a body-mind conflict where the mind believes it occupies a seriously defective or unsightly body. BDD would no longer be considered a psychological disorder.

In contrast, the dynamic unity approach to the human person counsels the BDD person to recognise that their mind is applying misconceived, often culturally derived, ideas of beauty to their body. Counselling would also seek understanding of other factors in the person's life that may be contributing to the condition and seek to have the self (as in the person's mind) accept and affirm their body. Standard counselling practice is to push back against BDD.

In 2018, the NSW state government announced it was looking to tighten regulations over the body-modification industry after a person was charged with genital mutilation over an allegedly botched procedure on a woman suffering BDD.[10]

7.4.2 Body integrity identity disorder (BIID)

A person with body integrity identity disorder (BIID) identifies as a disabled person who feels trapped in a fully functional body. Individuals with BIID are often so distressed by their fully capable bodies that they seek surgical amputation of healthy limbs, or the surgical severing of their spinal cord or seek to have other body organs disabled.

BIID sufferer Jewel Shuping, from North Carolina, USA, believed she was meant to be blind. Determined to make her desire a reality, in 2006 at age 21, Jewel "took matters into her own hands" and found a psychologist willing to ease her distress. He blinded her – an act which she compares to a deaf person wanting to get a cochlear implant – by putting drops of drain cleaner into her eyes.[11]

This is an example of a psychologist effectively adhering to the logic of the body-self dualism view of the human person. The logic of body-self dualism is that medical authorities should support the BIID patient to give priority to their mind over their body and assist them to disable part of their healthy body. This means that BIID would no longer be treated as a mental disorder.

In contrast, the logic of the dynamic unity approach to the human person is to counsel the BIID person to appreciate the intrinsic value of their able body. Counselling would also seek understanding of other factors in the person's life that may be contributing to the condition and seek to have the person accept and affirm their body. Standard counselling practice is to push back against BIID.

7.4.3   Anorexia nervosa

Anorexia nervosa particularly afflicts young women. A girl suffering with anorexia nervosa has the persistent and mistaken belief that she is obese. She refuses sufficient food to stay healthy, or regurgitates meals, or seeks liposuction for non-existent fat in her body, based on a false assumption about her body image.

The logic of body-self dualism is that a counsellor should respect the deeply held feelings of the anorexia patient, who chooses to prioritise the mind over the body. The patient should be counselled forward to liposuction, starvation and other acts that may be in accord with the patient's self-image but will never resolve their body-mind conflict. The inevitable end of this process is death.

Again, the dynamic unity view of the human person would be to counsel the anorexia patient to accept the intrinsic value of their body and to nourish it to a healthy state; that is, "to love the body they are in". Counselling would also seek understanding of other factors in the person's life that may be contributing to their condition and seek to have them accept and affirm their body. Standard counselling practice is to push back against anorexia nervosa.

7.4.4   Gender dysphoria

Gender dysphoria occurs when a person experiences distress due to a feeling of incongruence between their biological sex and their gender identity, causing them to seek professional help.

The logic of the body-self dualism view of the human person is that counselling supports the patient to convert, or transition, to the opposite sex or to another gender identity. In the case of full transitioning to the opposite sex, they would be counselled to undergo sex reassignment surgery. This removes the patient's healthy reproductive organs. The patient is sterilised, risks sexual impairment and becomes permanently dependent on medications, with many known and many unknown risks.

In contrast, the dynamic unity view proposes that a person with gender dysphoria be counselled to overcome their distress by affirming their body. Counselling would also seek understanding of other factors in the person's life that may be contributing to the condition. For example, autism is emerging as a factor among some people who experience gender dysphoria.

There is confusion in the health professions on how to counsel cases of gender dysphoria. Historically, most counselling pushed back against the condition, as with other identity disorders. As the transgender world view progresses, some professional associations now advocate that a person with gender dysphoria be counselled to convert from their birth sex to their desired sex or gender identity.

Indeed, in some jurisdictions, laws have been introduced to prevent counselling that pushes back against this condition and transgender advocates are pushing to have the *DSM* 5 and the WHO *Classification of Mental and Behavioural Disorders* no longer list gender dysphoria as a psychological disorder.

7.5 CONFUSION OVER CONVERSION VERSUS AFFIRMATION THERAPIES

In cases of BDD, BIID and anorexia nervosa, standard counselling practice is to push back against the disorder. This is called affirmation counselling; that is, encouraging the sufferer to affirm the body they are in. Conversion therapy would be to counsel a patient forward in their disorder.

Similarly, in the case of gender dysphoria, the dynamic unity view of the human person says that pushing back against the condition is affirmation therapy, while counselling forward to transitioning is conversion therapy. This is the logical meaning of conversion therapy as "trans" means "to convert", to change from one state (their birth sex) to another (to the opposite sex, or a to non-binary gender identity).

However, transgender activists have sought to reverse the meaning of language to conform with a transnormative world view, saying that counselling forward to transition is affirmation therapy, while pushing back against transitioning is conversion therapy. Transgender language is now being recognised in some laws that ban transgender conversion therapy.

7.6 CONCLUSION

Body self-dualism asserts that the mind can dominate the body, even so far as to redefine the sex or gender identity of a person. In such cases, it creates incongruence between the mind and the body, putting the mind at odds with the inherent biological reality of the person's own body. It is an assertion against the idea of normal, that which functions according to its design.

It is a belief, a social construct, an assertion without any theoretical or scientific imperative to say that it is true. Indeed, Diana Fuss (1989) admits that the belief that gender identity is a deeply felt part of a person's identity, such that a person can have a legally recognised gender identity other than their birth sex, "fail[s] to challenge effectively the traditional metaphysical understanding of identity as unity,"[12]; that is, as "dynamic unity".

While a person in a tolerant democracy is free to identify with any gender identity they choose, transgenderism proposes that counselling for gender dysphoria should give priority to recognising the mind over the body and support the patient being counselled to transition. Why is the practice of counselling for the gender dysphoria patient towards transitioning the one exception to treatments for similar body identity disorders that push back against such psychological disorders?

The scope of this question may have been restricted to methods of psychological and psychiatric counselling but for the fact that gender identity – a term that includes people with gender dysphoria, which is classified in the *DSM-5* as a psychological disorder – is now a protected attribute of the human person in various Australian anti-discrimination laws.

Consequently, psychiatrists and psychologists could be in breach of anti-discrimination laws and some health laws if they counsel a patient with gender dysphoria to affirm the body they are in instead of counselling them to undergo conversion/transitioning treatments, including sex-reassignment surgery. Further, such laws put patients at significant medical and psychological risk.

Endnotes

1. Robert P. George, "Gnostic Liberalism", *First Things*, December 2016. https://www.firstthings.com/article/2016/12/gnostic-liberalism Accessed 13 December 2016.

   For a more extensive discussion of the debate over body-self dualism and hylomorphism, see Patrick Lee and Robert P. George, *Body Self-Dualism in Contemporary Ethics and Politics,* Cambridge University Press, 2008.

2. Friedmann Pfäfflin, "Medical/Psychological Views", in *The Legal Status of Transsexual and Transgender Persons*, Jens M. Sharpe, (Editor), Intersentia Ltd, Cambridge, 2015; pg. 42.

3. For example, see Werner W. Franke and Brigitte Berendonk, "Hormonal doping and androgenization of athletes: a secret program of the German Democratic Republic government", *Clinical Chemistry* 43:7 1262–1279 (1997). https://www.ncbi.nlm.nih.gov/pubmed/9216474 Accessed 25 June 2018.

4. Kenneth Zucker, and Robbie Duschinsky, "Dilemmas encountered by the Sexual and Gender Identity Disorders Work Group for DSM-5: an interview with Kenneth J. Zucker", *Psychology & Sexuality*, 2016, 7 (1). pgs. 23-33. https://www.tandfonline.com/doi/abs/10.1080/19419899.2015.1024472?journalCode=rpse20 Accessed 2 April 2017.

5. Robert P. George, "Gnostic Liberalism", Op. cit.

6. De Anima ii 1, 412b6–9

7. King CD. The meaning of normal. *Yale Journal of Biology and Medicine* 1945; 18:493501, pgs. 493-494. https://www.ncbi.nlm.nih.gov/pmc/articles/PMC2601549/pdf/yjbm00493-0064.pdf Accessed 15 December 2017.

   Note: "Normal" is an objective term. Commonly, the word "normal" is misused as meaning "average" or "ordinary".

8. Professor Dr John Whitehall, "Childhood Gender Dysphoria and the Responsibility of the Courts", *Quadrant*, May 2017. https://quadrant.org.au/magazine/2017/05/childhood-gender-dysphoria-responsibility-courts/Accessed 5 August 2017.

9. "Body dysmorphic disorder (BDD)", Anxiety and Depression Association of America. https://www.adaa.org/understanding-anxiety/related-illnesses/other-related-conditions/body-dysmorphic-disorder-bdd Accessed 4 April 2017.

10. "NSW flags body modification crackdown", AAP and News.com, 3 May 2018. http://www.news.com.au/national/breaking-news/nsw-flags-body-modification-crackdown/news-story/af6e3f83444915384c43658399bb2895#.bxaw0 Accessed 9 May 2018.

11. "Psychologist blinds woman with drain cleaner - because she wanted to be disabled", *The Mirror*, 1 October 2015. https://www.mirror.co.uk/news/real-life-stories/psychologist-blinds-woman-drain-cleaner-6552282

    "Why Woman Who Put Drain Cleaner In Her Eyes Wanted To Be Blind", *Huffington Post*, 15 November 2015. https://www.huffingtonpost.com/entry/why-woman-who-put-drain-cleaner-in-her-eyes-wanted-to-be-blind_us_563af2cce4b0411d306fb1de Accessed 7 May 2018.

12. Fuss, Diana, *Essentially Speaking: Feminism, Nature and Difference*, New York, Routledge, 1989, pg. 103, cited in Annamarie Jagose, Queer Theory: An Introduction, Op. cit., pg. 83.

PART B

AUSTRALIA: WRITING THE TRANSGENDER WORLD VIEW INTO LAWS

Transgender ideology advocates are using the law as an instrument of social transformation. Australia has led the way for other countries – particularly the USA, Canada and the UK – to consider writing the transgender world view into law.

Australia is a case study of the human person being redefined by their gender identity rather than of their biological sex using three main legislative pathways.

First, anti-discrimination laws across many jurisdictions have been changed to legally protect a person's gender identity alongside or, arguably, in place of, their biological sex. Because of its wide coverage, particularly important were the 2013 changes to the federal *Sex Discrimination Act 1984* (SDA). Gender identity was made a protected attribute in the Act. Redefining of human sexuality in anti-discrimination laws is discussed in Chapter 8.

Second, some births, deaths and marriages registration (BDMR) laws have also been changed to allow a person to self-identify with a non-binary gender identity on their birth certificate. These changes were made following the 2013 changes to the SDA in the Australian Capital Territory (2014) and in South Australia (2016). The redefining of human sexuality in BDMR laws is considered in Chapter 9.

Third, in 2017, the definition of marriage in the federal *Marriage Act 1961* was changed to legalise both transgender marriage and same-sex marriage. Transgender marriage is the logical extension of changing sexual identity in BDMR and anti-discrimination laws, as discussed in Chapter 10.

Generally, the terms man and woman have not been defined in law.

Core international human rights instruments – like the *Universal Declaration of Human Rights* (1948) and the *International Covenant on Civil and Political Rights* (1966) – have regarded the definitions of man and woman as self-evident.

Some other countries are changing laws to recognise gender identity in accordance with the transgender world view.

In the UK and the USA, there are moves to recognise gender identity in law.

In the United States, a bill for an *Equality Act* was put to Congress in 2017. Its definition of gender identity is similar to the definition in the failed *Employment Non-Discrimination Act of 2009*[1] and to the definition inserted into Australia's *Sex Discrimination Act 1984* in 2013 (see Chapter 8.2.2). The *Equality Act* Bill defines gender identity as:

> the gender-related identity, appearance, mannerisms, or other gender-related characteristics of an individual, regardless of the individual's designated sex at birth.[2]

The Bill also defines sex, not as meaning the biological sex of a male or a female, but as:

(a) a sex stereotype;

(b) pregnancy, childbirth, or a related medical condition; and

(c) sexual orientation or gender identity.[3]

An increasing number of US states, cities and counties give legal recognition to a person's gender identity.[4]

In the UK, the House of Commons' Women and Equalities Committee report, *Transgender Equality* (2015-16), endorsed the Yogyakarta Principles' definition of gender identity (see Chapter 6.2.1) and proposed that the *Gender Recognition Act 2004* be amended to allow a person's self-defined gender identity to be recognised in the form of an X marker on British passports, just as they are recognised on Australian passports (see Chapter 8.3, including Footnote 23).

The report says:

> The UK must follow Australia's lead in introducing an option to record gender as "X" on a passport. If Australia is able to implement such a policy there is no reason why the UK cannot do the same. In the longer term, consideration should be given to the removal of gender from passports.[5]

The British Government's response was to endorse this recommendation.[6] Legislation is pending, depending on the outcome of an inquiry into the proposal.

The Canadian *Human Rights Act* was amended in 2017 to add "gender identity or expression" to the list of prohibited grounds of discrimination.[7]

Does it matter whether we are recognised in laws as biologically male or female, or recognised in transgender, self-defined, gender identity terms?

It matters because a matrix of federal, state and local government laws and regulations, as well as formal and informal policies and codes, bestow rights, protections and privileges (including the right to make complaints of discrimination against another person) and access to services are based on a person's sex as recorded on their official identity documents. This matrix has only been partially studied and documented.

It matters because, as parliaments and courts have retreated from the biological world view of the human person, opposing frameworks of competing and conflicted rights have been created. These conflicts are deep and being played out in law, education, workplaces and wide areas of public life, as summarised in Tables 1.1 and 18.1.

Endnotes

1. *Employment Non-Discrimination Act of 2009,* S.1584, 111th Congress (2009-2010), Sec. 3, Definitions, (a) (6). https://www.congress.gov/bill/111th-congress/senate-bill/1584/text

2. *Equality Act,* H.R.2282, Sec. 1101, Definitions and Rules, (a) (2). 115th Congress (2017/2018). https://www.congress.gov/bill/115th-congress/house-bill/2282/text

3. Ibid., Sec. 1101, Definitions and Rules, (a) (4).

4. A list of definitions of gender identity in various US jurisdictions can be found in the footnotes of "'Gender identity' legislation and the erosion of sex-based legal protections for females", Cathy Brennan and Elizabeth Hungerford, Gender Identity Watch, 2011. https://genderidentitywatch.com/gender-identity-legislation-and-the-erosion-of-sex-based-legal-protections-for-females/ Accessed 3 July 2018.

   A preliminary list of states, cities and counties with gender identity laws can be found at "US counties and cities with sexual orientation and gender identity protection", Wikipedia. https://en.wikipedia.org/wiki/File:US_counties_and_cities_with_sexual_orientation_and_gender_identity_protection.svg

5. *Transgender Equality* (2015-16), Women and Equalities Committee, House of Commons, pg. 63. https://publications.parliament.uk/pa/cm201516/cmselect/cmwomeq/390/390.pdf Accessed 3 July 2018.

6. "Government Response to the Women and Equalities Committee Report on Transgender Equality", Government Equalities Office, July 2016 pg. 22. https://assets.publishing.service.gov.uk/government/uploads/system/uploads/attachment_data/file/535764/Government_Response_to_the_Women_and_Equalities_Committee_Report_on_Transgender_Equality.pdf Accessed 3 July 2018.

7. Bill C 16, *An Act to amend the Canadian Human Rights Act and the Criminal Code,* Royal Assent 19 June 2017 http://www.parl.ca/DocumentViewer/en/42-1/bill/C-16/royal-assent Accessed17 July 2018.

CHAPTER 8

TRANSGENDERING THE FEDERAL
SEX DISCRIMINATION ACT 1984

Australians are now recorded as Male, Female, or X (Indeterminate, Unspecified, or Intersex) on all federal government documents since the Sex Discrimination Act 1984 was amended in 2013.

Can a man, who identifies as a woman, now claim the same rights, privileges, protections and access to services previously given only to biological women?

Arguably, the X category makes Male and Female cisgender terms rather than statements of biological reality.

8.1 INTRODUCTION

Profound changes were made to the federal *Sex Discrimination Act 1984* (the SDA) in 2013. These amendments give priority to legally defining Australians by their gender identity and gender orientation, rather than their biological sex.

These changes are redefining human sexuality in federal law.

The SDA changes have resulted in government documents recording a person by their gender identity, transgender policies being introduced in public schools, gender-neutral language being implemented in workplaces, institutions providing gender neutral toilets and other changes to many other areas of public life. In short, defining gender identity in law creates new transgender rights that conflict with the rights of people, particularly women and girls, who recognise their sex as inherently self-evident.

The SDA amendments were given Royal Assent on 28 June.[1] Three days later, the Attorney-General's Department issued the *Australian Government Guidelines on the Recognition of Sex and Gender* (1 July 2013) (the *Guidelines*). The *Guidelines* require all federal government departments to have official documents carry the "X" sex identifier, or sex marker, alongside Male and Female. X covers Indeterminate, Unspecified and Intersex.[2]

The *Guidelines* attribute the SDA changes to proposals from the Australian Human Rights Commission (AHRC). A series of AHRC reports paved the way for these changes, beginning with the 2008 *Sex and gender diversity issues paper*.[3]

Later, the 2009 *Sex Files: the legal recognition of sex in documents and government records* (the *Sex Files*) recommended the

> development of national guidelines concerning the collection of sex and gender information from individuals.[4]

The *Sex Files* advocated recording transgender identity on key identity documents such as

> passports, driver's licences and photo identity cards ... [that] are often used to open bank accounts, travel, access goods and services and for other day-to-day functions.[5]

This was followed in 2011 by the *Protection from discrimination on the basis of sexual orientation and sex and/or gender identity in Australia: Consultation Report*. It criticised the SDA for defining "man" and "woman" biologically, saying that these definitions did not identify "the full spectrum of sex diversity that exists"[6].

8.2   THE SEX DISCRIMINATION ACT 1984

8.2.1   Redefining objects of the Sex Discrimination Act

The original objective of the SDA was to eliminate, as far as possible, discrimination against biological women. It aimed "to give effect to certain provisions of the [UN] Convention on the Elimination of All Forms of Discrimination Against Women and to provisions of other relevant international instruments"[7].

The biological attributes of women were recognised as grounds for protection against discrimination. Women had faced workplace discrimination when they become pregnant, or when they were breastfeeding. They faced discrimination because of their biological sex, not because of social characteristics, mannerisms, dress, or other sex-related characteristics. To underscore the biological differences that singled out women for discrimination, the SDA incorporated definitions of man and woman. It said:

> *woman* means a member of the female sex irrespective of age
>
> *man* means a member of the male sex irrespective of age.[8]

Furthermore, the SDA was amended several times to define the key biological attributes, or associated attributes, by which women faced discrimination, particularly in the workplace. These amendments aimed to

> prohibit, so far as is possible, discrimination against people on the ground of sex, marital status, pregnancy or potential pregnancy, breastfeeding or family responsibilities ...[9].

As Gaze and Smith (2017) comment, these attributes are based on the fact that "[SDA] women, by virtue of their sex, are the only people who can become pregnant" and give birth to a child.[10]

Various cases clarified the SDA's area of operation after some men lodged discrimination claims against women-only services in the Act's early years. Gaze and Smith explain that some men had argued

> that specialist women's services, domestic violence support services, or women-only gyms or sessions in swimming pools were discriminatory ...
>
> Over time, however, such measures were clearly recognised not to be discriminatory ...[11] [under] special measures intended to achieve equality.[12]

The SDA aimed to overcome discrimination against women, protecting women according to biological, and associated, attributes by which they faced workplace discrimination. Defining a woman by her biological sex underscored the biological nature of these attributes. Together, these ensured that biological men could not claim equal access to women's-only services, protections and privileges.

The SDA still protects a biological woman in circumstances where she is pregnant, or because she has the potential to become pregnant, and when breastfeeding. Women will still have protections according to these defined attributes.

However, the 2013 amendments to the SDA fundamentally changed the objects of the Act and undermined the original protections given only to biological women in other circumstances covered by the Act.

8.2.2 Redefining men and women as fluid gender

The 2013 SDA amendment Bill defined and gave protected attribute status to gender identity and sexual orientation and repealed the biological definition of "man" and "woman".

Gender identity is defined in the SDA as

> the gender-related identity, appearance or mannerisms or other gender-related characteristics of a person (whether by way of medical intervention or not), with or without regard to the person's designated sex at birth.[13,14]

The Bill's Explanatory Memorandum made it clear the intention of the Bill was to

> ensure that 'man' and 'woman' are not interpreted so narrowly as to exclude, for example, a transgender woman from accessing protections from discrimination on the basis of other attributes contained in the SDA.[15]

There are many problems with the SDA definition.

First, the SDA says sex is "designated" (assigned, appointed) at birth, just as parents choose and designate (assign) a newborn's name, or as a person is chosen for a position. The SDA treats identification of sex at birth as a choice that can be changed (re-designated or reassigned) later, whereas science says sex is inherent, an immutable, biological fact. By making sex a choice, the SDA sets the ground for gender identity to be self-defined and fluid. Federal laws do not define sex, or gender which leads to further problems with the SDA definition of gender identity.

Second, as neither "sex" or "gender" are defined, it is unclear what "gender identity" means.

While the definition says "gender identity" means the "gender-related identity" of a person, this is a circular argument. It is like defining a table as an object that is table-like.

What does "gender-related appearance" mean? Should a woman who wears a suit be considered as having the gender identity of a man? Should a man who wears his hair in a "man bun" be considered as having the identity of a woman?

What do "gender-related mannerisms" mean? If a boy runs on the tips of his toes, or throws a ball underarm rather than overarm, should he be considered as having the gender identity of a girl?

What do "gender-related … characteristics" mean? Should a boy who plays with dolls instead of toy trucks be considered as having the gender identity of a girl rather than simply a boy who represents an exception to the typical patterns of male behaviour? Is a young girl who wears pants, short hair and plays with trucks instead of dolls to be considered a boy?

"Gender-related characteristics" appear to refer to characteristics based on a person's biological birth sex. Aren't gender-related mannerisms considered to be the mannerisms related to a person's sex?

Third, while sex and gender are not defined in federal laws, they have commonplace, self-evident definitions. Biological science defines sex as physical attributes such as chromosomes, hormone prevalence, and external and internal anatomy that distinguish biological male (who provides sperm) from biological female (who provides an ovum). Commonly, gender has referred to either of the two sexes (male and female), with reference to social and cultural differences rather than biological differences. At the same time, these social and cultural differences are characteristics that point back to biological sex differences.

Explicitly and implicitly, the SDA definition of "gender identity" relies on the fact of a person being biologically male or female in the first place.

Explicitly, the SDA says "gender identity" can be determined "with regard to the person's … sex at birth": presumably this refers to a person self-identifying as cisgender.

Implicitly, the SDA definition relies on a person's birth sex, saying that "gender identity" also can be "without regard to the person's … sex at birth". However, the gender identity of people who identify as non-binary, or on a spectrum of male to female or genderless, is measured against their birth sex; that is, "with … regard to their designated birth sex at birth". It recognises birth sex as the measure by which a person's gender identity is determined. All gender identity is defined against the biological reality of a person's immutable birth sex (see Chapters 4.4, 6.2.6).

Directly and indirectly, the SDA attempts to define a person's gender identity as separate from their sex, but the definition suffers from of definitional fallacies (sex being "designated"), failure to define key terms (sex and gender) and a definition that depends on the reality of immutable, biological sex. This attempt to define socially constructed gender identity against the reality of biological sex leads, once again, to the question: does a person have a gender identity (on a spectrum of male to female, or non-binary, or genderless), or is the person just biologically male or female? The SDA definition highlights, but does not solve, this conundrum.

This definitional conundrum leads to legal conundrums.

Gender identity refers to social characteristics that are personal and individual such that they should be considered personality traits. Such personal matters are not a matter for legal definition and regulation. Giving legal recognition to gender identity, with its many ambiguities, creates uncertainty in law.

The definition of gender identity in the SDA allows biological men who identify as women to claim the rights, privileges, protections and access to services previously granted only to biological women. This has undermined the integrity of the original Act, which aimed to protect biological women from discrimination by virtue of their sex.

The SDA definition of gender identity broadly corresponds with the ambiguous definitions of gender identity adopted by the Australian Human Rights Commission (AHRC), the Yogyakarta Principles, the American Psychological Association, the Safe Schools Coalition Victoria (see Chapter 6.2.1), the failed US *Employment Non-Discrimination Act 2009* and the 2017 US bill for an *Equality Act* (see Part B).

Sexual orientation becomes gender orientation: The 2013 SDA amendment Bill also inserted sexual orientation and made it a protected attribute in the SDA. It is said to be a person's sexual orientation towards:

(a) persons of the same sex; or

(b) persons of a different sex; or

(c) persons of the same sex and persons of a different sex.[16]

The Attorney-General's Explanatory Memorandum said the Bill deliberately used the term

> 'different sex', instead of 'opposite sex' as it is ... consistent with the protection of gender identity and intersex status, which recognises that a person may be, or identify as, neither male nor female.[17]

"Opposite" means "two" things not the same; for example, binary male/female. "Different" means "two or more" that are not the same; for example, "non-binary" which means other than two. This definition recognises an androgynous person sexually attracted to a gender queer person, or a demigirl-to-gender fluid orientation, or a gender queer-to-poligender orientation. These examples of "gender orientations" are consistent with a person being defined by their gender identity in place of their sex.

Consequently, "sexual orientation" in the SDA is better described as "gender orientation". As there are unlimited possible self-defined, fluid gender identities, there are unlimited possible "gender orientations".

Indeed, the Explanatory Memorandum said that the SDA definition of sexual orientation purposefully did not "use labels, such as homosexuality, lesbianism, bisexuality or heterosexuality" because these terms only recognise a person by their binary, biological sex, but not those with a non-binary gender identity.

However, it also claimed that it was "intended that the definition [of sexual orientation] cover each of these sexual orientations"[18]. But, if a man and a woman sexually attracted to each other are only recognised under the SDA as cismale and cisfemale, then the term heterosexual no longer describes sexual attractions between biological men and women.

Consequently, just as "gender identity" dissolves the meaning of sex, arguably, the SDA's definition of sexual orientation, meaning "gender orientation", also undermines, if not dissolves, the meaning of homosexual, lesbian, bisexual and heterosexual (see further discussion below).

8.3 GUIDELINES IMPLEMENTING THE SDA AMENDMENTS

Three days after the SDA was given Royal Assent, the *Australian Government Guidelines on the Recognition of Sex and Gender* (2013)[19] were issued by the Attorney General's Department with the purpose of changing identity recording on all official federal government documents and for collection of identity data.

The *Guidelines* require a person's sex identifier to be M, F, X (Indeterminate/Intersex/Unspecified) on official documents like passports, taxation forms, census forms and Medicare forms. If there is insufficient space for all these terms, then documents can record M, F, X.

The *Guidelines* are said to support "legal protections" for gender identity and intersex status, as defined in the SDA.[20] Further, this

> classification system is consistent with the Australian Government passports policy for applicants who are sex and gender diverse and Australian Standard AS4590 – Interchange of Client Information…[21].

The *Guidelines* go on to say:

> The X category refers to any person who does not exclusively identify as either male or female, i.e. a person with a non-binary gender identity or who identifies with the opposite to their sex at birth. People who fall into this category may use a variety of terms to self-identify.[22]

"Indeterminate" refers to

> someone whose biological sex cannot be unambiguously determined or someone who identifies as neither male nor female. Many terms are used to recognise people who do not fall within the traditional binary notions of sex and gender (male and female), including non-binary, gender diverse, gender queer, pan-gendered, androgynous and inter-gender.[23]

"Unspecified" is not defined in the *Guidelines*, but appears to apply

> in circumstances where a person is in the process of changing their identity from one sex and gender to another ('transitioning') or does not identify as having a sex.[24]

"Intersex" refers to people with a disorder of sexual development (DSD), as discussed in Chapter 5.2.

The *Guidelines* say that legal recognition only requires a statement from a registered medical practitioner or psychologist, a passport or Australian government travel document, an amended birth certificate, or a state or territory Gender Recognition Certificate or Recognised Details Certificate. "Sex reassignment surgery or hormone therapy are not prerequisites."[25]

The X marker not only appears on federal government documents. Variously, it has been adopted by some state and territory agencies.

Now the UK government says it must follow Australia's lead and introduce the X marker on British passports by amending the *Gender Recognition Act 2004* to allow a person to self-identify their legal gender identity in place of their birth sex (see Part B).

8.4   FURTHER EVIDENCE OF THE SDA AND GUIDELINES DISSOLVING BIOLOGICAL SEX, MAN AND WOMAN

What do the terms Male and Female mean on official federal government identity documents, when these terms appear next to the X marker?

Consider you are filling out a government form and you encounter the sex descriptors Male, Female, X (Indeterminate, Unspecified, Intersex). Automatically, the X term means that a person can choose to identify with a non-binary gender identity instead of their birth sex.

This means Male and Female are no longer fixed, immutable statements of a person's biological sex as recorded at birth. They are optional terms, "designated" or only "assigned" at birth. A person can choose to reassign them later. Effectively, the X marker changes Male to cismale and Female to cisfemale; that is, a person only chooses to self-identify with their biological sex.

Saying that a person is cisgender is like saying a person is cishuman (that they self-identify as human and not as some other species) as opposed to them saying, "I recognise that, of my nature, I is immutably human". Are people cisgender and cishuman, or are they just biologically male/female and human (see Chapter 2.3)?

The *Guidelines* reflect the gender identity conundrum in the SDA.

On the one hand, the *Guidelines* distinguish and separate biological sex ("chromosomal, gonadal and anatomical characteristics associated with biological sex") from gender identity ("outward social markers, including [a person's] name, outward appearance, mannerisms and dress")[26].

On the other hand, the *Guidelines* paradoxically say:

> Although sex and gender are conceptually distinct, these terms are commonly used interchangeably, including in legislation.[27]

Gender identity is an ambiguous term, confusing, if not dissolving, the meaning of male and female, and creating uncertainty in law.

8.5   CASES WHERE "GENDER IDENTITY" MAKES "SEX" AND "EQUALITY" AMBIGUOUS

Consider the case of a company/authority that plans to implement an affirmative action program that reserves five out of 10 senior management positions for women. There are three federal laws that could cover this program in the public or private sectors.[28]

The SDA has wide coverage and makes "sex" and "gender identity" protected attributes. It defines "gender identity", does not define "sex" and the 2013 amendment bill removed the definitions of "man" and "woman". Consequently, a biological man can self-identify as a "woman".

The federal *Equal Employment Opportunity (Commonwealth Authorities) Act 1987* covers "certain Commonwealth authorities" with the aim of promoting "equal opportunity in employment for women and persons in designated groups". The "designated groups" include Indigenous, disabled, migrant people and "any other class of persons prescribed by the regulations for the purposes of this definition"[29]. For the purpose of achieving one form of equality, as between women and men, the Act defines woman as "a member of the female sex irrespective of age"[30] but does not define "sex" or "man".

The federal *Workplace Gender Equality Act 2012*[31] broadly covers private sector employers with more than 100 employees. Equality indicators include "gender [sex] composition of governing bodies of relevant employers" and "equal remuneration between women and men"[32]. To achieve "gender equality" between women and men, the Act provides definitions: "*woman* means a member of the female sex irrespective of age" and "*man* means a member of the male sex irrespective of age"[33]. The Act does not define "sex".

Under these three federal laws, would the affirmative action program of a company/authority be considered discriminatory if it meant the five positions reserved for women were given only to biological women, or would the program be required to make it clear that, under the SDA definition of gender identity, transgender male-to-female could apply for these positions?

Which law would take priority? While the *Equal Employment Opportunity (Commonwealth Authorities) Act 1987* and *Workplace Gender Equality Act 2012* have provided definitions of "woman", these definitions rely on the meaning of the word "sex". Under the SDA, the definition of "gender identity" allows "sex" to include situations where a man self-identifies as a woman.

This is an example of uncertainty being created when "sex and gender" are "commonly used interchangeably" in Australian law.[34]

This ambiguity sets the stage for many other potential conflicts between the inherent right of biological women and the newly created rights of transgenders that flow from protecting a person's gender identity in the SDA.

8.6   CREATING WIDE CONFLICTS

The SDA definition of discrimination makes it an offence to treat an "aggrieved person less favourably than, in circumstances that are the same or are not materially different, the discriminator treats or would treat a person who has a different" gender identity, sexual orientation, sex, intersex status, relationship status, or who is pregnant, potentially pregnant, etc.[35] This is subject to the reasonableness test[36] and exemptions are made for a variety of agencies, organisations and services.

This means that people who identify as transsexual, non-binary or genderless cannot be treated "less favourably" in the same circumstances to people who regard their sexual identity as inherent and self-evident.

The SDA has wide coverage across areas of employment, education, provision of goods and services, accommodation, clubs, administration of Commonwealth programs, registered organisations, organisations granting occupational qualifications, sports and other areas.

Defining gender identity in the SDA and in some state and territory laws (see Table 8.1) creates new grounds for many conflicts. Examples include the following:

- What happens to the measures that have been recognised as not being discriminatory[37] under the SDA's special measure to achieve equality,[38] such as women's-only services, domestic violence shelters, gyms, or sessions in swimming pools?[39] Fernwood women's gyms have been granted exemptions to provide services only to women, not men.[40] Will men who identify as women or as non-binary be treated "less favourably" if they are not granted access to services like female gyms?

- Will teachers and principals in state schools face discrimination charges, or loss of professional qualifications and employment, if they deny a boy identifying as a girl access to female toilets, showers, change rooms and sports? How will the right of girls to their privacy be protected and respected?

- The SDA allows sporting authorities to refuse a male who identifies as a female from participating in a women's sport where their "strength, stamina or physique" gives them an unfair advantage.[41] Although this gives broad leeway for sporting authorities to act, the SDA also creates impetus for transsexual male-to-female participation in women's sports under conditions that are likely to be contested by biological women (see Chapter 17).

- In a workplace that invokes the SDA to impose gender-neutral language on staff, will a man married to a woman be required to refer to her only as his "partner" so as not to offend transgenders? Will he face social sanctions or refusal of new employment contracts if he fails to use gender-neutral language to describe his wife, son, daughter, friends and work colleagues?

Potentially, people can face penalties from discrimination charges or sanctions imposed by professional organisations, employers and other agencies covered by the SDA and/or covered by similar state and territory laws.

There are as many such examples as there are conflicts over rights, privileges, protections and access to services, as set out in Tables 1.1 and 18.1. More of these conflict cases are discussed in Part C of this book.

8.7   DOES GENDER IDENTITY MAKE HETEROSEXUAL, GAY, LESBIAN AND BISEXUAL AMBIGUOUS?

Defining a person by their gender identity makes man and woman cisgender terms and allows a person born male to identify as a woman and a person born female to identify as a man.

Consequently, "heterosexual" includes a cisgender male sexually attracted to a cisgender female, a cisgender male sexually attracted to a biological male who identifies as a woman, and a cisgender female sexually attracted to a biological female who identifies as a man.

"Gay" includes a cisgender male oriented to a cisgender male, a cisgender male oriented to a biological female who identifies as male, and a sexual attraction between two biological females who identify as males.

"Lesbian" includes a sexual attraction between two cisgender females, a cisgender female sexually attracted to a biological male who identifies as female, and a sexual attraction between two biological males who identify as females.

"Bisexual" means a combination of these possibilities.

In which case, the defining of a person by the gender identity appears to dissolve what most people would regard as the biological essence of their "sexual orientation". It appears to erase the common meaning of the terms heterosexual, gay, lesbian and bisexual.

8.8 AHRC AND LAW COUNCIL OF AUSTRALIA SUPPORTS THESE CHANGES

The Explanatory Memorandum of the 2013 SDA amendment Bill said that discrimination on the grounds of gender identity and sexual orientation were related to eight international conventions: to the *Convention on the Elimination of All Forms of Discrimination Against Women*, the *International Covenant on Civil and Political Rights*, the *International Covenant on Economic, Social and Cultural Rights*, the *Convention on the Rights of the Child*, the *International Labor Organisation* (ILO) Convention (No. 100), the *ILO Convention* (No. 111), the *ILO Convention* (No. 156) and *the ILO Convention* (No. 158) concerning Termination of Employment at the Initiative of the Employer.[42]

Despite this claim, none of these instruments refers to gender identity or sexual orientation. They only deal with discrimination based on biological sex.

Indeed, the AHRC admits that

> [t]here is no separate international human rights agreement that deals specifically with sexual orientation or gender identity.

Regardless, the AHRC says that

> all people have the same human rights regardless of their sexual orientation or gender identity.[43]

Despite not being mentioned in international law, the Law Council of Australia (2013) told a Senate inquiry into the SDA amendment Bill that it

> strongly supports the enactment of legislative protections against discrimination on the grounds of sexual orientation, gender identity, intersex status and relationship status.[44]

The Council invoked the Yogyakarta Principles, saying that they are "highly persuasive in interpreting existing international human rights obligations"[45], particularly in relation to governments adopting "legislative administrative and other measures" to legally protect a person by their gender identity.[46] However, the Yogyakarta Principles have no status in international law.

Here the Law Council admitted that each person's gender identity is "self-defined"[47]. Writing subjective gender identity into law creates uncertainty in law. Regardless, the Council followed the AHRC lead in advocating the recognition of gender identity in law.

8.9   LEGAL PARADOX

Defining a person by their gender identity in law, rather than by their birth sex, is comparable to the *Racial Discrimination Act 1975* recognising a person as self-defining their race, so that a person solely of English descent can self-identify as Aboriginal.

It is comparable to the *Age Discrimination Act 2004* allowing a person to change their age from, say, 40 to 70 to claim protections under the Act and gain access to the aged pension and welfare services available only to elderly people.

It is comparable to the *Disability Discrimination Act 1992* allowing a person to self-identify with a non-existent disability in order to claim protections under the Act and to access welfare payments and services available only to disabled people.

These discrimination acts recognise race, age and disabilities as facts, objectively determined. As they can be objectively determined, they provide certainty in law.

This begs a question: if the SDA allows a person to legally change their sex to a gender identity, why can't a person also change their race, or age, or self-identify as having a disability under the relevant anti-discrimination law?

8.10 STATE AND TERRITORY ANTI-DISCRIMINATION LAWS AND IDENTITY DOCUMENTS

State and territory anti-discrimination and equal opportunity laws vary in how they legally recognise a person, as outlined in Table 8.1.

Western Australia recognises persons by their biological sex, with an exception for transsexuals who have undergone sex-change surgery.

New South Wales, Victoria and Queensland recognise a person by their biological sex, and sex also includes socially or medically transitioned transsexuals.

Tasmania, South Australia and the Australian Capital Territory are broadly aligned with the federal SDA in defining a person by their sex and fluid gender identity. As with the amended SDA, "sex" appears to be a cisgender term, not a statement of biological reality.

Currently, the Northern Territory does not cover gender identity. However, a 2017 Attorney General's discussion paper recommends adopting definitions of gender identity and sexual orientation similar to those inserted into the federal SDA.

Further, South Australia and the ACT have amended their births, deaths and marriages registration laws to include not only male and female, but also "indeterminate sex", "unspecified sex" and "intersex" on birth certificates. SA also includes "non-binary" (see Chapter 9). It appears that these changes are to bring other identity documents into alignment with the SDA. In 2018, Queensland is considering changes similar to those in South Australia and the ACT.

Several state and territory transport departments are also adopting the federal *Guidelines'* X marker on drivers' registration forms. For example, WA Department of Transport *Change of Personal Details* form[48] and the SA *Driver's Licence/Learners Permit Application*[49] form allow a person to be recorded as Male, Female or X (see Table 8.1).

8.11 CONCLUSION

Largely without public debate, pathways have been created to legally define a person by their gender identity, with major consequences for all Australians in broad areas of public life. The amended SDA and the federal *Guidelines* have been the most significant.

The Australian Human Rights Commission (AHRC) has been a leading advocate for the transgender concept of gender identity being recognised in law. It has called for consistent coverage across all jurisdictions,[50] even though the AHRC itself admits "[t]here is no consensus about the definition of sex or gender …"[51]. The Law Council of

Australia has strongly supported federal legislative and administrative changes.

Theodore Bennett (2012) claims that the *Guidelines* accommodate both the biological world view, by having federal identity documents record Male and Female, and the transgender world view, by providing people with the X marker options.[52] To the contrary, the SDA and the *Guidelines* have brought the two world views into conflict. They have created new rights, protections, privileges and access to services that lead to social, legal and political conflicts.

One person's new right to a non-binary gender identity has become a biological person's loss of rights accorded to them by virtue of their biological sex.

This is creating grounds for legal prosecutions, professional sanctions and other punitive proceedings for people who cannot reasonably comply with laws that define a person by their self-identified, fluid, gender identity and their subjective gender orientation.

Endnotes

1. *Sex Discrimination Amendment (Sexual Orientation, Gender Identity and Intersex Status) Act 2013*.
   https://SDA.legislation.gov.au/Details/C2013A00098 Accessed 10 May 2018.

2. *Australian Government Guidelines on the Recognition of Sex and Gender* (July 2013, Updated November 2015), Attorney-General's Department, Australian Government, pg. 7.
   https://SDA.ag.gov.au/Publications/Documents/AustralianGovernmentGuidelinesontheRecognitionofSexandGender/AustralianGovernmentGuidelinesontheRecognitionofSexandGender.PDF Accessed 19 June 2017.

3. *Sex and gender diversity issues paper*, Human Rights and Equal Opportunity Commission, May 2008.
   https://SDA.humanrights.gov.au/our-work/projects/sex-and-gender-diversity-issues-paper Accessed 5 June 2017.

4. *Sex Files: the legal recognition of sex in documents and government records*, Australian Human Rights Commission 2009, pg. 9.
   https://SDA.humanrights.gov.au/our-work/sexual-orientation-sex-gender-identity/publications/sex-files-legal-recognition-sex Accessed 5 June 2017.

5. Ibid., pg. 20.

6. *Protection from discrimination on the basis of sexual orientation and sex and/or gender identity in Australia: Consultation Report*, Australian Human Rights Commission, April 2011, pg. 29.
   http://SDA.humanrights.gov.au/publications/consultation-protectiondiscrimination-basis-sexual-orientation-and-sex-andor-gender Accessed 5 June 2017, pg. 29.

7. *Sex Discrimination Act 1984*, Act No. 4 of 1984 as Registered 21 March 2012, C2012C00313, Section 3 (a).
   https://SDA.legislation.gov.au/Details/C2012C00313 Accessed 5 June 2017.

8. Ibid., Section 4.

9. Ibid., Section 3 (b).

10. Beth Gaze and Belinda Smith, *Equality and Discrimination Law in Australia: An Introduction*, Cambridge University Press, 2017, pg. 80.

11. Ibid., pgs. 77-78.

12. *Sex Discrimination Act 1984*, Act No. 4 of 1984 as Registered 21 March 2012, Op. cit., Section 7D.

13. *Sex Discrimination Act 1984*, as compiled on 1 July 2016, Section 4.
    https://SDA.legislation.gov.au/Details/C2016C00880

14. Note: The federal *International Criminal Court Act 2011* (Schedule, Part 1, Crime Against Humanity, 3) defines "gender" very differently to the SDA. It says "'gender' refers to both sexes, male and female, within the context of society, and does not indicate any different meaning", but only for the purpose of crimes against humanity.

15. Explanatory Memorandum, *Sex Discrimination Amendment (Sexual Orientation, Gender Identity and Intersex Status) Bill 2013*, then Federal Attorney General, Mark Dreyfus, pg. 13.
    http://parlinfo.aph.gov.au/parlInfo/search/display/display.w3p;query=Id%3A%22legislation%2Fems%2Fr5026_ems_1fcd9245-33ff-4b3a-81b9-7fdc7eb91b9b%22

16. *Sex Discrimination Act 1984*, as compiled on 1 July 2016, Op. cit., Section 4.

17 Explanatory Memorandum, *Sex Discrimination Amendment (Sexual Orientation, Gender Identity and Intersex Status) Bill 2013*, Op. cit., pg. 14.

18 Ibid., pg. 14.

19 *Australian Government Guidelines on the Recognition of Sex and Gender*, Op. cit.

20 Ibid., pg. 3.

21 Ibid., pg. 5.

   Note: The X marker was first introduced on Australian passports in 2003 for recognition of intersex people. In 2011, this was broadened to include a person with a new gender that was documented as indeterminate. This followed the 2008 International Civil Aviation Organisation's Machine Readable Travel Documents rule that requires that a person's sex be recorded on passports as "the capital letter F for female, M for male, or X for unspecified" (International Civil Aviation Organisation, Machine Readable Travel Documents, Doc 9303, Vol 1, 2008, pg. 14. https://www.icao.int/publications/Documents/9303_p4_cons_en.pdf Accessed 4 July 2018). In 2013, the *Guidelines* again broadened the X marker to include non-binary gender identities.

22 Ibid., pg. 5.

23 Ibid., Key Terms, pg. 9.

24 *Beyond the Binary: Legal Recognition of Sex and Gender Diversity in the ACT*, The ACT Law Reform Advisory Council (LRAC), 21 December 2012, pgs. 36, 38. http://SDA.justice.act.gov.au/publication/view/1897/title/beyond-the-binary-legal-recognition Accessed 30 May 2017.

25 *Australian Government Guidelines on the Recognition of Sex and Gender*, Op. cit. pg. 5.

26 Ibid., pg. 4.

27 Ibid., pg. 4.

28 Note: the federal *Acts Interpretation Act 1901*, Compilation date: 1 July 2016, does not define "man", "woman" or "sex".

29 The *Equal Employment Opportunity (Commonwealth Authorities) Act 1987*, Contents.
   https://SDA.legislation.gov.au/Details/C2016C00775

30 Ibid., Section 3.

31 *The Workplace Gender Equality Act 2012*, Section 3.
   https://SDA.legislation.gov.au/Details/C2016C00895

32 Ibid.

33 Ibid.

34 *Australian Government Guidelines on the Recognition of Sex and Gender*, Attorney General's Department, Australian Government, (July 2013, Updated November 2015) pg. 4, Op. cit.

35 *Sex Discrimination Act 1984*, as compiled on 1 July 2016, Op. cit., Sections 5, 5A, 5B, 5C, 6, 7, 7AA.

36 Ibid., Section 7B.

37 Beth Gaze and Belinda Smith, *Equality and Discrimination Law in Australia: An Introduction*, Op. cit., pgs. 77-78. 39.

38 *Sex Discrimination Act 1984*, as compiled on 1 July 2016, Op. cit., Section 7D.

39 Beth Gaze and Belinda Smith, Equality and Discrimination Law in Australia, Op. cit., pg. 80.

40. For example: *Fernwood Fitness Centre [1998] VADT 43* (9 January 1998). http://classic.austlii.edu.au/cgi-bin/sinodisp/au/cases/vic/VADT/1998/43.html?stem=0&synonyms=0&query=fernwood%20gyms

    Ex Parte Diana Williams and Fernwood Women's Health Club [2006] WASAT 180. https://www.slp.wa.gov.au/gazette/gazette.nsf/lookup/2006-149/$file/gg149.pdf

    Fernwood Women's Health Club Pty Ltd [2003] QADT 27 (27 November 2003). https://www.austlii.edu.au/cgi-bin/viewdoc/au/cases/qld/QADT/2003/27.html.

41. *Sex Discrimination Act 1984*, as compiled on 1 July 2016, Op. cit., Section 42.

42. Explanatory Memorandum, *Sex Discrimination Amendment (Sexual Orientation, Gender Identity and Intersex Status) Bill 2013*, Op. cit., pg. 18.

43. *Protection from discrimination on the basis of sexual orientation and sex and/or gender identity in Australia: Consultation report*, Australian Human Rights Commission, Op. cit., pg. 10.

44. Law Council of Australia, submission to the Senate Committee on Legal and Constitutional Affairs inquiry into the *Sex Discrimination Amendment (Sexual Orientation, Gender Identity and Intersex Status) Bill 2013*, 26 April 2013, pg. 4. https://www.lawcouncil.asn.au/docs/6440357b-e602-e711-80d2-005056be66b1/130426-Submission-2714-Sex-Discrimination-Amendment-Bill-2013.pdf Accessed 18 August 2017.

45. Law Council of Australia submission to the "Consultation on the protection from discrimination on the basis of sexual orientation and sex and/or gender identity" conducted by the Australian Human Rights Commission, 29 December 2010, pg. 12. https://www.humanrights.gov.au/sites/default/files/content/human_rights/lgbti/lgbticonsult/comments/Law%20Council%20of%20Australia%20-%20Comment%20132.doc Accessed 10 June 2017.

46. Law Council of Australia, submission to the Senate Committee on Legal and Constitutional Affairs inquiry into the *Sex Discrimination Amendment (Sexual Orientation, Gender Identity and Intersex Status) Bill 2013*, Op. cit., pg. 25.

47. Ibid., pg. 39.

48. Change of Personal Details P64, WA Department of Transport. https://www.police.wa.gov.au/~/media/Files/Police/Online-services/12-Traffic/Change-of-Personal-Details.pdf Accessed 7 May 2017.

49. Driver's Licence/Learners Permit Application MR205, South Australian Department of Planning Transport and Infrastructure. https://SDA.sa.gov.au/__data/assets/pdf_file/0020/17093/MR205.pdf Accessed 25 June 2017.

50. *Addressing sexual orientation and sex and/or gender identity discrimination: Consultation Report*, Australian Human Rights Commission, 2011, pg. 19. https://SDA.humanrights.gov.au/sites/default/files/document/publication/SGI_2011.pdf Accessed 1 June 2017.

    Sexual Orientation, Gender Identity and Intersex Rights: Snapshot Report, Background Paper 2014, Australian Human Rights Commission, 2014, pg. 6. http://SDA.humanrights.gov.au/sites/default/files/14.12.09%20FINAL%20SOGII%20Rights%20Discussion%20Paper%202014.pdf Accessed 1 June 2017.

51. *Sex Files: the legal recognition of sex in documents and government records*, Australian Human Rights Commission, Op. cit., pgs. 13-14.

52. Theodore Bennett, 'No man's land': Non-binary Sex Identification in Australian Law and Policy, Op. cit., pgs. 847-873.

TABLE 8.1
GENDER IDENTITY, SEXUAL/GENDER ORIENTATION AND SEX AS PROTECTED ATTRIBUTES IN ANTI-DISCRIMINATION AND EQUAL OPPORTUNITY LAWS

Jurisdiction	Gender identity: (gender identity, gender history, transgender, indeterminate, sexuality, sex)	Sexual orientation, gender orientation: (sexual orientation, gender orientation, sexuality)
Federal	Fluid gender identity recognised *Sex Discrimination Act* 1984 says "gender identity means the gender-related identity, appearance or mannerisms or other gender-related characteristics of a person (whether by way of medical intervention or not), with or without regard to the person's designated sex at birth"[1]. Gender identity recognises a person by their socially defined characteristics, including socially and medically transitioned transsexuals. It is unclear if "sex" means biological sex or cisgender, or either, particularly as the definitions of "man … a member of male sex" and "woman … a member of female sex" were removed from *Sex Discrimination Act* 1984 in 2013.[2] Intersex is recognised separately from gender identity in the *Sex Discrimination Act 1984*[3], although the Australian Government Guidelines on the Recognition of Sex and Gender (2013) conflates intersex as a fluid gender identity.[4]	Gender orientation, based on gender identity *Sex Discrimination Act* 1984 says "sexual orientation means a person's sexual orientation towards: persons of the same sex; or persons of a different sex; or persons of the same sex and persons of a different sex"[5]. "Different" means two or more that are not the same. "Different sex" recognises that a person may identify as neither male nor female and includes orientations between persons based on each person's socially defined gender identity.[6] Hence, sexual orientation is better described as "gender orientation". The change of meaning from sexual orientation to gender orientation was emphasised by removing the definitions of "man" and "woman" from the *Sex Discrimination Act* 1984 in 2013.[7]

TABLE 8.1

GENDER IDENTITY, SEXUAL/GENDER ORIENTATION AND SEX AS PROTECTED ATTRIBUTES IN ANTI-DISCRIMINATION AND EQUAL OPPORTUNITY LAWS

Jurisdiction	Gender identity: (gender identity, gender history, transgender, indeterminate, sexuality, sex)	Sexual orientation, gender orientation: (sexual orientation, gender orientation, sexuality)
New South Wales	Recognise transsexual (social and medical transitioning) "Transgender person" means a transsexual person, with or without medical intervention. It also means a person of "indeterminate sex"[†] who "identifies as a member of a particular sex by living as a member of that sex"[8] which appears to refer to an intersex person. Transgender recognises socially and medically transitioned transsexuals and intersex persons.	Sexual orientation, based on biological sex "Homosexual means male or female homosexual person"[9] and "homosexuality includes a reference to the person's being thought to be a homosexual person, whether he or she is, in fact, a homosexual person or not.[10] Homosexuality appears to define sexual orientations between two persons defined by their biological sex.

TABLE 8.1

GENDER IDENTITY, SEXUAL/GENDER ORIENTATION AND SEX AS PROTECTED ATTRIBUTES IN ANTI-DISCRIMINATION AND EQUAL OPPORTUNITY LAWS

Jurisdiction	Gender identity: (gender identity, gender history, transgender, indeterminate, sexuality, sex)	Sexual orientation, gender orientation: (sexual orientation, gender orientation, sexuality)
Victoria	Recognise transsexual (social and medical transitioning) "Gender identity means" a transsexual person, with or without medical intervention. It also means a person of "indeterminate sex"[†] who identifies "on a bona fide basis … as a member of a particular sex … by assuming characteristics of that sex"[11] which appears to refer to an intersex person. Gender identity recognises socially and medically transitioned transsexuals and intersex persons.	Sexual orientation, based on biological sex "Sexual orientation means homosexuality (including lesbianism), bisexuality or heterosexuality."[12] These appear to define sexual orientations between two persons defined by their biological sex.
Queensland	Recognise transsexual (social and medical transitioning) "Gender identity" means a transsexual person, with or without medical intervention. It also means a person of "indeterminate sex"[†], a person who "seeks to live as a member of a particular sex"[13] which appears to refer to an intersex person.[14] "Gender identity" recognises socially and medically transitioned transsexuals and intersex persons.	Sexual orientation, based on biological sex "Sexuality means heterosexuality, homosexuality, bisexuality."[15] These appear to define orientations between two persons defined by their biological sex.

TABLE 8.1
GENDER IDENTITY, SEXUAL/GENDER ORIENTATION AND SEX AS PROTECTED ATTRIBUTES IN ANTI-DISCRIMINATION AND EQUAL OPPORTUNITY LAWS

Jurisdiction	Gender identity: (gender identity, gender history, transgender, indeterminate, sexuality, sex)	Sexual orientation, gender orientation: (sexual orientation, gender orientation, sexuality)
South Australia	Fluid gender identity recognised The SA Act Interpretations Act 1915 says "gender identity means the gender-related identity, appearance or mannerisms or other gender-related characteristics of a person (whether by way of medical intervention or not), with or without regard to the person's designated sex at birth"[16]. In the SA Equal Opportunity Act 1984, it is unclear if "sex" means biological sex or cisgender, or either.[17] Intersex is defined separately from gender identity.[18]	Unclear if sexual orientation or gender orientation "Sexual orientation" is a protected attribute, but it is not defined in the SA Equal Opportunity Act 1984[19] or in the SA Act Interpretations Act 1915.

Table 8.1

TABLE 8.1
GENDER IDENTITY, SEXUAL/GENDER ORIENTATION AND SEX AS PROTECTED ATTRIBUTES IN ANTI-DISCRIMINATION AND EQUAL OPPORTUNITY LAWS

Jurisdiction	Gender identity: (gender identity, gender history, transgender, indeterminate, sexuality, sex)	Sexual orientation, gender orientation: (sexual orientation, gender orientation, sexuality)
Western Australia	Recognises transsexual, limited sex reassignment required "Gender history means ... a person identifies as a member of the sex opposite to their sex at birth by living or seeking to live as a member of the opposite sex"[20] following gender reassignment, as defined in the Gender Reassignment Act 2000.[21] Removal of internal reproductive organs is not required following the High Court of Australia ruling in AB & AH v the State of Western Australia (2011).[22,23] Intersex status not covered	Sexual orientation, based on biological sex "Sexual orientation ... means heterosexuality, homosexuality, lesbianism or bisexuality and includes heterosexuality, homosexuality, lesbianism or bisexuality imputed to the person."[24] "Man means a member of the male sex irrespective of age" and "woman means a member of the female sex irrespective of age"[25]. Consequently, sexual orientation appears to define orientations between two persons defined by their biological sex.

TABLE 8.1

GENDER IDENTITY, SEXUAL/GENDER ORIENTATION AND SEX AS PROTECTED ATTRIBUTES IN ANTI-DISCRIMINATION AND EQUAL OPPORTUNITY LAWS

Jurisdiction	Gender identity: (gender identity, gender history, transgender, indeterminate, sexuality, sex)	Sexual orientation, gender orientation: (sexual orientation, gender orientation, sexuality)
Tasmania	Fluid gender identity recognised	Unclear if sexual orientation or gender orientation
	"'Gender identity' means the gender-related identity, appearance or mannerisms or other gender-related characteristics of an individual (whether by way of medical intervention or not), with or without regard to the individual's designated sex at birth, and includes transsexualism and transgenderism."[26]	"'Sexual orientation includes heterosexuality; homosexuality; and bisexuality."[27]
	Gender identity recognises a person by their socially defined characteristics, including socially and medically transitioned transsexuals.	As "includes" means "part of a whole"; the Act may recognise more orientations than heterosexuality, homosexuality and bisexuality. It also may recognise orientations between persons based on their fluid defined gender identities.
	It is unclear if "sex" means biological sex or cisgender, or either.	

TABLE 8.1
GENDER IDENTITY, SEXUAL/GENDER ORIENTATION AND SEX AS PROTECTED ATTRIBUTES IN ANTI-DISCRIMINATION AND EQUAL OPPORTUNITY LAWS

Jurisdiction	Gender identity: (gender identity, gender history, transgender, indeterminate, sexuality, sex)	Sexual orientation, gender orientation: (sexual orientation, gender orientation, sexuality)
Australian Capital Territory	Fluid gender identity recognised The Discrimination Act 1991 says: "'Gender identity' means the gender-related identity, appearance or mannerisms or other gender-related characteristics of a person, with or without regard to the person's designated sex at birth"[28]. Gender identity recognises a person by their socially defined characteristics, including socially and medically transitioned transsexuals. At the same time, the Act says: "'man' means a member of the male sex irrespective of age" and "'woman' means a member of the female sex irrespective of age"[29]. "Man" and "woman" are defined biologically, while, at the same time, "gender identity" treats "sex" as person's choice, i.e. as cisgender.	Unclear if sexual orientation or gender orientation, or either "'Sexuality' means heterosexuality, homosexuality (including lesbianism) or bisexuality."[30] On the one hand, the Act defines "man" and "woman" biologically, which means the above terms are sexual orientations.[31] On the other hand, the Act also recognises a person by their self-defined gender identity in place of their biological sex, in which case the above terms are gender orientations.[32] It is unclear if "sexual orientation" means biologically based "sexual orientation", or "gender orientation", or either.

TABLE 8.1

GENDER IDENTITY, SEXUAL/GENDER ORIENTATION AND SEX AS PROTECTED ATTRIBUTES IN ANTI-DISCRIMINATION AND EQUAL OPPORTUNITY LAWS

Jurisdiction	Gender identity: (gender identity, gender history, transgender, indeterminate, sexuality, sex)	Sexual orientation, gender orientation: (sexual orientation, gender orientation, sexuality)
Northern Territory[‡]	Not covered Object is "to eliminate discrimination against persons on the ground of sex …"[33]. "Sexuality means having the characteristics or imputed characteristics of … transsexuality."[34] Is transsexuality a gender identity?	Sexual orientation, based on biological sexes "Sexuality" also "means having the characteristics or imputed characteristics of heterosexuality, homosexuality, bisexuality …."[35]. "'Man' means a member of the male sex irrespective of age and 'woman' means a member of the female sex irrespective of age."[36] Hence, "sexuality" appears to describe orientations between persons recognised by their biological sex.

[†] Note: "Indeterminate" is a term that has had three different meanings. First, formally or informally in some jurisdictions, birth certificates have allowed for "indeterminate sex" in cases where the sex of a still-born child, or miscarried child, cannot be determined.[37] Second, more recently in the above anti-discrimination laws, "indeterminate" appears to mean an intersex person whose sex has not been determined but who seeks to live as a person of a particular sex. Third, the Australian Government Guidelines on the Recognition of Sex and Gender (2013), based on amendments to the Federal *Sex Discrimination Act* 1984 in 2013, says "indeterminate" covers any self-defined, fluid gender identity.[38]

[‡] In September 2017, the Northern Territory Attorney General issued a Discussion Paper titled, Modernisation of the Anti-Discrimination Act.[39] The Discussion Paper outlines proposals to have NT law emulate the Federal *Sex Discrimination Act* 1984 (the SDA). It proposes removing the definitions of man and woman from the NT Anti-Discrimination Act 1992; inserting the same definitions of gender identity and sexual orientation as found in the SDA; making "it unlawful for a person to do an act, other than in private (for example at home), if the act is reasonably likely, in all the circumstances, to offend, insult, humiliate or intimidate another person or a group of people"[40] which reflects the Tasmanian Anti-Discrimination Act 1998 Section 17; and it recommends minimal exemptions.

Table 8.1

Endnotes

1. Federal *Sex Discrimination Act 1984*, Section 4, as compiled 1 July 2016.
   https://www.legislation.gov.au/Details/C2016C00880

2. Federal *Sex Discrimination Act 1984*, Section 4, as compiled 2 December 2012, prior to the 2013 amendments that removed the definitions of "man" and "woman".
   https://www.legislation.gov.au/Details/C2013C00012

3. Federal *Sex Discrimination Act 1984*, Section 4, as compiled 1 July 2016, Op. cit.

4. *Australian Government Guidelines on the Recognition of Sex and Gender*, Attorney General's Department, Australian Government, (July 2013, Updated November 2015), pgs. 4, 8, 9. Accessed 19 June 2017.
   https://www.ag.gov.au/Publications/Documents/AustralianGovernmentGuidelinesontheRecognitionofSexandGender/AustralianGovernmentGuidelinesontheRecognitionofSexandGender.PDF

5. Federal *Sex Discrimination Act 1984*, Section 4, as compiled 1 July 2016, Op. cit.

6. Explanatory Memorandum, *Sex Discrimination Amendment (Sexual Orientation, Gender Identity and Intersex Status) Bill 2013*.
   http://parlinfo.aph.gov.au/parlInfo/search/display/display.w3p;query=Id%3A%22legislation%2Fems%2Fr5026_ems_1fcd9245-33ff-4b3a-81b9-7fdc7eb91b9b%22

7. See Endnote 2.

8. NSW *Anti-Discrimination Act 1977*, Section 38A.
   http://www.austlii.edu.au/au/legis/nsw/consol_act/aa1977204/

9. Ibid., Section 4 Definitions.

10. Ibid., Section 49ZF.

11. Victorian *Equal Opportunity Act 2010*, Section 4 Definitions.
    http://www.austlii.edu.au/au/legis/vic/consol_act/eoa2010250/

12. Ibid.

13. Queensland *Anti-Discrimination Act 1991*, Schedule Dictionary at the end of the Act.
    http://www.austlii.edu.au/au/legis/nsw/consol_act/aa1977204/

14. Ibid.

15. Ibid.

16. South Australian *Acts Interpretation Act 1915*, Section 4, (as amended by the Statutes Amendment (Gender Identity and Equity) Act 2016.
    http://www.austlii.edu.au/au/legis/sa/consol_act/aia1915230/s4.html

17. SA *Equal Opportunity Act 1984*, Part 3.
    http://www6.austlii.edu.au/cgi-bin/viewdb/au/legis/sa/consol_act/eoa1984250/

18. South Australian *Acts Interpretation Act 1915*, Op. cit., Section 4.

19. South Australian *Equal Opportunity Act 1984*, Part 3. However, "sexual orientation" is not defined in the Equal Opportunity Act or the *Acts Interpretation Act 1915*.

20. Western Australia *Equal Opportunity Act 1984*, Section 35AA.
    http://www.austlii.edu.au/au/legis/wa/consol_act/eoa1984250/

21. Ibid., Section 4.

22 *AB & AH v the State of Western Australia* (2011) High Court of Australia 42. http://eresources.hcourt.gov.au/downloadPdf/2011/HCA/42

23 *AB v State of Western Australia & Anor* P15/2011; *AH v State of Western Australia & Anor* P16/2011 [2011] HCA 42, 6 October 2011. http://www.hcourt.gov.au/assets/publications/judgment-summaries/2011/hca42-2011-10-06.pdf

24 Western Australia *Equal Opportunity Act 1984*, Op. cit., Section 4.

25 Ibid., Section 4.

26 Tasmanian *Anti-Discrimination Act 1998*, Section 3. http://www.austlii.edu.au/au/legis/tas/consol_act/aa1998204/

27 Ibid.

28 ACT *Discrimination Act 1991*, Dictionary Endnotes. http://www.austlii.edu.au/au/legis/act/consol_act/da1991164/

29 Ibid.

30 Ibid.

31 Ibid.

32 Ibid.

33 NT *Anti-Discrimination Act 1992*, Section 3. http://www.austlii.edu.au/au/legis/nt/consol_act/aa204/

34 Ibid., 4.

35 Ibid., 4.

36 Ibid.

37 *Sex Files: the legal recognition of sex in documents and government records*, Australian Human Rights Commission, 2009, pg. 23. https://www.humanrights.gov.au/our-work/sexual-orientation-sex-gender-identity/publications/sex-files-legal-recognition-sex Accessed 5 June 2017.

38 *Australian Government Guidelines on the Recognition of Sex and Gender*, Op. cit., pg. 9.

39 *Discussion Paper: Modernisation of the Anti-Discrimination Act, Department of the Attorney General and Justice*, Northern Territory Government, September 2017. https://justice.nt.gov.au/__data/assets/pdf_file/0006/445281/anti-discrimination-act-discussion-paper-september-2017.pdf Accessed 23 October 2017.

40 Ibid., pg. 11.

CHAPTER 9

TRANSGENDERING BIRTH CERTIFICATES

A birth certificate establishes part of a person's genetic and family history and legally establishes a person's identity, rights and responsibilities in respect of services provided by the government and private sectors.

Male, Female, Indeterminate, Unspecified and Intersex are now recognised on some state and territory birth certificates.

9.1 INTRODUCTION

Following changes to the federal *Sex Discrimination Act* in 2013 to legally recognise a person by their gender identity, South Australia and the ACT changed their births, deaths and marriages registration (BDMR) laws to align with the SDA. They now recognise new forms of non-binary identities on birth certificates.

The new forms of identification reflect the X marker on all federal government documents, as introduced by the *Australian Government Guidelines on the Recognition of Sex and Gender* (2013) (see Chapter 8.3).

9.2 KEY SEX IDENTIFIERS OF THE HUMAN PERSON

A birth certificate is the cardinal identifier of a person. As noted by the Australian Human Rights Commission,

> Under Australia's identification systems the most important identity documents are known as cardinal documents ... [these] are birth certificates or change of name certificates ... Cardinal documents are the most trusted evidence of identity and citizenship.[1]

The *Birth Certificate Content* Review (2014), conducted by the NSW Registry of Births, Deaths and Marriages, explained how a birth certificate is a legal document that is

> used to establish identity and enable individuals to establish their rights and discharge their obligations in respect of services provided by the government and private sectors. A

birth certificate can also establish part of a person's genetic and family history.[2]

Among other things, a state or territory birth registration form typically includes a newborn's assigned name, recognised sex (male or female), place and date of birth; parents' names, sex and date of birth of parents; siblings' names, dates of birth and sex. A birth certificate is issued from a birth registration form by the registrar of births, deaths and marriages. The registrar can also issue a change-of-name certificate.

While some state and territory BDMR laws require that a child's sex be recorded, most BDMR acts and/or regulations refer indirectly to sex, with provisions for a person to change their sex. There are no BDMR laws or regulations that define sex, male or female. This is probably as these terms have been recognised as self-evident, axiomatic realities.

Birth certificates have been important for issuing other primary identity documents, like passports, marriage certificates and driver's licences.

9.3 AUSTRALIAN HUMAN RIGHTS COMMISSION ADVOCATES TRANSGENDER RECOGNITION ON BIRTH CERTIFICATES

The Australian Human Rights Commission (AHRC), formerly the Human Rights and Equal Opportunity Commission (HREOC), has advocated the recognition of gender identity on birth certificates.

In 2008, the HREOC's *Sex and gender diversity issues paper* argued that because transgenders have difficulty changing their "sex on some or all documents", a "third option" could be included on documents, like "birth certificates and passports"[3].

In 2009, the AHRC report, *Sex Files: the legal recognition of sex in documents and government records,* recommended that a person be allowed to "self-identify their sex ... so that surgery is not the only criteria [sic] for a change in legal sex", and that being married should not prevent a person from changing their "legal sex"[4]. It argued that a "person over the age of 18 years should be able to choose to have an unspecified sex noted on documents and records" and urged the federal government to "take a leadership role in ensuring that there is a nationally consistent approach to the legal recognition of sex ... particularly in relation to birth certificates ..."[5].

That approach was realised in the 2013 amendments to the *Sex Discrimination Act 1984,* which now recognises a person by their gender identity and sexual/gender orientation. This was followed immediately by the *Australian Government Guidelines on the Recognition of Sex and Gender* (2013, 2015),[6] which introduced the non-binary X marker on all federal government documents (see Chapters 8.2, 8.3).

In 2011, the AHRC consultation report on *Protection from discrimination on the basis of sexual orientation and sex and/or gender identity in Australia* cited the Law Council of Australia calling for "the right of trans people to change their gender by permitting the issuing of new birth certificates"[7].

In 2015, the AHRC national consultation report, *Resilient Individuals: Sexual Orientation, Gender Identity & Intersex Rights, National Consultation Report*, set out a "road map for inclusion". It called for

> all states and territories [to] legislate to require that a self-identified legal declaration, such as a statutory declaration, is sufficient proof to change a person's gender for the purposes of government records and proof of identity documentation [and that] relevant state and territory laws be amended to ensure that parents can be recognised on birth certificates (regardless of their SOGI status) and in adoption processes.[8]

In 2015, then President of the AHRC, Professor Gillian Triggs, called on all states and territories to align with the gender identity rules of the federal government and allow a person to change their gender identity without requiring approval of doctors and psychologists. Triggs said that some "state and territory laws currently prevent people from changing their gender on their birth certificate unless they have had gender-reassignment surgery and are unmarried" and called for the "removal of the legislative barriers to the legal recognition of their gender identity" so that transgender and gender-diverse people can have their "true gender" recognised, particularly on their birth certificates.[9]

The main argument for allowing a change of sex on a birth certificate is that medical treatments to change a person's sex are expensive and invasive for transsexuals.

However, the experience in the ACT (2014), South Australia (2016), Victoria (2016) and Tasmania (2016) has been that moves to amend BDMR laws to allow transsexuals to identify as members of the opposite sex, without medical intervention, have also included proposals for recognising non-binary gender identities on birth certificates.

In most states, birth certificates record Male or Female only. A High Court of Australia ruling has allowed for "Non-specific" sex to be also recorded in NSW (see Chapter 5.3.2), while the ACT and South Australia now record non-binary gender identities and intersex, as discussed below.

9.4 ACT RECOGNISES NON-BINARY ON BIRTH CERTIFICATES

In March 2014, the Australian Capital Territory (ACT) *Births, Deaths and Marriages Registration Act 1997* (the BDMRA) was amended to allow birth certificates to record a change of sex, or a gender identity, other than the person's sex as recorded at birth.

The ACT Birth Registration form now recognises Male, Female, Unspecified, Indeterminate, Intersex.[10] Although these terms are not defined in the BDMRA or regulations, they reflect the X marker required on federal government documents by the *Australian Government Guidelines on the Recognition of Sex and Gender* (2013, 2015) (see Chapter 8.3).

The amended BDMRA allows a person over the age of 18 to register a change of sex if "the person believes their sex to be the sex nominated in the application (the altered sex), and has received appropriate clinical treatment for alteration of the person's sex", or if the person is "intersex"[11]. Sex-reassignment surgery is not a requirement for registering a change of sex.

Parents of a child can apply to have a change of sex recorded for a child.[12] In both cases, "appropriate clinical treatment" is required from a doctor or psychologist.[13]

Change of sex can be done annually.[14] Other provisions allow for change of sex identifier for a person outside the ACT.

9.5 SOUTH AUSTRALIA LEGALISES TRANSGENDER RECOGNITION ON BIRTH CERTIFICATES

In 2016, South Australian (SA) amended the *Births, Deaths and Marriages Registration Act 1996*[15] (the BDMRA) to allow birth certificates to record a change of sex, or a gender identity, other than the person's sex as recorded at birth.

Gender identity is defined in the SA *Acts Interpretation Act 1915* to mean

> the gender-related identity, appearance or mannerisms or other gender-related characteristics of a person (whether by way of medical intervention or not), with or without regard to the person's designated sex at birth.[16]

Also, reflecting the X marker in the *Australian Government Guidelines on the Recognition of Sex and Gender*, the SA *Births, Deaths and Marriages Registration Regulations 2011*[17] says:

> For the purposes of Part 4A of the [BDMR] Act, each of the following is a recognised sex or gender identity:
>
> (a)　male;
>
> (b)　female;
>
> (c)　non-binary;
>
> (d)　indeterminate/intersex/unspecified.

The BDMRA allows for a "change of sex or gender identity" for "a person over the age of 18" born in SA. A person can change their "sex or gender identity" with appropriate clinical treatment, which "need not involve invasive medical treatment (and may include or be constituted by counselling)"[18].

A child under 18, who is registered in the state, can change their sex or gender if a

> court approves the making of the application.[19]
>
> … the Court is not bound by the rules of evidence, but may inform itself as the Court thinks fit. A child is to be taken to have the capacity to make an application.[20]

Other provisions allow for change of sex identifier for a person born outside SA.[21]

9.6　ARE MALE AND FEMALE ONLY CISGENDER TERMS ON SA AND ACT BIRTH REGISTRATION FORMS?

What does it mean to record a new-born as Male or Female if a child can also be recorded as Indeterminate, Unspecified or Non-Binary, or if a person can later change their sex after appropriate clinical treatment?

Arguably, it automatically means that Male and Female become cisgender terms. They are options open to being self-redefined, not innate and immutable terms fixed by biology at birth (see discussion in Chapter 8.4).

The non-binary options are not only for an adult to register a change of sex. They allow parents to register their child as neither male nor female or to register a child's change of sex. In 2016, the Victorian government sought to change the state's BDMR law to allow a parent to change a child's birth certificate with the child's consent[22] while, in Canada, a parent has sought to register a new-born without recording the child's sex.[23]

In all other Australian state and territory jurisdictions, birth registration forms record only Male or Female. This indicates that these are self-evident, biological terms.

What of recording intersex on birth registration forms? Intersex is a disorder of sexual development, not a sex. Further, as the Intersex Society of North America's *Guidelines* say, most intersex people identify with their sex assigned at birth (see Chapter 5.2.2). This raises an issue: can an intersex/DSD person be recorded both by their sex (as Male or Female) and as an intersex person on ACT and SA birth registration forms?

Changes to BDMR laws have been made without serious public debate. Most citizens in these jurisdictions remain unaware of how these changes redefine sex and create pressure for other laws to define new rights for people who identify as other than their birth sex. In turn, this creates conflicts with people who recognise their birth sex as inherent and self-evident.

9.7 FAILED ATTEMPT TO CHANGE BIRTH CERTIFICATES IN VICTORIA

In 2016, the *Births, Deaths and Marriages Registration Amendment Bill 2016* was defeated in the Victorian Upper House. The Bill proposed a new sex descriptor on birth certificates that recognised "male, female or any other sex"[24]

According to the accompanying *Explanatory Memorandum,* the Bill provided for the registration of Male, Female or any non-binary. Also, the Registrar had the discretion to refuse registration of a "prohibited sex descriptor … that is obscene or offensive"[25].

Supporters of the Bill said that it would allow transsexuals to transition and be recognised as a member of the opposite sex, without requiring invasive sex-reassignment surgery.

Victorian Liberal Upper House member and feminist, Louise Staley, was outspoken in opposing the Bill. She said that, as a feminist, she believed transgender people who didn't have surgery were not fully committed to being women. Staley said:

> The feminist in me objects strongly to a man changing his birth certificate to female because he feels enough of a woman to identify as one but not enough to take the step of permanently doing so.[26]

9.8 TASMANIAN EQUAL OPPORTUNITY COMMISSION OPTIONS PAPER FOR TRANSGENDER BIRTH CERTIFICATES

The 2016 Tasmanian Equal Opportunity Commission (TEOC) proposed amendments to the Tasmanian *Births, Deaths and Marriages Registration Act 1999* (the BDMRA) to allow a non-binary classification, as well as Male or Female, on the state's birth certificates.[27] The TEOC options paper, *Legal recognition of sex and gender diversity in Tasmania: Options for amendments to the Births, Deaths and Marriages Registration Act 1999*, generated considerable debate.

The TEOC options paper recommended that the BDMRA be amended so there would be "no requirement for surgical, medical or hormonal treatment to change sex classification"[28] because surgical treatment is invasive and expensive;[29] some gender-reassignment surgery is not approved in Australia, and is associated with high risks and a low rate of success;[30] others may have had gender-reassignment surgery that was not successful.[31]

The TEOC argued for a person to have the option of recording "a 'non-binary' classification category"[32] and for allowing a person to change their sex "once in a 12-month period"[33].

It offered four options as to how non-binary gender identities could be recorded on birth certificates:

- cease recording sex on birth certificates;

- additional sex categories so that adults could be legally recognised as neither male nor female, both male and female, indeterminate, or unspecified;

- introduce a free-text "other" category for a person to self-describe their gender identity;

- introduce an "'X' marker" to recognise "intersex/unspecified/indeterminate" gender identity options, alongside male and female.[34]

The TEOC argued that the X marker was the preferred option, to be consistent with the *Australian Government Guidelines on the Recognition of Sex and Gender* (2013, 2015).[35]

The TEOC options paper argued that the age at which children should be allowed to transition to the opposite sex should be in accordance with permission granted by the Family Court of Australia in the cases of *re Jamie* (aged almost 11 years),[36] *re Lucy* (aged 13 years)[37] and for two children in *re Sam and Terry* (both aged 16 years).[38]

There was concerted opposition to the TEOC discussion paper from the Women's Liberation Front (WoLF) Southern Tasmania. WoLF argued that

> 'gender identity' is not synonymous with 'sex' ... Birth Certificates do not record a person's gender identity; [they] record biological and familial facts about the birth of a child ... The Act does not provide any procedure for objective determination of a person's 'gender identity' therefore it must be assumed [it] is wholly subjective.[39]

WoLF argued that legally codifying "'gender identity' as synonymous with 'sex'" would be

> in contravention of the UN Convention on the Elimination of all Forms of Discrimination Against Women (CEDAW), which requires signatory states to take all measures to end practices, which are based on the idea of the inferiority or the superiority of either of the sexes or on stereotyped roles for men and women.[40]

Australia is a signatory to CEDAW, which was written into the Schedule of Section 3(a) of the Federal *Sex Discrimination Act 1984*. The primary objective of the Act was to implement the CEDAW precepts.[41] (Note: WoLF's submission was referring to the SDA before the 2013 amendments that removed the definitions of "man" and "woman" and inserted "gender identity" (see Chapter 8.2.1).

CEDAW aims to eliminate discrimination against women based on their being members of the female sex. WoLF argued that conflating sex with gender identity would undermine women's legal rights and reinforce negative sex stereotypes of women. It would

> result in a woman being defined as a person who has a particular appearance, mannerisms or characteristics most of which are defined according to feminine stereotypes ... such as caretaking, emotionalism, and weakness.

> [These stereotypes] have served as sufficient legal justification for women's exclusion from employment, participation in government, and many other critical social functions. Archaic stereotypes are directly responsible for the denial of female credibility and intellectual authority, in addition to causing the historical marginalisation of females, lower social status vis-a-vis males, and lack of power to engage equally with males.[42]

> The only definition of 'female' that does not rely on sex stereotypes for its meaning is ... in relation to biological sex.[43]

WoLF said that the TEOC failed to demonstrate that changing Tasmania's birth registration law "would reduce discrimination against transgender individuals"[44]. WoLF said, it is not "discriminatory for a person to have a sex marker that accurately reflects their biological sex, irrespective of their 'gender identity', and any subjectively perceived 'match' or 'mis-match' between the two"[45].

A WoLF concern was that the TEOC proposals would remove legally recognised female-only spaces and services, particularly the 15 women-only services or spaces operating in Tasmania[46] that have exemptions under the Tasmanian *Anti-Discrimination Act, 1998*.[47]

> Because the proposed changes would mean a person's legal sex is subjectively determined – being based entirely on self-identification – women would be prevented from accessing any legal remedy in defining the boundaries of their female-only spaces; effectively allowing any male the ability to access those spaces if they were to self-identify their sex as 'female'.[48]

Further, WoLF expressed concerns over the rights of women in prison, saying:

> Women's prisons are spaces in which women are confined and unable to escape unwanted attention from males. The fact that women may have to share cells and shower facilities with men who are seeking to transgender could be seen as an extra layer of punishment. Male prisoners in western countries are using human rights laws successfully to gain access to transgender treatment at public expense in prison, and the right to then transfer to the women's estate. These men are often precisely those who are most violent and dangerous to women's safety, having been convicted of grave crimes including the murder of women … there seems to be no acknowledgement here of the … serious and pressing right of women to avoid being compulsorily housed with violent men.[49]

Finally, the WoLF submission concluded:

> Unlike a change of a name, a change of sex alters legal relations between people. An individual changing their name has no bearing on the legal rights of others – a change of name is not comparable to a change of legal sex. Such a comparison is spurious at worst, and naively ill considered at best.[50]

9.9   CONCLUSION

BDMR laws and regulations have been changed in SA and the ACT to allow a person to identity as a member of the opposite sex, without requiring sex-change surgery, or with another non-binary gender identity, or as genderless. Similar proposals have been rejected in Victoria and Tasmania. A High Court case allowed for "non-specific sex" to be recorded on NSW birth certificates (see Chapter 5.3.2).

Recognition of markers such as unspecified, indeterminate and non-binary on a person's birth certificate means that biological sex (male/female) is no longer a necessary part of the cardinal identifier of a person. Furthermore, it appears that male and female are no longer biological terms but cisgender terms on SA and ACT birth registration forms.

Changing a person's sex identifier on their cardinal identifier sets in motion changes to the chain of documents that establish a person's identity and relationships. It redefines an array of rights, responsibilities, protections, privileges and access to services. Also, it redefines relationships, including marriage, as outlined in Chapter 10.

Adults are free to live and identify culturally as they please. If they wish to adopt a gender identity other than their biological sex, they have the liberty to do so in a tolerant democracy. Such choices can be respected. However, this book is concerned with the consequences of writing gender identity into law.

Endnotes

1. *The sex and gender diversity project: Concluding paper*, Australian Human Rights Commission, 2009, pg. 13.
   http://www.humanrights.gov.au/sites/default/files/document/publication/SFR_2009_Web.pdf Accessed 9 June 2017.

2. *Birth Certificate Content Review*, NSW Registry of Birth Deaths and Marriages,NSW Attorney General of Justice, NSW Government, 2014, pg. 3.http://www.bdm.nsw.gov.au/Documents/BDM-birth-cert-review-2014.pdfAccessed 12 June 2017.

3. *Sex and gender diversity Issues paper*, Human Rights and Equal Opportunity Commission, May 2008, pg. 6-7.
   https://www.humanrights.gov.au/our-work/projects/sex-and-gender-diversity-issues-paper Accessed 5 June 2017.

4. *Sex Files: the legal recognition of sex in documents and government records*, Australian Human Rights Commission 2009, Recommendations 1, 2, and 3.
   https://www.humanrights.gov.au/our-work/sexual-orientation-sex-gender-identity/publications/sex-files-legal-recognition-sex Accessed 5 June 2017.

5. Ibid: Section 2, Recommendations.

6. *Australian Government Guidelines on the Recognition of Sex and Gender*, Attorney General's Department, Australian Government, July 2013, Updated November 2015, pgs. 3-4.
   https://www.ag.gov.au/Publications/Documents/AustralianGovernmentGuidelinesontheRecognitionofSexandGender/AustralianGovernmentGuidelinesontheRecognitionofSexandGender.PDF Accessed 19 June, 2017.

7. *Protection from discrimination on the basis of sexual orientation and sex and/or gender identity in Australia: Consultation report*, Australian Human Rights Commission, April 2011, pg. 11.
   http://www.humanrights.gov.au/publications/consultation-protectiondiscrimination-basis-sexual-orientation-and-sex-andor-gender Accessed 5 June2017.

8. *Resilient Individuals: Sexual Orientation, Gender Identity & Intersex Rights, National Consultation Report*, 2015, Australian Human Rights Commission, 2015, pg. 3.
   https://www.humanrights.gov.au/our-work/sexual-orientation-sexgender-identity/publications/resilient-individuals-sexual Accessed 1 June 2017.

9. "Gender identity: Legal recognition should be transferred to individuals, Human Rights Commission says", ABC News, 7 April 2016.
   http://www.abc.net.au/news/2016-04-07/power-to-decide-gender-identity-'should-be-with-individuals'/7304120 Accessed 23 August 2016.

10. "Birth Registration Statement", Australian Capital Territory.
    https://www.accesscanberra.act.gov.au/app/answers/detail/a_id/2214/~/births%2C-deaths-and-marriages-forms-and-fees Accessed 6 June 2017.

11. Australian Capital Territory *Births, Deaths and Marriages Registration Act 1997*, Section 24 (1) (c) (I) (ii).
    http://www.legislation.act.gov.au/a/1997-112/current/pdf/1997-112.pdf

12. Ibid., 24 (2).

13. Ibid., 25 (1).

14 *Birth, Deaths and Marriages Practice Manual*, Justice and Community Safety, Australian Capital Territory Government, April 2014, pg. 42.
https://www.accesscanberra.act.gov.au/ci/fattach/get/45848/1433984222/redirect/1/filename/Births%20deaths%20and%20marriages%20practice%20manual.pdf Accessed 6 June 2017.

15 South Australian *Births, Deaths and Marriages Registration Act 1996*.
https://www.legislation.sa.gov.au/LZ/C/A/BIRTHS%20DEATHS%20AND%20MARRIAGES%20REGISTRATION%20ACT%201996/CURRENT/1996.6.UN.PDF

16 *Acts Interpretation Act 1915*, Section 4.
http://www.austlii.edu.au/au/legis/sa/consol_act/aia1915230/

17 *Births, Deaths and Marriages Registration Regulations 2011*, Section 7A, Under the *Births, Deaths and Marriages Registration Act 1996*.
https://www.legislation.sa.gov.au/LZ/C/R/BIRTHS%20DEATHS%20AND%20MARRIAGES%20REGISTRATION%20REGULATIONS%202011/CURRENT/2011.205.AUTH.PDF

18 South Australian *Births, Deaths and Marriages Registration Act 1996*, Op. cit., Section 29H.

19 Ibid., 29J 2 (b).

20 Ibid., Section 29J 6.

21 Ibid., Section 22O.

22 "Gender diverse win right to new birth certificates", *The Age*, 17 August 2016.
https://www.theage.com.au/national/victoria/gender-diverse-win-right-to-new-birth-certificates-20160817-gquvs8.html Accessed 12 May 2018.

23 "Parent fights to omit gender on B.C. child's birth certificate", *CBC News*, 6 July 2017.
http://www.cbc.ca/news/canada/british-columbia/parent-fights-to-omit-gender-on-b-c-child-s-birth-certificate-1.4186221 Accessed 12 May 2018.

24 Victorian *Births, Deaths and Marriages Registration Amendment Bill 2016*, Section 5. Bill is no longer on the web, but was at:
http://www.legislation.vic.gov.au/domino/Web_Notes/LDMS/Pub-PDocs.nsf/ee665e366dcb6cb0ca256da400837f6b/4d6b3e8bb0b7c5e-4ca25801300117077!OpenDocument

Explanatory paper available here:
https://www.parliament.vic.gov.au/publications/research-papers/summary/36-research-papers/13775-births-deaths-and-marriages-registration-amendment-bill-2016

25 *Births, Deaths and Marriages Registration Amendment Bill 2016*, Explanatory Memorandum, introduced 18 August, 2016, pg. 4-5. Was available at:
https://www.parliament.vic.gov.au/publications/research-papers/download/36-research-papers/13775-births-deaths-and-marriages-registration-amendment-bill-2016 Accessed 27 September 2016.

26 "Victoria MP Louise Staley under fire for trans comments", *Out in Perth*, 14 September 2016.
http://www.outinperth.com/victoria-mp-louise-staley-fire-trans-comments/ Accessed 16 September 2016.

27 *Legal recognition of sex and gender diversity in Tasmania: Options for amendments to the Births, Deaths and Marriages Registration Act 1999*, Equal Opportunity Tasmania, February 2016.
http://equalopportunity.tas.gov.au/__data/assets/pdf_file/0009/338490/EOT_Options_paper_on_legal_recognition_of_sex_and_gender_diversity_in_Tasmania_~_CONSULTATION_DOC.pdf Accessed 30 May 2017.

28 Ibid., pg. 3.

29 Ibid., pgs. 8-9.

30 At [15] in *AB v Western Australia [2011] HCA 42* (6 October 2011), cited in *Legal recognition of sex and gender diversity in Tasmania*, Op. cit., pgs. 8-9.

31 *Legal recognition of sex and gender diversity in Tasmania*, Op. cit., pgs. 8-9.

32 Ibid., pg. 4.

33 Ibid., pg. 3.

34 Ibid., pgs. 25-27.

35 Ibid., pg. 24, citing *Australian Government Guidelines on the Recognition of Sex and Gender* (July 2013, Updated November 2015). https://www.ag.gov.au/Publications/Documents/AustralianGovernmentGuidelinesontheRecognitionofSexandGender/AustralianGovernmentGuidelinesontheRecognitionofSexandGender.PDF

36 *re Jamie* [2013] FamCAFC 110 (31 July 2013).

37 *re Lucy* (Gender Dysphoria) [2013] FamCA 518 (12 July 2013).

38 *re Sam and Terry* (Gender Dysphoria) [2013] FamCA 563 (31 July 2013).

39 Women's Liberation Front (WoLF, Southern Tasmania), Comment on Options Paper, Legal Recognition of sex and gender diversity in Tasmania: Options for amendments to the Births, Deaths & Marriages Registration Act 1999, Equal Opportunity Tasmania (Options Paper), 2016, pg. 4. http://tasmaniantimes.com/images/uploads/WoLF_Comment_EOT_BDMR_Act.pdf Accessed 31 May 2017.

40 Ibid., pg. 6.

41 *Federal Sex Discrimination Act, 1984*, Section 3 (a). http://www.austlii.edu.au/au/legis/cth/consol_act/sda1984209/

42 Women's Liberation Front (WoLF, Southern Tasmania): Comment on Options Paper, Op. cit., pgs. 6-7.

43 Ibid., pg., 6.

44 Ibid., pg., 5.

45 Ibid., pg., 9.

46 Ibid., pg. 20, Appendix 1, list of organisations currently with exemptions under Tasmania's *Anti-Discrimination Act 1988*, available at http://equalopportunity.tas.gov.au/current_exemptions

47 *Anti-Discrimination Act, 1998*. http://www.austlii.edu.au/au/legis/tas/consol_act/aa1998204/

48 Women's Liberation Front (WoLF, Southern Tasmania): Comment on Options Paper, Op. cit., pg. 12.

49 "Briefing Paper on Equal Opportunity Tasmania, Options Paper", WoLF, 2016. http://tasmaniantimes.com/images/uploads/Briefing_Paper_on_Equal_Opportunity_Tasmania,_Options_Paper-_Legal_recognition_of_sex_and_gender_diversity_in_Tasmania.pdf Accessed 11August 2017.

50 Women's Liberation Front (WoLF, Southern Tasmania): Comment on Options Paper, Op. cit., pg. 14.

TABLE 9.1

TRANSGENDER RECOGNITION OF A PERSON ON BIRTH CERTIFICATES AND OTHER IDENTITY DOCUMENTS

Jurisdiction	Recognition on birth certificates	Recognition on transport department and key government identity documents
Federal	Not apply	Male, Female, X (Indeterminate, Unspecified, Intersex) Found on official federal government documents, including passports[1], tax[2] and Medicare forms.[3] Transsexual persons are recognised,[4] with or without medical intervention.[5]
New South Wales	Male, Female[6] Also, the High Court of Australia required NSW Birth Deaths and Marriages Registry to allow for the recording of "non-specific" sex in *re Norrie*.[7] Change of sex: medical transitioning required[8]	Male, Female Driver's licence only recognises male and female.[9] However, the application form says a federal government issued passport can be used for identification[10] (see above).
Victoria	Male, Female Male and female not defined in birth registration law, but recognised on birth certificate.[11] Change of sex: medical transitioning required[12]	Male, Female, Mx Mx (gender-neutral title and may be used by any person)[13]

TABLE 9.1
TRANSGENDER RECOGNITION OF A PERSON ON BIRTH CERTIFICATES AND OTHER IDENTITY DOCUMENTS

Jurisdiction	Recognition on birth certificates	Recognition on transport department and key government identity documents
Queensland	Male, Female[14] Change of sex: medical transitioning required[15]	Male, Female However, the Queensland Government "Change of Customer Details" form allows a change of "any other personal details". It is unclear if this "other details" includes change of sex, or change of gender identity, or either.[16]
South Australia	Male, Female, Non-Binary, Indeterminate, Intersex, Unspecified These forms of identity recognised following 2016 changes to the SA *Births Death and Marriages Registration Act 1996*[17] and are listed in the associated regulations.[18] Change of sex: social and medical transitioning recognised[19] Includes a child under 18 years, who can apply by themselves to a court for a change of sex or gender No minimum age requirement is specified for the child applicant.[20]	Male, Female, X 'X' - this option is available if a person does not identify their gender as either male or female.[21]

TABLE 9.1
TRANSGENDER RECOGNITION OF A PERSON ON BIRTH CERTIFICATES AND OTHER IDENTITY DOCUMENTS

Jurisdiction	Recognition on birth certificates	Recognition on transport department and key government identity documents
Western Australia	Male, Female[22] Change of sex: limited medical transitioning recognised[23] The *Gender Reassignment Act 2000* requires sex reassignment surgery[24], after which a gender recognition certificate is issued and presented to the Registrar of Births to amend the sex noted on the birth certificate.[25] However, in *AB & AH v the State of Western Australia* (2011),[26] the High Court of Australia said that, under the *Gender Reassignment Act 2000*, the only "gender reassignment procedure" required is the altering of the external physical characteristics that are socially recognisable. Removal of internal reproductive organs is not required.[27]	Male, Female, X "Your gender can be recorded as either M (male), F (female) or X (if you do not identify as either male or female)."[28]
Tasmania	Male, Female Birth registration law only refers to change of "sex". Birth certificate records child's sex as male or female.[29] Change of sex: medical transitioning required[30]	Male, Female[31]

TABLE 9.1
TRANSGENDER RECOGNITION OF A PERSON ON BIRTH CERTIFICATES AND OTHER IDENTITY DOCUMENTS

Jurisdiction	Recognition on birth certificates	Recognition on transport department and key government identity documents
Australian Capital Territory	Male, Female, Indeterminate, Unspecified, Intersex These forms of identity recognised following 2016 changes to the *Births Death and Marriages Registration Act 1997*.[32] These terms are not defined in any the BDMR act or regulations. Change of Sex: social and medical transitioning recognised[33] Parents or guardians of a child under 18 years can apply to the Registrar-General for alteration of the sex of their child.[34]	Male, Female The application form for a driver's licence recognises only male and female.[35] However, the primary proof of identity includes ACT birth certificate and federal government issued passport.[36] Both recognise non-binary gender identities.
Northern Territory	Male, Female[37] Change of sex: medical transitioning required[38]	Male, Female, Indeterminate/Intersex The application form for a driver's licence recognises "Male, Female, Indeterminate/Intersex"[39].

Endnotes

1. See "Sex and gender diverse passport applicants", Department of Foreign Affairs and Trade, Australian Government.
https://www.passports.gov.au/passports-explained/how-apply/eligibility-citizenship-and-identity/sex-and-gender-diverse-passport Accessed 26 June 2018.

2. "Update your gender", Australian Taxation Office, Australian Government. https://www.ato.gov.au/Individuals/Tax-file-number/Update-your-details/Update-your-gender/#bypost Accessed 26 June 2018.

3. Currently, Medicare says: "… our personal records system only allows us to record your gender as male or female. However, if you identify as a non-binary gender, we can add a note to your personal record about your gender details", "Updating your gender details with us", Department of Human Services, Australian Government.
https://www.humanservices.gov.au/individuals/enablers/updating-your-gender-details-us Accessed 26 June 2018.

4. *Australian Government Guidelines on the Recognition of Sex and Gender*, Attorney General's Department, Australian Government, (July 2013, Updated November 2015), pg. 10. Accessed 19 June 2017.
https://www.ag.gov.au/Publications/Documents/AustralianGovernmentGuidelinesontheRecognitionofSexandGender/AustralianGovernmentGuidelinesontheRecognitionofSexandGender.PDF

5. *Sex Discrimination Act 1984*, Act No. 4 of 1984 as registered 22 July 2016, C2016C00880, Section 4, gender identity.
https://www.legislation.gov.au/Details/C2016C00880

6. *Births, Deaths and Marriages Registration Regulation 2017*, Section 4 (a), under the Births, Deaths and Marriages Registration Act 1995.
httpos://www.legislation.nsw.gov.au/regulations/2017-434.pdf

7. NSW *Registrar of Births, Deaths and Marriages v Norrie* [2014] HCA 11, 2 April 2014.
http://www.hcourt.gov.au/assets/publications/judgment-summaries/2014/hca-11-2014-04-02.pdf

8. NSW *Births Deaths and Marriages Registration Act 1995*, Sections 32A, 32B.
http://www.austlii.edu.au/au/legis/nsw/consol_act/bdamra1995383/

9. "Licence Application" form, NSW Roads and Maritime Services.
http://www.rms.nsw.gov.au/documents/about/forms/45070018-licence-application.pdf Accessed 24 July 2017.

10. "Changing your personal details", NSW Roads and Maritime Services.
http://www.rms.nsw.gov.au/roads/licence/identity/change-details.html Accessed 24 July 2017.

11. John Symeopoulos, "Registering Victorian births," Births Deaths and Marriages Victoria, Maternal and Child Health Conference, 27 March 2014, Slide 8, Birth Registration Form.
http://www.education.vic.gov.au/Documents/childhood/professionals/profdev/Registering%20Victorian%20Births.pdf Accessed 24 July 2017.

12. Victorian *Births, Deaths, and Marriages Registration Act 1996*, S. 4(1) definition of sex affirmation surgery.
http://www.austlii.edu.au/au/legis/vic/consol_act/bdamra1996383/

13. "Change of gender", Vic Roads.
https://www.vicroads.vic.gov.au/licences/renew-replace-or-update/update-your-details/change-of-gender Accessed 24 July, 2017.

Table 9.1

14. Queensland Online birth registration form.
https://www.bdm.qld.gov.au/registration/birth/birth.m Accessed 24 July 2017.

15. Queensland *Births, Deaths and Marriages Registration Act 2003*, Schedule 2 Dictionary, Sections 22-24.
http://www.austlii.edu.au/au/legis/qld/consol_act/bdamra2003383/

16. "Change of Customer Details (Individual)", Queensland Department of Transport.
https://www.support.transport.qld.gov.au/qt/formsdat.nsf/forms/QF4214/$file/F4214_CFD.pdf Accessed 24 July 2017.

17. *Births, Deaths and Marriages Registration Act 1996*, Sections 29H-29U.
https://www.legislation.sa.gov.au/LZ/C/A/BIRTHS%20DEATHS%20AND%20MARRIAGES%20REGISTRATION%20ACT%201996/CURRENT/1996.6.AUTH.PDF

18. South Australian *Births, Deaths and Marriages Registration Regulations 2011*, Section 7A, under the *Births, Deaths and Marriages Registration Act 1996*.
https://www.legislation.sa.gov.au/LZ/C/R/BIRTHS%20DEATHS%20AND%20MARRIAGES%20REGISTRATION%20REGULATIONS%202011/CURRENT/2011.205.AUTH.PDF

19. South Australian *Births Deaths and Marriages Registration Act 1996*, Sections 29H–29U.
http://www.austlii.edu.au/au/legis/sa/consol_act/bdamra1996383/

20. Ibid., Section 29J (7).

21. "Updating vehicle registration or driver's licence", Government of South Australia.
https://www.sa.gov.au/topics/driving-and-transport/vehicles-and-registration/vehicle-registration/updating-your-details Accessed 24 July 2017.

22. WA "Birth Registration Application Form".
http://www.bdm.dotag.wa.gov.au/_files/BDM1_Birth_Applic_Form.pdf Accessed 24 July 2017.

23. West Australian *Gender Reassignment Act 2000*, Sections 3, 14–16.
http://www.austlii.edu.au/au/legis/wa/consol_act/gra2000200/

24. Ibid.

25. West Australian *Gender Reassignment Regulations 2001*, r 4.
https://www.slp.wa.gov.au/pco/prod/filestore.nsf/FileURL/mrdoc_35859.pdf/$FILE/Gender%20Reassignment%20Regulations%202001%20-%20%5B00-00-00%5D.pdf?OpenElement

26. *AB & AH v the State of Western Australia* (2011) High Court of Australia 42.
http://eresources.hcourt.gov.au/downloadPdf/2011/HCA/42

27. *AB v State of Western Australia & Anor* P15/2011; *AH v State of Western Australia & Anor P16/2011* [2011] HCA 42, 6 October 2011.
http://www.hcourt.gov.au/assets/publications/judgment-summaries/2011/hca42-2011-10-06.pdf

28. "Change my Gender", Western Australia Department of Transport.
http://www.transport.wa.gov.au/mediaFiles/licensing/LBU_P_FAQ_ChangeMyGender.pdf Accessed 24 July 2017

29. "Birth Registration Statement", under the *Births, Deaths and Marriages Registration Act 1999*, State of Tasmania. Accessed 21 November 2017.

30. Tasmanian *Births, Deaths and Marriages Registration Act 1999*, Sections 3 and Part 4.
http://www.austlii.edu.au/au/legis/tas/consol_act/bdamra1999383/

31 "Drivers Licence Application", Tasmanian Government. http://www.transport.tas.gov.au/__data/assets/pdf_file/0006/111120/MR_72_10_15_Driver_Licence_Application.pdf Accessed 24 July 2017.

32 "Birth Registration Statement", Australian Capital Territory. https://www.accesscanberra.act.gov.au/app/answers/detail/a_id/2214/~/births%2C-deaths-and-marriages-forms-and-fees Accessed 6 June 2017

33 Australian Capital Territory, *Births, Deaths and Marriages Registration Act 1997*, Sections 24 (1) (c), 25 (1). http://www.austlii.edu.au/au/legis/act/consol_act/bdamra1997383/

34 Ibid., Sections 24 (2)–(4), 25 (2).

35 "Application for a Driver Licence", Australian Capital Territory Road Transport Authority. https://www.getroadready.com.au/img.ashx?f=f&p=%2F10007+Application+for+a+Driver+Licence+06092012.pdf Accessed 24 July 2017.

36 "Australian Capital Territory driver licence and motor vehicle registration proof of identity and residency requirements", ACT Government. https://www.accesscanberra.act.gov.au/app/answers/detail/a_id/2917#!tabs-2 Accessed 24 July 2017.

37 "Birth Registration Statement", Registrar of Birth, Deaths & Marriages, Northern Territory.

38 Northern Territory, *Births, Deaths and Marriages Registration Act*, Part 4. http://www.austlii.edu.au/au/legis/nt/consol_act/bdamra383/

39 "Application for Northern Territory Drivers/Riders Licence", Northern Territory, Motor Vehicle Registry. https://nt.gov.au/__data/assets/pdf_file/0017/162512/l1-a4-black-application-for-nt-driver-rider-licence-1-january-2018.pdf Accessed 26 June 2018.

CHAPTER 10

LEGALISING TRANSGENDER MARRIAGE

The Australian Government legalised transgender marriage, or gender-fluid marriage, in December 2017.

One day later, the Federal Attorney General's Department issued a draft Notice of Intended Marriage form, which said that people would be eligible to marry as Male, Female, or X, where X recognises a person as Indeterminate, Unspecified or Intersex.[1]

10.1 NO DEBATE OVER TRANSGENDER MARRIAGE

There has been a 13-year history of bills to the Australian federal parliament for legalising both same-sex marriage and transgender marriage, or gender-fluid marriage.

Despite this, there was almost no public debate concerning transgender marriage during the 2017 national survey asking Australians if they supported same-sex marriage. Debate was solely around same-sex marriage; that is marriage between two biological men or two biological women.

The lack of debate and scrutiny is all the more extraordinary given the number of groups that supported transgender marriage, where "two people are eligible to marry by their gender identity in place of their biological sex.

10.2 THE ABS SURVEY ON TRANSGENDER MARRIAGE

In 2004, the federal government wrote into the *Marriage Act 1961* the definition of marriage, which had been taken as self-evident. The definition said that marriage was

> the union of a man and a woman to the exclusion of all others, voluntarily entered into for life.[2]

Subsequently, there were 14 bills to federal parliament to recognise both transgender marriage and same-sex marriage, four bills to recognise same-sex marriage and two bills to recognise foreign same-sex marriages (see Table 10.1).

Many of these bills aimed to legalise marriage between "two people", a term that was little understood either by the public or by many politicians.

The meaning was clarified early in 2017 when the Federal Attorney General's Department commented on the Draft Exposure *Marriage Amendment (Same-Sex Marriage) Bill 2016*. The federal government planned to put this Bill to parliament if a majority of Australians voted to change the definition of marriage in a compulsory national plebiscite.

The Attorney General's Department told a Senate inquiry into this Bill that "the union of 2 people" would allow people "of a non-binary gender … to marry"[3]; that is, that the Bill would legalise transgender marriage. Further, the Bill's Explanatory Memorandum said that it would allow

> two people the freedom to marry in Australia, regardless of their sex or gender …. Throughout this Explanatory Memorandum, reference is made to 'same-sex marriage'. The term 'same-sex marriage' should be read to include a marriage of two people regardless of their sex or gender, where the union is not that of a man and a woman.[4]

This means that the "union of two people" would mean legalising transgender marriage as well as same-sex marriage.

In 2016, after the Senate rejected the proposal for a compulsory plebiscite, pressure was exerted for parliament to decide the definition of marriage. In 2017, a bill for marriage between "2 people" from a group of government members led by Liberal MP Dean Smith, resulted in Prime Minister Malcolm Turnbull appointing the Australian Bureau of Statistics to conduct a national marriage survey.

The survey question did not provide a definition of marriage, or mention transgender marriage, or specify a bill that would be put to parliament in the event of a Yes vote. Rather, it asked the broad question:

> Should the law be changed to allow same-sex couples to marry?[5]

The result was that 61.6 per cent voted Yes to changing the definition of marriage and 38.4 percent voted No. The participation rate of eligible voters was 79.5 per cent.[6]

While Australians voted for same-sex marriage, it was the Dean Smith Bill for both transgender marriage and same-sex marriage that was passed by the federal parliament on 7 December 2017.

The following day, 8 December, in an interview with Melbourne 3AW radio host Neil Mitchell, Prime Minister Turnbull said the new definition of marriage included both transgender marriage and same-sex marriage.

> Neil Mitchell: I was talking to a young person at the celebrations this week, a non-binary person identifying as neither male nor female; they plan to marry. Can they?
>
> Malcolm Turnbull: Well, two people will be able to get married, regardless of their gender, yes.
>
> Neil Mitchell: So, even if you don't identify as male or female?
>
> Malcolm Turnbull: Well, two people, any two people will be able to get married, subject to the other restrictions that exist, obviously they have to be adults and so forth, but instead of marriage being defined as being between a man and a woman, I think under the bill that's being debated in the Senate, it is basically between two persons regardless of their gender, that's the proposal.[7]

10.3   RECOGNISING TRANSGENDERS ON MARRIAGE FORMS

Also on 8 December, the Attorney General's Department released a draft new Notification of Intended Marriage form. It replaced the Bridegroom and Bride identification categories for each party with Groom, Bride or Partner.[8]

Each party can self-identify as Male, Female or X, where X refers to indeterminate, intersex or unspecified sex.[9] This is the same sex identifier as required on all federal government documents by the *Australian Government Guidelines on the Recognition of Sex and Gender* (2013, 2015).

10.4   THE AMBIGUITY OF UNLIMITED FORMS OF TRANSGENDER MARRIAGE

Again, as discussed in Chapter 8.4, placing the X marker on a sex identifier makes Male and Female mutable, cisgender terms. Further, since the X marker allows people to self-identify with any fluid gender identity, marriage between two people allows:

- a biological man who socially identifies as a woman to marry a biological cisgender woman and be in a recognised lesbian marriage;
- two biological men who socially identify as women to be in a recognised lesbian marriage;

- a biological woman who socially identifies as a man to marry a biological cisgender man and be in a recognised gay marriage;
- two biological women who socially identify as men to be in a recognised gay marriage;
- a person who identifies as 60 per cent male and 40 per cent female to marry a person who is 22 per cent male and 78 per cent female;
- a person who identifies as agender and a person who identifies as gender fluid also to be in a non-binary marriage; or
- two persons legally recognised by their gender orientations to be in, for example, a gender questioning-to-agender orientation marriage.

If each person has their own unique gender identity, there are unlimited possible gender-fluid identities and gender orientations. Consequently, the new definition of marriage between two people recognises unlimited forms of marriage by gender identity and gender orientation.

> Furthermore, transgender marriage compounds the problem of defining heterosexual, gay and lesbian. Under the SDA, two biological men can legally identify as women, "whether by way of medical intervention or not", while, under transgender marriage, they can also marry and be legally recognised as being in a lesbian marriage. They have three protected attributes in the SDA: gender identity, sexual (gender) orientation, and marital or relationship status.[10]

Just as Meyer and McHugh (2016) concluded that a broad definition of gender identity, as found in the SDA, is a *reductio ad absurdum* that dissolves the meaning of sex,[11] the broad definition of marriage between two people, which recognises people by their gender identity and gender orientation, is a *reductio ad absurdum* that risks making marriage meaningless (see Chapter 6.2.5).

To put it another way, transgender marriage forces everyone to question their default assumptions about sexual identity and marriage. It forces everyone not only to confront and question the meanings of sex, an issue previously always taken for granted, but to consider all new possible forms of gender identity and all possible new forms of marriage based on the claim that people can have a gender identity other than their birth sex.

10.5 ANTI-DISCRIMINATION LAWS PROTECTING TRANSGENDER MARRIAGE

Worldwide, there has been considerable debate over the immediate effects of changing the legal definition of marriage on those who believe in man+woman marriage and who provide services for weddings. People have faced prosecution for conscientiously objecting to providing their services for new forms of marriage that conflict with their belief in heterosexual marriage.

Such cases include:

- Colorado cake maker Jack Phillips was convicted on discrimination charges for declining to bake a cake for a same-sex wedding.[12] His case was later overturned by the US Supreme Court.[13]

- Washington florist Barronelle Stutzman was prosecuted in a US court for not providing flowers for a same-sex wedding.[14] The US Supreme Court has ordered lower courts to reconsider her case.[15]

- Photographer Elaine Huguenin was convicted on discrimination charges for not providing her services for a same-sex commitment ceremony in New Mexico.[16]

- Cynthia and Robert Gifford were fined for not providing their farm in upstate New York for a same-sex wedding reception.[17]

However, much wider areas of public life are affected by the intersection of a transgender marriage law and transgender anti-discrimination laws like the SDA. Together, these laws create and protect new rights, protections, privileges, and access to services for people who identify as other than their birth sex. These created rights conflict with the inherent rights, protections, privileges, and access to services of people who hold to the biological world view. These conflicts occur in schools, workplaces, the public service, health, the provision of goods and services by the private sector, etc. (see Table 1.1).

10.6 CONCLUSION: LEGAL UNCERTAINTY AND CONFLICTS

Despite extensive advocacy for transgender marriage by the Greens, leading Liberal and Labor parliamentarians, and many groups that campaigned to redefine marriage, parliamentary and public debate focused almost exclusively on recognising same-sex marriage.

Yet the *Marriage Amendment (Definition and Religious Freedoms) Bill 2017* delivered a third type of marriage, that is, transgender marriage.

Because gender identity and gender orientation are ambiguous terms, defining marriage as the union of two people, regardless of their gender identity or sexual/gender orientation, introduces ambiguity into the meaning of marriage.

Transgender marriage further entrenches conflicts, already apparent from the SDA, deeper into law, politics and culture.

Endnotes

1. "Gender bending form for marriages", *SBS News*, 8 December 2017.
   https://www.sbs.com.au/news/gender-bending-form-for-marriages Accessed 8 December 2017.

2. *Marriage Act 1961*, Section 5.
   http://www.austlii.edu.au/au/legis/cth/consol_act/ma196185/s5.html Accessed 9 June 2017.

3. Submission from Federal Attorney General's Department to the 2016-17 Senate Select Committee on the Exposure Draft of the Marriage Amendment (Same-Sex Marriage) Bill, Submission 78.
   http://www.aph.gov.au/Parliamentary_Business/Committees/Senate/Same_Sex_Marriage/SameSexMarriage/Submissions

4. Explanatory Memorandum, *The Marriage Amendment (Definition and Religious Freedoms) Bill 2017*, pg. 2.

5. "Australian Marriage Law Postal Survey", 2017, 1800.0, Australian Bureau of Statistics.
   http://www.abs.gov.au/ausstats/abs@.nsf/mf/1800.0 Accessed 20 December 2017.

6. Ibid.

7. Neil Mitchell interview with Prime Minister Malcolm Turnbull, "Mornings with Neil Mitchell, 3AW radio", 17 November 2017.

8. "Notice of Intended Marriage", Attorney General's Department, Australian Government. Form used after 8 December 2017.
   https://www.ag.gov.au/FamiliesAndMarriage/Marriage/Documents/New-noticeof-intended-marriage.pdf

9. Ibid.

10. *Sex Discrimination Act*, 1984, Section 21 3(a).

11. Lawrence S. Mayer and Paul R. McHugh, "Sexuality and Gender: Findings from the Biological, Psychological, and Social Sciences", *The New Atlantis*, Number 50, Fall 2016, pg. 88.
    http://www.thenewatlantis.com/docLib/20160819_TNA50SexualityandGender.pdf

12. "Gay wedding cake case heads to US Supreme Court", *SBS News*, 8 September 2017.
    https://www.sbs.com.au/news/gay-wedding-cake-case-heads-to-us-supreme-court Accessed 26 December 2017.

13. "Supreme Court rules for Colorado baker in same-sex wedding cake case", CNN, 4 June 2018.
    https://edition.cnn.com/2018/06/04/politics/masterpiece-colorado-gay-marriage-cake-supreme-court/index.html Accessed 8 July 2018.

14. "The woman who refused to provide flowers for a same-sex wedding has appealed to the Supreme Court", *SBS News*, 18 July 2017.
    https://www.sbs.com.au/topics/sexuality/agenda/article/2017/07/17/woman-who-refused-provide-flowers-same-sex-wedding-has-appealed-supreme-court Accessed 26 December 2017.

15. "Supreme Court vacates florist's same-sex wedding case", *Washington Times*, 25 June 2018,
    https://www.washingtontimes.com/news/2018/jun/25/supreme-court-vacates-florists-same-sex-wedding-ca/ Accessed 8 July 2018.

16 "US supreme court declines appeal of photographer who refused gay couple", *The Guardian*, 8 April 2014.
https://www.theguardian.com/world/2014/apr/07/supreme-court-gay-marriage-new-mexico-photographer Accessed 26 December 2017.

17 "Couple fined for refusing to host same-sex wedding on their farm", *NYPost*, 10 November 2014. Accessed 26 December 2017.
https://nypost.com/2014/11/10/couple-fined-for-refusing-to-host-same-sex-wedding-on-their-farm/

TABLE 10.1:
BILLS FOR TRANSGENDER MARRIAGE AND SAME-SEX MARRIAGE

There have been 20 bills prepared for federal parliament to change the definition of marriage. Fourteen bills have been for transgender marriage and same-sex marriage, four have been for same-sex marriage and two have been for recognising foreign same-sex marriages.

TABLE 10.1:
BILLS FOR TRANSGENDER MARRIAGE AND SAME-SEX MARRIAGE

Act/Bill	Definition of marriage
Marriage Amendment (Definition and Religious Freedoms) Bill 2017 Prepared by: Dean Smith (Lib, WA) Tim Wilson (Lib, Vic) Warrant Entsch (Lib, Qld) Trevor Evans (Lib, Qld) Trent Zimmerman (Lib, NSW) Jason Wood (Lib, Vic) This Bill was passed by parliament in December 2017 following a national survey on marriage.	Transgender marriage and same-sex marriage Marriage is defined as "the union of 2 people to the exclusion of all others, voluntarily entered into for life". The Explanatory Memorandum says: "Throughout this Explanatory Memorandum, reference is made to 'same-sex marriage'. The term 'same-sex marriage' should be read to include a marriage of two people regardless of their sex or gender, where the union is not that of a man and a woman"[1]. Couples can register gender identity on a Notice of Intention to Marry form as Groom, Bride, Partner – Male, Female, or X where X means Indeterminate, Unspecified, Intersex.[2] As marriage between "two people" is irrespective of sex or gender, the sex identifier on a person's birth certificate is no longer necessarily relevant for the purposes of marriage. Most states and territories only record Male/Female on birth certificates (see Chapter 9). The Bill amends the *Sex Discrimination Act* 1984 (SDA) to allow ministers of religion the right to not solemnise a marriage by their sexual orientation, gender identity, intersex or marital status, with reference to Sections 5A, 5B, 5C or 6 of the *Sex Discrimination Act* 1984.[3]
Exposure Draft Marriage Amendment (Same-Sex Marriage) Bill (2016) George Brandis (Attorney General)	Transgender marriage and same-sex marriage Attorney-General's Department: "the union of two people, to the exclusion of all others, voluntarily entered into for life" would mean "[s]ame-sex couples, and couples including people who are intersex or of a non-binary gender, would be able to marry"[4].

TABLE 10.1:
BILLS FOR TRANSGENDER MARRIAGE AND SAME-SEX MARRIAGE

Act/Bill	Definition of marriage
Marriage Legislation Amendment Bill 2016 Adam Bandt (AG, Vic) Cathy McGowan (IND, Vic) Andrew Wilkie (IND, Tas)	Transgender marriage and same-sex marriage Marriage means the union of two people, to the exclusion of all others, voluntarily entered into for life. The object of this Act is to allow couples to marry, and to have their marriages recognised, regardless of sex, sexual orientation, gender identity or intersex status.[5]
Marriage Legislation Amendment Bill 2016 Bill Shorten (ALP, Vic)	Transgender marriage and same-sex marriage Marriage means the union of two people, to the exclusion of all others, voluntarily entered into for life. The object of this Act is to allow couples to marry, and to have their marriages recognised, regardless of sex, sexual orientation, gender identity or intersex status.[6]
Marriage Amendment (Marriage Equality) Bill 2016 Tanya Plibersek (ALP, NSW)	Transgender marriage and same-sex marriage Marriage means the union of two people, to the exclusion of all others, voluntarily entered into for life.[7] Explanatory Memorandum: the objective is to allow "Australians to marry regardless of their sex, sexual orientation, gender identity or intersex status"[8].

TABLE 10.1:
BILLS FOR TRANSGENDER MARRIAGE AND SAME-SEX MARRIAGE

Act/Bill	Definition of marriage
Marriage Legislation Amendment Bill 2015 Warren Entsch (LP, Qld) Teresa Gambaro (LP, Qld) Terri Butler (ALP, Qld) Laurie Ferguson (ALP, NSW) Adam Bandt (AG, Vic) Cathy McGowan (IND, Vic) Andrew Wilkie (IND, Tas)	Transgender marriage and same-sex marriage Marriage means the union of two people, to the exclusion of all others, voluntarily entered into for life. The object of this Act is to allow couples to marry, and to have their marriages recognised, regardless of sex, sexual orientation, gender identity or intersex status.[9]
Marriage Amendment (Marriage Equality) Bill 2015 Bill Shorten (ALP, Vic)	Transgender marriage and same-sex marriage Marriage means the union of two people, to the exclusion of all others, voluntarily entered into for life. The object of this Act is to allow Australians to marry regardless of their sex, sexual orientation, gender identity or intersex status.[10]
David Leyonhjelm (LDP, NSW)	Probably same-sex marriage Marriage means the union of two people, to the exclusion of all others, voluntarily entered into for life. The objects of this Act are … to ensure the Marriage Act 1961 allows all Australians the freedom to marry regardless of sex.[11]

TABLE 10.1:
BILLS FOR TRANSGENDER MARRIAGE AND SAME-SEX MARRIAGE

Act/Bill	Definition of marriage
Marriage Equality Amendment Bill 2013 Sarah Hanson-Young (AG, SA)	Transgender marriage and same-sex marriage Marriage means the union of two people, to the exclusion of all others, voluntarily entered into for life. The objects of this Act are: (a) to remove from the Marriage Act 1961 discrimination against people on the basis of their sex, sexual orientation or gender identity; and (b) to recognise that freedom of sexual orientation and gender identity are fundamental human rights …[12]
Marriage Equality Amendment Bill 2013 Sarah Hanson-Young (AG, SA)	Transgender marriage Marriage means the union of two people, to the exclusion of all others, voluntarily entered into for life. The objects of this Act are: (a) to remove from the Marriage Act 1961 discrimination against people on the basis of their sex, sexual orientation or gender identity; and (b) to recognise that freedom of sexual orientation and gender identity are fundamental human rights …[13]
Marriage Amendment Bill (No. 2) 2012 Carol Brown (ALP, Tas) Trish Crossin (ALP, NT) Gavin Marshall (ALP, Vic) Louise Pratt (ALP, WA)	Same-sex marriage Marriage means the union of two people, to the exclusion of all others, voluntarily entered into for life. The object of this Act is to amend the Marriage Act 1961 to ensure equal access to marriage for all adult couples, irrespective of sex, who have a mutual commitment to a shared life.[14] Explanatory Memorandum: the purpose of the bill is "to establish marriage equality for same-sex couples"[15].

TABLE 10.1:
BILLS FOR TRANSGENDER MARRIAGE AND SAME-SEX MARRIAGE

Act/Bill	Definition of marriage
Marriage Equality Amendment Bill 2012 Adam Bandt (AG, Vic) Andrew Wilkie (IND, Tas)	Transgender marriage and same-sex marriage Marriage means the union of two people, regardless of their sex, sexual orientation or gender identity, to the exclusion of all others, voluntarily entered into for life.[16]
Marriage Amendment Bill 2012 Stephen Jones (ALP, NSW)	Same-sex marriage Marriage means the union of two people, regardless of their sex, to the exclusion of all others, voluntarily entered into for life. The object of this Act is to amend the Marriage Act 1961 to ensure equal access to marriage for all adult couples irrespective of sex who have a mutual commitment to a shared life.[17]
Marriage Equality Amendment Bill 2010 Sarah Hanson-Young (AG, SA)	Transgender marriage and same-sex marriage Marriage means the union of two people, regardless of their sex, sexual orientation or gender identity, to the exclusion of all others, voluntarily entered into for life. The objects of this Act are … to recognise that freedom of sexual orientation and gender identity are fundamental human rights …[18]
Marriage Equality Amendment Bill 2009 Sarah Hanson-Young (AG, SA)	Transgender marriage and same-sex marriage Marriage means the union of two people, regardless of their sex, sexuality or gender identity, voluntarily entered into for life. The objects of this Act are … to recognise that freedom of sexual orientation and gender identity are fundamental human rights …[19]

TABLE 10.1:

BILLS FOR TRANSGENDER MARRIAGE AND SAME-SEX MARRIAGE

Act/Bill	Definition of marriage
Same-Sex Marriage Bill 2008 Natasha Stott Despoja (AG, SA) Andrew Bartlett (AD, Qld)	Same-sex marriage The Bill says: omit from the definition of marriage "a husband and wife" and substitute "two people". Same-sex marriages: To avoid doubt, nothing in this Act is intended to prevent the marriage of two people of the same sex under this Act.[20]
Marriage (Relationships Equality) Amendment Bill 2008 Kerry Nettle (AG, NSW)	Transgender marriage and same-sex marriage Marriage means the union of two persons, regardless of their sexual orientation or gender identity, voluntarily entered into for life. The objects of this Act are to: (a) remove from the Marriage Act 1961 discrimination on the basis of sexual orientation and gender identity; and (b) permit marriage regardless of sexual orientation and gender identity.[21]
Marriage (Relationships Equality) Amendment Bill 2007 Kerry Nettle (AG, NSW)	Transgender marriage and same-sex marriage Marriage means the union of two persons, regardless of their sexuality or gender identity, voluntarily entered into for life. The objects of this Act are to: (a) remove from the Marriage Act 1961 discrimination on the basis of sexuality and gender identity; and (b) permit marriage regardless of sexuality and gender identity.[22]

TABLE 10.1:
BILLS FOR TRANSGENDER MARRIAGE AND SAME-SEX MARRIAGE

Act/Bill	Definition of marriage
Same-Sex Marriage Bill 2006 Natasha Stott Despoja (AD, SA) Andrew Bartlett (AD, Qld)	Same-sex marriage The Bill says: omit from the definition of marriage "a husband and wife" and substitute "two people". Same-sex marriages: To avoid doubt, nothing in this Act is intended to prevent the marriage of two people of the same sex under this Act.[23] Andrew Bartlett's Second reading speech: the "to avoid doubt" clause "uses gender-neutral language to accommodate unions between both heterosexual and homosexual couples"[24]
Same-Sex Relationships (Enduring Equality) Bill 2004 Michael Organ (AG, NSW)	Same-sex marriage The Bill says: omit from the definition of marriage "a husband and wife" and substitute "two people". Same-sex marriages: To avoid doubt, nothing in this Act is intended to prevent the marriage of two people of the same sex under this Act. The object of this Act is to eliminate all forms of discrimination on the basis of sexuality.[25]
Marriage Act 1961, as amended in 2004 Phillip Ruddock, Attorney General	Heterosexual marriage Marriage means the union of a man and a woman to the exclusion of all others, voluntarily entered into for life.[26] Man and woman are not defined in the Marriage Act 1961 or in the Acts Interpretation Act 1901.

Endnotes

1. Explanatory Memorandum, *The Marriage Amendment (Definition and Religious Freedoms) Bill 2017*, pg. 2.

2. Notice of Intention to Marry, Attorney General's Department, Australia Government.
https://www.ag.gov.au/FamiliesAndMarriage/Marriage/Documents/New-notice-of-intended-marriage.pdf Accessed 12 February 2018.

3. *Marriage Amendment (Definition and Religious Freedoms) Bill 2017*, Section 63.
https://www.legislation.gov.au/Details/C2017A00129 Accessed 12 February 2018.

4. Submission from Federal Attorney General's Department to the Senate Select Committee on the Exposure Draft of the Marriage Amendment (Same-Sex Marriage) Bill, Submission 78, January 2017, pg. 2.
http://www.aph.gov.au/Parliamentary_Business/Committees/Senate/Same_Sex_Marriage/SameSexMarriage/Submissions Accessed 14 March 2017.

5. *Marriage Legislation Amendment Bill 2016*, Sections 2, 3.
https://www.legislation.gov.au/Details/C2016B00127 Accessed 14 March 2017.

6. *Marriage Legislation Amendment Bill 2016*, Sections 1, 2.
http://www.aph.gov.au/Parliamentary_Business/Bills_Legislation/Bills_Search_Results/Result?bId=r5708 Accessed 14 March 2017.

7. *Marriage Amendment (Marriage Equality) Bill 2016*.
http://parlinfo.aph.gov.au/parlInfo/search/display/display.w3p;query=Id%3A%22legislation%2Fbillhome%2Fr5660%22 Accessed 14 March 2017.

8. The Hon Tanya Plibersek, *Explanatory Memorandum, Marriage Amendment (Marriage Equality) Bill 2016*.
http://parlinfo.aph.gov.au/parlInfo/search/display/display.w3p;query=Id%3A%22legislation%2Fems%2Fr5660_ems_47d6e42e-cd4a-442b-845d-62ff251cf8fb%22;rec=0

9. *Marriage Legislation Amendment Bill 2015*.
http://parlinfo.aph.gov.au/parlInfo/search/display/display.w3p;query=Id%3A%22legislation%2Fbillhome%2Fr5512%22 Accessed 14 March 2017.

10. *Marriage Amendment (Marriage Equality) Bill 2015*.
http://parlinfo.aph.gov.au/parlInfo/search/display/display.w3p;query=Id%3A%22legislation%2Fbillhome%2Fr5470%22 Accessed 14 March 2017.

11. *Freedom to Marry Bill 2014*.
http://parlinfo.aph.gov.au/parlInfo/search/display/display.w3p;query=Id%3A%22legislation%2Fbillhome%2Fs983%22 Accessed 14 March 2017.

12. *Marriage Equality Amendment Bill 2013*.
http://parlinfo.aph.gov.au/parlInfo/search/display/display.w3p;query=Id%3A%22legislation%2Fbillhome%2Fs938%22 Accessed 14 March 2017.

13. *Marriage Equality Amendment Bill 2013*.
http://parlinfo.aph.gov.au/parlInfo/search/display/display.w3p;query=Id%3A%22legislation%2Fbillhome%2Fs905%22 Accessed 14 March 2017.

Table 10.1:

14 *Marriage Amendment Bill (No. 2) 2012.*
    http://parlinfo.aph.gov.au/parlInfo/search/display/display.
    w3p;query=Id%3A%22legislation%2Fbillhome%2Fs884%22 Accessed
    14 March 2017.

15 Senators Crossin, Brown, Pratt and Marshall, *Explanatory Memorandum,
    Marriage Amendment Bill (No. 2) 2012.*
    http://parlinfo.aph.gov.au/parlInfo/search/display/display.
    w3p;query=Id%3A%22legislation%2Fems%2Fs884_ems_58d703ff-d4ba-403e-
    b689-513df229f620%22 Accessed 30 July 2017.

16 *Marriage Equality Amendment Bill 2012.*
    http://parlinfo.aph.gov.au/parlInfo/search/display/display.
    w3p;query=Id%3A%22legislation%2Fbillhome%2Fr4748%22 Accessed
    14 March 2017.

17 *Marriage Amendment Bill 2012.*
    http://parlinfo.aph.gov.au/parlInfo/search/display/display.
    w3p;query=Id%3A%22legislation%2Fbillhome%2Fr4749%22 Accessed
    14 March 2017.

18 *Marriage Equality Amendment Bill 2010.*
    http://parlinfo.aph.gov.au/parlInfo/search/display/display.
    w3p;query=Id%3A%22legislation%2Fbillhome%2Fs792%22 Accessed
    14 March 2017.

19 *Marriage Equality Amendment Bill 2009.*
    http://parlinfo.aph.gov.au/parlInfo/search/display/display.
    w3p;query=Id%3A%22legislation%2Fbillhome%2Fs722%22 Accessed
    14 March 2017.

20 *Same-Sex Marriage Bill 2006 [2008].*
    http://parlinfo.aph.gov.au/parlInfo/search/display/display.
    w3p;query=Id%3A%22legislation%2Fbillhome%2Fs502%22 Accessed
    14 March 2017.

21 *Marriage (Relationships Equality) Amendment Bill 2008.*
    http://parlinfo.aph.gov.au/parlInfo/search/display/display.
    w3p;query=Id%3A%22legislation%2Fbillhome%2Fs614%22 Accessed
    14 March 2017.

22 *Marriage (Relationships Equality) Amendment Bill 2007.*
    http://parlinfo.aph.gov.au/parlInfo/search/display/display.
    w3p;query=Id%3A%22legislation%2Fbillhome%2Fs558%22 Accessed
    14 March 2017.

23 *Same-Sex Marriage Bill 2006.*
    http://parlinfo.aph.gov.au/parlInfo/search/display/display.
    w3p;query=Id%3A%22legislation%2Fbillhome%2Fs502%22 Accessed
    14 March 2017.

24 Senator Andrew Bartlett, *Same-Sex Marriages Bill 2006*, Second Reading speech,
    15 June 2006.
    http://parlinfo.aph.gov.au/parlInfo/search/display/display.w3p;query=Id%3A%2
    2chamber%2Fhansards%2F2006-06-15%2F0030%22 Accessed 30 July 2017.

25 *Same-Sex Relationships (Enduring Equality) Bill 2004.*
    http://parlinfo.aph.gov.au/parlInfo/download/legislation/bills/r2057_first/toc_
    pdf/04079b01.pdf;fileType%3Dapplication%2Fpdf Accessed 14 March 2017.

26 *Marriage Amendment Act 2004*, Schedule 1.
    https://www.legislation.gov.au/Details/C2004A01361 Accessed 26 June 2018.

CHAPTER 11

THE ROAD AHEAD

11.1 INTRODUCTION

Following the 2013 changes to the *Sex Discrimination Act 1984* (SDA), the Australian Human Rights Commission (AHRC) and the Federal Labor Party have advocated extending the legal, economic and cultural rights of persons who self-identify with a fluid gender identity.

11.2 THE AHRC'S "ROAD MAP FOR INCLUSION"

The AHRC's *Resilient Individuals* (2015) has set out an extensive "Road map for Inclusion"[1] across all jurisdictions and across many institutions.

Call for states and territories to conform to the SDA: Although the SDA provides for extensive coverage across areas of federal government jurisdiction, the AHRC has called for state and territory laws to provide the same protections for gender identity and sexual orientation as the SDA.[2] South Australia, the ACT and Tasmania protect gender identity, while the NT is considering proposals to align its anti-discrimination laws with the SDA.

Call for self-identification on identity documents: The AHRC called for all states and territories to recognise non-binary gender identities on birth certificates and identity forms, in accordance with each person's self-chosen, fluid gender identity.[3] It called for them to "legislate to require that a self-identified legal declaration, such as a statutory declaration, is sufficient proof to change a person's gender for the purposes of government records and proof of identity documentation"[4].

Call for children to begin medical transitioning without involving the courts: The AHRC has called for an alternative to the requirement for Family Court orders for children under the age of 18 seeking hormone treatment to transition to the opposite of their birth sex. "Adequate safeguards" would be "the opinion of relevant and appropriate medical practitioners and the views of the young person seeking treatment"[5]. In 2017, the Family Court decided that it would no longer exercise its jurisdiction in cases involving children seeking access to puberty blockers and cross-sex hormones in order to transition to the opposite sex to their sex recorded at birth.[6]

Medicare funding of transgender clinical services: The AHRC has proposed research on how Medicare could fund "specialist clinical service provision needs of trans and gender diverse people"[7].

Accommodation of trans people in prisons: The AHRC has called on all states and territories to allow trans and gender-diverse people who are in prison to be placed in the prison of their choice, and for such prisoners to access hormone therapy.[8]

Special training: The AHRC has called for gender identity, sexual orientation, intersex and diversity training to be incorporated into medical, health science and allied health courses, teacher and welfare courses in university and vocational training sectors, and in the National School Curriculum.[9]

Sport: The AHRC proposes that trans and intersex people be able play in the professional and community sports of their choice.

Training practitioners for medical transitioning: The AHRC has called for resources to build awareness of the specific therapeutic and medical needs of transgender and gender-diverse people aimed at those being trained and existing practitioners.[10]

Teacher and welfare courses: The AHRC wants specialist training on transgender issues in university and vocational training sectors, as well as being included in the professional development of current practitioners via the Australian Teachers Federation and other professional bodies.[11]

11.3 LABOR PARTY TRANSGENDER POLICY COMMITMENTS

The 2015, 47th Labor Party National Conference set out an extensive National Platform covering transgenderism. The platform is said to be "a clear statement of the Party's beliefs"[12]. In part, it is based on a commitment to the Yogyakarta Principles, which are described as providing "a substantial guide" for gender identity and sexual orientation rights in Australian law[13] and "at the Human Rights Council and the General Assembly of the United Nations"[14].

To this end, the platform makes a number of commitments.

Review anti-discrimination laws: The platform says that Labor will review national anti-discrimination laws to ensure that religious and faith exemptions "do not place Australians in a position where they cannot access essential social services". This is based on Labor's position that no religion, faith or belief should be "used as an instrument of division or exclusion, and condemning anyone, discriminating against anyone, vilifying anyone is a violation of the values we all share, a violation which can never be justified by anyone's faith or belief"[15].

Schools policy: Labor says it will continue to support national programs to support transgender students, "ensuring gender-diverse students are able to express the gender they identify with, including through preferred name and dress"[16].

Medicare funding for medical transitioning: Labor's policy is "to ensure that Medicare and the Pharmaceutical Benefits Scheme implement anti-discriminatory policies for lesbian, gay, bisexual, transgender, and intersex Australians and that same-sex couples and their families are not discriminated against in their access to or use of Medicare or the PBS [Pharmaceutical Benefits Scheme] … Cost should not be a barrier to accessing these services and/or surgery, and Labor commits to removing, wherever possible, out-of-pocket health expenses for transgender people incurred in relation to their gender identity"[17].

Surrogacy policy: Labor says it will seek national agreement on the recognition of transgender, lesbian, gay, bisexual, and intersex parents. The platform supports "access [to] assisted reproductive technology, to adopt, and to enter into domestic surrogacy arrangements, on an equal basis to cisgender heterosexual couples in every Australian State and Territory"[18].

Advocacy for transgenderism: The platform says Labor will "Investigate establishing a National Gender Centre, … investigate amending the *Australian Human Rights Commission Act* to establish a Commissioner for Sexual Orientation, Gender Identity and Intersex Status issues, with equivalent powers, responsibilities and funding to Commissioners within the Australian Human Rights Commission"[19] and "appoint a Global Human Rights Ambassador"[20].

Counselling policy: The platform contains a resolution that says that Labor will amend laws to deal with any psychological treatments to discourage "gender questioning", saying that "[c]urrent laws regulating false and misleading conduct in trade or commerce, or professional misconduct in the health professions, are inadequate to deal with perpetrators who can evade health regulations by not being registered, and evade consumer protection laws by claiming to be conducting religious activities". Labor holds that "conversion therapies" to "cure" gender questioning young people are to be regarded as "serious psychological abuse" and that "harms" suffered by such children in families will be treated "as domestic violence against the child"[21].

11.4 CONCLUSION

If these proposals are fully implemented, the cost to the Australian taxpayer of implementing the transgender world view is likely to be enormous.

Where is the evidence that these policies will resolve gender dysphoria, especially in the case of children believing they should transition to the opposite of their birth sex?

When a family encourages a child to desist from transitioning until the child can make their own mature decision in adulthood, why should that be treated as domestic violence against the child?

Endnotes

1. *Resilient Individuals: Sexual Orientation, Gender Identity & Intersex Rights: National Consultation Report*, Australian Human Rights Commission, 2015, pgs. 2-5.
   https://www.humanrights.gov.au/our-work/sexual-orientation-sex-gender-identity/publications/resilient-individuals-sexual Accessed 6 June 2017.

2. Ibid., pgs. 2-3.

3. Ibid., pg. 50.

4. Ibid., pg. 3.

5. Ibid., pg. 2.

6. *Re: Kelvin [2017]* FamCAFC 258 (30 November 2017)
   http://www9.austlii.edu.au/cgibin/viewdoc/au/cases/cth/FamCAFC/2017/258.html

7. *Resilient Individuals*, Op. cit., pg. 4.

8. Ibid., pg. 3.

9. Ibid., pg. 4.

10. Ibid., pg. 4.

11. Ibid., pg. 4.

12. *A smart, modern fair Australia*, ALP National Platform 2015, pg. 1.
    https://cdn.australianlabor.com.au/documents/ALP_National_Platform.pdf

13. Ibid., pg. 161.

14. Ibid., pg. 170.

15. Ibid., pg. 139.

16. Ibid., pg. 90.

17. Ibid., pg. 109.

18. Ibid., pg. 137.

19. Ibid., pg. 162.

20. Ibid., pg. 170.

21. Ibid., pg. 193.

PART C

CONSEQUENCES OF THE TRANSGENDER WORLD VIEW CHANGING THE CULTURE

Part B of this book examined how the transgender world view has been written into three areas of law:

- anti-discrimination laws, particularly the federal *Sex Discrimination Act 1984*;
- state and territory births, deaths and marriages registration laws and regulations; and
- the definition of marriage in the federal *Marriage Act 1961*.

These form a legal framework to create a transnormative culture, where the newly created transgender rights conflict with, or take priority, over the inherent rights of citizens who recognise their biological sex as the essence of their sexual identity. These laws impact on many areas of culture, as identified in Table 1.1. Also, this framework has been created by court rulings that have supported the transgender world view.

Part C examines the many areas where these conflicts are happening and how children and women are particularly affected.

Chapter 12 examines how transgender theory has been applied to education. Chapter 13 examines the controversial Safe Schools Coalition program as a case study of transgenderism in education.

Children are being encouraged to undergo medical treatments to transition. Court approval is no longer required for a child to transition to the opposite of their birth sex. The impact of transitioning treatments is discussed in Chapter 14 by paediatrician, Professor John Whitehall.

Lane Anderson (a pseudonym) is a practising psychotherapist in North America. In Chapter 15, she describes her experience of counselling transgender teenagers and their families over a decade. She describes her clinical insights into her clients, adolescent psychology, and the impact of the transgender phenomenon on society.

Chapter 16 examines how the rights of women to their privacy, safe spaces, health needs and recognition as biological females are compromised and undermined by transgender laws. If biological men can identity as women, feminism is undermined.

Chapter 17 examines how the more biological men who self-identify as women participate in women's sports, the more biological women are likely to be displaced from winners' podiums.

Chapter 18 asks whether the cultural conflicts between the biological and transgender world views can be resolved or if compromises can be found. It argues that the biological world view should be recognised in law.

Chapter 19 examines how the state adopting an ideological belief like transgenderism is comparable to governments establishing a state religion. This has consequences for basic freedoms.

Chapter 20 makes a distinction between two forms of social conflicts. There are the conflicts between the biological and transgender world views and, separately, there are conflicts over same-sex marriage. These are separate issues that require different resolutions.

Chapter 21 points out that Michel Foucault's assertion that there is no human nature means there are no universal human rights. This assertion is the foundation of transgender/queer theories and underpins the confusions and conflicts in law and culture between the transgender and biological world views.

CHAPTER 12

TRANSGENDERSIM:
FROM THEORY TO LAW TO EDUCATION

"Childhood has been recognized as a crucial emblematic function in neoliberal sexual politics, and it has been duly regularized as a central queer [transgender] concern: an arguable crucible or ground zero of all sexual politics."

Diederik Janssen, "Queer theory and childhood",
Oxford Bibliographies.[1]

12.1 INTRODUCTION

The transgender world view challenges the understanding that a child has an innate, fixed sex. Transgenderism contests the laws, regulations and cultural mores it deems as conditioning children in their sexual identity. It regards this contest as the "crucible or ground zero of all sexual politics"[2].

Progressively, laws in various Australian jurisdictions have adopted the transgender world view and provided pathways for transgender school policies. The most significant was the federal *Sex Discrimination Act 1984*, which legally defined a person by their gender identity. This profoundly affects children and schools. Consider the response of governments to the question: if a child believes they are in the "wrong body" and identifies as the opposite to their birth sex, then what services and facilities is the child legally entitled to access in a government school?

This chapter examines how state education department policies are answering this question and the conflict these policies create for students, teachers, principals, and parents. It also examines the queer/transgender theory claim that a child's sexual identity is fluid and the idea that a child has agency to decide their identity.

Under Australian law, the age of majority is generally 18. As well as rights, protections, privileges and access to services based on their biological sex, minors are given special protections in law and culture due to their immaturity and vulnerabilities.

12.2 NEW POLICIES ON ACCESS TO SCHOOL TOILETS, SHOWERS, CHANGE ROOMS

Four state education departments have issued education policies requiring school authorities to negotiate with transgender students as to which toilets, other facilities, and services they can access at school.

The departments say that these policies flow from the definition of, and protections for, "gender identity" inserted into the federal *Sex Discrimination Act 1984* (the SDA) in 2013 and apply regardless of age. Section 21 covers all government-run schools in Australia and says that a school cannot discriminate against a student on the basis of their gender identity or sexual orientation, by "refusing or failing to accept the person's application for admission" or by "denying the student, or limiting the student's access, to any benefit" the school provides, or by "expelling" or "subjecting the student to any other detriment"[3].

It appears that, if a child regards their gender identity as being other than their sex at birth, their gender identity is legally recognised and protected under the SDA and, in some cases, under state anti-discrimination laws.

The *Australian Government Guidelines on the Recognition of Sex and Gender* (2013, 2015), which followed the recognition of gender identity being defined in the SDA in 2013, say that "[s]ex reassignment surgery or hormone therapy are not prerequisites" for legal recognition.[4] The threshold for recognition of a change of sex is low, requiring only a statement from a registered medical practitioner or psychologist, a passport or Australian government travel document, an amended birth certificate, or a state or territory Gender Recognition Certificate or Recognised Details Certificate.[5]

A school student can claim new rights by self-identifying as any gender other than their natal sex.

Consequently, the Queensland Department of Education and Training "Diversity in Queensland Schools" policy says:

> When determining which toilets and change rooms a student will use, the school should discuss this with the student/parent/carer (where applicable) and consider options at the school based on available facilities e.g. the establishment of non-gender

specific toilets and change rooms where there are individual stalls or cubicles that can provide privacy for all users ...

The principal may require appropriate medical evidence of gender identity in relation to a student to support that the accommodations required are in the best interests of the student.[6]

Similarly, in 2014 the NSW Legal Services Directorate issued "Transgender students in schools – legal rights and responsibilities", advising the state NSW Department of Education and TAFE:

Students should not be required to use the toilets and change rooms used by persons of the sex they were assigned at birth if they identify as a different gender. Alternative arrangements may include using staff toilets or unisex toilets where possible. The exclusion of students who identify as transgender from the toilet or change rooms of their identified gender must be regularly reviewed to determine its continuing necessity.

If other students indicate discomfort with sharing single-sex facilities (toilets or change rooms for example) with a student who identifies as transgender, this should be addressed through the school learning and support team.[7]

The NSW policy also contains risk assessments and management proposals. It assessed the risk for "use of toilet and change rooms" as "high", suggesting that other students face not just "discomfort", but potentially more serious issues. It sets out how teachers are to manage the risk.

Doors provided to change room cubicles of their identified gender.
Student must change in cubicle.
Staff to monitor length of time in change room.
Staff and student to report any incidents in the change room to Principal ...
Zero tolerance to "skylarking" in change rooms ...

The Victorian Department of Education and Training "Gender Identity" policy says that "schools must support and respect a student's choice to identify as their desired gender when this does not align with their designated sex at birth" and that "a letter from a gender identity specialist may be requested by the school to support them in developing the plan".

The policy says:

Toilets, showers and change rooms are specific to each school. The arrangements for the use of these facilities should be made locally and documented in the school management plan. Careful consideration should be given to the use of facilities that are appropriate to the student's preferred or chosen gender.

Note: Regular use of disabled toilets by a student without disabilities can draw attention to the student and is not appropriate for these purposes.[8]

The SA Department for Education and Child Development procedure for "Transgender and intersex student support" says:

Young people under the age of 18 years have the legal capacity to make many decisions if they have the maturity and cognitive ability to do so. However, this can only be determined on a case-by-case basis informed by age and developmental capacity. Site leaders are best placed to make this determination. It can also be informed by advice from a health care professional ...

Transgender and gender diverse students should have the choice of accessing a toilet/change room that matches their gender identity ...

Schools may also have unisex/gender neutral facilities. While this is a helpful strategy for creating an inclusive school environment for gender diverse students broadly, it is not appropriate to insist that any student, including a transgender student, use this toilet if they are not comfortable doing so ...

The SA policy goes on to warn principals and teachers that

[f]ailure to provide transgender students with access to appropriate toilet and change facilities may breach anti-discrimination legislation.[9]

Presumably, this means that school authorities could face legal penalties for non-compliance with these policies.

12.3 APPLYING THE TRANSGENDER WORLD VIEW TO SCHOOLS

Authors of transgender school programs have claimed that laws recognising the transgender world view are grounds for transgender education programs in schools.

For example, the Australian Research Centre for Sex, Health and Society (ARCSHS) at La Trobe University has been a leading advocacy centre for transgender school programs. It developed the controversial Safe Schools Coalition Victoria program (see Chapter 13).

The Safe Schools' resource, *Guide to supporting a student to affirm or transition gender identity at school*, takes its definition of gender identity from the SDA, Section 4 (see Chapter 8.2.2), and says that the *Guide* aims to combat discrimination, as defined in the SDA.[10]

In academic literature, ARCHS academics and researchers have articulated how transgender/queer theory can be applied in education. Elizabeth Smith, Roz Ward, Jennifer Dixon, Lynne Hillier, Anne Mitchell and Dr Tiffany Jones co-wrote "School experiences of transgender and gender-diverse students in Australia" (2016). They say that queer/transgender theory is interested in "(de)constructions of sex and gender"[11]; that is, in deconstructing the idea that people are inherently male or female.

In "Saving rhetorical children: sexuality education discourses from conservative to post-modern", Tiffany Jones (2011)[12] examined the evolution of sex education from conservative, liberal, critical to post-modern, including post-modern diversity education and "queer" (or transgender theory) education.

Jones defines "sexuality" very broadly to include

> anything obliquely related to constructions of sexed and gendered bodies, identities and behaviours; sexual feelings, desires and acts; sexual knowledge, skills and information.[13]

She says that, in diversity education,

> [s]exuality and gender are not limited to a two-sex bi-polarised model. A whole school approach is taken to becoming inclusive for people with diverse sexualities and gender identification, including students, staff and families. Variety is celebrated. Constructions of 'family' are reconsidered.[14]

Jones says that queer (transgender) education

> Aims to disrupt/destabilise the structures (sex, gender, orientation) that uphold the illusion of heteronormativity through revealing their performative nature. This can be achieved through deconstruction and (re)creation of texts, including the self or others as texts.[15]

Here, Jones alludes to Judith Butler's literary notions of a person being like a "text" that can be reviewed, rewritten, and performed so that a person can create a new gender identity (see Chapter 6.2). Such new gender identities are at odds with the "illusion of heteronormativity"; that is, laws and culture that recognise a person by their biological nature as male or female which, in turn, define heterosexual, gay, lesbian and bisexual orientations. This world view is said to exclude transgenders, those who identify as other than their birth sex.

Jones says that teaching methods

> may include viewing of alternative texts, lectures and guest speakers from marginalised groups, activisms within and beyond the school (creation of posters, plays, speeches, etc.), through to camps and ceremonies ...

> Teachers may 'play devil's advocate' in relation to the student, acting as a 'deconstructor, not a mere supporter in the traditional sense of the word'.[16]

The aim is to

> develop in students an oppositional position in relation to the dominant order ...[17]

> Students can both de-construct and co-construct sexual 'truths' and systems, as all knowledge is seen as constructed and relational. Students are placed in an oppositional subject position through which they can interrogate constructions of 'reality' and intervene in their reconstitution.[18]

This proposes encouraging students to stand in opposition to the biological definition of a person as male or female and to critique "constructions" of the family.

12.4 HOW MANY CHILDREN ARE TRANSGENDER, EXPERIENCING GENDER DYSPHORIA?

The attention education departments have given to transgender policies prompts the question: how many children experience gender dysphoria and how many transition later in life?

The American Psychiatric Association's *DSM-5*, which is a manual of psychological disorders, says the prevalence is very low – between five and 14 in every 100,000 males and two to three in every 100,000 females.[19]

How many children with gender dysphoria will identify as transgender as adults and how many desist from transitioning?

Research by Korte et al (2008) found that most children with gender dysphoria don't transition to the opposite sex in adulthood. Between 80 and 97.5 per cent desist.[20]

Yet, sweeping school policies have been developed to support the very few students who identify with other than their birth sex, compared with other conditions that are more prevalent and affect a person's employment opportunities. Compare the incidence of gender dysphoria with colour blindness that affects one in 12 men and one in 200 women. In the UK, it makes people ineligible for some jobs, because they can't distinguish the colour of, among other things, traffic lights, fire extinguishers and electrical wires. Colour blind people cannot be employed to drive a commercial vehicle, or be an electrician, pilot, fire fighter, baggage handler, police officer or painter.[21] Given the much higher incidence of colour blindness, should there be extensive school policies, backed with government funding, in place to help children suffering from colour blindness?

Gender dysphoria is a complicated issue and concerns with children transitioning are discussed in Chapter 14. Transgender literature emphasises one factor, the risks transgender students face from bullying, leading to negative mental health issues and self-harm. Taking this literature at face value, is the solution to support gender-dysphoric school children to transition and encourage them to assert their transgender rights though political action to improve their self-esteem, as proposed by ARCSHS academics? Or, is the solution to counsel them to wait until they are adults, while implementing school anti-bullying programs that teach students that nobody should be bullied for any reason?

There has been a recent spike in the number of young people wanting to transition in Australia. The number of children referred to Melbourne's Royal Children's Hospital for gender dysphoria increased from one in 2003[22], with 300 referrals expected in 2017.[23]

Again, this prompts the question: has the push for transgenderism in law, schools and culture created a transgender cultural phenomenon? Has transgender become the new black?

12.5 CONFLICT OF RIGHTS

In relation to education policies, transgender theory emphasises the rights of transgenders to self-identify their sex/gender identity, and to access the toilets, change rooms, showers and sports of their choice for their comfort. The theory does not discuss the potential for abuse; for example, when a male imitates being a female, not because he is in the "wrong body", but to access female facilities for other nefarious reasons.

The NSW policy admits that the risks involved are "high". Is this because the threshold for a male to identify as a female is low? It appears from the policies of various education departments discussed above, that medical evidence "may" be requested (Queensland) of a child's sexual/gender identity, otherwise self-identification appears to be the threshold for a child or teenager to identify as other than their birth sex.

This push for transgender toilet, shower and change room policies in schools comes at a time when there is serious community concern over child-on-child sexual abuse in schools. In 2013, there were almost 1,000 reported cases of children abusing other children. Criminologist Dr Wendy O'Brien, a senior research fellow with the Australian Crime Commission, says that this figure is just the tip of the iceberg and that the problem is under-reported.[24]

What about school safeguards? The NSW policy attempts to put safeguards against abuse in place for children by requiring school "staff to monitor length of time in change room". This puts teachers in an invidious position. Are teachers to be rostered outside toilets? What happens to a male teacher's reputation if he finds it necessary to intervene in a female toilet, shower or change room? Following the findings made in the Royal Commission into Institutional Sex Abuse about incidents in certain educational institutions, teachers may feel inhibited in entering change rooms to "monitoring length of time in [a] change room".

What of the right of parents to expect a high-level duty of care for their children? What of parents having "a prior right to choose the kind of education that shall be given to their children", as set down in the *Universal Declaration of Human Rights* (1948)?[25] This parental right is also recognised in the *International Covenant on Civil and Political Rights* (1966) Article 18 (4) which says the liberty of parents "to ensure the religious and moral education of their children in conformity with their own convictions"[26] must be respected. Australia is a signatory to the Covenant.

What of the right of other students to privacy in toilets, showers and change rooms? What of the right of girls to fair play in sports?

This discussion illustrates how, under the SDA and similar state and territory anti-discrimination laws, transgender rights override rights based on the biological world view, even when it involves "high-risk" policies for children. Far from children of biological sex possessing the right of privacy and to enjoy facilities without fear of intimidation, they how have a duty to share such facilities with students of the opposite biological sex who claim transgender status.

12.6 CHILD AGENCY: BLURRING THE LINES BETWEEN CHILD AND ADULT

Transgender education theory emphasises that children, and young people before or early in adolescence,[27] have the mental and emotional capacity to make their own choices and decisions. In education parlance, the term used is "child agency". Agency refers to the capacity of individuals to act independently and to make their own free choices.[28] The SDA underscores child agency in making gender identity and sexual orientation protected attributes, regardless of age.

Some state education department policies[29] and some school resources on transgender students[30] have emphasised that children can be considered "mature minors", capable of being treated as adult decision makers who do not require parental consent (see Chapter 13.5).

Transgender/queer theory says that neoliberal laws have conditioned children into male and female roles from the time they are born. It opposes this conditioning and advocates for children making their own gender choices. As Diederik Janssen (2015) argues, child agency is not only "a central queer concern" but is "arguably the crucible, or ground zero, of all sexual politics"[31].

If children have "agency" to change their sex by taking puberty blockers and sex-change hormones, then should children be regarded as having the capacity (agency) to make other decisions that are considered the domain of adults? Should child labour laws be abolished so that children can exercise their "agency" and go to work when they please? It is an open question as to whether transgender/queer theory has the theoretical framework to make distinctions between child and adult decision making on such an issue.

Transgender theory blurs boundaries between the child, teenager and adult that have been important in the protection of younger people.

This romanticising of child agency discounts the power imbalances between children and adults, leaving children exposed and vulnerable to the very adult conditioning and exploitation from which transgender/queer theory was supposed to liberate them. Do children really have the maturity to join the army, drink alcohol, drive a car, or go out to work when they choose without facing risks considered unacceptable by society? Do they really have the foresight, like that of adults, to decide to change their sex and understand the consequences?

It also leaves transgender/queer theory blind to possible serious problems some children face. In cases where a child's gender dysphoria is associated with autism or bad experiences, queer theory emphasises celebrating their state of "diversity" rather than seeking treatment to resolve the child's problems. It appears that some ARCSHS transgender theorists dismiss the idea that transgender (as in gender dysphoria) can be a "disordered psychological" condition.[32]

12.7   WHAT HAPPENED TO SEX?

Chapter 3 asked: why does sex matter? The complementary biological nature of men and women, that provides the gametes necessary for human reproduction and sex, is the basis of deep and profound human relationships. Sex is defined by reproductive male and female functions (see Chapter 3.2).

Yet, in the transgender academic writings discussed above, reproduction and pregnancy are not mentioned or considered. It appears to treat reproduction as disconnected from sex.

Jones (2016) says that among the top issues identified by students as missing from sexuality education are "how to make sexual activity enjoyable for both partners ... dealing with relationship break-ups, and understanding the emotions in relationships"[33]. Ironically, these very issues are indicative of a person yet to mature intellectually and emotionally, and yet to comprehend the responsibilities that accompany pregnancy and child rearing.

Transgender theory does not deal with the deep emotional and relationship issues associated with reproduction. Perhaps this is not surprising, given that transgender/queer theory deals with what is not normal; that is, what are other than normal sexual identities and what are other than normal relationships that lead to pregnancy, child birth and the rearing of children. Rather, it stands in opposition to defining humans as male or female, critiquing all that is based on the biological understanding of male and female[34] (see Chapters 4.2, 4.3).

Removing reproduction from consideration of "sexuality" ignores one of the fundamental purposes of sex, while the focus on a person's fluid gender identity, at the expense of their inherent sexual identity, risks desexualising sex (see Chapter 6.2.5).

12.8   ISSUES FOR EDUCATORS

What do the transgender education policies of state education departments mean for teachers and school principals?

Four state education departments have made it clear that their transgender student policies are framed by anti-discrimination laws, particularly the SDA (see above). The South Australian policy explicitly warns principals and teachers that they may "breach anti-discrimination legislation" if they fail to provide transgender students with access to appropriate toilet and change facilities.[35]

Does this also mean that a teacher or principal would face disciplinary action by state education authorities responsible for the registration of teachers, if they fail to allow a biological boy who identifies as a girl access to the female facilities? Would this mean that their professional qualifications could be revoked, or that future state teacher employment contracts could be in jeopardy?

12.9   CONCLUSION

How children are identified and raised from birth as male or female is a central concern of transgenderism. It proposes that the human person can be reshaped from a young age into the transgender world view, particularly through the education system. Some theorists have made clear that they reject the diagnosis of gender dysphoria as a psychological condition, even though the *DSM-5* says gender dysphoria is a psychological disorder.

The legal recognition of a person by their self-defined gender identity – in anti-discrimination laws and laws governing birth certificates and marriage – has set the stage for new education policies and programs based on the transgender world view. Education department policies have been discussed above, and school programs are discussed in the next chapter.

Transgender education policies, based on making gender identity a protected attribute in the SDA, prioritise rights created under the transgender world view over the inherent rights historically recognised within the biological world view of the human person.

The conflicts concern the right to privacy and safety of students who recognise their biological sex as innate, versus those who claim new rights according to their gender identity.

Teachers could face legal action for not prioritising the created rights of transgenders over the rights of biological boys and girls.

The right of parents to determine the education of their children is being undermined by laws like the SDA.

Given the complicated nature of gender dysphoria: its rarity; the high percentage of gender-dysphoric children who go on to identify only with their birth sex in adulthood; and the conflicts and risks involved for all children, the considered conclusion by Jesse Signal (2016) suggests more cautious policies are needed in law, medicine and education.

> Childhood gender dysphoria … is complicated and deserves a nuanced public conversation. The increasingly popular belief that gender dysphoria *must* mean a child will identify as trans in the long run has the opposite effect. It renders a complicated subject simple; it makes it harder to ask the questions that need to be asked. That doesn't help anyone.[36]

Endnotes

1. Diederik Janssen, "Queer theory and childhood", *Oxford Bibliographies*, last modified 27 June 2017.
http://www.oxfordbibliographies.com/view/document/obo-9780199791231/obo-9780199791231-0022.xml?rskey=cd46Xp&result=121 Accessed 26 May 2016.

2. Ibid.

3. Federal *Sex Discrimination Act 1984,* Section 21, as compiled 1 July 2016.
https://www.legislation.gov.au/Details/C2016C00880

4. *Australian Government Guidelines on the Recognition of Sex and Gender* (July 2013, Updated November 2015), Attorney-General's Department, Australian Government, pg. 5.
https://www.ag.gov.au/Publications/Documents/AustralianGovernmentGuidelinesontheRecognitionofSexandGender/AustralianGovernmentGuidelinesontheRecognitionofSexandGender.PDF Accessed 19 June 2017.

5. Ibid.

6. "Diversity in Queensland Schools – information for principals", Queensland Department of Education and Training, undated but current as of 30 June 2017.
http://education.qld.gov.au/schools/inclusive/docs/diversity-in-qld-schools-information-for-principals.pdf Accessed 28 August 2017.

7. "Transgender students in schools – legal rights and responsibilities", *Legal Issues Bulletin No 55, December 2014,* Education and Communities, NSW Government.
https://education.nsw.gov.au/about-us/rights-and-accountability/media/documents/public-legal-issues-bulletins/LIB-55-Transgender-students-in-schools-legal-rights-and-responsibilities.pdf Accessed 18 August 2017.

8. "Gender Identity", Education and Training, Victorian Government, undated but current as of 15 March 2018.
http://www.education.vic.gov.au/school/principals/spag/health/Pages/genderidentity.aspx Accessed 18 August 2017.

9. "Transgender and intersex student support", SA Department for Education and Child Development.
https://www.decd.sa.gov.au/sites/g/files/net691/f/transgender-and-intersex-support-procedure.pdf Accessed 18 August 2017.

10. *Guide to supporting a student to affirm or transition gender identity at school,* Roz Ward, Joel Radcliffe, Matthew Parsons, Mel Gaylard, Dani Wright Toussaint, Safe Schools Coalition Australian, pg. 1.
https://www.studentwellbeinghub.edu.au/docs/default-source/guide-to-supporting-a-student-to-affirm-or-transition-gender-identity-at-school_oct-2015-pdf6fac6cd6d84a461db22d828cc47706f8.pdf?sfvrsn=0 Accessed 24 September 2016.

11. Tiffany Jones, Elizabeth Smith, Roz Ward, Jennifer Dixon, Lynne Hillier and Anne Mitchell,"School experiences of transgender and gender-diverse students in Australia", *Sex Education,* 2016, Volume 16, No. 2, pgs.156–171.
http://dx.doi.org/10.1080/14681811.2015.1080678 Accessed 26 May 2016.

12. Tiffany Jones, "Saving rhetorical children: Sexuality education discourses from conservative to post-modern", *Sex Education: Sexuality, Society and Learning,* Vol. 11, Issue 4, August 12, 2011: pgs. 369–387.
http://www.tandfonline.com/doi/abs/10.1080/14681811.2011.595229#.Vy7I1GR962w Accessed 26 May 2016.

13. Ibid., pg. 371.

14 Ibid., pgs. 379-80.

15 Ibid., pgs. 379-80.

16 Ibid., pg. 376.

17 Ibid., pg. 376.

18 Ibid., 372-73.

19 *Diagnostic and Statistical Manual of Mental Disorders (DSM-5)*, 2013, American Psychiatric Association. https://crashchaoscats.wordpress.com/2014/04/10/dsm-v-gender-dysphoria/ Accessed 14 May 2018.

20 Korte et al, "Gender Identity Disorders in Childhood and Adolescence: Currently Debated Concepts and Treatment Strategies", *Deutsches Arzteblatt International,* 2008, https://www.ncbi.nlm.nih.gov/pmc/articles/PMC2697020/ Accessed 17 August 2017.

21 "7 Jobs That You Are Prohibited from With Colorblindness", Rich, We Read Better, 5 June 2012. http://wereadbetter.com/7-jobs-that-you-are-prohibited-from-with-colorblindness/ Accessed 30 June 2018.

22 Kate Legge, *Making the Switch*, *The Weekend Australian Magazine,* 18-19 July 2015 pgs. 12-16.

23 "First regional gender clinic opens at Gateway Health Wodonga", *The Border Mail,* 21 April 2017. http://www.bordermail.com.au/story/4611243/first-regional-gender-service-clinic-opens-on-the-border/ Accessed 14 July 2017.

24 "Data reveals allegations of children sexually abusing peers at school, experts call for action", ABC News, 31 July 2014. http://www.abc.net.au/news/2014-06-03/calls-for-action-to-halt-child-on-child-sex-abuse/5497196 Accessed 19 September 2017.

25 *Universal Declaration of Human Rights,* Article 26 (c), United Nations, 1948. http://www.un.org/en/universal-declaration-human-rights/

26 International Covenant on Civil and Political Rights, United Nations, (1966) http://www.ohchr.org/EN/ProfessionalInterest/Pages/CCPR.aspx

27 Diederik Janssen, "Queer theory and childhood", Op. cit.

28 Chris Barker, *Cultural Studies: Theory and Practice*, Sage, London, 2005; pg. 448.

29 "Gender Identity", Education and Training, Victorian Government, Op.cit.

30 *Guide to supporting a student to affirm or transition gender identity at school,* Op. cit., pg. 1.

31 Ibid.

32 Tiffany Jones, Elizabeth Smith, Roz Ward, Jennifer Dixon, Lynne Hillier and Anne Mitchell, "School experiences of transgender and gender-diverse students in Australia", Op. cit., pg. 160.

33 Tiffany Jones, "Saving rhetorical children: Sexuality education discourses from conservative to post-modern", Op. cit., pg. 385.

34 "Homosexuality", *Stanford Encyclopedia of Philosophy,* 5 July 2015. https://plato.stanford.edu/entries/homosexuality/#QueTheSocConSex

35 "Transgender and intersex student support", SA Department for Education and Child Development, Op. cit.

36 Jesse Signal, "What's missing from the conversation about transgender kids", *The Cut*, 25 July 2016.
https://www.thecut.com/2016/07/whats-missing-from-the-conversation-about-transgender-kids.html Accessed 7 January 2018.

CHAPTER 13

SAFE SCHOOLS COALITION VICTORIA: A CASE STUDY OF TRANSGENDERISM IN SCHOOLS

13.1 INTRODUCTION

In 2010, the Victorian state government began funding the Safe Schools Coalition Victoria (SSCV) program in Victorian schools. Marketed as an LGBTI anti-bullying program, the program has:

- focused on sexuality and transgenderism, and connected students with LGBT organisations;

- attacked heteronormativity (the biological world view that humans are male or female) and promoted transnormativity (the belief that fluid gender identity defines human sexuality, not biological sex);

- promoted resources that provided links to internet porn and an online sex shop; and

- promoted child agency over the right of parents to determine their children's education and moral formation.

The program was produced by the Australian Centre for Sex, Health and Society (ARCSHS) at La Trobe University, with considerable additional resources from Minus18, described on its website as "Australia's largest youth-led organisation for GLBT youth"[1]. The Minus18 organisation has been effectively partnered with ARCSHS.

In August 2013, Safe Schools went national as Safe Schools Coalition Association (SSCA) with an $8 million grant from the federal Labor government of the time to expand the program into other states and territories.[2] The grant came within two months of the *Sex Discrimination Act 1984* (SDA) being amended to make gender identity, sexual orientation and intersex status protected attributes.

Since then, a number of Safe Schools Coalition publications have claimed that the program is now validated and backed by these new provisions in the SDA and by the *Australian Government Guidelines on the Recognition of Sex and Gender* (2013, 2015).[3] For example, the SSCA

Guide to supporting a student to affirm or transition gender identity at school says that "gender identity is broadly defined" in the SDA

> as meaning 'the gender-related identity, appearance or mannerisms or other gender-related characteristics of a person (whether by way of medical intervention or not), with or without regard to the person's designated sex at birth'...
>
> This law protects people from discrimination in regards to their gender identity. It does not matter what sex the person was assigned at birth, or whether the person has undergone any medical intervention. This includes people who identify as women, men or as neither male nor female. The terms people use to describe their gender identity may include transgender, gender non-binary or agender. Although the *Sex Discrimination Act* does not use these specific labels it is intended to cover these identities and more.[4]

Following revelations in federal parliament in February 2016 that the program provided school students with links to adult sex clubs, an online sex shop and pornographic websites, and to an organisation that ran a sex toy/sadomasochistic workshop for youth,[5] the Liberal-National government of Malcolm Turnbull ordered a review of the Safe Schools resources. This resulted in the removal of all links to outside organisations and websites from SSCA resources, the relocation of SSCA resources onto a federal government website[6] and the federal government announcing that there would be no further federal funding to the SSCA program.

Due to ongoing public controversy, the NSW government scrapped the program. Tasmania discontinued funding and is developing its own anti-bullying program.[7] A newly elected government in South Australia has announced that funding for the program would cease in mid-2018.[8] In other states, it is optional for schools to join the SSCA program or use SSCA resources.

Despite the public controversy, in early 2016,[9] and again, early in 2017, the Victorian government announced extra funding to expand the program into all Victorian state secondary schools by the end of 2018.[10] It made the original SSCV resources, still with links to outside organisations and websites, available on the Victorian Department of Education and Training (DET) website.

However, as of late 2017, the DET website said, "Safe Schools is not part of the Victorian Curriculum – it's a commitment that schools make to be inclusive places for all students", while official guidelines on the same website say that "[t]he Victorian Government has committed to expanding Safe Schools to all government secondary schools by the end of 2018"[11]

By early 2018, the DET website no longer listed the SSCV resources and describes the department's "Safe Schools" program, as distinct from the SSCV program and resources, as the government's commitment to "creating an inclusive and safe environment" for school community, including LGBTI students, families and teachers.[12] Rather, it said that the Safe Schools Unit in the DET assists schools in meeting this commitment by using the SSCV teaching and learning resource, *All of Us*,[13] which was produced by ARCSHS as part of the SSCV program. DET says it will provide resources to schools, which raises the question: will the resources include those of the SSCV that are no longer listed on the DET webpage?

Some of the original SSCV resources – which had been listed in the DET webpage – are now found on either the Minus18 webpage or the federal government's "Student Wellbeing Hub".

The discussion below considers the original SSCV program and resources.

13.2   FOCUS ON TRANSGENDERISM AND SEXUALITY

The SSCV's official *All of Us* is a lengthy, 56-page guide for Years 7 and 8 teachers. It suggests a student activity where they imagine they are over 16 and in different relationships.[14]

Students are encouraged to adopt a label such as gay, lesbian or pansexual. A student handout provides scales of sexual attraction and sexual behaviour, defined by "who do you get together with" as factors to consider in sexual identity.[15]

The *Guide to supporting a student to affirm or transition gender identity at school* (the *Guide*) sets out a 15-point plan for schools to support transgender and gender-diverse students. These points include the following actions/recommendations:

- ensure a student's privacy is maintained, as "There is no need for everyone in the school to know whether a student is transgender or gender diverse …";
- establish a time frame for transitioning;
- it is crucial for the whole school to use the right pronouns for students;

- transgender students should be able to use the school toilets, showers, change rooms, and school camp accommodation they feel comfortable with and to participate in school sport and other events, and wear a uniform according to which gender they identify as;
- school documents and records should allow for Male, Female and X categories. This is consistent with the *Australian Government Guidelines on Recognition of Sex and Gender* requiring all federal government official document sex identifiers to allow a person to record Male, Female, X (Indeterminate, Unspecified, Intersex);[16]
- staff need professional education about gender diverse and transgender students;
- support should be sought from other students, who also need to be educated about gender-diverse and transgender students;
- preparations should be made to respond to the concerns of parents and the community;
- have support for gender-diverse and transgender students written into school policies;
- have a safety plan to deal with discrimination and bullying;
- adopt a whole-school approach to including gender diversity, intersex and sexual diversity.[17]

Another SSCV resource, *OMG im Trans,* was originally available on the Victorian DET webpage but is now only available from Minus18[18]. It advises students on medical transitioning hormone treatments and sex-change surgery.

> When under 18, the first medical option available to you is puberty blockers. They're most effective for people in the early stages of puberty, if you're younger it's definitely worth discussing with your doctor ...
>
> If you're interested, once you're 18 you can start hormone replacement therapy (HRT). This is when you adjust hormone levels in your body to better reflect your identity ...
>
> Surgery is something you might consider too, and while it isn't for everyone, for some it can be hugely beneficial. For chest and genital surgeries you will need additional approvals from your psychiatrist. At present, both top surgery (surgery on your chest) and genital surgery can't actually be performed on anyone under 18 years of age in Victoria. Cosmetic surgeries

such as nose or chin reconstructions are not subject to special restrictions.[19]

OMG im Trans also gives advice on transitioning, chest binding for females to "your chest to make it appear flat/smaller", and penis tucking for males.[20]

It also uses explicit language describing sexuality and use of sex toys:

> Spoiler alert, it's a total lie that all guys have dicks, that all girls have vaginas, and that's what makes a relationship 'straight' or 'gay'…

> Trans young people sometimes have personal names for their body parts and it's important to be aware and respectful of what those are. I guess I've referred to mine as a 'girl-penis' before" …

> Being trans doesn't exclude you from safe sex, kiddo! Pregnancy and STIs are still a thing, and using protection (on your body and your toys) is still super important.[21]

Virtually all the SSCV resources advocate transgenderism and advocate that people, including students, can change from their sex at birth to another gender identity. Such materials include: *All of Us: Health and Physical Education Resource Understanding Gender Diversity, Sexual Diversity and Intersex Topics for Years 7 and 8; All of Us: Student Handouts; Stand Out; Gender is not Uniform; OMG I'm Trans; OMG I'm Queer;* and *OMG My Friend is Queer.*[22]

13.3   CONNECTING STUDENTS WITH LGBTQ ORGANISATIONS

SSCV resources direct students to the Minus18 organisation. It is effectively partnered with ARCSHS, having produced *All of Us* and other SSCV resources.

The Minus18 website contained the article, "When are you Ready to Do It?"[23] This article, which has been removed from the Minus18 website, can still be accessed on web archives. It mentions no minimum age for sex but gives a range of other advice for children about sex:

> Guys, I'm not going to lie – sex can be pretty damn fun!

> It may come as a surprise, but there is no strict definition for virginity, especially if you're queer. Penis-in-vagina sex is not the only sex, and certainly not the 'ultimate' sex.

> - Make sure you're both turned on and in the mood before you start.

- If there's any kind of fingering, cut those nails and remove any nail polish first!
- Use plenty of lube when there's penetration.

  Choosing when to have sex, if at all, is totally up to you and completely valid.

Minus18 has provided an online forum[24] that also acted as a customised social networking site.

Other articles are no longer available on Minus18, but are stored on web archives. "Dating on the down low" advised students about avoiding parents scrutinising their sexual activity.

> Unless your parents walk in on you two on top of each other (more talk about that later), you're going to be fine.[25]

Multiple partners were presented as acceptable and sexual advice was offered:

> It doesn't matter if someone sleeps with more girls, guys, or people who identify as neither. It's more about the fact that they have an attraction to more than one gender.[26]

> 'So how did you lose your virginity?' ... 'Oh goodness. I was about 12 [interviewer and interviewee laugh] she was an older girl at high school ...'[27]

The seriousness of sexually transmitted infections, some of which can leave a person sterile, was downplayed:

> So I done fucked up. Literally. One Grindr hook-up gone wrong, and that's how I got myself some gonorrhoea. But let's backtrack here so I can fill out some holes (pun intended) in my little life drama. ... Contracting such STIs are actually quite common. It wasn't the end of the world. It was just a part of life as a sexually active individual.[28]

Under the heading "Other Groups in Victoria", the Minus18 website linked[29] to the US-based Scarleteen website[30], saying that "Thousands of sexual health questions are answered for you – nothing is off limits!" Scarleteen is aimed at adolescents and answers questions about sex submitted by minors. The website contains recommendations on how to restrain a sex partner with rope[31], using sex toys such as dildos and vibrators[32], and how to improvise with electric shavers and toothbrushes.[33] Polyamorous relationships[34] are also promoted. Graphic advice is provided on how to engage in oral sex.[35]

Scarleteen provides message boards for communication as well as real-time messaging with staff and volunteers providing sex advice to children and adolescents.

Another Minus18 resource, "7 ways to bind your chest", advised on chest binding, which is a dangerous practice. It said:

> Binding can be a huge help for dealing with chest dysphoria, presenting as male in public spaces or even just cosplaying as a character with a flat chest.[36]

This Minus18 article also offered a list of "Useful Websites", a few "wicked websites … as somewhere to start", including the website of a sex shop named "Tool Shed"[37] which stocks a range of sex toys and sadomasochistic items such as restraints, gags and whips, as well as pornographic books and DVDs.[38] This link was removed from the article within hours of it being exposed in federal parliament by George Christensen MP in February 2016,[39] but the article and link are still available on web archive.[40]

Both *OMG I'm Queer*[41] and the *All of Us*[42] resources direct students to Twenty10, an LGBT organisation that works with people of all ages. In January 2016, Twenty10 hosted a "hands-on" sadomasochistic/sex toy workshop for youth.[43]

The GLBT organisation, Working It Out,[44] was directly involved in implementing the SSC program in Tasmania and students were directed to Working It Out in a number of SSC materials.[45,46]

Working It Out recommended[47] students view YouTube channels, such as "Princess Joules"[48] and "Uppercase Chase"[49], which feature sex toys and sexually explicit transgender content.

SSCV was promoted as an anti-bullying program. What has this sort of material got to do with countering bullying?

In part, SSCV does single out LGBTIQ students for anti-bullying protections. However, effective anti-bullying programs aim to prevent all forms of bullying, regardless of who the targets/victims are, and regardless of why they are targets. Respect for all people should be the aim of any anti-bullying program. A program that singles out just one group for protection against bullying risks creating resentment in other bullied students who are not included in the program.

13.4   OPPOSING THE "HETERONORMATIVE"

Safe Schools Coalition was promoted as an anti-bullying program for LGBTIQ students.

One of the outspoken co-founders of SSCA from ARCSHS was Roz Ward. After her connection with the program was severed in 2017, Ward told a Victoria University Pride Week gathering that the purpose of the program was to challenge "heteronormativity"[50].

Ward provided a plain English description of heteronormativity in a 2015 speech, saying that the dominant

> ruling class has benefited, and continues to benefit, from oppressing our bodies, our relationships, sexuality and gender identities alongside sexism, homophobia and transphobia.
>
> Both serve to break the spirits of ordinary people, to consume our thoughts, to make us accept the status quo and for us to keep living or aspiring to live, or feel like we should live, in small social units and families where we must reproduce and take responsibility for those people in those units ...
>
> Apart from social stigma and discrimination, almost every single structure in society is set up to accommodate only two possible genders, male or female.
>
> Everything from the toilets we use, the school uniforms, changing rooms, all official documents, passports ... everything is divided into these two limited gender options."[51]

Ward advocates for liberating everyone from this sexual oppression and creating a society "where human sexuality, gender and how we relate to our bodies can blossom in extraordinarily new and amazing ways that we can only try to imagine today ..."[52].

13.5   SAFE SCHOOLS AND CHILD AGENCY

The Safe Schools Coalition program promotes child agency; that is, children making their own decisions independently of their parents.

The *Guide to supporting a student to affirm or transition gender identity at school* (the *Guide*) says that gender identity "is broadly defined" in the SDA.[53]

The *Guide* goes on to say "[i]t may be possible to consider a student a mature minor and able to make decisions without parental consent". The concept of "mature minor" is based on the Gillick case (1985)[54], which effectively ruled that while children can be guided by their parents, a child has a right to autonomy which develops gradually as it grows and develops their capacity for making decisions. The Gillick case has been recognised in Australian jurisprudence.

The *Guide* says it is up to the school to decide "whether it would be appropriate to involve the students' parent(s) or guardian(s)"[55].

Minus18's "Cover Your Tracks", now only available on web archives, informed students about how to delete their internet browsing history.[56]

The Minus18 resource, *Stand Out*, asks:

> Can you access websites from school computers that give information about sexuality, being intersex or gender diversity? Some students don't have access to the internet at home, or it is monitored by their family so having access at school is really important.
>
> Try accessing the website minus18.org.au, safeschoolscoalition.org.au or some of the groups listed at the back of this guide. Are any of them blocked? If so, for what reason? Speak to a teacher about the importance of allowing students to access them at school, and let them know why this matters.[57]

As mentioned in Chapter 12, advocacy for child agency would appear to conflict with the *International Covenant on Civil and Political Rights* (Article 18.4), which says that the state must respect the liberty of parents "to ensure the religious and moral education of their children in conformity with their own convictions"[58].

13.6 CONCERN AT CHILDREN TRANSITIONING

Australians are tolerant of adults exercising their freedom to change their sex or gender identity, but are concerned at children transitioning.

A poll of 2,500 Australians by the Sexton Marking Group in December, 2016 (see Chapter 1.3) asked if a child of one to five years of age should be allowed to transition. Seventy-six per cent of respondents said "no"; only seven per cent said "yes" and 17 per cent were "undecided".

There was marginally less opposition for six to 12 year olds transitioning. However, even for school age 13 to 17 year olds, more opposed it (46 per cent) than supported it (30 per cent), while 24 per cent were undecided.

Similarly, Australians are opposed to schools promoting the idea of being transgender to school students and the direction of some sex education programs. The polling found

- 82 per cent were "very concerned or somewhat concerned" at kindy or schools teaching children "that they can choose whatever gender they want"
- 87 per cent were "very concerned or somewhat concerned" at "schools supporting children as mature minors to change their gender identity without parental consent"
- 88 per cent were "very concerned or somewhat concerned … if the sex education curriculum was heavily influenced by pro-transgender activists pushing their own cause"

- 86 per cent were "very concerned or somewhat concerned" at any proposals to allow "12 to 14 year olds to access websites at school that are blocked by parents at home, without parental consent, including teen sex advice websites that encourage sexual experimentation".

Yet the SSCV resources were produced by "pro-transgender activists". The resources teach students that gender is fluid and may differ from their biological sex. They say that schools may support "children as mature minors to change their gender identity without parental consent" and advised children on how to access websites from school that are normally blocked at home.

Although it was aimed at secondary school students, some Victorian primary schools signed up to the Safe Schools Coalition.

Further, Jo Hirst, author of the transgender children's book, *The Gender Fairy,* acknowledged with special thanks[59] the Safe Schools co-founder, Roz Ward. The book recognised Ward for "providing support to schools in affirming children and young people's gender identities, and creating more gender expansive educational settings"[60]. *The Gender Fairy* tells kindergarten children, "only you know if you are a boy or a girl. No one can tell you"[61].

The polling also found that Australians were concerned about the consequences of students transitioning and at the consequences for teachers:

- 79 per cent were "very concerned or somewhat concerned" at "allowing boys who identify themselves as girls to share the girls' toilets, showers and change rooms at school"
- 84 per cent were "very concerned or somewhat concerned ... if teachers were sacked for refusing to teach the more controversial aspects of the sex education curriculum.

Again, the Safe School Coalition and policies of four state education departments (see Chapter 12.2) support allowing boys who identify as girls to access girls' facilities.

13.7 OTHER TRANSGENDERISM SCHOOL PROGRAMS

A number of programs and various resources advocating transgenderism are being pushed into schools. These include:

- *The Practical Guide to Love Sex and Relationships,* from the Australian Research Centre for Sex, Health and Society (ARCSHS);

- *Resilience Rights and Respectful Relationships* (RRRRs), from the Victorian Department of Education;
- *Building Respectful Relationships* (BRRs), recommended by the RRRR program;
- Picture books about gender diversity for kindergartens and early primary (such as *The Gender Fairy*, an Australian picture book for children four years and up) and chapter books for middle primary.[62]

13.8   CONCLUSION

The SDA, as well as some state and territory anti-discrimination laws, have provided legal pathways for introducing transgender sex education programs into schools.

Variously, these programs purport to be anti-bullying or for prevention of domestic violence programs, but they also promote transgenderism.

The SSCV program and resources have been the most publicly debated and controversial of these programs. They have not only promoted transgenderism, but presented a sexualised program to students and promoted child decision making without parental involvement.

Not surprisingly, the Federal Government withdrew its commitment to renewed funding, while some states have abandoned the program. Victoria's DET no longer lists SSCV resources on its webpage, saying only that it will recommend resources to schools for its own "Safe Schools" program. It is unclear if any of the original SSCV resources, or what other resources, are being recommended.

Arguably, it promotes child agency on sexuality in accordance with transgender/queer theory, challenges the so-called heteronormative experience (of being male or female), and promotes a transnormative view of human sexuality.

Arguably, the SDA and programs like the Safe Schools Coalition, undermine parents' right to determine the education of their children, as set down in the *International Covenant on Civil and Political Rights* (Article 18.4).

Endnotes

1. Minus18 - Australia's Largest Youth-Led Organisation for LGBTQ Youth, Minus18, YouTube, 6 April 2013.
https://www.youtube.com/watch?v=VBPd-rt8mZs Accessed 30 June2018.

2. ALP Media Release, "$8 Million to Help Stop Homophobia in Schools", 30 August 2013,
http://www.alp.org.au/cm13_300813 Accessed 30 January 2016.

3. *Australian Government Guidelines on the Recognition of Sex and Gender* (July 2013, Updated November 2015), Attorney-General's Department, Australian Government, pg. 5.
https://www.ag.gov.au/Publications/Documents/AustralianGovernmentGuidelinesontheRecognitionofSexandGender/AustralianGovernmentGuidelinesontheRecognitionofSexandGender.PDF

4. *Guide to supporting a student to affirm or transition gender identity at school*, Roz Ward, Joel Radcliffe, Matthew Parsons, Mel Gaylard, Dani Wright Toussaint, Safe Schools Coalition Australian, pg. 1.
http://www.education.vic.gov.au/Documents/about/programs/health/GuideSupportingStudentAffirmTransition.pdf Accessed 14 January 2017.

5. "Claude: safe play workshop", Twenty10,
http://www.twenty10.org.au/youth, accessed 31 January 2016. See advertisement archived at
http://www.spamdex.co.uk/twenty10-org-au/125729-whats-on-in-january-@-twenty10-inc-glcs-nsw.html Accessed 18 January 2018.

6. "About Safe Schools Coalition Australia", Resource Detains, Student Wellbeing Hub, Funded by the Australian Government Department of Education and Training.
https://www.studentwellbeinghub.edu.au/resources/detail?id=f0774c22-d5c5-6d32-997d-ff0000a69c30#/

7. "Low sign-up rate for Safe Schools anti-bullying program in Victoria", *Herald-Sun*, 18 April 2017.
http://www.heraldsun.com.au/news/victoria/low-signup-for-safeschools-antibullying-program-in-victoria/newsstory/f1b44e9d771d483c45861e03ecfeaf45 Accessed 16 January 2018.

8. "Concern for program gap after cut to Safe Schools funding", *In Daily*, 18 June 2018.
https://indaily.com.au/news/2018/06/18/concern-program-gap-cut-safeschools-funding/ Accessed 5 July 2018.

9. "Victorian Premier guarantees future of Safe Schools program as Federal MPs call for scheme to be axed", *ABC News*, 16 March 2016.
http://www.abc.net.au/news/2016-03-16/victorian-premier-guarantees-safeschools-if-federal-funding-cut/7252272 Accessed 21 May 2018.

10. Ibid.

11. *Safe Schools: Guide to making your schools save for GLBTI students*, Education and Training, Victorian State Government, undated. pg. 6.
http://www.education.vic.gov.au/Documents/about/programs/health/safeschoolsguide.pdf Accessed 16 January 2018.

12. Safe Schools, Department of Education and Training, Victorian Government.
https://www.education.vic.gov.au/about/programs/Pages/safeschools.aspx?Redirect=2 Accessed 30 June 2018.

13. *Guide to Making your School Safe and Inclusive for LGBTI Students*, Department of Education and Training, Victorian Government. https://www.education.vic.gov.au/Documents/about/programs/health/safeschoolsguide.pdf Accessed 30 June 2018.

14. *All of Us: Health and Physical Education Resource Understanding Gender Diversity, Sexual Diversity and Intersex Topics for Years 7 and 8*, Safe Schools Coalition Australia and Minus18. http://www.education.vic.gov.au/Documents/about/programs/health/AllOfUs_UnitGuide.pdf Accessed 14 January 2018. Now available at https://www.minus18.org.au/images/ALL_OF_US.pdf

15. *All of Us: Student Hand Outs*, Safe Schools Coalition Australia and Minus18, Ibid., pg. 24.

16. *Australian Government Guidelines on the Recognition of Sex and Gender* (July 2013, Updated Nov 2015). https://www.ag.gov.au/Publications/Documents/AustralianGovernmentGuidelinesontheRecognitionofSexandGender/AustralianGovernmentGuidelinesontheRecognitionofSexandGender.PDF Accessed 19 June 2017.

17. *Guide to supporting a student to affirm or transition gender identity at school*, Op. cit., pgs. 2-4.

18. *OMG im Trans* order form at Minius18. https://www.minus18.org.au/index.php/resources/booklets/omg-im-trans Accessed 30 June 2018.

19. *OMG I'm Trans*, Margot Fink, Micah Scott (editors), Minus18, 2015, pg. 11. http://www.education.vic.gov.au/Documents/about/programs/health/OMG%20I%27m%20Trans.pdf Accessed 14 January 2018.

20. Ibid., pg. 30.

21. Ibid., pg. 24.

22. Note: *Stand Out*, OMG I'm Trans, *OMG I'm Queer* and *OMG My Friend is Queer* are now available from Minus18.

23. "When are you Ready to Do It?", Minus18, 1 October 2012 https://minus18.org.au/index.php/sex-love/item/109-doing-it Accessed 6 January 2016. Now found at http://pandora.nla.gov.au/pan/156947/20160816-0053/minus18.org.au/index.php/sex-love/item/109-doing-it.html Accessed 16 January 2018.

24. https://minus18.org.au/index.php/forums Accessed 9 January 2016.

25. Indigo Lamb, "Dating on the down low", Minus18, 15 September 2014. https://minus18.org.au/index.php/resources/sexuality-info/item/446-dating-on-the-down-low Accessed 13 December 2015. Available now at http://pandora.nla.gov.au/pan/156947/20160816-0053/minus18.org.au/index.php/resources/sexuality-info/item/446-dating-on-the-down-low.html Accessed 16 January 2018.

26. Argo Theoharis, "Where are my bisexuals at?", Minus18, 14 May 2015. https://minus18.org.au/index.php/resources/sexuality-info/item/591-where-are-my-bisexuals-at Accessed 13 December 2015. Available now at http://pandora.nla.gov.au/pan/156947/20160816-0053/minus18.org.au/index.php/resources/sexuality-info/item/591-where-are-my-bisexuals-at.html Accessed 16 January 2018.

27. MINUSTV: "Do You Think Virginity Matters?", Minus18. https://minus18.org.au/index.php/resources/minustv/item/373-virginity Accessed 26 December 2015.

28. "So You Got An STI. Now What?", Minus18, 11 February 2015, https://minus18.org.au/index.php/sex-love/item/513-so-you-got-an-sti-now-what? Accessed 13 December 2015. Now available at http://pandora.nla.gov.au/pan/156947/20160816-0053/minus18.org.au/index.php/sex-love/item/513-so-you-got-an-sti-now-what.html Accessed 16 January 2018.

29. Mica Scott, "Other Groups in Victoria", Scarleteen, Minus 18. https://minus18.org.au/index.php/resources/seek-support Accessed 7 February 2016. Now available at http://pandora.nla.gov.au/pan/156947/20160816-0053/minus18.org.au/index.php/resources/seek-support.html Accessed 16 January 2018.

30. Scarleteen, Minus 18. http://www.scarleteen.com/ Accessed 6 January 2016.

31. Sam Wall and Isabella Rotman, "DIY sex toys: the partnered edition", Scarleteen, 5 February 2015. http://www.scarleteen.com/article/sexuality/diy_sex_toys_the_partnered_edition Accessed 6 January 2016.

32. "Toy Queries", Scarleteen, 18 November 2015. http://www.scarleteen.com/article/bodies/toy_queries Accessed 6 January 2016.

33. Sam Wall and Isabella Rotman, "DIY sex toys: the self love edition", Scarleteen, 5 February 2015. http://www.scarleteen.com/article/sexuality/diy_sex_toys_the_selflove_edition Accessed 6 January 2016.

34. "Scarleteen E-cards", Scarleteen, http://www.scarleteen.com/ecards Accessed 6 January 2016.

35. Heather Corinna, "Mouthing off on oral sex", Scarleteen, 25 April 2017. http://www.scarleteen.com/article/sexuality/mouthing_off_on_oral_sex Accessed 14 January 2018.

36. Michael Way, "7 ways to bind your chest", Minus 18, 2014. https://minus18.org.au/index.php/resources/sexuality-info/item/441-how-to-bind-your-chest Accessed 26 December 2015. It is now available on web archive at https://web.archive.org/web/20150304182734/https://www.minus18.org.au/index.php/resources/sexuality-info/item/441-how-to-bind-your-chest Accessed 20 January 2018.

37. Ibid.

38. The Tool Shed, https://www.toolshedtoys.com/

39. George Christensen MP, speech on Safe Schools, House of Representatives, Federal Parliament, Hansard, 25 February 2016, pgs. 2305-06. http://parlinfo.aph.gov.au/parlInfo/download/chamber/hansardr/115c3603-d1aa-4e7e-8ec1-5ec3e40edc8a/toc_pdf/House%20of%20Representatives_2016_02_25_4137_Official.pdf;fileType=application%2Fpdf#search=%22chamber/hansardr/115c3603-d1aa-4e7e-8ec1-5ec3e40edc8a/0000%22 Accessed 20 January 2018.

40. 7 Michael Way, "7 ways to bind your chest", Minus 18, Op. cit.

41. *OMG im queer*, Minus18, Safe Schools Coalition Victoria, Ygender, headspace http://www.education.vic.gov.au/Documents/about/programs/health/OMG%20I%27m%20Queer.pdf Accessed 16 January 2018. 2014 edition available at http://youreteachingourchildrenwhat.org/wp-content/uploads/2017/08/Safe-School-Coalition-Aus-OMG-Im-Queer-2014-edition.pdf

42 *All of Us: Health and Physical Education Resource Understanding Gender Diversity, Sexual Diversity and Intersex Topics for Years 7 and 8*, Op. cit., pg. 14.

43 "Claude: safe play workshop", Twenty10, http://www.twenty10.org.au/youth, accessed 31 January 2016. See advertisement archived at http://www.spamdex.co.uk/twenty10-org-au/125729-whats-on-in-january-@-twenty10-inc-glcs-nsw.html Accessed 18 January 2018.

44 *Working it out*. http://www.workingitout.org.au/ Accessed 7 January 2016.

45 *All of Us*, Op cit., pg. 14. http://www.safeschoolscoalition.org.au/app/theme/default/design/assets/all-ofus/documents/student-handouts.pdf Accessed 2 February 2016.

46 Micha Scott, *OMG I'm Queer*, Minus18, pg. 33. http://www.safeschoolscoalition.org.au/uploads/1c319a8803b891fac1c455e6b87affa6.pdf Accessed 2 February 2016.

47 "Turning out the Quilt", Working it Out and Mind Out, pg. 9. http://static1.1.sqspcdn.com/static/f/1262237/26719177/1449444366130/Zine+template+with+inserted+articles+vFINAL+v1.1.pdf?token=JHx0UW-6LoSae8bWP5peHyRH4YDM%3D Accessed 7 January 2016.

48 Princess Joules. https://www.youtube.com/results?search_query=princessjoules. Accessed 7 January 2016.

49 Uppercase Chase. https://www.youtube.com/results?search_query=uppercase+chase. Accessed 7 January 2016.

50 "Ward departs La Trobe following program's scrapping", *The Australian*, 19 June 2017. http://www.theaustralian.com.au/news/nation/ward-departs-la-trobe-following-programs-scrapping/news-story/fbf7624b707d861b8a1bb3e9b16e903b Accessed 14 January 2017.

51 Roz Ward, speech to the Marxism Conference, 2-5 April 2015 Melbourne, reported in "Safer schools or a radical Marxist sexual revolution?", Patrick J Byrne, Online Opinion, 19 February 2016. http://www.onlineopinion.com.au/view.asp?article=18033&page=0

52 Ibid.

53 Guide to supporting a student to affirm or transition gender identity at school, Op. cit., pg. 1.

54 *Gillick v West Norfolk and Wisbech Area Health Authority and another*, House of Lords, [1985] 3 All ER 402.

55 Guide to supporting a student to affirm or transition gender identity at school, Op. cit., pg. 1.

56 Micah Scott, "Cover Your Tracks", Minus18, 31 December 2012. https://minus18.org.au/index.php/sex-love/item/144-cover-your-tracks Accessed 7 January 2016. Available now at http://pandora.nla.gov.au/pan/156947/20160816-0053/minus18.org.au/index.php/sex-love/item/144-cover-your-tracks.html Accessed 16 January 2018.

57 Roz Ward, Micah Scott, *Stand Out: Edition 2*, Safe Schools Coalition Victoria and Minus18, pg. 18. Accessed 24 September 2016. https://www.minus18.org.au/images/STAND_OUT.pdf Accessed 19 July 2018.

58 *International Covenant on Civil and Political Rights*, Article 18.2.
    http://www.ohchr.org/en/professionalinterest/pages/ccpr.aspx

59 Jo Hirst, *The Gender Fairy*, Oban Road Publishing, 2016. pg. 4.

60 Ibid., pg. 34.

61 Ibid., pg. 20.

62 The Rainbow Owl, books and resources for embracing and supporting trans and gender diverse children and young people.
    http://www.the-rainbow-owl.com/ Accessed 18 May 2018.

CHAPTER 14

CHILDREN TRANSITIONING: CHILDHOOD GENDER DYSPHORIA

By Dr John Whitehall

14.1 INTRODUCTION

Gender dysphoria is defined as "clinically significant distress or impairment in social, school, or other important areas of functioning" due to "a marked incongruence between one's experienced/expressed gender and assigned gender"[1].

Formerly rare, recently there has been a phenomenal increase in the number of children being brought to specially created gender dysphoria clinics in children's hospitals throughout the Western world, including Australia. This increase has been associated with much publicity of transgender options in the media, the web and in transgender sex education programs in schools. No one knows the cause for the epidemic but it bears the hallmarks of a behavioural fad. Nevertheless, it is dangerous because medical treatment can involve hormones that interfere with the brain as well as the body, and progress to irreversible surgery in the attempt to mimic external characteristics of the opposite sex. The fad is the ideology known as transgenderism.

Recent years have seen the growth of the drama of children alleged to be questioning their gender. Their plight emerges from the backdrop of a sensationalist and uncritical media, adulation for those transitioning on transgender websites, and transgender school programs like that of the Safe Schools Coalition Victoria (see Chapter 13). The drama is now enacted throughout society: requirements for gender-neutral language, birth certificates changed, anti-discrimination provisions made in law, and special clinics opened at children's hospitals to help children transition to the opposite of their birth sex.

It used to be considered that the claim by a child that it was not a member of the sex denoted by its genitals indicated that the child was considered to be suffering from Gender Identity Disorder, not dissimilar from Body Identity Disorder, in which some people want to have healthy body parts removed; or Anorexia Nervosa, in which sufferers are deluded that they are overweight (see Chapter 7.3). In 2013, however, proponents of the transgender ideology were able to convince opposition in various editorial committees of their belief that there was no such thing as fixed gender identity and, therefore, the claim to have been born in the wrong body did not denote a psychological disorder. Illness, if at all associated with this concept, was only due to the distress caused by failure of society to affirm a person's gender identity.

In 1980, the psychiatric texts diagnosed this condition as Gender Identity Disorder (GID). In 2013, GID was reassigned as a normal phenomenon unless there was associated distress, in which case the problem was to be known as Gender Dysphoria.[2] As failure of society to accept the phenomenon was claimed to be the cause of such distress, a program of preventative education would be necessary. At the same time, laws were being changed to protect a person's gender identity and to impose penalties on those who were considered as discriminating against those who wanted to be recognised by their gender identity, not their sex.

Just as the world has suffered from utopian political ideologies in the 20th century, the medical profession has a record of adopting practices it has later regretted, such as the widespread sterilisation for the simple minded, frontal lobotomies for the psychotic, and electric shock for the depressed.

14.2   HOW COMMON IS CHILDHOOD GENDER DYSPHORIA?

No one really knows the answer to this question because there is an absence of formal prevalence studies[3,4] and estimates vary greatly as increasing numbers are being brought to childhood gender dysphoria clinics each year[5].

The leader of Toronto's Transgender Youth Clinic at the Hospital for Sick Children, Dr Joey Bonifacio, declared that estimates based on attendance at adult dysphoria clinics range from 0.005-0.014 per cent of adult males who consider themselves female, and 0.002-0.003 per cent of women who identify as men (personal communication). Bonifacio's statistics are the same as those declared in *The Diagnostic and Scientific Manual of Mental Health* – Fifth Edition (DSM-5)[6], which the American Psychiatric Association says is "the manual used by clinicians and researchers to diagnose and classify mental disorders"[7]. Bonifacio (2015), however, claims the figures underestimate the real prevalence[8]. In a 2016 personal communication, Bonifacio claimed the figures underestimate the real prevalence.

In Australia, prominence has been given to a cross-sectional questionnaire distributed to 8,166 adolescents in New Zealand (Youth'12) which reported 1.2 per cent answered "Yes" to the question,

"Do you think you are transgender? This references a girl who feels she should have been a boy, or a boy who feels he should have been a girl." Of the rest, 94.7 per cent denied being transgender, 2.5 per cent replied they were "unsure", and 1.7 per cent declared they "did not understand" the question[9,10]. The estimate of 1.2 per cent is promoted by leaders of the gender dysphoria service at Melbourne Children's Hospital[11], but the prevalence appears to have been conflated to 4 per cent by the addition of the unsure 2.5 per cent by the promoters of the Safe Schools Coalition Victoria Program[12].

Results of such tick-in-the-box questionnaires are unreliable. A tick in a box to the question of "do you think you are transgender" cannot be compared in accuracy with the standard definition published in DSM-5 according to which childhood gender dysphoria is based on "a marked incongruence" between natal and perceived gender lasting "at least six months"; "manifested by at least six" features, including "a strong desire … and insistence" on, together with a "strong preference" for, the company, clothing and toys of the opposite sex and its role in fantasy play; and associated with rejection of the stereotypes of its natal sex, including anatomy. Also, to comply with "dysphoria", there should be "significant distress or impairment … in functioning".[13]

The unreliability of such tick in the box questionnaires is emphasised in the *Journal of Homosexuality* (2011) in its consideration of the prevalence of suicide in sexual minorities. The *Journal* warns conclusions based on such questionnaires must be limited because they are based on "retrospective" data; "do not effectively allow cause and effect relationships to be discerned", including "co-occurring mental disorders"; are "restricted" in the number of questions they can ask to elucidate facts, and are weakened by the possibility of incomprehension of questions.[14]

Does it surprise that the reliability of responses from adolescents has been questioned? In the NZ survey, deemed authoritative by some in Australia, 36.5 per cent of adolescents actually declared they did not understand the question as to whether they had ever been "hit or physically harmed by another person"[15]. This response is hard to believe coming from a land committed to participation by its youth in the aggressive contact sports of Rugby Union and League! Furthermore, it is impossible to believe one-third of New Zealand's youth are so uneducated they cannot understand the written word! It is easier to believe they could not be bothered to answer the questions properly.

Given the unreliability of such survey data, how can it be claimed that 1.2 per cent of the population is transgender, on the basis of the NZ survey? That would make the prevalence of childhood gender dysphoria similar to the 1-3 per cent of intellectual disability. It is dissembling to conflate the figure to 4 per cent, as the Safe Schools Coalition Victoria program claims, but a lot of the claims of the proponents of gender fluidity are not based on established social sciences research methods.

A prevalence of 4 per cent would mean one-in-25 of all children seen by paediatricians would be transgender. In contrast, a straw poll of 28 generalist paediatricians conducted by this author revealed only 12 cases could be recalled from a cumulative experience of 931 years. Ten cases were associated with significant mental co-morbidity, and two had suffered sustained sexual abuse.

In reality, childhood gender dysphoria has been a rare condition that was relatively unknown until the last few years when the numbers of children and adolescents being presented to gender dysphoria clinics in the Western world has increased almost exponentially each year.

The final irony in the claim by proponents that up to 4 per cent of children are transgender (and, by innuendo, may need special medical help) is revealed when it is compared with the statistics of adult prevalence published in DSM-5. If a 4 per cent prevalence in children falls to 0.002 per cent in adults, it means, mathematically, that over 99 per cent will "desist" from transitioning and revert to natal sex before adulthood as a natural process of life. Only a tiny minority would "persist" in their gender dysphoria.

It is important to note that not all desisters emerge with heterosexual orientation: a minority will emerge with gay and lesbian orientations. The declaration that life as a homosexual was much less complicated than that of a medicalised, surgicalised, transgendered person appears to be the reason Professor Kenneth Zucker, prominent academic and former Head of Toronto's Center for Addiction and Mental Health, was recently dismissed from his position. Recognised as an international expert in gender dysphoria and proponent of a "watchful, waiting" approach in expectation of reversion of the child to natal sex, if not heterosexuality, Zucker was stood down and his unit closed.[16] Zucker says that research and experience shows that

> [t]he majority of children followed longitudinally appear to 'lose' the diagnosis of (gender dysphoria) when seen in late adolescence or young adulthood, and appear to have differentiated a gender identity that matches their natural sex[17].

14.3 ARE THERE ANY OTHER CLINICAL PROBLEMS ASSOCIATED WITH GENDER DYSPHORIA?

Mental illness are strikingly associated with gender dysphoria, raising the question of which came first: whether gender dysphoria causes mental illness or is but a symptom of pre-existing, underlying pathology. Proponents of transgender ideology promote the idea that gender dysphoria is the root cause of the mental problems, and the root cause of the dysphoria is the failure of parents and society to accept gender non-conformity as a normal phenomenon. This is despite clear reports of psychological disorder preceding the symptom of gender dysphoria.

Nevertheless, psychological disorder is prevalent, if not characteristic. A study of Dutch children with dysphoria aged four to 11 revealed associated psychiatric conditions of at least one type in 52 per cent, with diagnoses including anxiety, phobias, mood disorders, depression, attention deficit and oppositional behaviour.[18] A study by school teachers reported significant behavioural and emotional problems in about one third of 554 dysphoric Dutch and Canadian children below 12 years[19]. At the first presentation to a US gender clinic of 97 children with mean age 14.8 years, 44.3 per cent had a history of psychiatric diagnoses, 37.1 per cent were already on psychotropic medications and 21.6 per cent had a history of self-injurious behaviour[20]. In an Australian study of 39 dysphoric children of mean age 10, "behavioural disorders [were observed] in one-quarter of children, with Asperger Syndrome in one in seven"[21].

A recent study by Becerra-Culqui et al (2018), published under the name "Mental Health of Transgender and Gender Nonconforming Youth Compared With Their Peers", considered American children aged from three to 17 years who had been diagnosed as "Transgender and Gender Non-confirming" (TGNC) by therapists in their health care provider, Kaiser Permanente[22]. The records of 1,333 children were examined, of whom 251 were aged three to nine, and 1,082 from 10 to 17.

Mental conditions were confirmed to be very common. The most common diagnoses for children and adolescents were attention deficit disorders (transfeminine, 15 per cent; transmasculine, 16 per cent) and depressive disorders (transfeminine, 49 per cent; transmasculine, 62 per cent).

Of the children from three to nine years, 31.7 per cent had received official diagnoses in accordance with *The International Classification of Diseases,* Ninth Edition (ICD-9). Most often, they suffered from attention deficit disorders (approximately 15 per cent), anxiety (14 per cent), and conduct and/or disruptive disorders. Five per cent of transfeminine children were autistic and 11 per cent of transmasculine suffered from depression.

Of the older group of 1,082 children, a huge 73 per cent had been medically diagnosed with mental disorders ranging from anxiety (approximately 38 per cent), attention deficit (19.6 per cent), depressive disorders (56 per cent), and autism (5 per cent). Frank psychoses had been diagnosed in 4.7 per cent and schizophrenia spectrum in 1.6 per cent. In all, 14.5 per cent of the children had been so badly affected by mental disorder, they had needed to be hospitalised.

However, Becerra-Culqui et al avoided the basic question of which came first: mental disorder or gender dysphoria? Surely a temporal relationship could have been drawn from their records? As if avoiding the question of cause and effect, the authors equivocated, declaring "children who receive meaningful gender identity support do not necessarily experience elevated rates of depression and anxiety". They do not define such "affirmative intervention" but seek to assure that its "follow-up" will permit its impact to be examined. Meanwhile, the authors remain in a state of "considerable uncertainty".[23] Did they choose uncertainty rather than ask the obvious question of which came first?

There are, however, substantial reports of gender dysphoria *following,* rather than preceding, the onset of mental disorder. For example, Kaltiala-Heino et al (2015) reviewed cases presenting to Finnish hospitals from 2011 to 2013 and found that 75 per cent "had been or were currently undergoing child and adolescent psychiatric treatment for reasons other than gender dysphoria when they sought referral". Sixty-four per cent had, or were having, treatment for depression; 55 per cent for anxiety disorders; 53 per cent for suicidal and self-harming behaviours; 13 per cent for psychotic symptoms; 9 per cent for conduct disorders; 4 per cent for substance abuse; 26 per cent for autism spectrum disorder, and 11 per cent for ADHD. Of these children, 68 per cent "had had their first contact with psychiatric services due to reasons other than gender identity issues"[24].

From a survey of the literature, Kaltiala-Heino et al (2018)[25] found an increased prevalence of autism spectrum disorders (ASDs), varying from ~6 per cent to over 20 per cent, had been reported among samples of adolescents referred to gender identity services[26,27,28,29]. This vastly exceeds the estimated prevalence of 0.6 per cent to 0.7 per cent[30] in the general population. Among children and early adolescents with ASDs, gender variance is more than seven times more common than among non-referred controls[31,32].

14.4 IS THERE AN INHERENT RISK OF SELF-HARM AND SUICIDE?

Risk of self-harm has been reported in gender-dysphoric children and is the argument for "treatment", and the threat against inaction. Is self-harm another manifestation of an underlying disorder, or is it due to frustration from gender dysphoria alone, or due to ostracism?

Proponents of affirmative treatment proclaim the latter and declare an "alarmingly high rate" of self-harm and suicide attempts, exemplified by highly publicised and tragic youth suicides in the US[33].

As with most data related to gender dysphoria in children, studies are limited by lack of numbers and methodological bias, and the true rate of self-harm due to external ostracism is unknown. Other factors are very common and important and seem neglected in the argument.

Therefore, despite claims of an "alarmingly high rate" of self-harm and suicide, exemplified by that highly publicised and tragic death of a young dysphoric person in the US who suicided,[34] in reality, Aitken et al (2016) declare "systematic data on completed suicides among adolescents with GD [gender dysphoria] are not known", emphasising that "few data are available on the prevalence of self-harm and suicidality in children with gender dysphoria"[35]. One London study by Holt et al (2016) retrospectively reviewed letters from referring doctors and its own notes regarding 218 gender-dysphoric children with a mean age of 14. Of 41 aged five to 11, it reported self-harm in 14.6 per cent, suicidal ideation in 14.6 per cent and suicidal attempts in 2.4 per cent. Of 177 adolescents aged 12 to 18, suicidal ideation was reported in 39.5 per cent, self-harm in 44.1 per cent and suicidal attempts in 15.8 per cent. The study, however, utilised no comparative groups and did not consider strength of intent which could, of course, range from seeking attention to seeking death. Finally, the authors wondered if the rates "simply reflect trends in the general population".[36]

Furthermore, although detailing living arrangements of the children, the authors do not comment on their influence, though the effect of family dysfunction on the mood of its offspring is well known. The study found only 36.7 per cent were living with both biological parents. Fifty-eight point three per cent "had parents who had separated". "Domestic violence was indicated in 9.2 per cent … maternal depression in 19.3 per cent … paternal depression in five per cent [and] parental alcohol/drug abuse in 7.3 per cent of cases".[37] Nor does the study consider the significance of autism it found in 12.2-17.1 per cent of its children.

Elsewhere, Mayers et al (2013) found 14 per cent of children with autism aged one to 16 years have been reported to experience suicide ideation or attempts, suggesting a rate 28 times greater than that for typical children (0.5 per cent)[38].

The NZ survey of adolescents, discussed above and deemed authoritative by some in Australia, asked about "self-harm" in the previous year. Twenty-three point four per cent of non-transgenders replied "Yes", as did 45.5 per cent of transgenders, but 23.7 per cent reckoned they did not understand the question. When asked about attempted suicide, 4.1 per cent of non-transgenders replied "Yes", as did 19.8 per cent of "transgenders", but 13.3 per cent declared incomprehension.[39]

Aitken et al (2016) found similar rates of ideation in Canada, though associated with a lower rate of self-harm or attempted suicide (17 versus 6.2 per cent). They concluded "older age, and more total behavior problems, but not poor peer relations, were significantly associated with the increased risk … but could not argue that social ostracism … was a unique correlate".

Neither study revealed features of self-harm and attempted suicide.[40]

A review of such trends reveals the great difficulties in getting reliable data from child and adolescent interviewees. Muehlenkamp (2012) found rates of non-suicidal self-injury vary from 12.5 per cent to 23.6 per cent, and deliberate self-harm from 12.2 per cent to 31.4 per cent, depending on the form of assessment.[41] Other studies have confirmed between 19 per cent[42] and 29 per cent[43] of ALL adolescents have announced a history of suicidal ideation, and between seven and 13 percent to have attempted "suicide", though what constitutes an attempt is not defined in these studies or in those from London and NZ.

Complicating all discussions of suicide in children with gender dysphoria are the associated rates of psychiatric co-morbidity in children. In the study from London by Holt et al (2016) mentioned above, for children below 11 years of age, autism spectrum disorder was diagnosed in from 12.2 to 17.1 per cent, attention deficit hyperactivity in 14.6 per cent, anxiety in 17.1 per cent, depression in 7.3 per cent and psychosis in 2.4 per cent with, on the whole, rates increasing with age. It reports bullying and abuse in almost half to two thirds of all children but does not discuss whether they were provoked by transgender characteristics or those associated with autism, hyperactivity and psychosis.[44]

The question, then, is whether transitioning of transgender children will ultimately reduce self-harm? While De Vries et al (2012) say the Dutch experience concludes "starting cross-sex hormones early … followed by gender reassignment surgery … can be effective and positive for general and mental functioning"[45], other centres report high rates of suicide in years following reassignment[46,47]. To be fair, those reassigned in these studies did not have such a developed "pathway" for affirmation, as in Holland. Nevertheless, suicide attempts have been reported to be more common after surgery than in the general population in Belgium (5.1 per cent versus 0.15 per cent)[48] and in Sweden[49].

Conversely, regarding suicide by adolescent members of sexual minorities, the *Journal of Homosexuality* concludes "very few suicide decedents [sic]" have been identified as having "minority sexual orientation" in studies in North America: three of 120 adolescent suicides in New York, and four of 55 in Quebec"; and warns conclusions based on "small numbers ... must be regarded as tentative".

The conclusion of the *Journal of Homosexuality* is valid. Numbers are small and data is obscure.[50] No one knows how often real suicide attempts occur or their relationship with internal and external factors in gender dysphoria. When I raised the issue with one experienced therapist, it was denounced as "rubbish", merely a "weapon used by ideologues".

Nevertheless, for whatever cause, children with gender dysphoria are at risk and deserve compassion, support and close monitoring for the possibility of self-harm. Even if gender confusion, per se, has not been demonstrated to generate an increased rate of suicide in affected children, all their other mental issues and family disruptions are known to place them at risk.

14.5 WHAT ARE THE PERSONALITY CHARACTERISTICS OF PARENTS BRINGING CHILDREN TO GENDER DYSPHORIA CLINICS?

Few studies are available on the characteristics of parents bringing children to gender dysphoria clinics despite numerous studies on their children. It is imagined gender confusion in a child must deeply affect its parents, and the phrase common to those seen interviewed on television, "gut wrenching", is easy to accept. But, some other parents do not seem that upset by their child's identity with the opposite gender and evince an enthusiasm for transitioning that extends into the media. Sometimes, the parent, usually the mother, appears as a cheerleader for the promotion of the child as poster trans boy or girl for the school.

In 2016, I interviewed Kenneth Zucker, who headed the American Psychiatric Association's committee that drafted the DSM-5 position on diagnosis and treatment of gender dysphoria. I asked Zucker whether there are any distinguishing characteristics in parents of children with gender dysphoria. His published opinion is worth considering in detail with regard to "psychopathology in the parents"[51]. He writes

> As is true for many other psychopathologies of childhood, the severity of parental psychopathology of psychiatric impairment is a risk factor with regard to therapeutics. Thus, I have been particularly attentive over the years to assessing the function of the parents and have a great deal of empirical data in this regard. As one example, using the Diagnostic Interview Schedule, a

> highly structured method of assessing psychopathology in adults ...
>
> I have found that about 50 per cent of the mothers of GID boys had two or more DIS diagnoses and about 25 per cent had three or more DIS diagnoses. A composite measure of maternal psychopathology was a very strong correlate of a general measure of the child's psychopathology[52].

Earlier, Zucker had reported:

> The etiology of gender identity disorder remains a source of debate ... One of the psychosocial factors deemed important concerns parental attitudes and behaviours regarding psychosexual socialisation. A consistent empirical and clinical observation is that parents are prone either to tolerate or to encourage the emerging cross gender behaviour, which ultimately appears to contribute to the consolidation of a cross gender identity in the child.
>
> The reasons for such tolerance or encouragement seem to vary. In some instances, it appears related to an intense desire on the parent's part, particularly the mother's, to have a child of the opposite sex ...[53].

Another study by Marantz (1991) also points to a high incidence of Borderline Personality Disorder and depression in mothers of dsyphoric boys. Comparing mothers of dysphoric boys to those of "normal boys" revealed 53 per cent of mothers of dysphoric boys met the diagnosis for Borderline Disorder or depression compared with 6 per cent of other mothers. Moreover, with regard to child rearing practices and attitudes, the mothers of dysphoric children "had attitudes and practices that encouraged symbiosis and discouraged autonomy"[54].

With regard to "Children with gender identity disorder: Is there a best practice?", Zucker (2008) writes:

> For ... parents ... in which the child's gender identity difficulties are embedded in a great deal of ambivalence, the focus of sessions can be to explore the underlying dynamics. Very often, what is weaved into this is the broader complexity of the family system, the parents' relationship, and the individual problems of each parent. In these cases, the therapeutic work is much more complex, challenging and long term.[55]

Parental acceptance of the child's identification with non-natal gender leads to early social transitioning. Toronto's Dr Bonifacio says many have progressed far into transitioning before attending his clinic: parents are dressing and entertaining the child as the opposite sex, applying new pronouns and a new name. Such commitment, he explains, paves the way for further treatment.

Zucker (2018) is more explicit: he would argue

> that parents who support, implement or encourage a gender transition (and clinicians who recommend one) are implementing a psychosocial treatment that will increase the odds of long-term persistence.[56]

He predicts that, "in children who socially transition prior to puberty … the persistence rate will be extremely high"[57]. As considered below, the problem with persistence is that it most likely means entering the medical pathway of treatment known as the Dutch Protocol, with all is complications.

14.6 WHAT OPTIONS ARE THERE FOR TREATMENT OF CHILDREN WITH GENDER DYSPHORIA?

Basically, there are three options. The first, known as "conversion therapy" or "reparative therapy", is the active attempt to make the child more comfortable in its natal sex and to dissuade the child from identification with the opposite sex. The second may be called "waiting and watching", while making the child comfortable in its natal sex in expectation provided by the statistics that it will grow out of its gender dysphoria through puberty. In both the first and second options, Zucker (2008, 2012) says the reasons for the gender dysphoria are explored with the child and their parents with the aim of reducing the intensity of the dysphoria.[58,59]

Ristori and Steensma (2016) say the third treatment option is called "affirmative therapy", which involves actively supporting transition to the opposite sex[60] (see Definitions and Terms).

The first option, "conversion" or "reparative" therapy, in which children are encouraged to be comfortable with their natal sex, is anathema to transgender activists. In some states of North America, laws prevent "conversion" or "reparative" therapy. The Australian Labor Party's national platform is to make such therapy illegal, when next in government (see Chapter 11.3).

Evoking spectres of past brutal aversion therapy of transgender and homosexual adults, activists declare that anything less than affirmation in transgender children is inhumane, futile and may provoke suicide. Their argument is that transgender is fixed before, and unchangeable after, birth. Affected children "are born into the wrong body", something parents must accept as both normal and unchangeable: so much so that attempts to resist the transitioning constitute child abuse. Therefore, the term "conversion therapy" has a pejorative, political clamour to it. Indeed, the term is wielded more like an ideological weapon than as a description of a medical alternative which might, in fact, be as unthreatening as sympathetic reassurance.

The second treatment option involves keeping the child as happy as possible within its "own skin" or natal sex, in the expectation it will "grow out of it". It allows a child to dress and play with toys of the opposite sex but without active encouragement and with limitations to place and time. It allows that a minority will "persist" into homosexuality but perceives life as a homosexual as less complicated than that of the medicalised transgender.

The third treatment option, "affirmation", excludes the first two and comprises a medical "pathway" towards physical simulation of the opposite sex that may be seen to progress through five phases. This pathway is known as the Dutch Protocol. It evolved from treatment of dysphoric children in a gender clinic in Holland but it now serves as the standard template for medical affirmation of a child towards the opposite sex (De Vries and Cohen-Kettenis, 2016).[61]

Note: The language of "conversion therapy" and "affirmation therapy" is often confusing because the meaning of words are based on a the transgender world view, not on the science of biology. In the transgender world view, "conversion" means orientating the child back towards the sex with which it was born. "Affirmation" means orientating the child towards its chosen, new gender. Failure to promote "affirmation therapy" is "conversion therapy" by default and, therefore worthy of similar censure under the law.

Indeed, proponents of transgender ideology do not accept any middle ground. Either a therapist actively assists the child towards the opposite gender or the therapist is guilty of "conversion therapy" by omission. Therefore, on flimsy grounds, the current "standards of care" (Coleman et al, 2011) declare

> treatment aimed at trying to change a person's identity ... to become more congruent with sex assigned at birth, has been attempted in the past without success ... such treatment is no longer considered ethical.[62]

Zucker (2018) is not surprised that proponents of transition take "umbrage at the mere idea of a treatment arm designed to reduce a child's gender dysphoria via psychotherapeutic methods".[63] He declares preference for the summary statement of the American Academy of Child and Adolescent Psychiatry:

> different clinical approaches have been advocated for childhood gender discordance ... there have been no randomized controlled trials of any treatment ... the proposed benefits of

treatment to eliminate gender discordance ... must be carefully weighed against ... possible deleterious effects.[64]

The problem is that proponents for active transitioning do not seem to recognise many of the deleterious effects.

14.7 WHAT DOES THE DUTCH PROTOCOL INVOLVE?

Phase 1 of the Dutch Protocol involves the social transitioning of a dysphoric child to the name, pronouns, dress and persona of the opposite sex.

Phase 2 follows with the administration of drugs which block the release of hormones from the pituitary gland which should travel to the gonads to stimulate production of sperm and ova, as well as the production and secretion of the sex hormones (testosterone and oestrogen) that bring about and sustain the physical and mental characteristics of puberty and, then, reproductive adult life. These drugs are known as puberty blockers and are usually given at the onset of puberty. The youngest child reported to receive them in Australia did so at 10½ years of age.

Phase 3 involves the administration of hormones of the opposite sex with the intention of evoking the physical characteristics of that sex. In time, exposure of the gonads to the hormones of the opposite sex will lead to chemical castration. Although international guidelines suggest irreversible surgery be delayed until 18 years of age, at least five girls in Australia have undergone bilateral mastectomy before that age as part of Phase 3 therapy.[65] Termed "top surgery", bilateral mastectomies are being permitted at these younger ages under the sophistry that they are "partially reversible". However, the ability to breastfeed is, of course, irreparably lost, even if some of the shape of the breasts might be restored by artificial implants of various kinds.

Phase 4 involves surgical remodelling of the genitalia and other features of the natal sex, such as the masculine "Adam's apple" and distribution of hair. Not all children with gender dysphoria submit to this degree of surgery.

Phase 5 does not feature in transgender literature. Those emerging from Phase 4 face a life-time commitment to supervision of hormonal therapy, maintenance of urogenital plumbing to deal with the problems of leaks and blockages, and, possibly, psychological support.

14.8 WHAT PROBLEMS MAY A CHILD ENCOUNTER ON THE DUTCH PATHWAY?

Phase 1: social transitioning. The association with psychological disorder cannot be overemphasised: a large percentage of dysphoric children are actually given an associated psychiatric diagnosis. The very definition of "dysphoria" implies the rest are suffering significant disturbance. Proponents would maintain the psychological disturbance is secondary to gender confusion. This is despite many reports revealing the earlier onset of a psychological condition of which gender dysphoria is a later symptom, as discussed above.

In any case, to suffer from a psychological condition at variance with physical reality is normally considered delusional and, normally, authority figures in a child's life do not seek to sustain the delusion. They do not encourage, flaunt or participate in the delusion but seek to minimise its magnitude and propensity for harm.

For example, no one participates in the delusion of a child's anorexia nervosa and, if school authorities facilitated its manifestations by creating special areas for the minimal consumption of food or private vomiting of the stomach's contents, their actions would be considered criminal. Also criminal would be a surgeon's participation in the delusion of obesity by the placing of gastric bands to reduce the intake of food in order to satisfy the identity disorder (see Chapter 7.3).

But the converse applies to the delusions in which a child claims to belong in the body of the opposite sex. The dangers of fortifying a mental delusion were once obvious, but are no longer. How can a child re-orientate to the instructions of their chromosomes and hormones if there is a concerted drive by adult authorities to undermine biology's message of binary difference in the sexes?

Even if the child's mental co-morbidity does permit some lucidity of thought, how might a child escape the adopted and re-enforced identity when the hormones of puberty begin to impact on the sexual centres of its brain? Complications with "second transitioning" after time spent as the opposite gender are easily imagined (Steensma and Cohen-Kettenis, 2011)[66]. What happens if a child changes its mind and wants to desist from transitioning, as research shows is happening in the vast majority of cases? How does the child resist those authority figures who had participated, if not encouraged, the delusion?

Worse, what if the child is so intimidated by the fear of coming out against the delusion that passive acceptance of the next phase of the Dutch pathway seems the only possibility? Or, what if the vulnerable child has been so mentally influenced that it has no idea how to live in its natural sex, despite the urgings of its hormones? As Zucker declared above, once a child has entered social transitioning, the chances of desisting are reduced.

Phase 2: the blocking of puberty. The induction of puberty begins deep in the brain where it is started by a biological clock and involves a cascade of hormones with various checks and balances. Where and how it starts is unknown, but chemical messengers ultimately influence nerve cells in the hypothalamus to release hormones in pulsatile fashion to initiate the cascade of effects.

They stimulate cells in the nearby pituitary gland to secrete other hormones that travel to stimulate the gonads (the testes and ovaries) to release yet other hormones that travel to evoke secondary sex characteristics in the body, and to activate and energise awaiting sex centres in the brain.

The hormones released by the pituitary gland to stimulate the gonads are called "gonadotropins". The suffix "tropins" is derived from the Greek and effectively means "causing the gonads to grow and mature". The hormones that are secreted by cells in the hypothalamus to cause the release of the gonadotropins from the pituitary are called "gonadotropin-releasing hormones", abbreviated to GnRH.

The GnRH hormones secreted by the hypothalamus act on receptors on the surface of the cells in the pituitary. Their pulsatile secretion (every 60 to 90 minutes) allows time for the pituitary receptors to reset after they have become fatigued sending messages to the nuclei of their cells. If they are continuously stimulated, the receptors become exhausted, messages are no longer relayed to the nuclei of the pituitary cells, gonadotropins are no longer released, and puberty stalls.

The chemical composition of GnRH was elucidated in the early 1970s and found to be comprised of 10 molecules known as peptides. Cleverly, scientists soon learned how to swap the last peptide in the chain for another, with the effect that the new GnRH would engage with the receptors and stimulate the gland, but would not permit those receptors to be restored to their functional self on the cell wall. In other words, scientists were able to create a chain of peptides which would exhaust the pituitary and thus stop the production of gonadotropins for as long as the abnormal chain was administered.

Known as GnRH "agonists", because they first stimulate the production of gonadotropins, the GnRH agonists are manufactured in injectable form and will exhaust the production of gonadotropins for weeks after administration. If injected every month or so, puberty may be stalled for years on end.

Since the 1980s, these drugs have been used to block puberty when it has begun too early. This condition is known as precocious puberty and is associated with psychological disturbance, interference with growth and a higher incidence of sexual abuse. Blockers have been used with good effect in these rare cases and it appears puberty itself may pick up after limited exposure. Any effects of exposure to the drug on the developing brain have, however, been difficult to assess because of the mental and societal stress associated with precocious puberty and the rarity of the condition.

However, the fact that puberty may restart has emboldened proponents to declare the effects of blockers in childhood gender dysphoria are "safe and entirely reversible". The international Endocrine Society (Hembree et al, 2011) is not so effusive in reassurance, declaring passively that "prolonged pubertal suppression … should not prevent resumption" upon cessation[67]. More significantly, the Society warns there are no data regarding how long it might take for active sperm and ova to appear after prolonged blockage.

After discovery, blockers were soon employed to block the secretion of the sex hormones from the gonads in conditions known to be worsened by their action, such as the effect of oestrogens on endometriosis in women and testosterone in cancer of the prostate. The use of blockers in these situations has been reported to have been associated with both psychological instability and reduced executive function (Grigorova et al, 2006; Nelson et al, 2008; Craig et al, 2007)[68,69,70], but the confounding effect of ageing, medication and worry about the disease have made it difficult to assess the individual contribution of GnRH blockers.

Unexpectedly, outside their effects on the central nervous system, Ohlsson (2016) has shown that the use of blockers affects the nervous system of the bowel in women taking them to reduce the production of gonadal oestrogen whose excess was believed to exacerbate the gynaecological condition of endometriosis. An unexpected increase in gastro-intestinal problems was reported in these women and intestinal biopsies revealed a marked reduction in the nerve cells responsible for intestinal mobility.[71]

This effect was confirmed in animal studies (Sand et al, 2015)[72] (see below) and believed to suggest a role for GnRH beyond the isolated and specific responsibility of stimulation of the pituitary to a general responsibility for the maintenance of nerve cells in varying parts of the body. In other words, the role of GnRH cannot be reduced to the single effect of stimulating the pituitary to produce gonadotropins. GnRH appears to have widespread effects and these should be considered when blockers are administered.

Though neglected in medical research on humans, there has been much work in laboratory bench studies and on animals to elucidate the broad effects of GnRH, and answer the question of what might happen when they are blocked. Studies on animals have revealed that branches of the brain cells that secrete GnRH extend well beyond the pituitary to areas of the brain concerned with sexuality, cognition, memory, emotion and executive function (Jennes et al, 2009; Casoni et al, 2016; Jennes et al, 1994; Kauffman 2004; Quintanar et al, 2007)[73,74,75,76,77]. Activity of GnRH in those regions was substantiated by finding the presence of its appropriate receptors (Stopa et al, 1991; Ban et al, 1990)[78,79]. That GnRH could be found in the cerebrospinal fluid that bathes the brain suggested that fluid could be another medium for widespread distribution, beyond the actual presence of GnRH secretary cells (Caraty 2008)[80].

Subsequently, injection of GnRH into specific sites of the brain resulted in specific effects. In particular, injection into regions concerned with sexuality was found to facilitate sexualised behaviour in both male and female animals (Pfaff et al. 1973; Moss et. al. 1973; Pfaff 1973; Maney et. al. 1997; Schimi et. al. 2000; Riskind et. al. 1979; Argiolas et. al. 2013)[81,82,83,84,85,86,87]. Conversely, sexualisation was reduced by blocking the effect of GnRH with special antibodies, and the special inhibiting hormone that is believed responsible for influencing seasonal sex behaviour in animals (Bentley 2006)[88]. It appears GnRH turns sexualisation on, and its blocking turns it off.

A more general influence of GnRH on sexual identity and behaviour was generated by the finding that various odours (pheromones) of the opposite sex could stimulate the release of GnRH to act on local sex centres in the brain, as well on the pituitary, to bring about the secondary release of the gonadal sex hormones with their added sexualising effect (Martin et al, 1986; Ungerfeld 2007)[89,90]. Soon, however, it was found that other "sociosexual stimuli" for gender identity and behaviour existed in the "rich and complex social environment that is full of the sights, sounds, and smells of their neighbours, mates and offspring" of mammals (Hawken et al, 2012)[91]. Thus, in sheep, it went on to be revealed that the presence of an odourless member of the opposite sex could cause an immediate release of GnRH, as could an odourless, unobserved member. Even a photograph of a ram could induce sexualisation in a ewe, as could the mask of a ram on the face of her sister.

These investigations on sheep pointed to poorly understood "sociosexual" stimulation of sexualisation involving the mind, memory, emotions and senses, impacting on hormones, being exacerbated by their response, all under the direction of the original complement of chromosomes. Though not understood, the force of these stimuli is obvious. The poetic description by Eugene E Brussell of love as "A beautiful dream with glandular activity" is physiologically apt.

As well as investigating the broad role of GnRH in the development and maintenance of sexuality, some researchers were looking at the specific effects on the brains of sheep which had been administered blockers in early stages of life.

In veterinary schools in universities in Glasgow and Oslo, over 10 years ago, a broader anatomical and behavioural effect was being demonstrated on such sheep. Those on blockers revealed lasting damage to the amygdala component of the limbic system to which branches of the cells that produce GnRH had been proven to reach. The limbic system integrates cognition, memory and emotions, and leads to appropriate "executive function". On blockers, the amygdala hypertrophied, and the function of many of its component genes was shown to be altered. The affected sheep demonstrated sustained reduction in memory and an increase in emotional lability (Nuruddin et Al, 2013; Nuruddin et Al, 2013; Nuruddin et al, 2013; Evans 2 et Aa, 012; Hough et al, 2017; Wojniusz et al, 2011)[92,93,94,95,96,97,98].

Recently, bench studies in other laboratories have confirmed a deleterious effect of blockers on the integrity of nerve cells from the hippocampus, another part of the limbic system. Perhaps by influencing delicate cascades of enzymes within those cells, exposure to blockers has resulted in deformation of the tiny extensions through which nerve cells communicate with each other and, ultimately, contribute to the function of the brain (Prange et al, 2008; Quintanar et al, 2016; Naftolin et al, 1971)[99,100,101].

Much, indeed most, remains unknown about the widespread function of GnRH, but there is sufficient evidence for a maintenance role in widespread neuronal function, as well as a specific role in sexual identity and reproductive function to challenge its experimental administration to the growing brains of children.

Therefore, how can a blocked young brain be expected to comprehend a sexual future?

The gender clinics administer puberty blockers with the argument they provide the young person with more time for better consideration of future gender identity and procreation, while reducing the provocation of unwanted sexual characteristics. The question is: how can a child who is maintained in a neutered state, from as early as 10½ years of age, be expected to understand such things when denied the sexually orientating effects of natural hormones? And, how can the child be expected to "think straight" when denied the sustaining effect of, in particular, GnRH, on various parts of the brain that integrate memory, cognition, and emotion into rational action? According to bench and veterinary literature, administration of blockers may be expected not only to block the outward signs of puberty but also:

1. the sexually orientating and energising effect of general "sociosexual stimuli" on the brain, as mediated by GnRH secretion

2. facilitation of sexualised behaviour by the specific action of GnRH upon local "sex centres" within the brain

3. the secondary effects of testosterone and oestrogen in their selective energising of a pubescent brain that has been quietly awaiting them, as organised and directed by the body's chromosomes since the early weeks of foetal life

4. the timely exposure of the brain to those gonadal hormones, according to the natural orchestration of the pubertal symphony. Late arrival has been shown to reduce their effect in sexualisation

5. the capacity of the limbic system to fully integrate cognition, memory and emotion and exert "executive function" in favour of the propagation of the species.

While the natural process of strengthening of gender identity is blocked, the neutered child remains exposed to the sustained pressure for transition exerted by its principal authorities: the child's parent(s), teachers, doctors, therapists, advisors, internet websites and the weight of the experience from presenting and living as a member of the opposite sex. Denied the orientation of natural hormones while exposed to such powerful influences, it is not surprising that studies reveal that, once started on blockers, medical escalation continues towards the other sex.

Phase 3: the administration of cross-sex hormones. Cross-sex hormone therapy means giving enough hormones of the opposite sex to evoke and sustain its external characteristics, such as the development of breasts in a male, or a beard in a female. The hormones are given for life and must be monitored for side effects.

According to The World Professional Association for Transgender Health (WPATH), feminising hormones carry likely increased risks that include venous thromboembolic disease, gallstones, elevated liver enzymes, weight gain, and hypertriglyceridemia. There is a likely increased risk for cardiovascular disease with the presence of additional risk factors. There are possible increased risks of hyperprolactinemia and hyperprolactinemia or prolactinoma, and Type 2 diabetes with the presence of additional risk factors.

WPATH says that masculising hormones carry likely increased risks that include polycythemia, weight gain, sleep apnoea and balding. There are possible increased risks of elevated liver enzymes and hyperlipidemia. Possible risks with additional risk factors include destabilisation of certain psychiatric disorders, cardiovascular disease, hypertension and Type 2 diabetes.[102]

By suppression of gonads, there is a slow process of chemical castration and, therefore, the desire for reproduction needs to be effected by the collection and cryopreservation of ova and sperm before the cross-sex hormones are administered. Then, ova and sperm need to be stored in a frozen state to be artificially administered to a subsequent partner.

According to international practice, cross-sex hormones may follow and then accompany blocking therapy, and be initiated around 16 years of age. Some clinics, however, commence therapy as early as 14 years (Shumer 2016)[103].

This "earlier" trend obeys a certain "affirmative" logic: if the child is determined to change gender, and if parents and authority figures agree, why make the child wait? After all, if puberty is blocked, the child will remain in an immature state while all his or her peers are growing in height and developing sexual characteristics. Surely, this period of stagnation is unnecessary. Would it not be more merciful to give the sex hormones that will produce external characteristics of the chosen gender sooner rather than later?

On this logic, affirmation therapy is creeping into earlier ages despite recommendations of the Endocrine Society: "Given the high rate of remission ... [of gender dysphoria] ... after the onset of puberty, we recommend against a complete social role change and hormone treatment in prepubertal children" (Hembree 2009)[104].

Are there side effects of cross-sex hormones on the brain?

Though proponents of transgender therapy are open about the general metabolic effects of cross-sex hormones, such as propensity to thrombosis, hypertension, and osteoporosis, few references are made to the effect of cross-sex hormones on the growing brains of young people (Chew et al, 2018)[105]. Nevertheless, there is sufficient evidence from adult human and veterinary studies to warn that the impact is great, even if the reason is poorly understood.

Surprisingly, it has been revealed that nerve cells of the brains of both males and females manufacture the female sex hormone, oestrogen, which was traditionally considered only to be produced by distant gonads in mature females[106,107]. It has been shown that this locally produced oestrogen (known as a neurosteroid) is basic to the function of the neurons, in as yet unknown ways (Spencer et al, 2008)[108]. More surprising is that testosterone, conveyed from the testes in large quantities to the brain cells in males, and small quantities from the adrenal glands in females, is metabolised in those cells into oestrogen, contributing to its local concentration (Garcia-Segura 2008)[109].

Thus, the female hormone, oestrogen, is believed to regulate differentiation of neurons and their supporting cells. It "generates sex differences in neuronal circuits controlling ... reproduction" as well as local development of the extensions from the neurons and the way they communicate, in their many thousands, to each other (Terasawa et al, 2012)[110].

Interruption of the neuronal concentration of oestrogen results in deformation of the communicating branches of the neurons, similarly to the observed effect of puberty blockers on neurons in bench studies (Quintanar 2016)[111]. Possibly, GnRH supports nerve cells by maintaining the balance of testosterone and oestrogen, but this is yet to be investigated.

The question arises: what will happen to the function of the individual neurons and their summation into a brain, if bathed in volumes of cross-sex hormones while deprived of the presence of those it was programmed to expect? Again, knowledge is limited because of the scarcity of underlying research. It is known that a balance of sex hormones is responsible for the differentiation of an early foetus into a male or female, and for a sex-specific organisation of the brain that continued into early infancy to then await further development and specific sex hormone activation in puberty. Can the growing adolescent brain adapt to concentrations of cross-sex hormones its chromosomal design was not expecting?

At first, cross-sex hormones were advised to be restricted until the age of 16 but now, in Australia, there is no age limit and it would appear early administration is likely. The approval of the Family Court of Australia was required for administration of cross-sex hormones to children under 16 but, in November 2017, the Court, following assurances from children's gender clinics, decided it would no longer intervene in cases where children have the permission of their parents and their treating doctors.[112] Now, the administration of these drugs and practice of mastectomies is accountable only to those who prescribe them and any reporting of their administration will not necessarily be available for public scrutiny.

So, what effect might be expected from administration of cross-sex hormones to the growing brain? As mentioned, there are few relevant studies but imaging of brains of adult transgenders has revealed shrinkage of male brains exposed to oestrogens at a rate ten times faster than ageing, and has revealed enlargement of female brains exposed to testosterone (Zubiaurre-Elorza et al, 2014; Rametti et al, 2 2012; Hulshoff et al, 2006)[113,114,115].

Hulshoff et al (2006) investigated brain morphology of eight males and six females who had been on cross-sex hormones and were about to undergo genital surgery, and published their results in a paper named "Changing your sex changes your brain: influences of testosterone and oestrogen on adult human brain structure". Their ages ranged from 16 to 45, with an average of 25 years. The natal males had received oestrogen and an anti-adrenergic drug, cyproterone. The natal females had received testosterone. Brain volumes were assessed on high resolution magnetic resonance images obtained "prior to and during cross-sex hormone treatment after a four-month interval" and were compared to those of healthy comparison subjects. The experiment revealed a decrease in "hypothalamus and total brain volumes" in males on cross-sex hormone therapy of a "magnitude" (31ml over a four-month period) which was "striking, since it signifies a decrease in brain volume, which is at least ten times the average decrease of around 2.5ml per year in healthy adults". Moreover, the authors emphasise that, in younger adults, shrinkage associated with age is "normally small" compared with older adults. Testosterone administered to natal females resulted in an increase in overall brain volume.[116]

These changes in volumes were associated with (in natal males) reduction in size of the internal third and lateral ventricles, and (in natal females) with an increase in their volumes. This suggested "that the total ... changes are at least in part due to changes in medial brain structures (including but not limited to the hypothalamus ... (involving) both alterations in nerve cells as well as in axonal fibers". The authors were not surprised that there were also "changes in total brain size" as cells influenced by oestrogen and androgens exist throughout the brain.[117]

Thus, the cross-sex hormones resulted in changes in brain volumes towards natural difference between males and females, but the changes cannot be described as "natural" because cell death is implicated. Pondering on the effect on the brain cells, the authors declare

> the most important mechanism by which steroid hormones alter neuron number in sexually dimorphic regions is by influencing cell death. In addition, they are involved in neuronal migration, neurogenesis, and neurotransmitter plasticity.[118]

Hulshoff's work is supported by references to effects of cross-sex hormones on animals (Raisman et al, 1971; Block et al, 1988; Nottebohm 1980)[119,120,121] and has been considered in some depth because references to such effects on the brain are not available in the promotional literature for transgendering.

My personal review of all published cases of considerations of childhood gender dysphoria by the Family Court of Australia revealed no references to the deleterious effects of cross-sex hormones on brain morphology. It is as if they do not exist. Their importance is particularly relevant for children and adolescents transgendering with cross-sex hormones because it should be noted the effects in Hulshoff's study were revealed after only four months of treatment: transgendering youth will be administered these hormones for life.

Phase 4: surgery. According to international guidelines, "sex-realignment surgery" may be performed from 18 years, though there are reports of it occurring earlier in private clinics (Milrod 2014)[122]. Mastectomy, however, may be performed at a younger age if developing breasts increase dysphoria.

As the significance of realignment surgery may not be appreciated by a non-medical audience, it may be helpful to consider some details of the fate towards which children on affirmation therapy may be headed (Weissler et al, 2018)[123]. There are various components and not all patients progress to the final package, but the project will usually include relatively simple surgical procedures of castration, removal or augmentation of breast tissue, reduction in the size of the Adam's apple, and alteration of body hair.

Surgical construction of alternate genitals is difficult, often multi-staged, fraught with complications, and limited in outcome.

Creating ersatz female genitals is easiest: an orifice is created in the perineum, lined with skin from a filleted penis and, sometimes, deepened by transplanted bowel. The scrotum forms labia. The glans is grafted above the orifice and the urethral tube is shortened.

Creating male genitals is harder. One surgeon declared "the task assumes nearly Herculean dimensions" (Rashid et al, 2013)[124], but this underestimates the ingenuity and range of objectives while exaggerating results. Hercules was always successful: creation of a penis is not. Some patients settle for a clitoris enlarged by male hormones. Others aspire to a penetrative organ, or at least one that can deliver urine when its owner is standing. In these cases, a shaft may be attempted from tissue grafted from thigh or even forearm and stiffened with a length of bone. A glans may be fashioned from a graft of inner skin and the tube that delivers urine may be lined with mucous membranes from the mouth. The appearance of a scrotum may be achieved by creating a sac from the labia and inserting two artificial testicles.

Though techniques are improving with practice, complications are protean. Grafts may die, holes fill in, tubes obstruct, openings appear, bones protrude, bowels perforate and germs invade but, all in all, these are high-risk procedures undertaken in the attempt to produce an "aesthetically and functionally pleasing" result for the recipient.

14.9 IS THERE EVIDENCE THE DUTCH PROTOCOL IS BENEFICIAL?

Despite the magnitude of the intervention into the minds and bodies of children comprised in the Dutch Protocol, it has no underpinning in the "scientific method" that should accompany any medical intervention.

Normally, the process to validate any medical intervention begins in physiological plausibility, then to studies in laboratories, then to studies on animals, then to pilot studies on humans; then, finally, to cross-over, blinded studies adjudicated by disinterested researchers whose results are analysed statistically. All the while, side effects are sought and balanced against putative gain. A reasonable observer would imagine such stringent practices would apply to the regime of treatment that begins by the giving of hormones that might affect the brain as well as the body, would entail chemical castration, and may lead to massive surgical enterprise in which physical castration is inherent. However, that is not the case.

A recent article by Chew et al (2018)[125] in *Pediatrics*, the prestigious journal of the American Academy of Pediatrics, emphasises the lack of normal scientific appraisal. It is named "Hormonal Treatment in Young people with Gender Dysphoria: a systemic review" and is a summation of international literature on the "psychosocial, cognitive and/or physical effects". It is a significant article in the Australian context because its authors are associated with such prominent institutions as the Royal Children's Hospital in Melbourne, which appears to be at the forefront of the Dutch Protocol in this country.

For Chew et al to declare in their introduction that such studies are "scarce" is an understatement: in the 70 years from January 1946 to June 2017, they could find only 13 publications of any relevance. They find this scarcity to be "problematic" because "adolescence is a period of rapid development across multiple domains" to which hormonal therapy in transgendering adults may not "translate". The problem lies in the virtual absence of scientific literature that pertains to the intervention that may be about to be inflicted on brains of children undergoing the cerebral growth spurt of puberty and adolescence.

The authors categorised their findings under several headings.

Physical effects: The authors introduce the actions of puberty blockers and cross-sex hormones and detail some physical effects, concluding, "overall, hormonal treatments for transgender youth were observed to be relatively safe". Then they undermine that assurance by acknowledging "the relatively short follow-up duration of the studies". They consider the effect on bone growth to be of particular concern, but also warn of "various metabolic and cardiovascular effects" known to be associated with cross-sex hormones in adults.[126]

Psychosocial effects: The authors' report claims that transgendering therapies were "associated with significant improvements in multiple psychological measures, including global functioning, depression ... and behavioural and/or emotional problems". However, they report the studies revealed "unclear effects on anger and anxiety" and "no significant effect on symptoms of GD (gender dysphoria)". Indeed, one study suggested "an increase in GD and body image difficulties"[127].

However, the authors do not discuss weaknesses in the studies claiming psychological benefit, merely admitting that there is a knowledge "gap". These weaknesses include the limited number of children studied, the limited time of study, the lack of controls, and the possibility of observer bias. When those who are diagnosing, treating and measuring outcome (without comparison) on a relatively small cohort of suffering children who must be well known to all, the possibility of observer bias is obvious. Compassion, alone, would inspire optimistic thinking.

Another major confounder of psychological benefit is the large number of children suffering from associated psychological disorder, as emphasised by Becerra-Culqui et al (2018).[128] The effect of concentrated, compassionate, professional support, by a team of adults committed to increasing a child's happiness, is likely, by itself, to be positive, and thus skew results. Moreover, any undisclosed psychotherapeutic medicines the children might also be taking are likely to skew results.

Cognitive effects: The authors could find only two references, both pertaining to very weak studies, on the cognitive effects of transitioning therapy; that is, on the brain power and behaviour of the recipient. One study examined "executive function" in eight children on blockers and, though it found "significantly reduced accuracy" in transfemale adolescents, the importance of this negative finding was downplayed by arguing the number of children was too small for validation. The other study examined visio-spatial ability, which is generally believed to be greater in males, and was reported to have been enhanced in natal females who had received testosterone for 10 months. No other effects of steroids on the growing brain were assessed.

The quality and risk of bias of the 13 studies were independently assessed by two of the Australian authors, who concluded: "In all studies, there was a medium to high risk of bias" because of the small numbers of subjects, absence of controls, loss of follow up, retrospectivity, absence of randomisation and "no blinding" of researchers.[129]

Appropriately, the Australian team proclaimed the need "to reassess and expand on the findings of the existing studies". They explained the inability of blockers to reduce symptoms of gender dysphoria to be "probably not surprising", arguing it would be unreasonable to expect blockers to "lessen the dislike" of existing sexual features and to "satisfy ... desire" for the physical features of the opposite sex. They did not discuss the inability of blockers to alleviate innate mental disorder of which the dysphoria might have been but a symptom.[130]

With regard to the effect of cross-sex hormones on cognition, apart from the minimal reference to testosterone, reviewers could find no relevant literature.

Overall, the Australian authors conclude the existing studies have "neglected several key outcomes". These include "psychological symptoms ... which is a critical knowledge gap"; the impact of treatment on fertility; the possibility of other physical side effects, including growth and cardiovascular function; and the manner of withdrawal from treatment, especially with regret.[131]

It should be emphasised that the above article reporting scarcity of studies is not unique. Other publications in mainstream paediatric literature complain of "lack of consensus regarding appropriate intervention or even appropriate goals of intervention" (Shumer et al, 2013)[132], "limited long term data" (Costa R et al, 2015)[133] "small numbers from only one clinic" (de Vries et al, 2014)[134], "reliance on clinical impressions" (Schwartz 2012)[135]. Thus, there is a lack of randomised controlled studies that provide definitive recommendations for treatment options. Therefore, the best evidence available is characterised as "expert opinion", which is influenced by prevailing cultural belief systems and theoretical orientations (Milrod 2013)[136].

In a Special Review in the *Journal of Homosexuality* of "The treatment of gender dysphoric/gender variant children and adolescents", David Schwartz (2012)[137], a child psychiatrist from New York, emphasised the lack of scientific data regarding medical intervention and concluded with the reassurance that affected children would naturally desist. He declared

> the long-term psychological and physiological consequences of ... (the medical pathway) ... are unknown and, as is the case with all self-selected populations, very difficult to assess owing to problems of (lack of experimental) control and limited sample numbers.

Schwartz highlighted concerns, including dependence on "clinical impression", "usage of anecdotal data", suspension of "natural scepticism" in "favor of literality" of children's and adolescents' claims, unquestioning "certitude", and lack of consideration of "potential disadvantages"[138].

Yet another review of recent research by Fuss et al (2015) concluded that

> more longitudinal research ... is needed to compare different strategies of care and to see long term results especially in those minors with comorbid psychiatric disorders. The lack of evidence is even more pressing considering ... the dramatically increasing number of referrals to gender clinics ...[139].

14.10   IS ANYTHING ELSE AT RISK?

Apart from the health of children, is anything else at risk? The answer is yes. Transgender ideology is challenging basic human rights and freedoms. Beginning in the US and Canada, laws have been passed which oblige a medical practitioner to direct a dysphoric child towards transitioning.

14.10.1 What does the law have to say in North America?

In California, in September 2012, a law was passed "to prohibit a mental health provider ... from engaging in sexual orientation change efforts ... with a patient under 18 years of age" which included "transgender youth, as well as lesbian, gay and bisexual young people". Such efforts included "efforts to change behaviors or gender expressions" which were deemed "unprofessional conduct and shall subject the provider to discipline". The Bill cited various national organisations of paediatricians, psychologists and psychiatrists which described such activities as conversion or reparative therapies.[140]

Similar laws have been enacted in New Jersey, Illinois, Oregon, and Washington. In 2015, the state of Ontario, Canada passed an "anti-reparative" and "anti-conversion" law. It opposed any attempt to re-orientate sexuality or to affirm a child in their natal sex in order "to save children's lives".

In effect, US President Barack Obama joined the affirmation team, responding to a petition banning "dangerous ... conversion therapy" after the suicide by a 15-year-old natal male adolescent who had sought to identify as a female and allegedly underwent "conversion" therapy at his parent's church. The White House said that the "Obama administration supports efforts" to ban conversion therapy for minors "because overwhelming evidence demonstrates" it "is neither medically nor ethically appropriate"[141].

It is hard to gauge the effect of the laws. No charges have yet been laid but many therapists uncommitted to active affirmation are now reported to be unwilling to care for transgender children because they do not want the worry of the medico-legal risk (personal communication). The result of their withdrawal in the face of increasing public demand is that children and their parents are funnelled towards those willing to continue or initiate the stages of transition.

One definite association with the development of the law in Ontario was the dismissal of the international leader in management of gender dysphoria, Dr Kenneth Zucker, and the closure of his long-established clinic in Toronto for allegedly practising conversion therapy. This has brought immeasurable weight to the law.

This law, known in Ontario, Canada, as the *Affirming Sexual Orientation and Gender Identity Act, 2015*[142] was passed unanimously and in a "miraculously" short time according to its promoter, parliamentarian, The Reverend Cheri DiNovo. When I interviewed The Rev DiNovo in 2016, she explained that "Bills may take up to years to pass but this one succeeded in only two months". The Rev DiNovo, who entered Parliament in March 2006, has been a prominent advocate for many issues, including recognition of the Stalin-imposed famine on Ukraine as "genocide", and is also prominent for "pass[ing] most LGBTQ legislation in Canada". She has conducted a weekly radio program, received literary awards, earned a Master's degree in divinity, a doctorate in ministry from the University of Toronto, and been a minister of the United Church of Canada since 1995[143].

All her educational achievements are relevant to the discussion we shared. Concisely, she declared the object of her "gender" law was not punitive but "instructional": to save children's lives, gender identity had to be affirmed. "Reparative or conversion" attempts should, therefore, be dissuaded and certainly not remunerated under the state's *Health Insurance Act 1990*.

I asked about clauses in the Act declaring that the reparative therapy ban "does not apply if the person is capable with respect to the treatment and consents to the provision of the treatment". The Rev DiNovo was unclear in her response. I asked at what age would a child be deemed capable of consent to reparative treatment? Up to what age would a child be incapable of consent and therefore have to rely on the judgement of parents and affirmative therapists? DiNovo would not approximate, merely repeating, and now, with many words, that the law was "instructional".

More disturbing was the response of this educated politician to my question as to why active, affirmative, transitioning therapy should be applied when studies show the vast majority of children with gender dysphoria were going to "grow out of it" and only identify with their natal sex in adulthood? "I did not know that," she declared. I continued by presenting a book written by Dutch leaders in the field who attest to the majority desisting. She declared she had not heard of them. I left her office perplexed. Could one so prominent not know most children would desist from transgender confusion?

14.10.2 What does the law have to say in Australia?

In February 2017, a *Health Complaints Act* became law in Victoria in which complaints may be raised against fraudulent and negligent practices which will include, according to Health Minister Jill Hennessy, "conversion" therapy.

She explained the Act will "provide the means to deal with those who profit from the abhorrent practice of "gay conversion therapy ... which inflicts significant emotional trauma and damages the mental health of young members of our community. This bill will enable the new Commissioner to investigate and crack down on anyone making dangerous and unproven claims that they can "convert" gay people. Though she specified "gay people" and did not define age, the declaration attributed to Hennessy that "any attempts to make people uncomfortable with their own sexuality is completely unacceptable"[144], suggests a broad intent for the law, in line with North American legislation.

More intimidating than the American laws, the Victorian Act will transfer the onus of proof to the accused who will need "reasonable excuse" to avoid investigation after a complaint has been laid. In other words, the Victorian Parliament has overturned the hard-won human right of being innocent until proven guilty, as declared in Article 11 of the *Universal Declaration of Human Rights*.

In response to whether presumption of guilt would confront Human Rights, Hennessy convolutedly explained:

> The reverse onus is required in relation to these offences as the 'reasonable excuse' exception relates to matters which are particularly within an accused's knowledge and introduce additional facts from the subject matter of the offence, which would be unduly onerous for a prosecution to investigate and disprove at first instance. Once the accused has pointed to evidence of a reasonable excuse, which they should have access to if the excuse is applicable, the burden shifts back to the prosecution who must prove the essential elements of the offence to a legal standard. I am of the view that there is a negligible risk that these provisions would allow an innocent person to be convicted of any of these offences. Accordingly, I am of the view that these offence provisions are compatible with the charter[145].

More broadly than Ontario's *Affirming Sexual Orientation and Gender Identity Act 2015,* which focuses on therapists receiving National Insurance funding, the Victorian *Health Complaints Act 2017* will embrace any person or organisation beyond the classical health care providers that offer "general health services"[146] to "maintain or improve a client's health or wellbeing"[147], including "mental or psychological health or status"[148]. Given the antagonism of transgender activists to affirming children in their natal sex, sooner rather than later any person advising "watchful waiting" of a transgender child may be asked for a "reasonable excuse".[149]

Not only are medical practitioners, psychologists and counsellors at risk, so too are school teachers and parents. According to the NSW Department of Education, teachers are reminded of their mandatory obligation to report suspected child abuse to their principals who, in turn, are reminded of their responsibility to report abuse to authorities in Family and Community Services. According to a department *Legal Issues Bulletin* (2014),

> Should a teacher have "reasonable suspicion": that a transgender student is at "suspected risk of harm ... relat[ing] to the parent's stated response to their child identifying as transgender, [then] school staff should inform their principal of any concerns about a student who may be at suspected risk of harm[150].

14.11 WHAT DOES THE FUTURE HOLD?

The draft Platform prepared by the Australian Labor Party for its National Conference later in 2018 includes a provision regarding gay conversion therapy. It says: "Labor opposes the practice of so-called conversion and reparative therapies on LGBTIQ+ people and seek[s] to criminalise these practices".[151]

The ALPs Federal health spokesperson, Catherine King has been reported to have declared that stopping conversion therapy would be a "personal priority" if Labor wins the next election.[152] The policy refers to transgenders, as well as gays and lesbians, so the policy applies to anyone who is transgender, including children with gender dysphoria.

Labor's 2015 National Platform commits the party to ensuring "child protection authorities acknowledge attempts to 'cure' Gender Questioning children and young people as serious psychological abuse, and would acknowledge these harms, when suffered within the family as domestic violence against the child".[153]

It should be emphasised that "conversion therapy" is Orwellian double-speak for any attempt to reduce gender dysphoria by helping the child become comfortable with its natal identity, and not ushering the child onto the pathway of affirmation. Merely encouraging a gender confused child to wait for the orientating effects of puberty to be worked through may be considered a form of child abuse. In the future, it may become very dangerous for a child to express confusion of gender: no-one will be able legally to protect it from gender transitioning protocols that are backed by the state. The irony is that the state will sanction any transition to any gender, as frequently and momentously as the client wishes, as long as the direction is away from that decreed by chromosomes.

Such punitive bias is not shared by the highest of international organisations: no less than the international Endocrine Society acknowledges a middle path between "complete social role change and hormone treatment" on the "affirmative" end of the spectrum and punitive attempts to dissuade on the other. Implying that for "most children", gender dysphoria "does not persist" if parents are patient, the Society recommends children should not "be entirely denied to show cross-gender behaviours" and should not "be punished for exhibiting such behaviors".[154] While Australian politicians cannot be expected to have full understanding of therapies (even Canada's Rev Cheri DiNovo claims she has never heard that most gender dysphoric children only identify with their natal sex in adulthood), the commitment of some to such intervention in the healing arts is surprising. Their dedication to one single option despite varying opinions must be credited to the astonishing success of transgender activism.

Ironically, some homosexuals are beginning to perceive their future eroding. In a conversation with a mother of a gender confused child, she reported to me the consternation of a homosexual friend. The male friend said, "I am glad I grew up in an earlier era, otherwise my preference for softer clothing, colours and play, and the company of female children, could have led to my transition!" Had he grown up in the pending era, his parents could have been charged with child abuse for not submitting him to the Protocols, and any resistant doctor could have been deregistered.

Social and medical transitioning treatments constitute an experiment that appears to be based on the Dutch Protocol of therapy for childhood gender dysphoria. The Dutch Protocol appears to have overlooked important international codes of medical research ethics on human experimentation, including the ancient Hippocratic Oath, the Belmont report (1978), the Declaration of Geneva (1948), the Declaration of Helsinki (1964) and the Nuremberg Principles (1949).

The Nuremberg Code and related Declaration of Helsinki are the basis for the US Code of Federal Regulations issued by the United States Department of Health and Human Services for the ethical treatment of human subjects. In addition, the idea of informed consent has been universally accepted and now constitutes Article 7 of the United Nations' *International Covenant on Civil and Political Rights*. It is also the basis for International Ethical Guidelines for Biomedical Research Involving Human Subjects proposed by the World Health Organisation.

Against key protections of these codes, questions have to be asked about children transitioning.

Against the requirement for a subject "understanding consent", how can a child on puberty blockers understand their sexual future? How can a child with a psychological disorder comprehend transitioning and the permanent changes to their future?

Against the necessity for an outcome that cannot be achieved in any other way, why is medical transitioning vigorously pursued when most children will revert to identifying with their natal sex in adulthood? Who can predict that "compassionate, supportive, watching and waiting" until the child reaches adulthood will not be effective?

Against the requirement that experimentation is based on previous knowledge, including animal studies, there is virtually no previous knowledge, and animal studies that ought to be dissuasive are being ignored.

Against the requirement that an experiment ought not to exceed expected benefits, animal studies show risk of sustained cerebral damage. Conversely, there is no long-term evidence that dysphoric children will be advantaged by medical transitioning, while there is long-term evidence that transgendered adults have an inordinate rate of suicide.

Against the necessity that staff must be fully qualified, the very recent tsunami of childhood gender dysphoria means very few therapists possess long-term, corporate expertise.

Against the requirement that medical staff must stop the experiment when they observe the experiment is dangerous, given the absence of traditional study design, how will the staff know when things have gone wrong? In the absence of such standard trials, frontal lobotomies were pursued enthusiastically for a long time at the cost of tens of thousands of interventions.

Against the necessity that subjects should be free to leave the study at any time, what child will be able to walk away from a new identity, the persuasion of drugs and the commitment of authority figures?

Endnotes

1. *Diagnostic and Statistical Manual of Mental Disorders, Fifth Edition.* (DSM-5) American Psychiatric Association. Washington. DC 2013, pg. 452.

2. Ibid.

3. Ristori J, Steensma TD. Gender dysphoria in childhood. Int Rev Psych. 2016;28 (1):13-20. Doi 10.3109/09540261.2015.1115754

4. Shumer D, Spack NP. Current management of gender identity disorder in childhood and adolescence: guidelines, barriers and areas of controversy. Curr Opin Endocrinol, Diabetes and Obes. 2013;20(1):69-73. Doi 10.1097/MED.0b013e32835c711e

5. Eade DM, Telfer MM, Tollitt MA. Implementing a single session nurse led assessment clinic into a gender service. Transgender Health. 2018;3(1):43-46. Doi 10.1089/trgh.2017.0050

6. DSM-5. 2013, Op. cit., pg. 454.

7. "Gender Dysphoria", American Psychiatric Association. https://www.psychiatry.org/File%20Library/Psychiatrists/Practice/DSM/APA_DSM-5-Gender-Dysphoria.pdf Accessed 12 July 2018.

8. Bonifacio HJ, Rosenthal SM. Gender variance and Dysphoria in Children and Adolescents. Pediatr Clin North Am. 2015. 62(4):1001-1016. Doi 10.1016/j.pcl.2015.04.013

9. Clark T, Lucassen M, Bullen P et al. The Health and Well-Being of Transgender High School Students: Results From the New Zealand Adolescent Health Survey (Youth'12). J Adolescent Health. 2014;55:93-99.

10. Clark TC, Fleming T, Bullen P, et al. Youth'12 prevalence tables: The health and wellbeing of New Zealand secondary school students in 2012. Auckland, New Zealand: University of Auckland; 2013. Accessed 14 July 2018.

11. Telfer M, Tollit M, Feldman D. Transformation of health-care and legal systems for the transgender population: The need for change. JPCH.2015. 51;1051-1053.

12. *All of Us: Health and Physical Education Resource Understanding Gender Diversity, Sexual Diversity and Intersex Topics for Years 7 and 8,* Safe Schools Coalition Australia and Minus18, pg. 8. http://www.education.vic.gov.au/Documents/about/programs/health/AllOfUs_UnitGuide.pdf Accessed 14 January 2018. Now available at https://www.minus18.org.au/images/ALL_OF_US.pdf

13. DSM-5. 2013, Op. cit., pg. 452.

14. Haas A, Eliason M, Mays V et al. Suicide and Suicide Risk in Lesbian, Gay, Bisexual, and Transgender Populations: Review and Recommendations. J Homosex. 2011;58:10-51. Doi: 10.1080/00918369.2011.534038

15. Fan X et al. An exploratory study about inaccuracy and invalidity in adolescent self-report surveys. Field Methods. Savon-Williams and Joyner. 2006;18(3):223-244. Doi 10.1177/152822X06289161

16. "Gender identity debate swirls over CAMH psychologist, transgender program", *The Globe and Mail.* 14 February 2016. https://www.theglobeandmail.com/news/toronto/gender-identity-debate-swirls-over-camh-psychologist-transgender-program/article28758828/ Accessed 14 July 2018.

17. Zucker KJ, Wood H, Singh D, Bradley SJ. A developmental biopsychosocial model for the treatment of children with gender identity disorder. J Homosex. 2012;59(3):369-397. Doi 10.1080/00918369.2012.653309

18 Wallien MS, Swaab H, Cohen-Kettenis PT. Psychiatric comorbidity among children with gender identity disorder. J Am Acad Child Adolesc Psychiatry. 2007;46(10):1307-1314. Doi 10.1097/chi.0b013e3181373848

19 Steensma TD, Zucker KJ, Kreukels BP et al. Behavioural and emotional problems on the Teacher's Report Form: a cross-national, cross-clinic comparative analysis of gender dysphoric children and adolescents. J Abnorm Child Psychol. 2014;42(4):635-647. Doi: 10.1007/s10802-013-9804-2

20 Spack NP, Edwards-Leeper L, Feldman HA, et al. Children and adolescents with gender identity disorder referred to a pediatric medical center. Pediatrics. 2012;129(3):418-425. Doi 10.1542/peds.2011-0907

21 Hewitt JK, Paul C, Kasiannan P et al. Hormone treatment of gender identity disorder in a cohort of children and adolescents. Med J Aust. 2012;196(9):578-581. Doi 10.5694/mja12.10222

22 Becerra-Culqui TA, Liu Y, Nash R et al. Mental Health of Transgender and Gender Nonconforming Youth Compared With Their Peers. Pediatrics. 2018;141(5). Doi 10.1542/peds. 2017-3845

23 Ibid.

24 Kaltiala-Heino R, Sumia M, Tyolajarvi M et al. Two years of gender identity service for minors: overrepresentation of natal girls with severe problems in adolescent development. Child Adol Psych Mental Health. 2015.9(9). Doi: 10.1186/s13034-015-0042-y

25 Kaltiala-Heino R, Bergman H, Työläjärvi M, and Frisén L. Gender dysphoria in adolescence: current perspectives. Adolesc Health Med Ther. 2018; 9: 31–41. Doi https://doi.org/10.2147/AHMT.S135432

26 Kaltiala-Heino R, Sumia M, Tyolajarvi M, Lindberg N. Two years of gender identity service for minors: overrepresentation of natal girls with severe problems in adolescent development. Child Adolesc Psychiatry Ment Health. 2015;9:9. Doi 10.1186/s13034-015-0042-y

27 Chen M, Fuqua J, Eugster EA. Characteristics of referrals for gender dysphoria over a 13-year period. J Adolesc Health. 2016;58(3):369–371. Doi 10.1016/j.jadohealth.2015.11.010

28 Holt V, Skagerberg E, Dunsford M. Young people with features of gender dysphoria: demographics and associated difficulties. Clin Child Psychol Psychiatry. 2016;21(1):108–118. Doi 10.1177/1359104514558431

29 Van Der Miesen AI, Hurley H, De Vries AL. Gender dysphoria and autism spectrum disorder: a narrative review. Int Rev Psychiatry. 2016;28(1):70–80. Doi 10.3109/09540261.2015.1111199

30 Lai M, Lombardo MV, Baron-Cohen S. Autism. Lancet. 2014;383(9920):896–910. Doi 10.1016/S0140-6736(13)61539-1

31 van Der Miesen AI, et al. 2016, Op. cit.

32 Strang JF, Kenworthy L, Dominska A, et al. Increased gender variance in autism spectrum disorders and attention deficit hyperactivity disorder. Arch Sex Behav. 2014;43(8):1525–1533. Doi 10.1007/s10508-014-0285-3

33 Karasic D, Ehrensaft D. We must put an end to gender conversion therapy for kids. *Wired*. 2015. Htp://www.wired.com/2015/07/must-out-an-end-gender-conversion-therapy-kids/ Accessed 18 October 2016.

34 Ibid.

35 Aitken M, VanderLaan DP, Wasserman L, Stojanovski S, Zucker KJ. Self-harm and suicidality in children referred for gender dysphoria. J Am Acad Child Adolesc Psychiatry. 2016;55(6):513-520. Doi 10.1016/j.jaac.2016.04.001

36 Holt V, Skagerberg E, Dunsford M. Young people with features of gender dysphoria: demographics and associated difficulties. Clin Child Psychol Psychiatry. 2016;21(1):108-118. Doi 10.1177/1359104514558431

37 Ibid.

38 Mayes SD, Gorman AA, Hillwig-Garcia J et al. Suicide ideation and attempts in children with autism. Res Autism Spec Dis. 2013;7(1):109-119. Doi 10.1016/j.rasd.2012.07.009

39 Clark TC (2013) Op. cit.

40 Aitken M, VanderLaan DP, Wasserman L, Stojanovski S, Zucker KJ. Self-harm and suicidality in children referred for gender dysphoria. J Am Acad Child Adolesc Psychiatry. 2016;55(6):513-520. Doi 10.1016/j.jaac.2016.04.001

41 Muehlenkamp JJ, Claes L, Havertape L, Plener PL. International prevalence of adolescent non-suicidal self-injury and deliberate self-harm. Child Adoles Psychiatry Ment Health. 2012;6(10). Doi 10.1186/1753-2000-6-10

42 Lewinsohn PM, Rohde P, Seeley JR. Adolescent suicidal ideation and attempts: risk factors and clinical implications. Clin Psychol Sci Pract. 1996;3(1):25–46. Doi 10.1111/j.1468-2850.1996.tb00056.x

43 Faulkner AH, Cranston K. Correlates of same-sex sexual behavior in a random sample of Massachusetts high school students. Am J Public Health. 1998 Feb;88(2):262–266. Doi 10.2105/AJPH.88.2.262

44 Holt V et al (2016), Op. cit.

45 De Vries AL, Cohen-Kettenis PT. Clinical management of gender dsyphoria in children and adolescents: the Dutch approach. J Homosex. 2012;59(3):301-320. DOI:10.1080/00918369.2012.653300

46 Murad MH, Elamin MB, Garcia MZ, Mullan RJ, Murad A et al. Hormonal therapy and sex reassignment: a systematic review and meta-analysis of quality of life and psychosocial outcomes. Clin Endocrinol (Oxf) 2010;72(10): 214–231. Doi 10.1111/j.1365-2265.2009.03625.x

47 Dhejne C, Lichtenstein P, Boman M et al. Long-Term Follow-Up of Transsexual Persons Undergoing Sex Reassignment Surgery: Cohort Study in Sweden. PLOS 1. 2011;6(2): e16885. Doi 10.1371/journal.pone.0016885

48 De Cuypere, Elaut E, Heylens G, et al. Long term follow up: psychosexual outcome of Belgian transsexuals after sex reassignment surgery. Sexologies. 2006;15:126-133. Doi: 10.1016/j.sexol.2006.04.002

49 Dhejene C, Lichtenstein P, Boman M et al. Long-Term Follow-Up of Transsexual Persons Undergoing Sex Reassignment Surgery: Cohort Study in Sweden. PLOS 1. 2011;6(2):e16885. Doi 10.1371/journal.pone.0016885

50 Haas A (2011), Op. cit.

51 Zucker KJ. Children with gender identity disorder. Is there a best practice? Neuropsychiatrie de l'enfance et de l'adolescence. 2008;56(6):358-364. Doi 10.1016/j.neurenf.2008.06.003

52 Zucker KJ, Lambert S, Bradley SJ et al. Risk factors for general behavior problems in boys with gender identity disorder. Presented at 19th Symposium of the Harry Benjamin International Gender Dysphoria Association. 2005. Bologna Italy.

53 Zucker KJ, Bradley SJ, Moshe I. Delayed naming of a baby boy. J of Psychology: human sexuality. 1990;6(1):57-68. Doi: 10.1300/J056v06n01_04

54. Marantz S, Coates S. Mothers of boys with gender identity disorder: a comparison of matched controls. J Am Acad. Child and Adolescent Psychiatry. 1991;30(2):310-315. Doi 10.1097/00004583-199103000-00022

55. Zucker KJ. Children with gender identity disorder. Is there a best practice? Neuropsychiatrie de l'enfance et de l'adolescence. 2008;56(6):358-364. Doi 10.1016/j.neurenf.2008.06.003

56. Zucker KJ. The myth of persistence: response to 'a critical commentary on follow-up studies and 'desistance' theories about transgender and gender non-conforming children; by Temple Newhook et al. International Journal of Transgenderism. 2018;19 (2):231-245. Doi:10.1080/15532739.2018.1468293

57. Ibid.

58. Zucker KJ, Wood H, Singh D, Bradley SJ. A developmental, biopsychosocial model for the treatment of children with gender identity disorder. Journal Homosex. 2012;59(3);369-397. Doi 10.1080/00918369.2012.653309

59. Zucker KJ, 2008. Op. cit.

60. Ristori J, Steensma TD. Gender dysphoria in childhood. Int Rev Psych. 2016;28 (1):13-20. Doi 10.3109/09540261.2015.1115754

61. De Vries AL, Cohen-Kettenis PT. Clinical management of gender dsyphoria in children and adolescents: the Dutch approach. J Homosex. 2012;59(3):301-320. DOI:10.1080/00918369.2012.653300

62. Coleman E, Bockting W, Boltzer M et al. Standards of care for the health of transsexual, transgender and gender non-conforming people. Version 7. International Journal of Transgenderism 2011;13:165-232. Doi:10.1080/15532739.2011.700873.

63. Zucker, 2018. Op. cit.

64. Practice parameter on gay, lesbian, or bisexual sexual orientation, gender noncormfority, and gender discordance in children and adolescents. American Academy of Child and Adolescent Psychiatry. 2012;51:957-974. Doi:10.1016/j.jaac.2012.07.004

65. "Transgender children are rare, but we're being told ...", *Daily Telegraph*, 12 September 2017. https://www.dailytelegraph.com.au/rendezview/what-madness-can-justify-mutilating-our-children/news-story/ =84c7426daf4c543d1074a08fd9bf3d41 Accessed 10 July 2018.

66. Steensma TD, Cohen-Kettenis PT. Gender transitioning before puberty. Arch Sex Behav. 2011;40(4):649-650. Doi 10.1007/s10508-011-9752-2

67. Hembree WC, Cohen-Kettenis P, Delemarre-van de Waal HA et al. Endocrine treatment of transsexual persons: an Endocrine Society Clinical Practice Guideline. J Clin Endocrinol Metab. 2009 Sep;94(9):3132-3154. Doi 10.1210/jc.2009-0345

68. Grigorova M, Sherwin BB, Tulandi T. Effects of treatment with leuprolide acetate depot on working memory and executive functions in young premenopausal women. Psychneuroendocrinology. 2006;31(8):935-947. Doi 10.1016/j.psyneuen.2006.05.004

69. Nelson CJ, Lee JS, Gamboa MC et al. Cognitive effects of hormone therapy in men with prostate cancer: a review. Cancer. 2008;113(5):1097-1106. Doi 10.1002/cncr.23658

70 Craig MC et al. Gonadotropin hormone releasing hormone agonists alter prefrontal function during verbal encoding in young women. Psychoneuroendocrinology. 2007;32(8-10):116-1127. Doi 10.1016/j.psyneuen.2007.09.009

71 Ohlsson B. Gondadotrophin-releasing hormone and its physiological and pathophysiological roles in relation to the structure and function of the gastro-intestinal tract. European Surgical Research. 2016;57:22-33 https://doi.org/10.1159/000445717

72 Sand E, Linninge C, Lozinska L et al. Buserelin treatment to rats causes enteric neurodegeneration with moderate effects on crf-immunoreactive neurons and enterobacteriaceae in colon, and in acetylcholine-mediated permeability in ileum. BMC research notes. 2015;8:824. https://doi.org/10.1186/s13104-015-1800-x

73 Jennes et al. *The Gonadotrophin-releasing hormone and its receptor. Hormones, Brain and Behaviour 2nd edn.* Pfaff DW (ed) Academic Press 2009; pgs. 1645-1668.

74 Casoni F, Malone SA, Belle M et al. Development of the neurons controlling fertility in humans: new insights from 3D imaging and transparent fetal brains. Development. 2016;143(21):3969-3981. Doi 10.1242/dev.139444

75 Jennes L, Conn P. Gonadotropin releasing hormone and its receptors in the rate brain. Front Neuroendocrinol. 1994;15(1):51-77. Doi 10.1006/frne.1994.1003

76 Kauffman AS. Emerging functions of gonadotropin releasing hormone II in mammalian physiology and behaviour. J Neuroendocrinol. 2004;16(9):794-806. Doi 10.1111/j.1365-2826.2004.01229.x

77 Quintanar JL, Salinas E, Gonzalez R. Expression of gonadotropin-releasing hormone receptor in cerebral cortical neurons of embryos and adult rats. Neurosci Lett. 2007;411(1):22-25. Doi 10.1016/j.neulet.2006.06.077

78 Stopa EG, Koh ET, Svendsen CN, Rogers WT, Schwaber JS, King JC. Computer-assisted mapping of immunoreactive mammalian gonadotropin-releasing hormone in adult human basal forebrain and amygdala. Endocrinology. 1991;128(6):3199–3207. Doi 10.1210/endo-128-6-3199

79 Ban E, Crumeyrolle-Arias M, Latouche J et al. GnRH receptors in rat brain, pituitary and testis; modulation following surgical and gonadotropin releasing hormone agonist induced castration. Mol Cell Endocrinol. 1990;70(1):99-107. Doi 10.1016/0303-7207(90)90063-E

80 Caraty A, Skinner DC. Gonadotrophin-releasing hormone in third ventricular cerebrospinal fluid: endogenous distribution and exogenous uptake. Endocrinology. 2008;.149(10):5227-5234. Doi 10.1210/en.2007-1636

81 Pfaff D, Lewis C, Diakow C et al. Neurophysiological analysis of mating behavior responses as hormone sensitive reflexes. Prog Physiol Psychol. 1973;5:253-297.

82 Moss RL MCann SM. Induction of mating behavior in rats by luteinizing hormone releasing factor. Science. 1973;181(4095):177-179. Doi 10.1126/science.181.4095.177

83 Pfaff DW, Luteinizing hormone-releasing factor potentiates lordosis behavior in hypophysectomized ovariectomized female rats. Science. 1973;182(4117):1148-1149.

84 Maney DL, Richardson RD, Wingfield JC. Central administration of chicken gonadotropin-releasing hormone-11 enhances courtship behavior in a female sparrow. Horm Behav. 1997;32(1):11-18. Doi 10.1006/hbeh.1997.1399

85 Schimi PA, Rissmin EF. Effects of gonadotropin-releasing hormones, corticotrophin-releasing hormone and vasopressin on female sexual behavior. Horm Behav. 2000;37(3):212-220. Doi 10.1006/hbeh.2000.1575

86 Riskind P, Moss RL. Midbrain Central Gray: LHRH infusion enhances lordotic behavior in estrogen-primed ovariectomized Rats. Brain Res Bull. 1979;4(2):203-205. Doi 10.1016/0361-9230(79)90282-X

87 Argiolas A, Melis MR. Neuropeptides and central control of sexual behavior from past to present: a review. Prog neurobiol 2013;108:80-107. Doi: 10.1016/j.pneurobio.2013.06.006

88 Bentley GE, Jensen JP, Kaur GJ et al. Rapid inhibition of female sexual behavior by gonadotropin-inhibiting hormone (GnIH). Horm Behav. 2006;49(4):550-555. Doi 10.1016/j.yhbeh.2005.12.005

89 Martin GB, Oldham CM. Cognie Y et al. The physiological response of anovulatory ewes to the introduction of rams – A review. Live Prod Sci. 1986;15(3):219-47. Doi 10.1016/0301-6226(86)90031-X

90 Ungerfeld R. Socio-sexual signaling and gonadal function: opportunities for reproductive management in domestic ruminants. Soc Reprod Fertil Suppl. 2007;64(1):207-221. Doi: 0.5661/RDR-VI-207

91 Hawken PA, Martin GB. Sociosexual stimuli and gonadotropin-releasing hormone/luteinizing hormone secretion in sheep and goats. Domest Anim Endocrinol. 2012;43(2):85-94. Doi 10.1016/j.domaniend.2012.03.005

92 Nuruddin S, Bruchhage M, Ropstad E et al. Effects of peripubertal gonadotropin-releasing hormone agonist on brain development in sheep ... a magnetic resonance imaging study. Psychoneuroendocrinology. 2013;38(10):1994-2002. Doi 10.1016/j.psyneuen.2013.03.009

93 Nuruddin S, Wojniusz S, Ropstad E et al. Peri-pubertal gonadotropin-releasing hormone analog treatment affects hippocampus gene expression without changing spatial orientation in young sheep. Behav Brain Res. 2013;242(1):9-16. Doi 10.1016/j.bbr.2012.12.027 ·

94 Nuruddin S, Krogenaes A, Brynildsrud OB et al. Peri-pubertal gonadotropin-releasing hormone agonist treatment affects sex based gene expression of amygdala in sheep. Psychoneuroendocrinology. 2013;38(12).3115-3127. Doi 10.1016/j.psyneuen.2013.09.011

95 Evans NP, Robinson JE, Erhard HW et al. Development of psycophysiological motoric reactivity is influenced by peripubertal pharmacological inhibition of GnRH action-results of an ovine model. Psychoneuroendocrinology. 2012;37(11):1876-1884. Doi 10.1016/j.psyneuen.2012.03.020

96 Hough D, Bellingham M, Haraldsen IRH et al. 2017 Spatial memory is impaired by peripubertal GnRH agonist treatment and testosterone replacement in sheep. Psychoneuroendocrinology. 2017;75(1):173-182. Doi 10.1016/j.psyneuen.2016.10.016

97 Hough D, Bellingham M, Haraldsen IRH et al. A reduction in long-term spatial memory persists after discontinuation of peripubertal GnRH agonist treatment in sheep. Psychoneuroendocrinology. 2017;77(1):1–8. Doi 10.1016/j.psyneuen.2016.11.029

98 Wojniusz S, Vogele C, Ropstad E et al. Prepubertal gonadotropin-releasing hormone analog leads to exaggerated behavioral and emotional sex differences in sheep. Hormones and Behaviour. 2011;59(1):22-27. Doi 10.1016/j.yhbeh.2010.09.010

99 Prange-Kiel J, Jarry H, Schoen M et al. Gonadotropin releasing hormone regulates spine density via its regulatory role in hippocampal oestrogen synthesis. J Cell Biol. 2008;180(2):417-426. Doi 10.1083/jcb.200707043

100 Quintanar JL, Calderón-Vallejo D, Hernández-Jasso I. Effects of GnRH on Neurite Outgrowth, Neurofilament and Spinophilin Proteins Expression in Cultured Spinal Cord Neurons of Rat Embryos. Neurochem Res. 2016;41(10):2693-2698. Doi 10.1007/s11064-016-1983-0

101 Naftolin F, Ryan KJ, Petro Z. Aromatization of androstenedione by the diencephalon. J Clin Endocrinol Metab. 1971;33(2):368-370. Doi 10.1210/jcem-33-2-368

102 The World Professional Association for Transgender Health. Standards of Care for the Health of Transsexual, Transgender, and Gender Nonconforming People. Version 7. https://www.wpath.org/media/cms/Documents/SOC%20v7/SOC%20V7_English.pdf Accessed 14 July 2018.

103 Shumer DE, Nokoff NJ, Spack NP. Advances in care of transgender children and adolescents. Adv Pediatr. 2016;63(1):79-102. Doi 10.1016/j.yapd.2016.04.018

104 Hembree WC et al. 2009. ibid.

105 Chew D, Anderson J, Williams K et al. Hormonal Treatment in Young people with Gender Dysphoria: a systematic review. Pediatrics 2018;141(4). Doi 10.1542/peds.2017-3742

106 Neurosteroids. Special Issue. J Steroid Biochemistry and molecular biology. 2012;131. https://www.sciencedirect.com/journal/the-journal-of-steroid-biochemistry-and-molecular-biology/vol/131/issue/3

107 Fester L, Prange-kiel J, Jarry H, Rune GM. Estrogen synthesis in the hippocampus. Cell Tissue Res. 2011;345(3):285-294. Doi 10.1007/s00441-011-1221-7

108 Spencer JL, Waters EM, Romeo RD et al. Uncovering the mechanisms of estrogen effects on hippocampal function. Front Neuroendocrinol. 2008;29(2):219-237. Doi 10.1016/j.yfrne.2007.08.006

109 Garcia-Segura LM. Aromatase in the brain: not just for reproduction anymore. J Neuroendocrinol. 2008;20(6):705-712. Doi 10.1111/j.1365-2826.2008.01713.x

110 Terasawa E, Kenealy BP. Neuroestrogen, rapid action of estradiol, and GnRH neurons. Front Neuroendocrinol. 2012;33(4):364-375. Doi 10.1016/j.yfrne.2012.08.001

111 Quintanar JL, Calderón-Vallejo D, Hernández-Jasso I. Effects of GnRH on Neurite Outgrowth, Neurofilament and Spinophilin Proteins Expression in Cultured Spinal Cord Neurons of Rat Embryos. Neurochem Res. 2016;41(10):2693-2698. Doi 10.1007/s11064-016-1983-0

112 "Trans teenagers no longer need judge's approval for hormone therapy, court rules", ABC News, 30 November 2017. http://www.abc.net.au/news/2017-11-30/trans-teens-no-longer-need-court-approval-for-hormone-therapy/9212072 Accessed 14 July 2018.

113 Zubiaurre-Elorza L, Junque C, Gomez-Gil E, & Guillamon A. (2014). Effects of cross-sex hormone treatment on cortical thickness in transsexual individuals. J Sex Med, 2014;11(5):1248–1261. Doi https://doi.org/10.1111/jsm.12491

114 Rametti G, Carrillo, B, Gomez-Gil E, Junque C, Zubiaurre-Elorza L, Segovia S., Gomez A, Karadi K, Guillamon, A. Effects of androgenisation on the white matter microstructure of female-to-male transsexuals. A diffusion tensor imaging study. Psychoneuroendocrinology, 2012;37, 1261–1269. Doi 10.1016/j.psyneuen.2011.12.019

115 Hulshoff Pol HE, Cohen-Kettenis PT, Van Haren NE, et al. Changing your sex changes your brain: Influences of testosterone and estrogen on adult human brain structure. Eur J Endocrinol. 2006;155(1):S107–S111. Doi 10.1530/eje.1.02248

116 Ibid.

117 Ibid.

118 Ibid.

119 Raisman G, Field PM. Sexual dimorphism in the preoptic area of the rat. Science. 1971;173(3998):731-733. Doi 10.1126/science.173.3998.731

120 Block GJ, Gorski RA. Estrogen/progesterone treatment in adulthood affects the size of several components of the medial preoptic area in the male rat. J Comp Neurol. 1988; 275(4):613-622. Doi 10.1002/cne.902750409

121 Nottebohm F. Testosterone triggers growth of brain vocal control nuclei in adult female canaries. Brain Res. 1980;189(2):429-436. Doi 10.1016/0006-8993(80)90102-X

122 Milrod C. How young is too young: Ethical concerns in genital surgery of the transgender MTF adolescent. J Sex Med. 2014;11(2):338-346. Doi 10.1111/jsm.12387

123 Weissler JM, Chang BL, Carney MJ et al. Gender affirming surgery in persons with gender dysphoria. Plast reconstr surg. 2018;141(3):388e-396e, Doi 10.1097/PRS.0000000000004123

124 Rashid M, Tamimy MS. Phalloplasty: the dream and the reality. Indian J Plast Surg. 2013;46(2):283-293. Doi 10.4103/0970-0358.118606

125 Chew D, Anderson J, Williams K et al. Hormonal Treatment in Young people with Gender Dysphoria: a systematic review. Pediatrics 2018;141(4). Doi 10.1542/peds.2017-3742

126 Ibid.

127 Ibid.

128 Becerra-Culqui, et al. Mental Health of Transgender and Gender Nonconforming Youth Compared With Their Peers. 2018 Op. cit.

129 Chew D, et al. Hormonal Treatment in Young people with Gender Dysphoria: a systematic review, 2018. Op. cit.

130 Ibid.

131 Ibid.

132 Shumer DE, Spack NP. Current management of gender identity disorder in childhood and adolescence: guidelines, barriers and areas of controversy. Curr Opin Endocrinol Diabetes Obes. 2013;20(1):69-73. Doi 10.1097/MED.0b013e32835c711e

133 Costa R, Dunsford M, Skagerburg E et al. Psychological support, puberty suppression, and psychosocial functioning in Adolescents with Gender Dysphoria. J Sex Med. 2015;12(11):2206-2214 Doi 10.1111/jsm.13034

134 de Vries AL, McGuire JK, Steensma TD et al. Young adult psychological outcome after puberty suppression and gender reassignment. Pediatrics. 2014;134(4):696-704.Doi 10.1542/peds.2013-2958

135 Schwartz D. Listening to children imagining gender: observing the inflation of an idea. J Homosexuality. 2012;59(3):460-479. Doi 10.1080/00918369.2012.653314

136 Milrod C. How young is too young: Ethical concerns in genital surgery of the transgender MTF adolescent. J Sex Med. 2014;11(2):338-346. Doi 10.1111/jsm.12387

137 Schwartz D. Listening to children imagining gender: observing the inflation of an idea. J Homosexuality. 2012;59(3):460-479. Doi 10.1080/00918369.2012.653314

138 Ibid.

139 Fuss J, Auer MK, Briken P. Gender dysphoria in children and adolescents: a review of recent literature. Curr Opin Psychiatry. 2015;28(6):431-434. Doi 10.1097/YCO.0000000000000203

140 California Senate Bill 1172, Chapter 835, 30 September 2012. http://leginfo.legislature.ca.gov/faces/billNavClient.xhtml?bill_id=201120120SB1172 Accessed 14 July 2018.

141 "Barack Obama calls for end to 'dangerous' practice of conversion therapy for gay minors", ABC News, 9 April 2015. http://www.abc.net.au/news/2015-04-09/obama-calls-for-end-to-conversion-therapy-for-lgbt-youth/6380424 Accessed 14 July 2018.

142 Ontario's *Affirming Sexual Orientation and Gender Identity Act, 2015* https://www.ontario.ca/laws/statute/S15018

143 Cheri DiNovo, Wikipedia. https://en.wikipedia.org/wiki/Cheri_DiNovo Accessed 19 October 2016.

144 "Zero tolerance: Andrews to crack down on gay 'conversion' therapy," *The Age* 24 January 2016. https://www.theage.com.au/national/victoria/zero-tolerance-andrews-to-crack-down-on-gay-conversion-therapy-20160123-gmcimw.html Accessed 20 October 2016.

145 Parliamentary debates, (Hansard) Legislative Assembly. 58th Parliament, First session. Wednesday, 10 February 2016, pg. 97. https://www.parliament.vic.gov.au/images/stories/daily-hansard/Assembly_2016/Assembly_Daily_Extract_Wednesday_10_February_2016_from_Book_1.pdf

146 *Health Complaints Act 2017*, Section 3.

147 Ibid, Section12 (2) (a)

148 Ibid., Section 3.

149 Ibid., Section 39 (3).

150 Transgender students in schools – legal rights and responsibilities", *Legal Issues Bulletin No 55*, December 2014, Education and Communities, NSW Government. https://education.nsw.gov.au/about-us/rights-and-accountability/media/documents/public-legal-issues-bulletins/LIB-55-Transgender-students-in-schools-legal-rights-and-responsibilities.pdf Accessed 18 August 2017.

151 "ALP National Platform: Consultation Report", April 2018, pg. 183.
https://d3n8a8pro7vhmx.cloudfront.net/australianlaborparty/pages/121/attachments/original/1524719995/2018_ALP_National_Platform_-_Consultation_Draft.pdf?1524719995 Accessed 14 July 2018.

152 "Federal Labor vows to crack down on gay conversion therapy", *Sydney Morning Herald,* 21 April 2018.
https://www.smh.com.au/national/federal-labor-vows-to-crack-down-on-gay-conversion-therapy-20180421-p4zawu.html Accessed 14 July 2018.

153 *A smart, modern fair Australia,* ALP National Platform 2015, pg. 193.
https://cdn.australianlabor.com.au/documents/ALP_National_Platform.pdf

154 Hembree WC. et al. (2009), Op. cit.

CHAPTER 15

EXILES IN THEIR OWN FLESH: A PSYCHOTHERAPIST SPEAKS[1]

By Lane Anderson (a pseudonym)[2]

I am a licensed psychotherapist. I'm writing this article (2015) on my last day at a teen health clinic, where I've seen patients and their families for nearly a decade.

In recent years especially, it's become increasingly clear to me that I cannot uphold the primary value of my profession, to do no harm, without also seriously jeopardizing my standing in the professional community. It's a terrible and unfortunate conflict of interest. I've lost much sleep over the fact that, for a significant portion of my clients and their parents, I am unable to provide what they profess to come to me seeking: sound clinical judgement. Increasingly, providing such judgement puts me at risk of violating the emergent trans narrative which–seemingly overnight and without any explanation or push-back of which I am aware–has usurped the traditional mental health narrative.

When I am suddenly, and without warning, discouraged from exploring the underlying causes and conditions of certain of my patients' distress (as I was trained to do), and instead forced to put my professional stamp of approval upon a prefab, one-size-fits-all narrative intended to explain the complexity of my patients' troubles, I feel confused. It's as if I am being held hostage. No longer encouraged or permitted to question, consider or discuss the full spectrum of my patients' mental health concerns, it has occurred to me that I am being used, my meagre professional authority commandeered to legitimize a new narrative I may or may not wish to corroborate.

It's been perilous to simply admit to not fully understanding it all– let alone *disagree* with the trans narrative. There was no training or teaching. I was just suddenly told that some of my patients thought they were trapped in the wrong body and that was that.

After much soul searching, I felt I had no choice but to remove myself from this crippling work setting. Being told to exercise my clinical judgement with some clients, while ignoring it with others, made me feel like a fraud.

Throughout my career, I have come to my work with these thoughts in mind: that life is complex, that people are complex. But, in one way or another, most people tend to balk at that kind of ambiguity. I try to assist people in flexing a little, try to help them find ways to manage life's grey areas, and the occasional distress that comes from simply being conscious. But, at the end of the day, I couldn't deny it was a little weird for me to go on believing I could effectively teach others to be less rigid, more free people facing their lives head on, when I myself, their humble guide, was being exploited, tongue-tied by a new party line.

There are so many complex forces, from many different realms, coming into play with this trans wave. Most people are completely unaware of these intersecting interests.

Unfortunately, the culture war has done a number on the concept of critical thinking. I have considered myself liberal my entire adult life, and I still am. But, for a long time, I couldn't find anyone questioning this trans explosion who wasn't on the far right. It made me feel like only conservatives were allowed to think, to consider this issue but, ultimately, their thoughts were rendered meaningless due to their branding by the culture war. It's essential that left-leaning people model critical thinking for the masses in this regard.

It's important to link people like us together, who have been silenced, so we can resume contact with our critical thinking skills and reduce our growing sense of self-doubt. Divide and conquer is best accomplished through silencing, through calling into question those who speak out. There is so much of this attached to the trans movement. Even just *wondering* about a profound concept such as transgender is labeled transphobic. What I think has happened is that people are now phobic about their own gut responses to life. We are being systematically separated from our own intuition. This is fatal for a civilization, I think. Not that our intuition always tells the truth with a capital T, but it is a critical piece of who we are. Without it, we remain profoundly directionless, and more susceptible to coercion of all types.

What frightens me most about the trans movement is that the establishment has gotten involved and is leading it. I think that's really weird. Clearly, they are benefiting from it financially. So sad. It disturbs me to see how giddy my former medical director is to be part of this growing craze. We used to treat kids with mental health problems, but now it's all about validating their emergent and shifting identities. As professionals, if we don't loudly prioritize their identities as being the most important thing about them (and identities do shift constantly in kids and teens), we risk coming across as unsupportive and even immoral. Identity development has always been a teen task but, in the past, it wasn't necessarily supposed to become a lifestyle, or colonize the entirety of your existence.

Our world is in a profound state of flux. We can't begin to comprehend what the Internet has done to how we see ourselves. People are looking for ways to belong, ways to understand who they are in place and in time. They are looking to reduce the anxiety that comes when too much change happens all at once. I try and look at trans folks as people who are seeking to answer the new questions that have emerged in this early 21st century. I have been trying to find a way to understand their urges to detach from their bodies, to undo that feeling of exile they experience in their own flesh. We all want to get back to ourselves; it is our duty to reconnect with those weighty parts that inevitably sink to the depths of us, the parts too heavy to remain on the surface of our lives.

From what I can see, the age-old human task to reclaim that which has gone missing appears to be manifesting with great prominence in the trans community. The problem is this: we all look for short cuts to finding the lost treasure. It's human nature to resist the long and serpentine journey to our own sense of personal truth. In our fear, in our self-doubt, we calculate the risk and often decide it is preferable to be shown what another person – a "helping professional" or an activist – bills as a sure thing, a direct path to what we sense we lack. We all, on some level, hold a child-like fantasy that someone else has figured it out and can provide us a direct map to ourselves. And that's what the trans narrative does. It promises to guide the follower to their essential, authentic self. But this, unfortunately, doesn't happen, because the essential self, whatever that is, is not created from another's road map, but can only be comprised of the trails we forge ourselves.

What saddens me the most is the way children are being trained to think their parents do not love them if mom and dad don't jump aboard the trans train. To me, this is a brutal aspect of a near-dictatorship being foisted on everyone. The kids are too young to see that there are no other people who will have their backs, throughout life with lasting devotion, in the unique way their families will. They think these new friends they've made online understand them perfectly. And, in believing this unquestioningly, they find themselves lulled by the frictionless experience delivered most powerfully by group think.

Of course, I'm describing the pull of all cults; that deep human desire to be known through and through and through. The cult experience seeks to end the frustration that naturally comes when we mature and begin to see ourselves as separate beings. In our separateness, we must do the hard work of truly learning to know another. Group think reduces the fear that comes when we are unsure if we will be located by another, when we remain unable to locate *ourselves.*

Cults and closed narratives neutralize and tame what we see as the unknown. I think somebody needs to put a refresher out there on the cult mindset and group think. People seem to have forgotten that we are all very easily influenced by each other. Carl Elliot wrote about this in relation to body dysmorphic disorder (people wanting to amputate their own limbs because they dis-identify with them) in the *Atlantic*, "A new way to be mad".

One common trait I've noticed in nearly all the trans kids I've met has been their profound sense of being different, and too alone. They often have had little success with making friends, or what I would call contact with "the other". Because of their psychic isolation, they are prime targets for group think narratives. But, in addition to looking for a way to belong, they are also craving protection and the stamp of legitimacy, perhaps because they feel a profound lack of it.

Now that the government and medical communities are involved in the creation of who trans folks are, this class of individuals have finally found their safe havens. Now, rather than being merely invisible and awkward, they have been transformed into veritable leaders of a revolution. Now, rather than cower in the shadows, they have commandeered the narratives of others into a similar dark and brooding place where they once were. The tables, as they lived and viewed them, have now turned.

It's got to be dizzying for these formerly "ugly ducklings" to find themselves at the center of a flock of swans. To become a part of the movement, to finally be seen and found as whole, alive, and most importantly, *wanted*, all they have to do is renounce the very bodies in which they feel they have been imprisoned. In doing so, the promised payoff is very big, for they have finally found a way to render mute all those who once discounted and disbelieved them. Through silencing others who threaten them, they have unearthed a means of silencing their own self-hate. Rather than being afraid of themselves, they make others fear what they have become.

Psychologically, these interpersonal tactics would once upon a time have been categorized as immature, "primitive" defenses erected by an undifferentiated self that cannot see the self or others as whole creatures. But, as I witness it in my own practice, this is the basic thinking underlying the psychology of the trans narrative. In her recent blog post, "My Disservice to My Transgender Patients", Dr. Kathy Mandigo talks about feeling threatened by some of her MTF (male-to-female) patients. Many of the trans kids I've worked with will joke about how they and their friends are dictators, "masters of the universe"! I find that clinically significant.

This is something toddlers do when they are first discovering they are separate from their rulers (parents). Rather than fear the parent, they seek to control the parent, exert their will on the parent and co-opt the parent's power as their own. In doing this, they hide from view their terror at facing their own powerlessness. Ideally, the child will gradually outgrow this urge to control, will gradually relinquish the dictatorial need to create safety through controlling the external realm. When that happens, we say it is a sign of maturity. As our own sense of agency grows, we are better able to forfeit the habit of controlling others. We also begin to feel guilt at the idea of controlling others, as we begin to see them as separate from us, 3D human beings instead of mere props on our psychic stage.

Unfortunately, some people have a hard time making this shift. They get stuck or addicted to manipulating their external environment, and will continue to create inner safety through the constant and relentless work of controlling others.

Last week, in a team meeting, our medical director said he was meeting with a girl who identifies as FTM (female-to-male) to discuss top surgery and testosterone treatment. Apparently, according to the director, the girl's mom is slowing down the process of transition. Bad mom, right? The director added that the girl's mom told her that *nine* out of *nine* of her daughter's friends also identify as FTM.

At this point, I couldn't hold my tongue any longer. I said, "Can we not be honest and see that we are dealing with a trend?" Of course, everyone else at the table was mute. Considering I'm leaving my post, I felt bold enough to say that I found it infuriating we couldn't discuss this topic clinically. More silent colleagues (except their eyes were wide as if they wanted me to keep talking and taking the risk for them). I said that what we were doing as a medical community was potentially very harmful, and made mention of some of the videos I'd watched featuring transmen who decided to go off testosterone. The medical director prides himself in providing special services for those patients he deems unjustly marginalized by society. But he can't see how the medical community has become complicit in the oppression he earnestly seeks to remedy.

A large part of the problem comes with the revolution in health care. More and more, we are giving people the power to define their own treatments. This is good in many ways, but the trans movement is using this moment, and is actively recruiting young, psychologically undefined and frightened people to push their agenda through the medical community. It's clearly not that difficult to do. These kids are just pawns. That's how it looks to me, anyway. The trans community needs more converts so that the narrative becomes more cohesive. I'm guessing the push for this comes from a need to further cohere so they will have more members to fully cement a fragile, constructed reality.

We – people who don't identify as trans – are the external realm that must be controlled to bring the trans community the inner peace they now lack. But they don't get that they will never find calm or strength this way. You cannot find yourself through coercing others. You cannot extinguish your fears by turning from them. The trans community must face their own fears, face themselves and their own demons. They can't wipe out their fear that they are not really transitioning by censoring the thoughts and expressions of others. If they believe they are trans, they shouldn't need to spend so much effort foisting that belief on others.

The fact that they do dictate to others is, to me, diagnostic of their very condition. They are uncertain about who and what they are. No sin in that. That's human. The transgression comes in refusing to accept this uncertainty, and in sacrificing the lives and consciences of others to nullify your own self-doubt.

Endnotes

1. "Exiles in their own flesh: A psychotherapist speaks", was originally published on the web page,4thWaveNow, 22 August 2015.
https://4thwavenow.com/2015/08/22/exiles-in-their-own-flesh-a-psychotherapist-speaks/ Accessed 19 April 2017. It is published with permission of Lane Anderson.

2. Lane Anderson also recommends, "Listening to Children Imagining Gender: Observing the Inflation of an Idea", by David Schwartz PhD., Journal of Homosexuality, Volume 59, 2012, Issue 3, a special issue on The Treatment of Gender Dysphoric/Gender Variant (GD/GV) Children and Adolescents. http://dx.doi.org/10.1080/00918369.2012.653314

CHAPTER 16

ABOLISHING WOMEN'S SAFE SPACES

If we cannot name a phenomenon, we certainly cannot fight it. Gender ideology is harmful to women and girls.

Mary Lou Singleton[1]

16.1 INTRODUCTION

One result of writing gender identity into law is to allow biological males who identify as females to be legally recognised as women.

This has knock-on effects for women and girls as many of the rights, protections, privileges and access to services – that respect women's privacy and provided them safety – are now also bestowed on biological men who identify as women. Many feminists have argued that this effectively erases the identity of women as biological females in many areas of the culture.

This chapter examines how women from diverse backgrounds, and in many different circumstances, have reacted to transgender laws that allow biological men to identify as women.

16.2 US MIDWIVES REPLACE "PREGNANT WOMAN" WITH "PREGNANT PERSON"

The Midwives Alliance of North America (MANA) was formed in 1982 as a professional organisation for midwives, student midwives and other healthcare providers.

In 2014, MANA replaced the term "pregnant woman" in its *Midwives Alliance Core Competencies* document with "birthing parent", "pregnant people", "pregnant person" and "pregnant individuals". This was to avoid offending transgenders, particularly female-to-males who become pregnant, and biological men who identify as women.[2]

The *Core Competencies* document did not make a complete transformation to gender-neutral language. Somewhat inconsistently, it still used terms like "mother", meaning "a mother related to her child or children"[3]; and "midwifery" and "midwife", meaning "a person, typically a woman, who is trained to assist women in childbirth"[4].

Reacting to the changes, the Woman-Centered Midwifery group issued an Open Letter to MANA opposing the changes in August 2016. The letter said that "women are all but missing from the language" due to the "erasure" of the word "woman". The letter added:

> We know as midwives that biological sex occurs at the level of our DNA and the gametes we produce, and is immutable. By embracing the idea that any human other than those in a class called women carry offspring to term, give birth to them and nurse them, we are prioritizing gender identity over biological reality ...
>
> The very few gender-identified males that have given birth or accessed an abortion have only done so because they are female-bodied people, and that scientific fact cannot be erased.[5]

The Woman-Centered Midwifery website elaborated on this biological reality, saying:

> [P]regnancy and birth can never be 'biologically neutral'[6] ...
>
> We understand that a "woman" is a mature human female and that only females are capable of conceiving, gestating, and birthing children.[7]

The Woman-Centered Midwifery Open Letter was criticised by transgender female-to-male and parent of two, Trevor MacDonald.

Born female, MacDonald transitioned to male by taking testosterone and undergoing chest surgery. When MacDonald and partner decided to start a family, MacDonald stopped hormone therapy and was able to become pregnant. MacDonald did not plan to breastfeed, assuming it would not be possible, but decided to try after learning that "even a small amount of milk could be really valuable to my baby", and that "breastfeeding is about more than the milk. It can be a relationship too and a whole way of parenting"[8].

> In 2012, MacDonald founded the international support group, Birthing and Breast or Chestfeeding Trans People and Allies[9] and, in 2014, formed a research team through the University of Ottawa, which obtained funding from the Canadian Institutes of Health Research. The purpose was to conduct qualitative research about transmasculine individuals' experiences of pregnancy, birthing, and feeding their newborns.[10]

MacDonald supported the MANA *Core Competencies* inclusion of gender-neutral language that would not offend "transgender, genderqueer and intersex" recognition, while labelling the Woman-Centered Midwifery objection as "transphobia in the midwifery community"[11].

16.3 AUSTRALIAN MIDWIVES REJECT "PERSON-CENTRED" CARE

In 2017, Australia's Nursing and Midwifery Board, representing 30,000 midwives, issued a new draft code of conduct that proposed replacing references to "woman-centred care" with "person-centred care"[12].

The Advertiser newspaper asked the Board to explain the reasons for the proposed change in language. The response from a Board "spokesperson" was not couched in terms of avoiding discrimination against transgenders, but argued that proposed changes in the codes of conduct for both nursing and midwifery were to recognise both the person receiving care and the person's family and others. However, the change would have accorded with the trangenderism push for gender-neutral language.

The Board received submissions from the profession, academics and individuals opposing the proposed changes.

University of South Australia midwifery professor Mary Steen told *The Advertiser*:

> Midwife means with woman. The woman is at the centre of a midwife's scope of practice, which is based on the best available evidence to provide the best care and support to meet individual women's health and wellbeing needs.[13]

Professor Alison Kitson, vice-president and executive dean of the College of Nursing and Health Sciences at Flinders University, agreed, saying:

> Retaining the "woman-centred" term is important to remind us all that our care is focused on the women and the significant life-changing experience they are about to have.[14]

Selena Pregarc, who was 32 weeks pregnant and under the care of an obstetrician and a midwife, said:

> The most feminine thing to do is to carry a baby. Women are really the only ones who can have children and midwives are there to help women through.[15]

Dr Caroline Homer, from the Centre for Midwifery at Sydney's University of Technology, argued:

> Person-centred care also removes the woman from the central role in her child-bearing experience and renders her invisible.[16]

The Australian College of Midwives argued similarly:

> Once we start moving down the road of talking about women as persons, we lose women's identity – that fundamental essence.

> Women are struggling to have their voices heard enough as it is. It's another chip at women's identity.[17]

Following a flood of submissions, the Australia's Nursing and Midwifery Board said it would change the code for nurses, but not for midwives. While the nursing code will use the term "person-centred" care, the midwifery code is retaining "woman-centred" care.[18]

Australia has a number of hospitals serving women's health. Would a shift to gender-neutral language for women's health services lead to women's hospitals being renamed in gender-neutral terms? Would Melbourne's Royal Women's Hospital be renamed the Royal Person's Hospital? Would Melbourne's Mercy Hospital for Women be renamed the Mercy Hospital for Persons?

16.4   US RESTROOM AND CHANGE ROOM PRIVACY CONFLICTS

In the United States, the conflict between new transgender rights and the privacy of biological women came into focus when parents and school authorities resisted the claim by a transgender female-to-male student, Gavan Grimm, for the right to use male restrooms.

In June 2015, Grimm sued the Gloucester County, Virginia School Board because it would not allow him access to the boys' restroom.

Originally, the district had allowed Grimm access to male facilities but, after complaints by families of children at the school, the decision was revised to allow only biological girls to use the female facilities and only biological boys to use the male facilities. Instead, the school's three single-occupancy bathrooms, which were available for any student at the school, were offered to any transgender students.

Grimm did not accept this attempt at a compromise arrangement and sued the school district for alleged unlawful discrimination.[19]

In 2016, the Obama administration's Departments of Justice and Education added to the controversy when it sent a "Dear Colleague" letter to American schools. The letter declared that schools must allow "students to participate in sex-segregated activities and access sex-segregated facilities consistent with their gender identity" because "both federal agencies treat a student's gender identity as the student's sex for purposes of enforcing Title IX"[20]. Title IX is a 1972 law banning discrimination on the basis of sex in federally funded education programs.[21]

In early 2017, President Donald Trump rescinded the Obama administration's letter.[22] In mid-2017, the Grimm case was taken to the US Supreme Court, which sent the case off to a lower court,[23] where it appears to have faltered.

Of interest is some of the testimony presented to the courts in the Grimm case by concerned females who had faced similar situations to those faced by girls at the Gloucester County school.

Consider the statement of a teenage girl, identified as S.H.

> I previously attended a public middle school in Illinois. I am 14 years of age. My former public middle school feeds into a public high school which permits males into female restrooms, based upon whether they profess a female gender identity. The high school district adopted this policy a couple of years ago, without notifying the parents of this change. The school district also let one student have access to locker rooms formerly reserved for the opposite sex.
>
> The idea of permitting a person with male anatomy –regardless of whether he identifies as a girl – in girls' locker rooms, showers and changing areas, and restrooms, makes me extremely uncomfortable and makes me feel unsafe as well.
>
> Even the idea that a boy or man is allowed in those areas makes me anxious and fearful, regardless of whether I ever encounter them in any of those places. I feel unsafe because I am concerned that a boy or man can access the girls' facilities by just professing a female identity, and that would allow them to take advantage of the school's policies in order to see me and my friends as we have to undress for school.
>
> They could take pictures of us with their phones and then post them to the internet. I would feel especially violated in the event that the school district's policy enabled a person with male genitalia, regardless of what gender that person professes, to see me partially or fully undressed. I also do not want to be exposed to male genitalia in any way while in facilities formerly designated for girls only.[24]

Consider also the statement of J.S., a survivor of childhood sexual abuse, in an amicus brief from Safe Spaces for Women. Her comments were in relation to a similar situation to that of the Grimm case, a Washington Administrative Code allowing men who gender identify as female to enter women's locker rooms, spas, and restrooms.

> As a survivor of childhood molestation and rape, the passage of this [Washington] law left me feeling vulnerable and exposed in areas [in which] I should be protected.
>
> I worked for many years to heal from the emotional, physical, and spiritual effects of the trauma inflicted by my childhood attacker. Depression, panic attacks, suicidal thoughts, Post Traumatic Stress Disorder, and physical phantom pains are a legacy of my past abuse. I had been panic-attack free for over a decade when Washington's law went into effect.
>
> Now, using a public bathroom is very difficult and has led to many panic attacks. I have not entered a public women's locker room in over a year. Before Washington's law was passed, if I encountered a man in the women's bathroom or locker room, management, staff, police and the general public would all have been there to protect my privacy and safety. This is no longer the case. To be in a position where I am left exposed, separate from others and no longer have a voice, is the same position I was in as a child of eight.[25]

These testimonies express the concerns of women in jurisdictions where laws, regulations and state policies are granting transgenders access to the restrooms of their choice. They echo the concerns of women recorded at the very start of this book in Chapter 1.1.

The restroom controversies have spread to many US States.

North Carolina enacted a law mandating that, in government buildings, including schools, people use only bathrooms that correspond to their sex as recorded on their birth certificate. While the North Carolina *Public Facilities Privacy & Security Act* was approved into law in 2016, portions of the measure were later repealed in 2017 as part of a compromise between the Democratic governor and Republican-controlled Legislature. Celebrities and corporations reacted by boycotting North Carolina.

Similar moves in other states have been stymied.

The issue is not about acceptance or rejection of transgenders. It is about the safety of biological women and their right to privacy.

16.5   AUSTRALIAN TOILET CONTROVERSIES

In Australia, the federal *Sex Discrimination Act 1984* (SDA), and some state and territory anti-discrimination laws that recognise a person by their gender identity, are being claimed as grounds for the provision of gender-neutral toilets and change rooms, or as grounds for allowing a transgender person to use the facilities of their choice.

There are many examples.

In recent years, the education departments of NSW, Victoria, Queensland and South Australia have said that federal and state laws require that, if a biological boy identifies as a girl, then this child must be allowed to use female facilities; conversely for females (see Chapter 12.2).

In May 2015, the Australian Human Rights Commission's (AHRC) *Resilient Individuals* reported that some universities had introduced progressive initiatives like "gender neutral toilets ... Others, however, have some way to go"[26].

In 2016, Melbourne University, with 42,000 students, planned to designate 37 bathrooms at its main campus as "all gender" facilities. Other universities are making similar changes.[27]

By 2017, sections of the federal public service had plans to introduce gender-neutral bathrooms. The federal Department of Environment and Energy was planning to install "inclusive" bathrooms at its Canberra headquarters, while the Treasury building was to be fitted out with unisex bathrooms as part of a refurbishment.[28]

In 2017, the National Building Codes Board received a submission to make gender-neutral toilets compulsory in all public and commercial buildings. The matter was to be referred for consideration at the Building Minister Forum in early 2018. A spokesperson for Parents and Friends of Lesbians and Gays (PFLAG) said gender-neutral toilets are an essential part of creating an inclusive society.[29]

Once a person is recognised by their gender identity in law, access to toilets, showers and change rooms involves either:

(a) separate Male, Female and Unisex/Other restrooms, an option ruled out by some transgenders; or

(b) transgenders choosing to use the Male or Female restroom of their choice; or

(c) making all restrooms Unisex.

The arguments for these options vary.

One view is that making a person use the restroom identified by their birth sex causes embarrassment and discrimination against transgenders. The counter view is that it violates the right to privacy and physical safety of those who regard their birth sex as self-evident.

In the case of (c), the 2017 BBC two-part documentary, *No more boys and girls: can our kids go gender free?*, experimented in various way with breaking down sex differences in a UK primary school. One method was to have the school experiment provide only gender-neutral toilets. The organiser of the program admitted that "[t]he children didn't like the [unisex] toilet"[30]. The girls were particularly uncomfortable. Arguably, this experiment confused cultural differences that are not based on biological sex – boys wear blue, girls pink; boys play with trucks, girls with dolls – with cultural practices that are biologically based, such as providing separate Male/Female restrooms to respect privacy concerns of men and women. In reality, it doesn't matter if some girls wear blue and some boys play with dolls. It does matter that their privacy is respected and they are protected when they are most vulnerable.

It is claimed that, as unisex toilets usually are floor-to-ceiling cubicles, privacy and safety are preserved. It's also the case that females can be trapped in such a cubicle by a male, and many girls and women don't like sharing the common washbasin area with males.

Once again, this is the imposition of uniformity, the opposite of diversity.

16.6 MEDICAL TRIALS AND TREATMENTS ACCORDING TO SEX-BASED BIOLOGY

Men can suffer from different medical conditions from women. Women are subject to cervical, uterine, and ovarian cancers, while men can develop prostate cancer. However, the medical issues go beyond diseases associated with reproductive organs.

As discussed in Chapter 3.2, around 6,500 human genes have been found to express differently in men and women. Hence, it is not surprising that medical research has found that men and women also differ in certain patterns of illness and disease risk factors, and respond differently to many forms of medical treatments. This underscores the importance of distinguishing between men and women in medical trials. These differences have been considered so important in medicine that it has led to a new branch of science called sex-based biology.

Liu and Mager (2016) conducted a review of "the history and progress of women's inclusion in clinical trials for prescription drugs" and presented "considerations for researchers, clinicians, and academicians on this issue". They concluded that "[t]he importance of considering the differences between the male and female sex in clinical decision-making is crucial"[31].

They cited the US Institute of Medicine, now the National Academy of Medicine, which, in 2001, published *Exploring the Biological Contributions to Human Health: Does Sex Matter?* The Academy's Committee on Understanding the Biology of Sex and Gender Differences

> examined biology from the cellular to the organismal and behavioral levels, and concluded that differences do occur and can have important consequences. They concluded that sex (being male or female) should be recognized as an important variable in research and increased knowledge in this area should be cultivated. The growth of knowledge has become a branch of science known as sex-based biology ...

Liu and Mager indicated important areas of difference between biological men and women:

> Sex differences can be observed in various disease states in prevalence, diagnosis, severity, and outcomes ...
>
> [T]here may be differences in patient outcomes or responses to treatment between men and women ...
>
> [T]he differences between the sexes in circulating levels of endogenous hormones, such as testosterone and estradiol, can affect pharmacokinetic or pharmacodynamic parameters ...
>
> Pharmacodynamic differences between the sexes have been observed for particular drugs ... Although detected pharmacokinetic and pharmacodynamics differences may not indicate clinically meaningful outcomes, there are still differences that may be clinically significant yet remain unknown ...
>
> Health disparities are also observed between men and women, which may be due to biological, cultural, social, or economic factors.[32]

How is medical research to proceed in the interests of combatting sex-specific diseases, and measuring the different responses of biological women and men to medical trials, if identity documents fail to record people as biologically male or female? Will medical and pharmaceutical trials conducted according to a person's birth sex be considered discrimination against transgender persons?

What are the rights of patients under new transgender laws? Consider sensitive, sex-specific medical examinations and treatments. In January 2018, a British woman went public after a transsexual nurse with stubble and tattoos was sent to perform her pap smear at a London health clinic. The female patient said she was "embarrassed and distressed" and lodged a complaint. Her complaint was not about the nurse's gender or physical appearance. Rather, "[p]eople who are not comfortable about this are presented as bigots and this is ... kind of how I was made to feel about it", she said.[33]

Under transgender anti-discrimination laws, will women have the right to ask for females to take pap smears and carry out other intimate examinations and treatments? Or will women be accused of discrimination against transsexual male-to-females if they ask for biological females to carry out intimate medical examinations and treatments?

16.7 WOMEN'S PRISONS

Should transgenders be accommodated in sex-specific prisons according to their birth or according to how they identify as opposite to their birth sex?

Gender identity anti-discrimination laws suggest that they have some claim to the prison of their choice. There is considerable documentation of sexual assaults on transsexuals in prisons, particularly in male prisons.[34]

Further, the British Association of Gender Identity Specialists told the recent UK Parliamentary Transgender Equality Inquiry that the Association was concerned about "patients who were charged with crimes, convicted and who ended up on the sex offenders register when we thought that the same thing wouldn't have happened if they weren't a trans person"[35]. The Association numbers over a hundred members and comprises the overwhelming majority of clinicians working in gender identity clinics in the British Isles, including speech therapists, psychologists, psychiatrists, surgeons, psychosexual counsellors, nurses, occupational therapists, endocrinologists, general practitioners and social workers.

On the other hand, accommodating biological males who identify as females in prisons puts at risk biological women prisoners.

Consider these cases.

In Australia, Maddison Hall (born Noel Crompton in 1964) shot and killed hitchhiker Lyn Saunders at Gol Gol, New South Wales. After being convicted in 1989, Hall began hormone treatment while in prison, and was transferred to the women's Mulawa Correctional Centre in 1999, where it was alleged that Hall had sexual relations with several female prisoners. After three months, Hall was alleged to have raped a woman and was returned to a male prison. Hall was charged with rape, but a case did not proceed after the alleged victim was released, returned to New Zealand and refused to press charges. After being returned to a male prison, Hall sued the state of NSW claiming psychological trauma, and received an out-of-court settlement for $25,000, which was used to fund Hall's sex-reassignment surgery in 2003.[36]

In the UK, Martin Ponting, who was sentenced to life in 1995 for the rape of two girls under the age of 16, was moved to the all-women prison of Bronzefield in Surrey in 2017 because he now identifies as a woman and goes by the name of Jessica Winfield.[37] He received a £10,000 National Health Service sex change in prison. He started molesting inmates almost immediately after transferring to a women's prison. He has since been segregated.[38] One of the women he victimised stated, "To assume the identity of a woman after what he did is a kick in the teeth"[39]. Some pro-trans observers have criticised the media for "deadnaming" Ponting; that is, mentioning his old name, Martin Ponting, rather than solely using his new name, Jessica Winfield.[40]

Ian Huntley, a serial rapist and child molester who murdered two 10-year-old girls in 2002,[41] now goes under the name Lian and says he wants to change gender so he can live in a women's prison.[42]

A 2017 report by the UK campaign group Fair Play for Women suggests that placing transwomen in female prisons may be even more risky for the other inmates. The report was produced by *Dr Nicola Williams, a research scientist specialising in human biology who has held a number of senior scientific positions within the pharmaceutical industry.* Williams found that, despite the imprecision of prison figures, 41 per cent of trans male-to-female prisoners in England and Wales are sex offenders, compared with a proportion of 17 per cent in the prison population as a whole.[43]

The Times has also reported:

> In previously unpublicised evidence to the Commons women and equalities committee, the British Psychological Society warned that some biological men convicted of sex crimes had "falsely claimed" to be transgender "as a means of demonstrating reduced risk and so gaining parole" or in rare cases it has been thought that the person is "seeking better access to females and young children through presenting in an apparently female way"[44].

Further, the British Association of Gender Identity Specialists warned the UK parliament's Transgender Equality Inquiry in the UK Parliament of an ever-increasing tide of referrals of patients in prison serving long or indeterminate sentences for serious sexual offences. These vastly outnumber the number of prisoners incarcerated for more ordinary, non-sexual offences. It has been rather naïvely suggested that nobody would seek to pretend transsexual status in prison if this were not actually the case.

> There are, to those of us who actually interview the prisoners, in fact very many reasons why people might pretend this. These vary from the opportunity to have trips out of prison through to a desire for a transfer to the female estate (to the same prison as a co-defendant) through to the idea that a parole board will perceive somebody who is female as being less dangerous through to a [false] belief that hormone treatment will actually render one less dangerous through to wanting a special or protected status within the prison system and even (in one very well evidenced case that a highly concerned Prison Governor brought particularly to my attention) a plethora of prison intelligence information suggesting that the driving force was a desire to make subsequent sexual offending very much easier, females being generally perceived as low risk in this regard. I am sure that the Governor concerned would be happy to talk about this.[45]

In her book, *Gender Hurts* (2004), Sheila Jeffreys, former Professor of Feminist Politics in the School of Social and Political Science at the University of Melbourne, says:

> The men who are being given the right to live alongside women in prison include some of the most dangerous to women's safety – men who have been convicted of crimes of grave violence including the murder of women.[46]

In 2010, Italy resolved the vexed issue of transsexual prisoners by converting an under-utilised, medium-security women's prison into a specially equipped detention centre for transgender inmates. It was estimated that Italy had about 60 transgender prisoners at the time. Leading gay rights groups said they welcome the new prison as a dedicated space providing the psychological support transgender prisoners need.[47]

In the absence of other such prisons, will anti-discrimination laws see state authorities face legal action by prisoners for refusing to allow men who identify as women, "whether by way of medical intervention or not", to be accommodated in women's prisons?

While allowing transsexual prisoners to access the prison of their choice is said to be in the interests of protecting transsexuals in prisons, such policies are open for any man identifying as a woman for any reason to gain access to a women's prison and, in some cases, putting the safety of biologically female prisoners at risk.

16.8 WOMEN'S SERVICES, SAFE SPACES, AFFIRMATIVE ACTION

In many Australian jurisdictions, anti-discrimination laws allow for

> a general exemption in relation to special services, benefits or facilities that are designed to meet the special needs of people with a particular attribute or to prevent or reduce a disadvantage suffered by those people in their education, accommodation, training or welfare. For example, special measures may exist for women, people with a disability or people within a particular age or religious group.[48]

Overwhelmingly, exemptions to anti-discrimination laws are to provide safe spaces and specialist services to women.

For example, the Anti-Discrimination Board of NSW lists 89 exemptions to the NSW *Anti-Discrimination Act 1977*. Approximately 80 are for women's organisations, such as refuges, gyms, career education, medical services, disability services, leadership training, education scholarships and female swimming classes. Exemptions have also been granted to some men's sporting and support organisations and for some gay clubs.[49]

Until recently, anti-discrimination laws have aimed to protect biological women against discrimination, allowing for exemptions to provide safe spaces and specialist services to women. Gaze and Smith (2017) point out that, after the *Sex Discrimination Act* was passed in 1984, "some early complaints were from men who argued that specialist women's health services, domestic violence support services, or women's-only gyms or sessions in swimming pools were discriminatory"[50]. These claims were rejected on the grounds that certain female spaces and services were necessary to provide substantive equality for women.

A leading case in the issue of women's-only services concerned Fernwood Fitness Centres, a large provider of women's gyms. In 1996, the Victorian Civil and Administrative Tribunal ruled that it could provide health and fitness gyms catering for women only and to permit those centres to be staffed by women only under the Victoria's *Equal Opportunity Act*.[51] This was one of a number of exemptions granted periodically to Fernwood in different states.

However, where laws like the Federal *Sex Discrimination Act 1984*, as amended in 2013, give legal protection to persons by their gender identity, men who identify as women can claim access to these services and spaces, unless a court provides an exemption.

So, what happens if a man identifying as a woman seeks to access a women's safe space such as a homeless shelter or other women's space?

As Ruth Barrett et al argue in the recent book, *Female Erasure* (2016), this is erasing women and girls from the public square.[52]

16.9   ERASING FEMALE, FEMINISM, GAY, LESBIAN

Erasing feminism: If a biological man can identify as a woman, then this allows any man who chooses to self-identify as a woman to claim all the rights, protections, privileges and access to services once reserved only for biological women. The logic of the claim by transgender/queer theory that sex is only a social construct, and of laws recognising a person by their gender identity, is that the essence of what it is to be a "woman" is blurred, if not erased (see Chapter 8.7).

If there is no biological female as distinct from biological male, there is no feminism. If there is no sex, there can be no "sexism", no male patriarchy, no male discrimination against women. A biological man who identifies as female can say, "you cannot accuse me of sexism because I am the same as you".

As Carol Downer comments in *Female Erasure* (2016),

> A close reading of Judith Butler, one of the main queer activists and theorists, reveals that she wants the feminist movement to cease its efforts against the oppression of women on the basis of sex ... I suspect that few feminists or genderqueer people realise that this is queer theory's position ...[53]

> Categorising people by gender [identity], rather than sex, erases female experience.[54]

Erasing lesbian and gay: Gays and lesbians have been the "load-bearing wall" of LGBTIQ rights. However, legally recognising people by their gender identity, rather than their sex, blurs, if not erases the meaning of lesbian and gay (see Chapter 8.7). The terms "lesbian" and "gay" are defined as sexual attractions between biological women and sexual attractions between biological men, respectively.

As Annamarie Jagose (1994) has noted, the logic of queer/transgender theory is that

> [b]y persistently denaturalising gender and sexuality, [Judith] Butler problematises many of the cherished assumptions of gay liberation and lesbian feminism ...[55].

16.10   CONCLUSION

While the federal SDA provides exemptions for some organisations, the recognition of gender identity has created conflicts between the newly created rights of a biological man who identifies as a woman and the rights of biological women in many institutions.

Mary Lou Singleton is an active member of the US Women's Liberation Front, a radical feminist organisation that filed a lawsuit against the Obama administration in an attempt to restore rights to women and girls. Speaking on a panel at the conservative Heritage Foundation, Singleton summed up the impact of transgenderism on biological women.

> Transgender ideology tells us there is no such thing as biological sex and robs us of our ability to name the class of people who suffer sex based oppression. If we cannot name a phenomenon, we certainly cannot fight it. Gender ideology is harmful to women and girls.[56]

Endnotes

1. Mary Lou Singleton, cited in Ryan T Anderson, *When Harry Became Sally*, Encounter Books, New York, 2018, pg. 208.

2. *Midwives Alliance Core Competencies*, Midwives Alliance of North America. https://mana.org/resources/core-competencies Accessed 7 May 2017.

3. "mother", *English Oxford Living Dictionaries*. https://en.oxforddictionaries.com/definition/mother Accessed 7 May 2017.

4. "midwife", *English Oxford Living Dictionaries*. https://en.oxforddictionaries.com/definition/midwife Accessed 7 May 2017.

5. "Open Letter to MANA – Sign-On", Women-Centered Midwifery. https://womancenteredmidwifery.wordpress.com/take-action/ Accessed 7 May 2017.

6. "Pregnancy and birth can never be 'biologically neutral'", Women-Centered Midwifery. https://womancenteredmidwifery.wordpress.com/ Accessed 7 May 2017.

7. About Women-Centered Midwifery. https://womancenteredmidwifery.wordpress.com/about/ Accessed 7 May 2017.

8. "Manitoba father who breastfeeds shares story to promote tolerance", *CBC News,* 28 September 2015. http://www.cbc.ca/news/canada/manitoba/manitoba-father-who-breastfeeds-shares-story-to-promote-tolerance-1.3246720 Accessed 17 May 2017.

9. "Transgender dad shares his comforting path to pregnancy", Toronto's *The Star,* 19 May 2016. https://www.thestar.com/life/parent/2016/05/19/transgender-dad-shares-his-path-to-parenthood-in-new-book.html Accessed 13 March 2018.

10. Trevor MacDonald, Joy Noel-Weiss, Diana West, Michelle Walks, MaryLynne Biener, Alanna Kibbe, Elizabeth Myler, "Transmasculine individuals' experiences with lactation, chestfeeding, and gender identity: a qualitative study", *BMC Pregnancy and Childbirth*, 16 May 2016, 16 (1): 1–17. doi:10.1186/s12884-016-0907-y Accessed 13 March 2018.

11. Trevor MacDonald, "Transphobia in the Midwifery Community", *Huffington Post,* 15 September 2016. http://www.huffingtonpost.com/trevor-macdonald/transphobia-in-the-midwif_b_8131520.html Accessed 7 May 2017.

12. "Midwives rail against proposal to call women persons in new code of conduct", *News.com*, 24 November 2017. http://www.news.com.au/lifestyle/parenting/pregnancy/midwives-rail-against-proposal-to-call-women-persons-in-new-code-of-conduct/news-story/0c3b37b55934effcfc48498b64a1256f Accessed 11 March 2018.

13. Ibid.

14. Ibid.

15. Ibid.

16. Ibid.

17. Ibid.

18. Ibid.

19. Ryan T Anderson, A brave new world of transgender policy, *Harvard Journal of Law & Public Policy*, Vol. 41. No. 1, 2017, pgs. 309-354. http://www.harvard-jlpp.com/wp-content/uploads/2018/01/Anderson_FINAL-Copy.pdf This journal article contains details of the case and subsequent appeals. Accessed 17 May 2017.

20. "Dear Colleague Letter on Transgender Students Notice of Language Assistance", U.S. Department of Justice and U.S. Department of Education, 13 May 2016. https://www2.ed.gov/about/offices/list/ocr/letters/colleague-201605-title-ix-transgender.pdf Accessed 17 May 2017. U.S. Departments of Education and Justice Release Joint Guidance to Help Schools Ensure the Civil Rights of Transgender Students, 13 May 2016, https://www.ed.gov/news/press-releases/us-departments-education-and-justice-release-joint-guidance-help-schools-ensure-civil-rights-transgender-students Accessed 17 May 2017.

21. Education Amendments of 1972, Pub. L. No. 92-318, §§ 901–907, 86 Stat. 235, 373–75 (codified as amended at 20 U.S.C. §§ 1681–1688 (2012).

22. "Trump Rescinds Rules on Bathrooms for Transgender Students", *New York Times,* 22 February 2017. https://www.nytimes.com/2017/02/22/us/politics/devos-sessions-transgender-students-rights.html Accessed 9 July 2018.

23. "High court sidesteps ruling on transgender rights", *Politico*, 3 June 2017. https://www.politico.com/story/2017/03/supreme-court-scraps-transgender-bathroom-rights-235712 Accessed 1 July 2018. Accessed 9 July 2018.

24. Defendant's and Intervenor-Defendants' Brief, "Exhibit Q: Declaration of S.H.," pgs. 1–3, Gloucester County School Board v. G.G., Supreme Court of the United States, No. 16-273, January 2017, cited in Gender Identity Policies in Schools: What Congress, the Courts, and the Trump Administration Should Do Ryan T. Anderson, PhD, and Melody Wood, *Backgrounder,* Heritage Foundation, 23 March 2017, pg. 17. http://www.breakpoint.org/wp-content/uploads/2017/03/Gender-Identity-Policies-in-Schools-What-Congress-the-Courts-and-the-Trump-Administration-Should-Do.pdf Accessed 11 March 2018.

25. Brief of Amicus Curiae Safe Spaces for Women Supporting Neither Party, p. 14. r, Gloucester County School Board v G.G., Supreme Court of the United States, No. 16-273, January 2017, cited in "Gender Identity Policies in Schools: What Congress, the Courts, and the Trump Administration Should Do", Ryan T. Anderson, PhD, and Melody Wood, Ibid., pgs. 17-18.

26. *Resilient Individuals: Sexual Orientation, Gender Identity and Intersex Rights, National Consultation Report,* Australian Human Rights Commission, 2015, pg. 45. https://www.humanrights.gov.au/sites/default/files/document/publication/SOGII%20Rights%20Report%202015_Web_Version.pdf Accessed 6 June 2017.

27. "Transgender Australians can choose any bathroom they want, but not everyone is happy about it", *Washington Post,* 18 June 2016. https://www.washingtonpost.com/news/worldviews/wp/2016/06/18/transgender-australians-face-ingrained-biases-even-if-the-bathroom-issue-hasnt-spawned-legal-debate/?utm_term=.5b6d9ea9e1d3 Accessed 15 March 2018.

28. "Public service push for gender-neutral bathrooms", *Sydney Morning Herald*, 13 May 2017. https://www.smh.com.au/politics/federal/public-service-push-for-genderneutral-bathrooms-20170511-gw2taq.html Accessed 15 March 2018.

29. "LGBTIQ push for gender-neutral toilets goes to National Building Codes Board", *Courier Mail,* 16 December 2017. http://www.couriermail.com.au/news/queensland/lgbtiq-push-for-genderneutral-toilets-goes-to-national-building-codes-board/news-story/bcd5ba2d04a5b50f6dcd45eb15cc2c2b Accessed 15 March 2018.

30. "The school that went gender neutral: In a unique TV experiment, a class of seven-year-olds was taught to forget all the differences between the sexes. A lesson for us all – or just PC lunacy?", *Daily Mail,* 6 August 2017. http://www.dailymail.co.uk/news/article-4764198/The-school-went-gender-neutral.html Accessed 1 July 2018.

31. Katherine A. Liu and Natalie A. Dipietro Mager, "Women's involvement in clinical trials: historical perspective and future implications", Pharm Pract (Granada). 2016 Jan-Mar; 14(1): 708. Published online 15 March 2016. https://www.ncbi.nlm.nih.gov/pmc/articles/PMC4800017/ Accessed 16 July 2017.

32. Ibid.

33. "U.K. patient 'distressed by transsexual nurse with stubble", *Newsweek,* 1 January 2018. http://www.newsweek.com/uk-patient-distressed-transsexual-nurse-stubble-767385 Accessed 19 January 2018.

34. "'I had to undo eight years of being a woman': how LGBT prisoners are lost in the system", *The Conversation,* Nicola Carr, Siobhan McAlister, Tanya Serisier, 5 February 2016. https://theconversation.com/i-had-to-undo-eight-years-of-being-a-woman-how-lgbt-prisoners-are-lost-in-the-system-54134 "'Absolutely terrifying': transgender people and the prison system", Jeremy Story Carter and Damien Carrick, *Law Report,* ABC, 4 April 2016 http://www.abc.net.au/radionational/programs/lawreport/transgender-people-and-the-prison-system/7284154 Accessed 19 January 2018.

35. Written evidence submitted by British Association of Gender Identity Specialists to the Transgender Equality Inquiry, Dr. James Barrett, President, British Association of Gender Identity Specialists, 20 August 2015. http://data.parliament.uk/writtenevidence/committeeevidence.svc/evidencedocument/women-and-equalities-committee/transgender-equality/written/19532.html Accessed 9 July 2018.

36. "Prisoner Noel Crompton, Known as Maddison Hall", *NSW Parliament Hansard,* 21 September 2006. http://23.101.218.132/Prod/parlment/hansart.nsf/V3Key/LC20060921025?open&refNavID=HA8_1 Accessed 11 July 2017.

    "Male criminals who become women behind bars", *The Advertiser,* 11 April 2013. http://www.adelaidenow.com.au/news/weird/call-me-michelle-the-killers-who-become-women-behind-bars/news-story/99e8bebf0bcf70579f9173ea21ab9424?sv=69e959af0483bfe72029975427920727 Accessed 11 July 2017.

    "Did Hall get fellow prisoner pregnant?" *Sydney Morning Herald,* 21 September 2006. http://www.smh.com.au/news/national/did-hall-get-fellow-prisoner-pregnant/2006/09/21/1158431837244.html Accessed 11 July 2017.

    "Sex change killer Maddison Hall to be free as a bird", *Daily Telegraph,* 3 April 2010. https://www.dailytelegraph.com.au/news/nsw/sex-change-killer-to-be-free-as-a-bird/news-story/b1fecc9a9a4717607de6e980980e0ba5?sv=e95663cd723e2f8ffa0caa3329e03203 Accessed 11 July 2017.

37 "A rapist in a women's prison? Society has lost the plot", Brendan O'Neil, *Spiked*, 11 September 2017.
http://www.spiked-online.com/newsite/article/a-rapist-in-a-womens-prison-society-has-lost-the-plot/20310#.W0MDG7Gr3MU Accessed 11 July 2017.

38 Trans Prison Swap on Good Morning Britain, Fair Play for Women, Dr Nicola Williams, 21 November 2017.
https://fairplayforwomen.com/trans-prison-swap-piers-morgan/ Interview on YouTube,
https://www.youtube.com/watch?v=2fGDqtwaUdQ&t=6s Accessed 9 July 2018.

39 "'A kick in the teeth': Victims' fury as double rapist who attacked two young girls is moved to a women-only jail after £10k NHS sex change op", *The Sun*, 20 March 2017.
https://www.thesun.co.uk/news/3137217/victims-fury-as-double-rapist-who-attacked-two-young-girls-is-moved-to-a-women-only-jail-after-10k-nhs-sex-change-op/ Accessed 11 July 2017.

40 "A rapist in a women's prison? Society has lost the plot", Brendan O'Neil, *Spiked*, 11 September 2017, Op. cit.

41 "Huntley named as serial rapist in 1999", *The Telegraph*, 27 February 2004.
https://www.telegraph.co.uk/news/uknews/1455421/Huntley-named-as-serial-rapist-in-1999.html Accessed 17 March 2018.

42 "Murderer Ian Huntley wants to change gender so he can live in a women's prison", *Cosmopolitan*, 16 January 2017.
https://www.cosmopolitan.com/uk/reports/news/a48830/ian-huntley-sex-change-womens-prison/ Accessed 17 March 2018.

Trans Prison Swap on Good Morning Britain, Fair Play for Women, Dr Nicola Williams, 21 November 2017.
https://fairplayforwomen.com/trans-prison-swap-piers-morgan/ Interview on YouTube,
https://www.youtube.com/watch?v=2fGDqtwaUdQ&t=6s Accessed 9 July 2018.

43 "Up to half of trans inmates may be sex offenders", *The Times*, https://www.thetimes.co.uk/article/up-to-half-of-trans-inmates-may-be-sex-offenders-26rz2crhs Accessed 9 July 2018. 19 November 2017.

"Half of all transgender prisoners are sex offenders or dangerous category A inmates", *Dr Nicola Williams*, Fair Play for Women, 9 November 2017.
https://fairplayforwomen.com/transgender-prisoners/ Accessed 9 July 2018.

44 "Up to half of trans inmates may be sex offenders", *The Times*, 19 November 2017, Ibid.

45 Written evidence submitted by British Association of Gender Identity Specialists to the Transgender Equality Inquiry, Dr. James Barrett, Op. cit.

46 Shelia Jeffreys, *Gender Hurts: A feminist analysis of the politics of transgendersim*, Routledge, 2014, pg. 157.

47 "Italy 'to open first prison for transgender inmates'", BBC, 12 January 2010.
http://news.bbc.co.uk/2/hi/europe/8455191.stm Accessed 9 July 2018.

48 Discrimination in the Law, Inquiry under section 207 of the Equal Opportunity Act 1995, Victorian government.
https://www.parliament.vic.gov.au/archive/sarc/Equal_Opportunity/Discussion/chapterfour.htm#text75 Accessed 12 March 2018.

49 Current section 126A exemptions, Anti-discrimination Board of NSW.
http://www.antidiscrimination.justice.nsw.gov.au/Pages/adb1_antidiscriminationlaw/adb1_exemptions/s126av2.aspx Accessed 12 March 2018.

50 Beth Gaze and Belinda Smith, *Equality and Discrimination Law in Australia: An Introduction,* Cambridge University Press, 2017. pg. 77.

51 *Stevens v Fernwood Fitness Centres Pty Ltd* (1996), EOC 92-782.

52 Ruth Barrett (Editor), *Female Erasure: What you need to know about gender politics' war on women, the female sex and human rights,* foreword by Germaine Greer, Tidal Tide Publishing, LLC, Pacific Palisades, CA, USA, 2016.

53 Carol Downer, *Female Erasure,* Op. cit., pgs. 336-337.

54 Ibid., pg. 351. Note: Judith Butler uses discursive arguments to say she is not abolishing feminism but, as many feminists have pointed out, if the idea of biological female is abolished, then feminism is also abolished.

55 Annamarie Jagose, *Queer Theory: an introduction,* Melbourne University Press, 1996, pg. 85.

56 Mary Lou Singleton, cited in Ryan T Anderson, *When Harry Became Sally,* Op. cit.

CHAPTER 17

TRANSGENDERING WOMEN'S SPORTS

> To have one's dreams erased by unfair advantage
> or unsafe conditions is unacceptable.
>
> Kathy Crocco[1]

17.1 TRANSGENDER MALE-TO-FEMALES IN FEMALE SPORTS

In November 2016, 36-year-old, transgender, male-to-female cyclist, Jillian Bearden, won the women's division of the El Tour de Tucson.

Third-place finisher, Suzanne Sonye, said she would take on Bearden any time, but

> I feel bad about saying it but, no, I do not think it's fair play and I question her integrity knowing that she's going into these events knowing that she is going to be stronger.
>
> I'm sure [Bearden] had a rough go at it. It's very difficult to be transgender. But [when it comes to racing] it's problematic to me that she [transitioned] only a couple [of] years ago, and has lived 30 years as a man. Regardless of testosterone levels, she's got muscle memory and a lung capacity that I could never build up. She was a Cat 1 as a male. I could never match a pro man. How fair is that to her female competitors?[2]

New Zealand weightlifter, Gavan Hubbard, competed in men's elite events until transitioning at age 35 as Laurel Hubbard. In 2017, Hubbard won the Australian international women's competition lifting 591 pounds, 19 pounds more than the biological woman who came second. Deborah Acason, from the Australian Weightlifting Federation, told 1 News Now her concerns.

> We all deserve to be on an even playing field. It's difficult when you believe that you're not. If it's not even, why are we doing the sport?[3]

In 2014, male-to-female transgender, mixed martial arts (MMA) fighter, Fallon Fox (then aged 39), overpowered female opponent Tamikka Brents in three minutes. Brents suffered potentially career-ending injuries, including concussion and a broken orbital bone requiring seven staples. Afterwards, Brents said,

> I've fought a lot of women and have never felt the strength that I felt in a fight as I did that night. I can't answer whether it's because she was born a man or not, because I'm not a doctor. I can only say I've never felt so overpowered ever in my life, and I am an abnormally strong female.[4]

Ronda Rousey has been the Ultimate Fighting Champion (UFC) women's bantamweight leader. She says that she could "knock out anyone in the world" but that she will not fight a man transgendered as a woman.[5]

In 2015, eight members of an Iranian women's national football team were biological men awaiting sex-reassignment surgery.[6]

17.2 HOW DO MALE AND FEMALE BODIES DIFFER?

The transgender world view that a biological man can become a woman raises the question: do differences in strength and physical performance warrant separate men's and women's sports? Do transitioning treatments equalise transsexual male-to-females and biological women?

The current men's 100 metre world record of 9.58 seconds was set by Jamaica's Usain Bolt in 2009, while the women's world record of 10.49 seconds was set by American Florence Griffith-Joyner in 1988. The 0.91-second (9.5 per cent) difference indicates the different physiologies and mechanics of male and female bodies.

Biological sex is a "major factor influencing best performances and world records," say Thaibault et al (2010) in the *Journal of Sports Science & Medicine*.[7] The authors analysed 82 quantifiable events since the beginning of the Olympic era. For each event in swimming, athletics, track cycling, weightlifting and speed skating, the gap between men and women was fitted to compare male and female records. The study also examined the best performance of the top 10 performers for men and women in swimming and athletics.

Overall, the study observed a gap in world records

> after 1983, at a mean difference of 10.0% ± 2.94 between men and women for all events… [t]he gap ranges from 5.5% (800-m freestyle, swimming) to 36.8% (weightlifting) … [The] top ten performers' analysis reveals a similar gender gap trend with a stabilization in 1982 at 11.7%.

The study concluded that "[r]esults suggest that [biological] women will not run, jump, swim or ride as fast as [biological] men"[8].

Table 17.1 (see page 301) compares differences in times, heights and lengths in a selection of male and female athletics in swimming and cycling competitions.

Chris Schwirian (2015), a Biological Sciences lecturer at Ohio University since 1966, has been involved in the physiological testing of athletes, including runners, cyclists, swimmers, and rowers, at almost every level of competition. Schwirian says:

> Faster men's times for 100 to 800 meters are mostly due to men, on average, having greater muscle mass – and a larger portion of it is fast-twitch [muscle], which allows them to generate greater force, speed, and anaerobically produced energy. At all distances beyond 800 meters, the main reason for the gap is men's higher aerobic capacity [VO_2max], on average, which is due to their typically having less body fat, more haemoglobin and muscle mass, and larger hearts and lungs than women ...[9]

Schwirian confirms the above finding of Thibault et al (2010), saying that the "gap [between men and women] has been stable for the past few decades, although it is not necessarily stable across all age groups"[10].

Furthermore, as UK Fair Play for Women (2017) has pointed out:

> Men's bones are bigger and stronger in size and density. The legs are longer and straighter and attach to the knees at a different angle. The shoulder and elbow joints are also differently arranged, and the ligaments that hold the skeleton together are far stronger in men – which is why women are more flexible.
>
> We have different muscle to fat ratios and men have far more of the fast twitch muscle fibres. Even with intensive training women cannot match the bulk and explosive strength of men.
>
> Larger hearts and higher lung capacity, and greater levels of haemoglobin within their blood, allow men another 15-25% increase in their ability to utilise oxygen.
>
> All these factors affect performance and give men a mechanical advantage over women which cannot be changed by reducing testosterone levels. Endocrinologists estimate that it would take 15 years of hormone suppression in addition to surgery to see any significant changes in bone density.[11]

17.3 EVOLVING IAAF AND OLYMPIC POLICIES ON ELIGIBILITY FOR WOMEN'S COMPETITIONS

Controversy over athlete eligibility rules of the International Olympic Committee (IOC) and the International Association of Athletics Federations (IAAF), and judgements on these rules by the Court of Arbitration for Sport (CAS), has revolved around the eligibility of both female intersex athletes and transsexual male-to-females to play in women's competitions. Some intersex women, like South Africa's Caster Semenya and India's Dutee Chand, can have elevated testosterone levels.

These testosterone rules for female intersex athletes are described here because they are relevant to rule requirements of transsexual male-to-females competing with biological women. For female-to-male athletes, there are no restrictions.

A 2011 rule – that required intersex women to have a testosterone level below 10 nmol/L (nanomoles per litre) – was nullified by CAS in the case of *Dutee Chand v. Athletics Federation of India (AFI) & IAAF* (2014).

A new 2018 policy requires female intersex athletes to have a testosterone level below 5 nmol/L for the 400 metre to 1,500 metre and one mile track and field events. These requirements do not apply to other events for the 2020 Olympics.

In 2003, an ad hoc committee convened by the IOC Medical Commission established new guidelines[12] for participation of athletes who had undergone sex reassignment. It required that "surgical anatomical changes have been completed, including external genitalia changes and gonadectomy", and that the person's sex reassignment had been legally recognised by the appropriate official authorities.

The Rules also required that "hormonal therapy appropriate for the assigned sex has been administered in a verifiable manner and for a sufficient length of time to minimise gender-related advantages in sport competitions". Further, a person would be eligible to participate in women's competitions "no sooner than two years after gonadectomy"[13].

Individuals who have "undergone sex reassignment of male to female before puberty" are to be "regarded as girls and women (female)"[14].

In 2011, the IAAF introduced additional rules that required an Expert Medical Panel to make recommendations to the IAAF on a transsexual male-to-female's eligibility to compete in the women's competition. The Panel was to consider "details of any sex-reassignment procedure undertaken (including date of orchidectomy or other surgical procedure), ... evidence of acquired sex under applicable law, ... details of any post re-assignment treatment (name of treatment, dosage and periodicity), and details of any post-reassignment monitoring of treatment"[15].

Also, the Panel was to consider "the age of the athlete, ... the period since ... sex reassignment, ... whether the athlete's sex reassignment took place pre- or post-puberty, ... and the athlete's androgen levels"[16]. Early transitioning treatments would reduce normal muscle growth in adolescent males.

In 2015, an IOC Consensus Meeting substantially changed the rules in two ways.[17] First, the new rules said that, for a transsexual male-to-female to participate in women's events,

> surgical anatomical change as a pre-condition to participation is not necessary to preserve fair competition and may be inconsistent with developing legislation and notions of human rights.[18]

Second, it applied the same testosterone rule that had been introduced in 2011 for intersex women. The Consensus statement said that an athlete must consistently demonstrate that a "total testosterone level in serum has been below 10 nmol/L for at least 12 months" prior to their first competition.[19]

While the 10 nmol/L was dropped for intersex women for the 2016 Olympics, as a result of the CAS ruling on Dutee Chand, it remained in place for transsexual male-to-females.

In April 2018, at the same time that the IAAF changed its policy to lower the required testosterone levels for intersex women to 5 nmol/L, the IAAF announced that it "is currently reviewing and updating those regulations ... and expects to issue updated regulations on this topic in the coming months"[20].

At the time of this book, it is not clear whether the anticipated new IAAF/IOC rules for transsexual male-to-females will see the testosterone level for these athletes also reduced to 5 nmol/L for them to be eligible to play in women's competitions.

17.4   SIGNIFICANCE OF TESTOSTERONE

Table 17.2 (see page 304), based on data cited by the IAAF, shows that transsexual male-to-females with a testosterone level of 10 nmol/L would have 10 times the average testosterone of women who are not intersex.

Do higher testosterone levels in men give them a competitive advantage over women? Does reducing testosterone levels in biological males also reduce their muscle strength to that of women?

Two views were presented in *Bloody Elbow* (2013), in articles on transsexual male-to-female mixed martial arts fighter, Fallon Fox.

Dr Marci Bowers – a male-to-female transgender and pioneer of sex-reassignment surgery – argued that, after several years of hormone therapy, "most measures of physical strength minimize, muscle mass decreases, bone density decreases, and they become fairly comparable to women in their musculature"[21].

However, an endocrinologist and hormone specialist, Dr Ramona Krutzik, suggests that the advantages accumulated over 20 years of physical development as a male won't disappear after a few years of androgen blocking.

Krutzik has pointed out that men are completely developed by the age of 22, giving them considerable advantage in muscle formation in their early years of development. She said:

> Typically, you're looking at about 15 years after androgen suppression and SRS [sex-reassignment surgery] to really start to see significant changes in bone density.[22]

Indeed, the 2018 IAAF report on *Eligibility regulations for the female classification*[23] says the new 5 nmol/L rule for intersex women is based on science that confirms the importance of testosterone. The Explanatory Notes/Q&A (2018) accompanying the report cited the CAS *Chand v IAAF & AFI* decision to explain why there are separate men's and women's competitions. It said:

> [M]en have significant advantages in size, strength and power over women, due in large part to men's much higher levels of circulating testosterone from puberty onwards. Because of the impact that such advantages can have on sporting performance, it is generally accepted that competition between male and female athletes would not be fair and meaningful, and would risk discouraging women from participation in the sport. Therefore, in common with many other sports, the IAAF has created separate competition categories (or 'classifications') for male and female athletes …[24].

> To the best of our knowledge, there is no other genetic or biological trait encountered in female athletics that confers such a huge performance advantage.[25]

However, while the 2018 IAAF requirement for intersex women to have a testosterone level below 5 nmol/L reduces their disparity with other women and male-to-female athletes, this is still five times the average level of testosterone in other women. A new rule for transgender athletes, due to be announced in 2018, will clarify eligibility requirements for the 2020 Olympics.

Testosterone is only one measure of advantage biological men have over women. Lung capacity, muscle type, bone density, limb length and other male biological attributes contribute to the male advantage in sports.

17.5 AUSTRALIAN SPORTING POLICIES

The Australian Sports Commission has been working with the Australian Human Rights Commission to develop policies for national sporting organisations since 2016.[26]

In April 2014, the organisers of the Bingham Cup – a biennial, international, non-professional, gay rugby union tournament first held in 2002 – brought together the chief executives of Football Federation of Australia, Cricket Australia, the Australian Rugby Union, the National Rugby League and the Australian Football League. The codes committed to finalise and implement their own policies consistent with the *Anti-Homophobia & Inclusion Framework for Australian Sport.*[27]

Controversy over male-to-female transgenders playing in women's sports have started in the recently formed Australian Football League (AFL) women's competition with a transsexual male-to-female playing in the Victorian women's competition.

The AFL includes transgenders in its *National Sexuality and Pregnancy Guidelines 2013*. The *Guidelines* say that legal advice will be sought in the case of transgender players, given that

> [t]here is debate over whether a male to female transgender person obtains any physical advantage over other female participants ...

> The exclusion of Transgender Members from participation in Australian Football events and activities may have significant adverse implications for their health, wellbeing and involvement in community life and on Australian Football. In general, Members must facilitate the participation by Transgender persons in Australian Football with the gender with which they identify.[28]

In 2015, the Australia's National Rugby League (NRL) also adopted a code for transgenders in sport, saying:

> The NRL is aware that the International Olympic Committee (IOC) has established criteria for selection and participation in the Olympic Games. Where a transgender person intends to compete at an elite level, we will encourage them to obtain

advice about the IOC's criteria, which may differ from the position we have taken.[29]

The NRL women's competition began in the 2018 season.

17.6 WIDER FEMALE-TRANSGENDER CONFLICTS

Many women are concerned about the future of women's sports with transgender male-to-females playing in female sports. However, in some cases, the issue appears to extend beyond just the physical advantage of males-to-females.

Website Gender Trender (18 September 2014) gave some disturbing background to the fight between transgender Fallon Fox and lesbian Tamikka Brents.

Gender Trender said the level of brutality in the fight between them was "unlike anything seen in Women's MMA". It accused Fallon Fox of

> posting … anti-gay screeds online which center on the 'unfairness' of lesbian women declining relations with males like himself who are transgender…
>
> As bizarre and unlikely as Fox's public campaigns may seem to the average citizen outside of the LGBT, this sort of over the top anti-gay, anti-lesbian, anti-female "Men's Rights" campaigning is an activity that is well within the mainstream of transgender activism. For example: The largest organized protest by far in the entire history of the transgender rights movement was *not* against the political foes of transgender rights, but instead centered on a single private lesbian gathering that is for females only (Michigan Women's Music Festival).
>
> Everyone within the LGBT knows: there is nothing heterosexual male "lesbians" like Fallon Fox hate more than an actual female lesbian. It may seem counterintuitive to the average person's conception of "males who identify as female", but such males actually *do not like* women and find the lives and existence of real females disruptive to their male gender fantasies. Lesbians receive the worst of their ire for the obvious reason: that lesbian sexuality and culture is not inclusive of males, regardless of their feelings or any cosmetic surgery procedures they may undergo. This is why males in the transgender community (those that fancy themselves "male lesbians") were so invested in seeing Tamikka Brent battered by a fellow "male lesbian".
>
> This is why a heterosexual, white, male, transgender, AJ McKenna, published nine successive blog posts prior to the Fox vs. Brents match calling "for blood" against black lesbian

Tamikka Brents and calling her an "enemy" of men like himself. This is why he contacted her sponsors and supporters and demanded that they stop supporting the lesbian fighter. This is why he posted a video (which he removed after Tamikka was hospitalized) where he likened Tamikka to rapist Mike Tyson because McKenna felt that her failure as a gay female to accept males as potential romantic partners "rapes" their identity as male lesbians.

To those outside the LGBT this all sounds absurd and unbelievable. Actually, it sounds absurd and unbelievable to most of us. Unfortunately, this is the state of the mainstream rhetoric of the transgender movement towards lesbians and women in general.[30]

Gender Trender went on to give a much longer account of the conflict between lesbians and male-to-female transgenders.

17.7 CONCLUSION

This book does not resolve the issue of intersex women participating in female sports. The IAAF and IOC have policies that are evolving with the scientific evidence. Rather, it examines legal issues in relation to male-to-female athletes participating in female competitions.

In Australia, the Federal *Sex Discrimination Act 1984*, Section 42, provides for excluding transgender "persons from participation in any competitive sporting activity in which the strength, stamina or physique of competitors is relevant"[31].

However, the decisions of the IOC and CAS have opened the way for biological men, with or without medical intervention, to play in women's sport. This is despite men typically outpacing women in running, throwing, lifting, jumping, rowing, boxing, martial arts and football, to name just a few sports.

Arguably, even with medical intervention, it would take 15 years or more for the muscle strength levels of male-to-female athletes to be reduced to the strength levels of women.

Chris Judd (2018) – now a sports commentator who has captained the West Coast Eagles and Carlton in the Australian Football League (AFL) – says the issue is fairness to women and that difference is not discrimination.

> I understand that at an individual level, it is unfair transgender athletes can't play in the AFLW [AFL Women's game]. It excludes them just because of the way they were born. But if the

policy were to be reversed, it would be unfair on other AFLW players.

We should continually look to make society as fair as practically possible, but the idea that the world will ever be a completely just place, while ideologically sound, is fanciful. People with unsymmetrical faces will never become models, short people don't play in the NBA and, on the more extreme side of it, anyone born in Syria would be only too aware of just how unfair life can be.

In Australia, our problems are minor by comparison. But if we've become a society where people can't have adult conversations around sensitive topics and remain open to other points of view, we'll have plenty of bigger problems to deal with in the future.[32]

Kathy Crocco (2016) was an aspiring athlete who had her hopes dashed by a life-changing knee injury at age 18. Her critique of the CAS and IOC decisions to allow male-to-female transsexuals to play in women's competitions helps to sum up the issue.

[F]or every male-to-female there is a biological female athlete who must let go of her dreams based on something other than science and medical evidence. I cannot support the erasure of biological women's dreams based on bad science and inadequate or incompetent research.

If an aspiring athlete's dreams are altered by injury, as mine were, or by being defeated in fair and safe competition, then that is the way of the athlete.

To have one's dreams erased by unfair advantage or unsafe conditions is unacceptable.[33]

Endnotes

1. Kathy Crocco, "Pseudoscience supplants female athlete's Olympic dreams", *Female Erasure: What you need to know about gender politics' war on women, the female sex and human rights,* Ruth Barrett (Editor) Tidal Tide Publishing, LLC, Pacific Palisades, CA, USA, 2016, pg. 262.

2. "Paving the way for transgender cyclists: The story of Jillian Bearden", *Cycling Tips*, 10 December 2016. https://cyclingtips.com/2016/12/paving-the-way-for-transgender-cyclists-the-story-of-jillian-bearden/ Accessed 21 March 2018.

3. "'She has every right to compete with women': Transgender weightlifter sparks criticism after competition win", *Yahoo 7 News*, 20 March 2017. https://au.news.yahoo.com/a/34720066/kiwi-transgender-weightlifter-laurel-hubbards-win-causes-stir-among-female-aussie-competitors/ Accessed 21 March 2018. Now available at https://au.news.yahoo.com/a/34720066/kiwi-transgender-weightlifter-laurel-hubbards-win-causes-stir-among-female-aussie-competitors/ Accessed 20 July 2018.

4. "Allowing transgender Olympians is unfair to women", *The Federalist,* 27 January 2016. http://thefederalist.com/2016/01/27/allowing-transgender-olympians-is-unfair-to-women/ Accessed 21 March 2018.

5. "UFC Women's Champ Refuses to Fight Trans Athlete Fallon Fox", *OUT*, 17 July 2016. http://www.out.com/sports/2015/7/16/ufc-womens-champ-refuses-fight-trans-athlete-fallon-fox Accessed 21 March 2018.

6. "Eight of Iran's women's football team 'are men'", *The Telegraph,* 30 September 2015. https://www.telegraph.co.uk/news/worldnews/middleeast/iran/11903290/Eight-of-Irans-womens-football-team-are-men.html Accessed 21 March 2018.

7. Valérie Thibault, Marion Guillaume, Geoffroy Berthelot, Nour El Helou, Karine Schaal, Laurent Quinquis, Hala Nassif, Muriel Tafflet, Sylvie Escolano, Olivier Hermine, and Jean-François Toussaint, "Women and Men in Sport Performance: The Gender Gap has not Evolved since 1983", *Journal of Sports Science & Medicine,* 2010 June; 9(2): 214–223. https://www.ncbi.nlm.nih.gov/pmc/articles/PMC3761733/ Accessed 15 May 2017.

8. Ibid.

9. Chris Schwirian, "Running: Why Are Men Faster than Women?" *Arts and Science Forum, Ohio University,* 10 March 2015, reported from *Runner's World* 2015. https://www.ohio-forum.com/2015/03/running-why-are-men-faster-than-women/ Accessed 24 March 2018.

10. Ibid.

11. "Our day in parliament – MPs are invited to hear the other side of the story", Fair Play for Women, 11 November 2017 https://fairplayforwomen.com/the-gender-recognition-act/ Accessed 24 March 2018.

12. "Statement of the Stockholm consensus on sex reassignment in sports", ad hoc committee convened by the International Olympic Committee Medical Commission, 28 October 2003. https://stillmed.olympic.org/Documents/Reports/EN/en_report_905.pdf Accessed 21 March 2018.

13 Ibid.

14 Ibid.

15 *IAAF regulations governing edibility of athletes who have undergone sex reassignment to compete in women's competitions,* IAAF, 1 May 2011, pg. 2. https://www.google.com.au/url?sa=t&rct=j&q=&esrc=s&source=web&cd=3&ved=0ahUKEwid9JiFr4rbAhVLipQKHfgDBAgQFgg2MAI&url=https%3A%2F%2Fwww.iaaf.org%2Fdownload%2Fdownload%3Ffilename%3De08ef22e-09ff-43eb-a338-fe127e99fc28.pdf%26urlslug%3DIAAF%2520Regulations%2520Governing%2520Eligibility%2520of%2520Athletes%2520Who%2520Have%2520Undergone%2520Sex%2520Reassignment%2520to%2520Compete%2520in%2520Women&usg=AOvVaw25DOgjparBnJwQSPJbAGWI Accessed 16 May 2018.

16 Ibid., pg. 8.

17 "IOC Consensus Meeting on Sex Reassignment and Hyperandrogenism", IOC, November 2015. https://stillmed.olympic.org/Documents/Commissions_PDFfiles/Medical_commission/2015-11_ioc_consensus_meeting_on_sex_reassignment_and_hyperandrogenism-en.pdf Accessed 16 May 2018.

18 Ibid.

19 Ibid.

20 *Eligibility regulations for the female classification (athletes with differences of sex development): Explanatory Notes Q&A,* IAAF, 23 April 2018. Download at https://www.iaaf.org/news/press-release/eligibility-regulations-for-female-classifica Accessed 16 May 2018.

21 "Leading sex-reassignment physicians weigh in on Fallon Fox", *Bloody Elbow,* 8 March 2013. https://www.bloodyelbow.com/2013/3/8/4075434/leading-sex-reassignment-physicians-weigh-in-on-fallon-fox Accessed 22 March 2018.

22 "Dr. Ramona Krutzik, M.D. discusses possible advantages Fallon Fox may have", *Bloody Elbow,* 20 March 2013. https://www.bloodyelbow.com/2013/3/20/4128658/dr-ramona-krutzik-endocrinologist-discusses-possible-advantages-fallon-fox-has https://www.bloodyelbow.com/2013/3/20/4128658/dr-ramona-krutzik-endocrinologist-discusses-possible-advantages-fallon-fox-has Accessed 22 March 2018.

23 *Eligibility regulations for the female classification (athletes with differences of sex development),* IAAF, 23 April 2018. https://www.iaaf.org/download/download?filename=2ff4d966-f16f-4a76-b387-f4eeff6480b2.pdf&urlslug=IAAF%20Eligibility%20Regulations%20for%20the%20Female%20Classification%20(Athletes%20with%20Differences%20of%20Sex%20Development)%20in%20force%20as%20from%201st%20November%202018 Accessed 16 May 2018.

24 *Eligibility regulations for the female classification (athletes with differences of sex development): Explanatory Notes/Q&A,* IAAF, 23 April 2018, pg. 1, citing *Chand v IAAF & AFI* (CAS 2014/A/3759), pg. 1. https://www.google.com.au/url?sa=t&rct=j&q=&esrc=s&source=web&cd=1&ved=0ahUKEwiY8pKogZHcAhXHy7wKHWzdBRAQFggtMAA&url=https%3A%2F%2Fwww.iaaf.org%2Fdownload%2Fdownload%3Ffilename%3Dc402eb5b-5e40-4075-8970-d66fccb10d41.pdf%26urlslug%3DExplanatory%2520Notes%253A%2520IAAF%2520Eligibility%2520Regulations%2520for%2520the%2520Female%2520Classification&usg=AOvVaw27XDESdCzgYQ818vhuESul Accessed 9 July 2018.

25 Ibid, pg. 6.

26 "Australian Sports Commission developing transgender athlete guidelines", *Canberra Times*, 19 October 2017.
http://www.canberratimes.com.au/sport/act-sport/australian-sports-commission-developing-transgender-athlete-guidelines-20171018-gz3njg.html Accessed 16 May 2018.

27 *Resilient Individuals: Sexual Orientation, Gender Identity and Intersex Rights, National Consultation Report,* Australian Human Rights Commission, 2015, pg. 22.
https://www.humanrights.gov.au/sites/default/files/document/publication/SOGII%20Rights%20Report%202015_Web_Version.pdf Accessed 15 September 2017.

28 "National Sexuality and Pregnancy Guidelines 2013", Australian Football League (AFL) pg. 4.
http://s.afl.com.au/staticfile/AFL%20Tenant/AFL/Files/Schedule%209%20-%20National%20Sexuality%20&%20Pregnancy%20Guidelines.pdf Accessed 9 July 2018.

29 "National Rugby League Member Protection Policy", NRL, Updated July 2015.
https://playnrl.com/media/1939/nrl-member-protection-policy-revised-27072015-002.pdf Accessed 9 July 2018.

30 "Fallon Fox: why hormones don't make a woman", Gender Trender, 18 September 2014.
https://gendertrender.wordpress.com/2014/09/18/fallon-fox-why-hormones-dont-make-a-woman/ Accessed 9 July 2018.

31 *Sex Discrimination Act 1984,* Act No. 4 of 1984 as Registered 21 March 2012, C2012C00313, Section 42.
https://www.legislation.gov.au/Details/C2012C00313.

32 Chris Judd, "Are some more equal than others?" *The Age,* 7 May 2018.
https://www.theage.com.au/sport/afl/are-some-more-equal-than-others-20180507-p4zdus.html Accessed 10 May 2018.

33 Kathy Crocco, "Pseudoscience supplants female athlete's Olympic dreams", *Female Erasure,* Op. cit., pg. 262.

TABLE 17.1
DIFFERENCES IN MALE AND FEMALE WORLD RECORDS IN A REPRESENTATIVE SAMPLE OF SPORTS

Event	Male	Athlete, year	Female	Athlete, year	Difference Actual	%
ATHLETICS[1]						
100m	9.58	Usain Bolt 2009	10.49	Florence Griffith-Joyner 1998	0.91	9.5
200m	19.19	Usain Bolt 2009	21.34	Florence Griffith-Joyner 1998	2.15	11.2
400m	43.03	Wayde Van Niekerk 2016	47.60	Marita Koch 1985	4.57	10.6
800m	1:40.91	David Rudisha 2012	1:53.28	Jarmila Kratochvilova 1983	12.37	12.3
1,500m	3:26.00	Hicham El Guerrow 1998	3:50.07	Genzebe Dibaba 2015	24.07	11.7
10,000m track	26:17.53	Kenenisa Bekele 2005	29:17.45	Almaz Ayana 2016	179.9	11.4
10km road	26:44	Leonard Patrick Komon 2010	29.43 Mx	Joyciline Jepkosgei 2017	179	11.2
Marathon	2:02.57	Dennis Kipruto Kimetto 2014	Time 2:15.25 Mx	Paula Radcliffe 2003	12.28	10.1
High jump	2.45m	Javier Sotomayor 1993	2.09	Stefka Kostadinova 1987	-0.36	-14.7
Pole vault	6.16m	Renaud Lavillenie 2014	5.06	Elena Isinbaeva 2009	-1.1	-17.9
Long jump	8.95m	Mike Powell 1991	7.52	Galina Chistyakova 1988	-1.43	-16.0
4 x 100m relay	36.84	Jamaica 2014	40.82	United States 2012	3.98	10.8

TABLE 17.1
DIFFERENCES IN MALE AND FEMALE WORLD RECORDS IN A REPRESENTATIVE SAMPLE OF SPORTS

Event	Male	Athlete, year	Female	Athlete, year	Difference Actual	%
ATHLETICS[1]						
4 x 200m relay	1:18.63	Jamaica 2014	1:27.46	United States "Blue" 2000	8.83	11.2
4 x 1,500m relay	14:22.22	Kenya 2014	16:33.58	Kenya 2014	131.3.6	15.2
SWIMMING[2]						
50m freestyle	20.91	Cesar Cielo 2009	23.67	Sarah Sjöström	2.76	13.2
100m freestyle	46.91	Cesar Cielo 2009	51.71	Sarah Sjöström	4.8	10.2
1,500m freestyle	14:31.02	Yang Sun 2012	15:25.48	Katie Ledecky	54.46	6.3
50m backstroke	24.04	Liam Tancock 2009	27.06	Jing Zhao	3.02	12.6
200m backstroke	1:51.92	Aaron Peirsol 2009	2:04.06	Missy Franklin	12.14	10.9
50m breaststroke	25.95	Adam Peaty 2017	29.40	Lilly King	3.45	13.3
200m breaststroke	2:06.67	Ippel Watanabe	2:19.11	Rikke Moeller-Pedersen	12.44	9.8
4 x 100m freestyle	3:08.24	United States	3:30.65	Australia	22.41	11.9
4 x 200m freestyle	6:58.55	United States	7:42.08	China	43.53	10.4
CYCLING, ELITE COMPETITION[3]						
200m flying	9.347	Francois Pervis 2013	10.384	Kristina Vogel 2013	1.037	11.1

Mx: mixed male-female race.

Note: As men and women use differently weighted javelin, discus, shotput and hammer (in the hammer throw), records are not included in this table. Similarly, in cycling, the some events differ in distance for men and women. The 4,000m flying is run over 4,000 meters for men and 3,000 meters for women.[4]

Table 17.1

Endnotes

1. World Records, International Association of Athletics Federations (IAAF).
   https://www.iaaf.org/records/by-category/world-records Accessed 29 April 2018.
   List of world records in athletics, Wikipedia.
   https://en.wikipedia.org/wiki/List_of_world_records_in_athletics Accessed 29 April 2018.

2. FINA 50-meter World Records, International Swimming Federation.
   http://www.fina.org/sites/default/files/wr_50m_oct_11_2017.pdf Accessed 29 April 2018.

3. Track Records, Cycling Australia. Men's Records.
   http://www.cycling.org.au/Track/Track-Records-Male Women's Records.
   http://www.cycling.org.au/Track/Track-Records-Female Accessed 29 April 2018.

4. Olympic cycling – why do men's and women's events differ?" David Rouffet, PhD, Sport Performance Analysis, *The Conversation*, 6 August 2012.
   https://theconversation.com/olympic-cycling-why-do-mens-and-womens-events-differ-8470 Accessed 29 April 2018.

TABLE 17.2

COMPARING NORMAL RANGE OF TESTOSTERONE LEVELS (NMOL/L) FOR WOMEN AND MEN WITH OLYMPIC/IAAF LEVELS FOR INTERSEX FEMALE AND MALE-TO-FEMALE ATHLETES

Normal range of testosterone in women and men	nmol/L
Range for women (including elite female athletes who are not intersex/DSD)[1]	0.12 – 1.79
Range for men[2]	7.7 – 29.4

IAAF/Olympic maximum testosterone levels for intersex women and male-to-female athletes	nmol/L
February 2017 to April 2018 for 2018 Winter Olympics, South Korea: maximum testosterone level for intersex female and male-to-female athletes in all events[3]	10.0
IAAF rule for 2020 maximum testosterone level for intersex females, 400m-1,500m track and field only[4]	5.0
IAAF rule for 2020 Olympics for male-to-females athletes	Pending

Table 17.2

Endnotes

1   *Eligibility regulations for the female classification (athletes with differences of sex development)*, IAAF, 23 April 2018, citing Handelsman, Hirschberg and Bermon, "Circulating Testosterone as the Hormonal Basis of Sex Differences in Athletic Performance", *Endocrine Reviews*, 2018 (publication pending). https://www.iaaf.org/download/download?filename=2ff4d966-f16f-4a76-b387-f4eeff6480b2.pdf&urlslug=IAAF%20Eligibility%20Regulations%20for%20the%20Female%20Classification%20(Athletes%20with%20Differences%20of%20Sex%20Development)%20in%20force%20as%20from%201st%20November%202018 Accessed 16 May 2018.

2   Ibid.

3   *IOC Consensus Meeting on Sex Reassignment and Hyperandrogenism*, International Olympic Committee, November 2015. https://stillmed.olympic.org/Documents/Commissions_PDFfiles/Medical_commission/2015-11_ioc_consensus_meeting_on_sex_reassignment_and_hyperandrogenism-en.pdf Accessed 16 May 2018.

4   *Eligibility regulations for the female classification (athletes with differences of sex development): Explanatory Notes Q&A*, IAAF, 23 April 2018. Download at https://www.iaaf.org/news/press-release/eligibility-regulations-for-female-classifica Accessed 16 May 2018.

CHAPTER 18

CAN CONFLICTED BIOLOGICAL VERSUS TRANSGENDER RIGHTS BE RESOLVED?

18.1 CONFLICTED WORLD VIEWS, CONFLICTED SOLUTIONS

Can the wide array of legal and cultural conflicts between the biological and transgender world views be resolved? Or, can compromises be made? Can the two world views co-exist?

Options for each world view are considered in Table 18.1, along with objections to each option from the opposing world view.

Readers can make their own judgements as to which of the suggested options offer reasonable compromises. However, it should be pointed out that, for each option there are strong objections from the opposing world view, which suggests that satisfactory compromises are difficult to find. In most instances, the two world views are deeply conflicted.

In most areas of contention listed in Table 18.1, a person failing to comply with the transgender world view can face legal penalties and/or professional sanctions that could lead to loss of professional qualifications and loss of employment.

Conflicts arise in several ways.

18.2 THREE FORMS OF CONFLICTS

A. Conflicts over access to women's services and private spaces: Historically, various rights, privileges, protections and access to services have been bestowed on women according to their biological sex. Women's-only services have been considered an inherent right.

Conflicts occur when a man identifies as a woman and claims access to women's-only toilets, showers, change rooms, sports, gyms, domestic violence shelters, lesbian organisations, affirmative action programs and accommodation for female prisoners.

Just as Table 18.1 offers solutions according to each world view, there are strong objections from the opposing world view.

For example, how can the conflicting claims for access to toilets, showers and change rooms be resolved? Either women concede their rights to privacy and safety, by sharing their facilities with biological men who identify as women, or transgender male-to-females continue to use male facilities. Or, does a third category of unisex facilities, alongside male and female facilities, provide a compromise solution? Some male-to-female transgenders claim that this discriminates against their right to access female facilities (see Chapter 16.4).

How can the conflict over participation in women's sports be resolved? The International Association of Athletics Federations, the International Olympic Committee and the Court of Arbitration for Sport have struggled to find solutions, and many biological women have objected to their solutions (see Chapter 17).

The requirement that men who identify as women have access to women's-only services effectively erases the differences between men and women. It treats men and women as the same.

Similarly, some laws support women's affirmative action policies to achieve workplace equality between biological men and women. Others aim to provide equality between transgenders and biological men/women, such that a man who identifies as a woman can presumably take advantage of women's affirmative action policies. Which laws will be given priority (see Chapter 8.5)?

There is an overlap between this category, dealing with who has "access" to services, and the last section below, which deals with "provision" of a range of services.

B. Conflicts over use of language: Conflicts occur over how a person is identified. If everyone is on a male-female spectrum, or identifies as non-binary or genderless, then how are such identities to be recorded?

Generally, the idea of having a free-text "other" category for a person to self-describe their gender identity has been rejected. Victoria considered allowing for "any other sex" for birth registrations (see Chapter 9.7), while a Tasmanian proposal considered the "other" category for a person to self-describe their gender identity (see Chapter 9.8). Allowing for umlimited types of gender identity is mostly considered impractical. The compromise solution has been to have the X category to recognise Indeterminate, Unspecified and Intersex.

Using the "X" or "other" categories still leaves a problem. How are people of diverse genders to be addressed with an appropriate pronoun? The solution has been to introduce gender-neutral pronouns that do not identify any sex or gender.

Given that gender-neutral language is now required in some workplaces and educational institutions, conflict happens when a person does not want to be addressed, or refer to their family and friends, in gender-neutral language; that is, when a person recognises that their own sex, and that of their family and friends, is immutable, not cisgender. Conflict occurs when everyone is required to use gender-neutral language so as not to treat transgenders differently.

The logical extension of recognising people by their gender identity is that language is made gender neutral. Language becomes uniform.

Table 18.1 shows that conflicts occur in the workplace and across the culture when people are recorded on birth certificates, marriage forms, school records, passports and other official documents by their gender identity in place of their biological sex.

In 2018, Dr David Mackereth, a 55-year-old who worked as a doctor for more than two decades, had his contract terminated as a medical assessor for the UK Department of Work and Pensions in Dudley. In refusing to address transgenders with gender neutral pronouns, he was said to be non-compliant with the UK *Equality Act 2010*.[1]

C. Conflicts over provision of services. Conflicts occur over the provision of services when a service provider is required to provide services to men/boys who identify as women/girls in many situations.

For example, how are the rights of teachers, students and parents who hold the biological world view to be respected when the law recognises the transgender world view: a belief that a person's gender identity replaces their sex? This is not an academic question as the policies of several state education departments now require schools to allow boys who identify as girls to access girls' sports and facilities (see Chapter 12.2). Such policies conflict with a teacher's right to follow their conscience and belief and a parent's right to determine the education of their children, as defined in the *International Covenant on Civil and Political Rights* (ICCPR, Articles 18: see Chapter 19.2).[2]

What happens when there are conflicts over the provision of health services? In 2015, psychologist and sexologist, Professor Kenneth Zucker, was stood down as head Toronto's Centre for Addiction and Mental Health (CAMH) gender identity health clinic, the largest in Canada, and his unit was then closed. Zucker headed the American Psychiatric Association committee to establish the diagnosis and treatment of gender dysphoria for the *DSM-5* (see Chapters 7.2, 14.2). He supported use of hormones and surgery for transitioning teenagers and adults, but adopted a "watch and wait" approach to counselling children with gender dysphoria, based on evidence showing that most children with gender dysphoria identify only with their birth sex in adulthood (see

Chapter 6.2.11). His dismissal came after an "inconclusive" CAMH review, prompted by and activist campaign against Zucker and his unit over their "watch and wait" approach.

As Table 8.1 shows, conflicts over provision of services affect principals and teachers, counsellors, doctors and other health professionals, medical researchers, wedding celebrants, wedding service providers and female beauty service providers. In a variety of situations, these people are required to treat men and women, boys and girls, the same rather than provide services that respect and treat them differently according to their biological sex, or their psychological condition.

Again, with all proposed solutions, there are objections from the opposing world view.

18.3 OTHER AREAS OF CONFLICT

Many dilemmas are created when a biological man can be legally recognised as a woman.

- How does the "#Me Too"[3] movement deal with a biological male who identifies as female, then sexually assaults women, or if a biological male sex abuser changes his sex to female after abusing women?

- If a biological man can identify as a woman and a woman can identify as a man, on which side of the gender (male-female) pay gap will such people be considered to be?

- What happens to half a century of affirmative action policies for biological women if biological men can legally identify as women and claim the same rights as women, as allowed for in the South Australian *Acts Interpretations Act 1915* for "appointments to statutory bodies"?[4]

- Does International Women's Day become International Person's Day?

- Are women's hospitals renamed persons' hospitals?

- Where a biological woman is assaulted by a husband/partner who was born male but identifies as female, is this to be recorded as a case of male-on-female or female-on female domestic violence?

- Should violent rapists who were born male, but who now identify as female, be accommodated in women's prisons? Should all prisons be made gender neutral?

- Will a girls' school be accused of discrimination against transgenders if it refuses to enrol boys who identify as girls and if it refuses to allow them access to girls' toilets, showers, change rooms, sports, camps and dormitories?

- Will women's associations and safe spaces be required to include biological men who say they are women?

- In the future, will women's-only gyms be required to give biological men who identify as women, with or without sex-change surgery, access to their facilities?

Even though all definitions of gender identity are ambiguous – based on the transgender world view, which has no scientific or theoretical foundation to validate its claims – this world view has been given priority in many laws.

This raises important questions. Should one world view be prioritised in law over the other? How is tolerance shown towards the other world view?

18.4 SOLUTION: WRITE DEFINITIONS OF "MAN", "WOMAN" AND "SEX" INTO LAW AND TOLERATE TRANSGENDERISM IN CULTURE

Given the deep conflicts between the transgender and biological world views, why should the transgender world view, representing a fraction of one per cent of the population (see Chapter 6.2.10), be given priority in law at the expense of the rights of the 99 per cent plus who regard biological sex as self-evident and immutable?

This book has provided many cases that demonstrate why laws should give priority to the biological world view. Male and female are factual descriptions of men and women based on the systematic study of the structure and behaviour of human beings through observation and experiment.[5]

A man is objectively defined as being "a member of the male sex"; a woman is defined as "a member of the female sex". Sex is objectively defined according to the biological reproductive functions of men and women.

This definition of sex applies not only to humans, but to all mammals. The fact that some people have a disorder of sexual development, or that some people are transsexuals, is not grounds for claiming that sex cannot be defined (see Chapter 5).

These definitions provide certainty in law by recognising the inherent nature and rights of the vast majority of people who regard their birth sex as immutable and fixed. Consequently, these definitions should be written into anti-discrimination and other laws in place of gender identity.

In the absence of man, woman and sex being defined in law, the vast majority of people, who are not transgender, are at risk of legal and/or professional sanctions for non-compliance with the transgenderism world view in many of the areas listed in Table 18.1.

18.5   TRANSGENDERISM'S OBJECTIONS TO RECOGNISING THE BIOLOGICAL WORLD VIEW IN LAW

Objection 1: The biological world view does not protect the legal right of people to be transgender and express diversity.

Answer: This claim confuses "rights" with "liberties". A person has the liberty to adopt any gender identity they choose. Liberty means "the state of being free within society from oppressive restrictions imposed by authority on one's way of life, behaviour, or political views"[6]. A liberty for a person to transgender and express their diversity is better than a legal "right" that restricts the liberties and rights of everyone else.

Further, it is inappropriate for laws to regulate matters that are personal, based on feelings, emotions and personal preferences, like friendship, or family size, or gender identity. In this way, personal liberty allows for diversity on all matters personal, whether it is a person's friendships, or how many children a couple have, or their chosen gender identity.

Conversely, claiming gender-identity rights leads to demands for gender-neutral language, unisex restrooms and sports, and so on. This imposes uniformity, or homogeneity, on everyone. This is the opposite of diversity. It is comparable to a government legally imposing a uniform family size on all families.

This underscores the importance of recognising the biological world view in law, and thereby recognising people by their biological sex at birth on legal identity documents, which does not restrict the freedom of a person to socially identify as transgender.

By *not* turning liberties and freedoms into legally defined gender identity rights, freedoms and liberties are maximised. Sexual diversity is recognised and maintained.

Objection 2: How are the rights of gender-diverse people – to access the sports and restrooms of choice, for example – to be protected?

Answer: This requires an understanding of human rights.

Laws don't "create" rights. Laws only recognise, codify, protect and extend rights that are inherent to every person because they are human.

An inherent human right is "a permanent, essential, or characteristic attribute"[7] derived from the dignity of the human person. Both the *Universal Declaration of Human Rights* (1948) and *the International Covenant on Civil and Political Rights* (1966) begin by recognising the "inherent dignity" of all people and go on to recognise the inherent equal rights of "men and women".

As an example of such rights, anti-discrimination laws based on the UN *Convention on the Elimination of Discrimination Against Women* recognise the inherent rights of biological women and provide positive measures to ensure women receive equal pay to men for equal work.

Or, again, freedoms of association and movement are inherent human rights, while slavery is a violation of these rights.

At least until recent changes to law, it has been self-evident that inherent rights are automatically bestowed on men and women according to their biological sex.

This contrasts with the transgender ideological "belief" that the law should define newly created rights for people according to their socially constructed gender identity.

In this case, laws like the *Sex Discrimination Act 1984* (as amended in 2013) provide grounds for newly created rights (for example, men identifying as women accessing women's change rooms) to conflict with inherent rights, (for example, biological women having their own change rooms to ensure their right to privacy and bodily safety and integrity).

The more *constructed* rights for a minority are protected in law, the more the *inherent* rights of the majority of people are restricted.

Conversely, the less that laws regulate matters of personal feelings, preferences and taste, the more that freedoms, liberties and diversity are preserved.

The logic of the transgender world view is that men and women are treated as all being the same, which is the opposite of diversity.

Objection 3: How are transgenders to be protected from discrimination?

Answer: The biological world view does not impose sexual conformity on people. It doesn't say "a person cannot be transgender". If it doesn't impose restrictions, it preserves liberty and freedoms and allows for diversity. A person can be transgender, socially recognised and addressed with pronouns appropriate to their gender identity without imposing gender-neutral language on everyone.

Defamation laws, anti-vilification laws, employment laws, etc. protect all people.

Effective anti-bullying laws, policies and education programs teach people not to bully anyone; to respect all people.

These are the legal and cultural hallmarks of a tolerant society. Tolerance – that is, being broadminded about the existence, opinions, beliefs or behaviour of people with whom you disagree – is a necessary condition for a liberal democracy.

While the two world views appear to be mutually exclusive and conflicted, only the biological world view in law preserves diversity and gives transgenders the liberty to identify and live as they please.

Objection 4: Isn't the biological world view also a "belief" about human sexuality that is imposed on society by the state?

Answer: Defining "woman", "man" and "sex" in law recognises inherent, self-evident characteristics of the human person. Hence, the law is only recognising biologically verifiable "facts" about men and women to protect their inherent rights, privileges, protections and access to services based on their birth sex. Biological sex is objectively verifiable, just as a table is scientifically verifiable as being a flat surface with legs for the purpose of eating, writing or working at.

Facts are verifiable. Beliefs don't have to be verifiable. Many beliefs cannot be verified.

Hence, the state is not adopting a "belief" about the human person by defining "man", "woman" and "sex" in law; it is only recognising inherent facts or realities.

In contrast, gender identity is a social construct that does not have a scientific or theoretical foundation to provide a consensus definition. It is a contested, subjective "belief" about human identity.

A tolerant democracy allows all "beliefs" to be expressed and manifest in the public square.

Tolerating a belief is very different from protecting a "belief" in law, which is comparable to imposing a state-established "religion" on society. It risks changing a tolerant democracy into an authoritarian state.

18.6   CONCLUSION

Table 18.1 indicates the conflicts between the two world views. Few, if any, of these conflicts can be resolved to the satisfaction of both world views.

In part, these conflicts arise when gender identity, a subjective and ambiguous concept that has no theoretical or scientific foundation, is written into law. It is not a verifiable scientific "fact" but a "belief" that cannot be verified.

In part, these conflicts occur because of a misunderstanding about the nature of rights. Rights are inherent to every person by virtue of the inherent human dignity of every person. Laws don't create these rights; they can only recognise, codify and protect human rights.

Consequently, if laws should define "man", "woman" and "sex", they make clear the basis of inherent rights according to a person's biological sex. Until recently, most laws have regarded the meaning of these terms as self-evident.

In contrast, writing gender identity into law creates conflicts over rights, protections, privileges and access to services between the vast majority of people, who regard their biological sex as immutable and self-evident, and the minority who identify as other than their sex at birth. It restricts the freedoms and liberties of the majority in the interests of a minority.

Further, when the state writes gender identity into law, it creates and protects a new state "belief" where people can be prosecuted or lose their professional registration for non-compliance. This restricts the freedoms of thought, belief, conscience, religion, speech and association of those who recognise the biological world view.

When a democracy creates an established state belief, it no longer provides a neutral, public square for all beliefs and risks morphing into an authoritarian state.

Endnotes

1. "One word ended Dr David Mackereth's 26-year career. Now he wants to have his say", *Mamamia*, 17 July 2018.
https://www.mamamia.com.au/doctor-fired-transgender-pronouns/ Accessed 20 July 2018.

2. *International Covenant on Civil and Political Rights,* Article 18.
http://www.ohchr.org/en/professionalinterest/pages/ccpr.aspx

3. "Interview: Alyssa Milano on the #MeToo movement: 'We're not going to stand for it any more'", *The Guardian*, 1 December 2017.
https://www.theguardian.com/culture/2017/dec/01/alyssa-milano-mee-too-sexual-harassment-abuse Accessed 20 May 2018.

4. South Australian *Acts Interpretation Act 1915,* Section 4, (as amended by the *Statutes Amendment (Gender Identity and Equity) Act 2016.*
http://www.austlii.edu.au/au/legis/sa/consol_act/aia1915230/s4.html

5. Based on the definition of "science", *Oxford Living Dictionaries.*
https://en.oxforddictionaries.com/definition/science Accessed 15 April 2018.

6. "liberty", *Oxford Living Dictionaries.*
https://en.oxforddictionaries.com/definition/liberty Accessed 15 April 2018.

7. "inherent", *Oxford Living Dictionary.*
https://en.oxforddictionaries.com/definition/inherent Accessed 15 April 2018.

TABLE 18.1:
OPTIONS FOR RIGHTS, PRIVILEGES, PROTECTIONS AND ACCESS TO SERVICES ACCORDING TO THE BIOLOGICAL WORLD AND THE TRANSGENDER WORLD VIEW. WHICH WORLD VIEW SHOULD BE PRIORITISED?

	Access to services and spaces, employment and identity documents	Proposals prioritising: (a) the biological world view (BWV) where persons are immutably, biologically Male or Female (M/F); and then (b) the transgender world view (TWV) where people identify by their fluid gender identity	Objections from: The biological world view (BWV) and the transgender world view (TWV)
1	Birth certificate sex identifier	BWV: M/F	TWV objection: Non-binary gender identities and genderless are not recognised on identity documents.
2	Sex identifier on official documents	TWV: M/F, X (Indeterminate, Unspecified, Intersex); or M/F, Other Indeterminate covers non-binary	BWV objection: The X marker automatically changes/degrades the meaning of M/F from immutable, biological sex to cisgender terms that are mutable, fluid and lack certainty.

Table 18.1:

	Access to services and spaces, employment and identity documents	Proposals prioritising: (a) the biological world view (BWV) where persons are immutably, biologically Male or Female (M/F); and then (b) the transgender world view (TWV) where people identify by their fluid gender identity	Objections from: The biological world view (BWV) and the transgender world view (TWV)
3	Access to toilets, showers, change rooms	BWV: Person uses M/F facility according to biological sex at birth.	TWV objection: Transgenders cannot access the facilities that match their gender identity.
		TWV (1): Provide Unisex (gender-neutral) faculties for transgenders, separate from M/F facilities.	BWV objection (1): Transgenders cannot use the facilities that match their gender identity. Disabled people can object to being required to share facilities with transgenders.
		TWV (2): Allow transgenders to use the restroom of their choice.	BWV objection (2): Biological women and girls required to have men who identify as women using female facilities and female private, intimate spaces and putting them at risk of sexual assault from males who pretend to be male-to-female transgenders. Biological men and boys required to have women and girls who identify as males using male facilities and lose male private spaces.
		TWV (3): Abolish M/F facilities and have only Unisex (gender-neutral) facilities.	BWV objection (3): Biological women, girls, men and boys required to share facilities and object to their loss of privacy.

317

	Access to services and spaces, employment and identity documents	Proposals prioritising: (a) the biological world view (BWV) where persons are immutably, biologically Male or Female (M/F); and then (b) the transgender world view (TWV) where people identify by their fluid gender identity	Objections from: The biological world view (BWV) and the transgender world view (TWV)
4	Access to sex-specific schools	BWV: Boys attend boys' schools. Girls attend girls' schools.	TWV objection: Transgenders cannot attend a school that matches their gender identity.
		TWV: Transgenders attend schools according to the sex with which they identify, e.g. a boy identifying as a girl attends a girls-only school.	BWV objection: A sex-specific girls' school required to accommodate boys who identify as girls, and either provide separate unisex restroom facilities or allow these biological males to access girls' facilities and sports.
5	School sex education	BWV: Teach male and female biology, reproduction and aspects of heterosexual/gay/lesbian sexuality.	TWV objection: Transgenders are not recognised and object that children are not taught that they can change their sex/gender identity.
		TWV: Teach that gender identity is independent of biological sex, or that sex and gender identity are social constructs.	BWV objection: Parents don't want children taught the belief that gender identity is independent of sex, or that people can change their sex or that sex is solely a social construct.
6	School dormitories and camps	BWV: Sex-specific dormitories and camp facilities	TWV objection: Transgenders cannot access dormitories and camp faculties that match their self-defined gender identity.
		TWV: Person accesses dormitories and camp faculties that match their self-defined gender identity.	BWV objection: Parents, students and teachers holding the BWV are required to have biological males who identify as female access to girls' dormitories and camps, violating girls' right to privacy and putting girls at risk of sexual assault from males who pretend to be male-to-female transgenders.

Table 18.1:

	Access to services and spaces, employment and identity documents	Proposals prioritising: (a) the biological world view (BWV) where persons are immutably, biologically Male or Female (M/F); and then (b) the transgender world view (TWV) where people identify by their fluid gender identity	Objections from: The biological world view (BWV) and the transgender world view (TWV)
7	Marriage application form	BWV: Groom, Bride, Partner	TWV objection: Transgender (gender-fluid) marriage is not recognised.
		TWV: Groom, Bride, Partner: M/F, Indeterminate, Unspecified, Intersex	BWV objection: People who hold the BWV object that Indeterminate, Unspecified means that M/F become mutable, fluid cisgender terms, not statements of immutable, fixed, biological reality. This allows two men to identify as women and be in a lesbian marriage.
8	Services to weddings	BWV: Marriage celebrants and wedding service providers (reception places, food suppliers, photographers, etc.) holding a BWV choose to service weddings according to their conscience, thought, belief or religion.	TWV objection: People choosing not to service transgender weddings because of their BWV accused of discrimination against transgender couples.
		TWV: All wedding service providers are required by law to service transgender (gender-fluid) weddings.	BWV objection: Service providers who hold to the BWV are required to service transgender (gender-fluid) weddings, violating their right to freedom of conscience, thought, belief and religion, as set out the in the International Covenant on Civil and Political Rights.

	Access to services and spaces, employment and identity documents	Proposals prioritising: (a) the biological world view (BWV) where persons are immutably, biologically Male or Female (M/F); and then (b) the transgender world view (TWV) where people identify by their fluid gender identity	Objections from: The biological world view (BWV) and the transgender world view (TWV)
9	Transgender marriage counselling	BWV: Counsellors holding the BWV should be free to provide marriage counselling according to their conscience.	TWV objection: Counsellors holding to the BWV who choose not to counsel transgenders can be accused of discrimination against transgender couples.
		TWV: Counsellor should be required to provide marriage counselling to couples, regardless of their gender identity.	BWV objection: Counsellors holding to the BWV are required to counsel according to the TWV, violating their right to freedom of conscience, thought, belief and religion, as set out in the International Covenant on Civil and Political Rights.
10	Language of sex and gender	BWV: People are free to identify persons in terms that recognise by their biological birth sex, with no threat of detriment, or to identify a person by their preferred pronouns and non-binary terms.	TWV objection: Transgenders are not recognised by their preferred pronouns and non-binary terms.
		TWV: By law, or under threat of professional sanctions, people are required to address both transgenders, and people who regard their sex as immutable, using either gender-neutral pronouns or in terms by which the transgender person chooses to be recognised.	BWV objection: People holding the BWV are required to (a) address transgenders by their preferred pronouns in all circumstances, and (b) refer to themselves, their family and friends in gender-neutral terms.

Table 18.1:

	Proposals prioritising: (a) the biological world view (BWV) where persons are immutably, biologically Male or Female (M/F); and then (b) the transgender world view (TWV) where people identify by their fluid gender identity	Objections from: The biological world view (BWV) and the transgender world view (TWV)
Access to services and spaces, employment and identity documents		
11 Access to sex-specific sports, women-only clubs and organisations	BWV: A person plays in male or female sport, or becomes a member of men's or women's clubs, according to their birth sex.	TWV objection: Transgenders cannot play in the sport, or access organisations, that match self-defined gender identity.
	TWV: A person plays in male or female sport that matches their self-defined gender identity. A biological man who identifies more as a woman plays in female-only sport.	BWV objections: Biological women claim that transsexual male-to-females have an unfair strength and bio-mechanical advantage, even after sex-change surgery and hormonal treatments, over biological women. Biological women are required to compete with transsexual male-to-females in female-only sports and accept them as members of female-only organisations.
12 Provisions of health services such as female pap smear test	BWV: Biological women permitted to ask for biological females to take pap smears and carry out other intimate examinations and treatments.	TWV objection: Biological women can be accused of discrimination against transsexual male-to-female medical personnel if they ask for biological females to carry out intimate medical examinations and treatments.
	TWV: Laws recognise male-to-female medical persons as female and require women patients to accept services from transgender medical personnel.	BWV objection: This requirement violates a woman's right to privacy and possibly risks her safety.

	Proposals prioritising: (a) the biological world view (BWV) where persons are immutably, biologically Male or Female (M/F); and then (b) the transgender world view (TWV) where people identify by their fluid gender identity	Objections from: The biological world view (BWV) and the transgender world view (TWV)
Access to services and spaces, employment and identity documents		TWV objection: Transgenders can object if they are not recognised by their transitioned identity. Health professionals can be accused of discrimination for asking a transsexual/ transgender person their birth sex in order to provide medical treatments specific to that person's biological sex.
13 Medical treatments, referrals, provision of pharmaceuticals	BWV: Diagnose medical conditions and treat patients according to their biological sex, given that men and women are subject to some different diseases, can present with very different symptoms for the same condition and respond differently to the same treatments. TWV: Diagnose medical conditions and treat patients according to their transitioned gender identity, i.e. medically treat male-to-female as female and female-to-male as male.	BWV objection: Health professionals can be held accountable for misdiagnosis and/or mistreatment if they fail to diagnose and treat a transgender person according to their biological birth sex.
14 Medical research	BWV: The new scientific field of sex-based biology says it is important to conduct diagnosis, pharmaceutical trials and other medical treatments separately on biological men and biological women as diagnosis and responses to treatments can be different because of their biological differences (see Chapter 16.6). TWV: For the purposes of medical research, transgenders are identified by their gender identity, not their birth sex.	TWV objection: Conducting diagnosis, pharmaceutical trials and other medical treatments on persons according to their biological birth sex discriminates against people whose gender identity is different from their birth sex. BWV objection: If medical trials cannot test different responses of male and females, then the medical treatments cannot be effectively tailored to provide the most effective results to all men and women.

Table 18.1:

	Proposals prioritising: (a) the biological world view (BWV) where persons are immutably, biologically Male or Female (M/F); and then (b) the transgender world view (TWV) where people identify by their fluid gender identity	Objections from: The biological world view (BWV) and the transgender world view (TWV)
Access to services and spaces, employment and identity documents		
15 Psychological counselling of, doctors' referrals for, pharmacies' provision of pharmaceuticals for, people (including children) transitioning to the opposite sex	BWV: Gender dysphoria is listed in the DSM-5, a manual of psychological disorders, along with anorexia and body identity disorder. Counselling treatments push back against the transitioning, i.e. conversion to the opposite to the person's birth sex. Doctors should not be required to provide prescriptions or referrals for transgenders and pharmacists not required to dispense transitioning pharmaceuticals. TWV: Gender dysphoria is resolved by supporting a person to transition to a gender identity other than their birth sex.	TWV objection: Counselling that pushes back against transitioning is considered discrimination against transgenders. ALP policy is to be that families discouraging a child from transitioning will be considered as domestic violence against the child (see Chapter 11.3). Doctors should be required to provide prescriptions or referrals; pharmacists required to dispense transitioning pharmaceuticals. BWV objection: Counsellors who object – pointing to how gender dysphoria is classed as a psychological disorder in the DSM-5 and to studies showing that most children with gender dysphoria desist transitioning and, as adults, identify only with their biological sex at birth – can be accused of discrimination and risk sanctions.
16 Female beauty salon services, like waxing	BWV: Biological women can choose to have a biological female provide some intimate salon services, like waxing. TWV: Biological women required to accept a transsexual male-to-female providing intimate salon services.	TWV objection: Biological women can be accused of discrimination against transsexual male-to-females if they ask for biological females to provide intimate salon services. BWV objection: Biological women claim a right to privacy and a right to choose who carries out intimate services.

	Proposals prioritising: (a) the biological world view (BWV) where persons are immutably, biologically Male or Female (M/F); and then (b) the transgender world view (TWV) where people identify by their fluid gender identity	Objections from: The biological world view (BWV) and the transgender world view (TWV)
Access to services and spaces, employment and identity documents		
17 Access to female-only safe spaces; for example, female gyms, domestic violence shelters	BWV: Biological women only have access to female safe spaces. TWV: Transsexual male-to-females are to be treated the same as biological women and given access to female-only safe spaces.	TWV objection: Biological women can be accused of discrimination for refusing transgender males-to-females access to female-only safe spaces. BWV objection: Biological women claim a right to privacy and to safe spaces for biological females only.

Table 18.1:

		Proposals prioritising: (a) the biological world view (BWV) where persons are immutably, biologically Male or Female (M/F); and then (b) the transgender world view (TWV) where people identify by their fluid gender identity	Objections from: The biological world view (BWV) and the transgender world view (TWV)
18	Access to services and spaces, e.g. employment and identity documents Affirmative action, e.g. women's scholarships, jobs, preselection for parliament	BWV Only biological women are beneficiaries of affirmative action policies. Transgender male-to-females are not eligible.	TWV objection: Transgender males-to-females claim they are discriminated against if they are refused access to affirmative action programs.
		TWV: Transgender male-to-females claim the same privileges granted to biological women under affirmative action programs.	BWV objection: Biological women object that this undermines, or destroys, the idea of affirmative action as a man can self-identify as a woman and claim privileges given to women only.
19	Accommodation in prison	BWV: Prisoners are housed in prison that match their biological sex. Prisons provide sex-specific showers and toilets.	TWV objection: Transgenders claim that they are discriminated against by being denied accommodation in prisons that match their self-defined gender identity.
		TWV (1): Transgender prisoners accommodated in prisons according to their self-defined gender identity.	BWV objection (1): Biological women object to having transgender male-to-females accommodated in their prison (a) violating their right to privacy in showers, toilets and change rooms, and (b) placing biological women at risk in cases where these biological males are in prison for violent crimes against women.
		TWV (2): Transgender prisoners accommodated in special prison for transgenders, as in Italy.	BWV objection (2): Possibly, transgenders claim that they are discriminated against by being denied accommodation in prisons that match their self-defined gender identity.

325

	Access to services and spaces, employment and identity documents	Proposals prioritising: (a) the biological world view (BWV) where persons are immutably, biologically Male or Female (M/F); and then (b) the transgender world view (TWV) where people identify by their fluid gender identity	Objections from: The biological world view (BWV) and the transgender world view (TWV)
20	Access to lesbian-only organisations, spaces, events	BWV: Biological, female lesbians have exclusive access to lesbian organisations, spaces, events.	TWV objection: Biological men who identify as women and as lesbians can claim they are discriminated against if refused access to lesbian-only organisations, spaces, events.
		TWV: Transgender male-to-females who identify as lesbians claim access to lesbian organisations, spaces, events.	BWV objection: Biological, lesbian women object to having transgender male-to-females accessing lesbian organisations, spaces, events.
21	Employment	Under various anti-discrimination and equal opportunity laws, employers can face charges of discrimination against transgenders, on the basis of their fluid gender identity, and employees and professionals can face workplace discipline, or loss of professional accreditation. These could apply in the areas above: 3, 4, 5, 6, 8, 9, 10, 11, 12, 13, 14, 15, 16, 17, 18, 19, 20.	

CHAPTER 19

TRANSGENDERISM LAWS UNDERMINING A TOLERANT DEMOCRACY

Liberal democracy is founded on the state being tolerant of all beliefs and religions in the public square. The neutral state is essential for keeping the peace in a diverse, pluralist society.

For a just and equitable society, laws must recognise what are verifiable, immutable facts while tolerating opposing views or beliefs.

19.1   EVOLUTION OF TOLERANT DEMOCRACIES

The modern tolerant democracy and codifying of inherent rights didn't just happen. They were forged from centuries of conflicts and bloodshed.

The 16th and 17th century Wars of Religion, or the wars of the Reformation and Counter-Reformation, cost millions of lives in Europe and Britain. The combatants were influenced by rival religious beliefs, although the divisions were not solely religious and, in most cases, religion was only one contributor to the conflict.

These wars ended with a series of treaties, which profoundly affected the shape of emerging democracies over subsequent centuries. Either people tolerated each other's beliefs and lived alongside each other peacefully, or countries would face endless wars.

"Tolerance" means to "allow the existence, occurrence, or practice of (something that one dislikes or disagrees with) without interference".[1] It derives from the Latin, *tolerantia*, meaning to bear with, or endure with.

Tolerance became a foundation principle of modern democracy.

A tolerant democracy allows for a "pluralist" society that recognises "autonomy for individual bodies in preference to monolithic state control"[2] where "members of minority groups maintain their independent cultural traditions"[3].

A tolerant democracy has no established official religion or belief. The state remains neutral and maintains an open public square in which all beliefs and faiths can be held and manifested. Or, if there is an established religion, the state does not discriminate against other religions or beliefs.

As British philosopher and theologian Rabbi Jonathan Sacks has explained, a tolerant state

> aims not so much at truth but at peace. It is a political necessity, not a religious imperative, and it arises when people have lived through the alternative: the war of all against all.[4]

A further bulwark for free, tolerant democracies was created after the bloody horrors of World War II (1939–45), which saw the deaths of 50-70 million people at the unbelievable rate of 200,000-250,000 per week.

Driven by the cry of "never again", the *Universal Declaration of Human Rights* was drafted as a visible, worldwide testimony of the dignity and inherent rights of every human being by a group of remarkable international contributors under Eleanor Roosevelt. In 1948, it was ratified through a proclamation by the United Nations General Assembly on 10 December 1948, with a count of 48 votes to none, with eight abstentions and two did not vote.[5]

The UDHR Preamble says:

> Whereas disregard and contempt for human rights have resulted in barbarous acts which have outraged the conscience of mankind, and the advent of a world in which human beings shall enjoy freedom of speech and belief and freedom from fear and want has been proclaimed as the highest aspiration of the common people …[6].

In 1966, the *International Covenant on Civil and Political Rights* (ICCPR) transformed the UDHR into an international legal instrument. Australia is a party to the ICCPR, but has not incorporated the Covenant into federal law, although some provisions have been incorporated into the federal *Privacy Act 1988*[7] and the *Disability Discrimination Act 1992*.[8]

UDHR and ICCPR have added protections for human rights in international and domestic law, setting standards for governments to respect rights based on the inherent dignity of the human person.

19.2 MAN, WOMAN AND BELIEFS RECOGNISED IN THE UDHR AND ICCPR

The UDHR Preamble made it clear that the *Declaration* cannot create rights, it can only recognise that

> the *inherent* dignity and ... the equal and *inalienable* rights of all members of the human family is the foundation of freedom, justice and peace in the world ...[9] (author emphasis).

Dignity, "the state or quality of being worthy of honour or respect",[10] is *inherent*, "a permanent, essential, or characteristic attribute"[11], and rights derived from that dignity are *inalienable*, they cannot "be taken away ... or even given away"[12].

Both the UDHR and ICCPR state that the dignity of the human person is the basis of human rights, including the equal rights of "men and women" [13,14].

Both the UDHR and ICCPR regard the biological nature of men and women as self-evident and part of the inherent dignity of the human person. Human biological nature is recognised prior to any legal definitions of man and woman and prior to bestowing different rights, privileges, protections and access to services on men and women.

At the same time, both the UDHR and ICCPR[15] protect freedom of "belief", regardless of whether a belief is verifiable or not. The UN Human Rights Committee (1994) explains that freedom of belief

> is far-reaching and profound; it encompasses freedom of thought on all matters, personal conviction and the commitment to religion or *belief*, whether manifested individually or in community with others[16] (editor emphasis).

Consequently, the right to hold transgenderism as a "belief" is protected by the UDHR and ICCPR. This "belief" does not have to be based on science, or be verifiable in other ways.

In summary, these UN instruments recognise man and woman as biological, immutable "facts", while protecting the rights of people to hold contrary and contested "beliefs" like the belief that a person can have a gender identity as well as, or in place of, their biological sex. These instruments of international law require governments to tolerate, and ensure the liberty of all people to hold, a chosen belief.

However, ensuring a person's liberty to hold a belief is very different from the state defining this belief in law. In doing so, the state imposes one "belief" on its citizens.

Hence, where the state defines gender identity in law, it brings the *created* rights of transgenders into conflict with the *inherent* rights of people who recognise their biological nature as men or women.

Table 18.1 describes the areas of conflict this creates in the culture.

19.3   GENDER IDENTITY AS A NEW STATE-ESTABLISHED "BELIEF"

The distinction between a law recognising verifiable "facts" as compared with a law recognising an unverifiable, ideological "belief" is important to the functioning of democracy.

To ensure plurality, or diversity, of beliefs in the public square, the state must remain neutral. It does not become entangled in matters of personal preference, like family size, choice of marital partner, choice of friends, secular and religious beliefs, or social aspects of a person, like their gender identity.

In being relaxed about personal matters, it avoids establishing a state religion or "belief" that is imposed on society.

In contrast, what does it mean for the state to define the human person by their gender identity? What does it mean for democracy to write an ideology like transgenderism into law?

It means that the state establishes transgenderism as a "belief".

It is analogous to the state making the Catholic belief a protected attribute in anti-discrimination law. This would mean that state schools would be forced to teach the Catholic faith, and atheist organisations would be forced to employ Catholics. Effectively, the government would be making Catholicism a state religion intolerant of other people who hold any different belief.

This would mark a return to the authoritarian form of state that a tolerant, neutral democracy is supposed to avoid.

As law professor Iain Benson (2017) pointed out:

> To allow the state (i.e. comprised by law and politics) to interfere unduly in the domestic sphere, will shift the state from being one that is "open" to one that is authoritarian or "total" ...[17].

19.4   CONCLUSION

The more that the created rights of the transgenderism world view are inserted into law, the more the freedoms and rights of people who recognise their sex as inherent are restricted.

The more that people fear, or suffer, legal sanctions or loss of their professional accreditation and employment, the more freedom of speech, association, belief, thought, conscience and religion are threatened.

This is precisely what the neutral democratic state is supposed to avoid. It marks the devolution of a tolerant democracy towards an authoritarian state.

The risk is not a military war, but a legal and cultural conflict of all against all.

Endnotes

1. "tolerate", *Oxford Living Dictionaries*.
   https://en.oxforddictionaries.com/definition/tolerate Accessed 15 April 2018.

2. "pluralist", *Oxford Living Dictionaries*.
   https://en.oxforddictionaries.com/definition/pluralist

3. "pluralism", *Oxford Living Dictionaries*.
   https://en.oxforddictionaries.com/definition/pluralism Accessed 15 April 2018.

4. Jonathan Sacks, *The Home We Build Together*, Continuum, London, 2007, pg. 199.

5. "Questions and answers about the Universal Declaration of Human Rights", United Nations Association in Canada.
   https://web.archive.org/web/20120912162219/http://www.unac.org/rights/question.html Accessed 15 April 2018.

6. *Universal Declaration of Human Rights*, Preamble.
   http://www.un.org/en/universal-declaration-human-rights/

7. *Privacy Act 1988*.
   https://www.legislation.gov.au/Details/C2018C00034

8. *Disability Discrimination Act 1992*.
   https://www.legislation.gov.au/Details/C2018C00125

9. *Universal Declaration of Human Rights*, Preamble, Op. cit.

10. "dignity", *Oxford Living Dictionaries*.
    https://en.oxforddictionaries.com/definition/dignity Accessed 15 April 2018.

11. "inherent", *Oxford Living Dictionaries*.
    https://en.oxforddictionaries.com/definition/inherent Accessed 15 April 2018.

12. "inalienable", *Oxford Living Dictionaries*.
    https://en.oxforddictionaries.com/definition/inalienable Accessed 15 April 2018.

13. *Universal Declaration of Human Rights*, Preamble.

14. *International Covenant on Civil and Political Rights*, Article 3.
    http://www.ohchr.org/en/professionalinterest/pages/ccpr.aspx

15. Ibid., Article 18 (3).

16. Human Rights Committee, General Comment 22, Article 18 (Forty-eighth session, 1993). Compilation of General Comments and General Recommendations Adopted by Human Rights Treaty Bodies, U.N. Doc. HRI/GEN/1/Rev.1 at 35 (1994). Note: the meaning of belief and how beliefs are protected is explained in this document by the HRC, Comment 22.

17. *Religion, Liberty and the Jurisdictional Limits of Law*, General Editors Iain T. Benson, Barry W. Bussey. LexisNexis Canada Inc., August 2017.

CHAPTER 20

CONCLUSION: TWO PROTECTIONS FOR RIGHTS, LIBERTIES AND FREEDOMS

20.1　INTRODUCTION

There have been public debates in many countries over the legalisation of same-sex marriage. These same-sex marriage debates have overshadowed and masked the wider issue of transgenderism, which has been subject to little public debate.

To grasp the distinction between the transgender world view and same-sex marriage, consider the LGBTIQ acronym. Same-sex marriage involves issues of sexual orientation (LGB); that is, of sexual relationships. Transgenderism – transgender, queer, questioning (TQ) – involves the issue of sexual/gender identity.

Each involves different conflicts over rights and freedoms, as indicated in Table 1.1, and requires different solutions. The I (intersex) issue is different again (see Chapter 5.2).

20.2　LIVING WITH DIFFERENT VIEWS OF MARRIAGE

Conflict over the definition of marriage concerns what sexual relationships or orientations should be legally recognised as marriage.

In part, the conflict involves different *beliefs* about marriage. Some people claim that heterosexual, same-sex (and transgender) forms of marriage should be recognised in law. Others hold that the law should recognise only heterosexual marriage.

In countries where same-sex marriage has been legalised, significant numbers of people still hold that marriage should only mean heterosexual marriage. They claim a right to freedom of thought, belief, conscience or religion about marriage.

In part, the conflict also involves the right to *manifest* (make plain or clear in the public eye) their belief; that is, the right freely to express, without impairment, their belief about marriage. The right to manifest a belief requires the right to freedom of speech, association and other forms of expression.

For example, ministers of religion and civil celebrants argue that they should not be compelled to marry same-sex couples or, in fact, to marry any couple. Similarly, some wedding service providers – bakers, florists, photographers – argue that they should not be required to provide their services to same-sex weddings, or any weddings, against their right publicly to manifest their belief only in heterosexual marriage (see Chapter 10.5).

The *International Covenant on Civil and Political Rights* (ICCPR) recognises these freedoms and rights. Article 18 states:

1. Everyone shall have the right to freedom of thought, conscience and religion. This right shall include freedom to have or to adopt a religion or belief of his choice, and freedom, either individually or in community with others and in public or private, to manifest his religion or belief in worship, observance, practice and teaching.

2. No one shall be subject to coercion which would impair his freedom to have or to adopt a religion or belief of his choice.[1]

Conversely, the ICCPR says that people should not be forced to act against their religion, belief, conscience or thought.

3. Freedom to manifest one's religion or beliefs may be subject only to such limitations as are prescribed by law and are necessary to protect public safety, order, health, or morals or the fundamental rights and freedoms of others.[2]

Some teachers argue that they should not be compelled to teach that same-sex marriage is equal to heterosexual marriage. This would be contrary to the ICCPR protections for freedom of belief for teachers, as well as the rights of parents to determine the moral education of their children. Article 18 goes on to say:

4. The States Parties to the present Covenant undertake to have respect for the liberty of parents and, when applicable, legal guardians, to ensure the religious and moral education of their children in conformity with their own convictions.[3]

Some same-sex marriage advocates say that civil celebrants and wedding service providers should be required to provide their services to gay and lesbian weddings. They argue that to refuse their services constitutes discrimination; that is, such refusals may offend or treat same-sex couples differently or less favourably.

Advocates for heterosexual marriage argue that legally requiring them to provide their services to same-sex weddings would force them to *manifest* a *belief* that they do not have in same-sex marriage.

People who decline to supply services to a same-sex wedding because they hold a belief in heterosexual marriage risk being prosecuted under the Federal *Sex Discrimination Act 1984*, which says the test for discrimination is where

> the discriminator treats the aggrieved person less favourably than, in circumstances that are the same or are not materially different, the discriminator treats or would treat a person who has a different sexual orientation. ... [or] imposes, or proposes to impose, a condition, requirement or practice that has, or is likely to have, the effect of disadvantaging persons who have the same sexual orientation as the aggrieved person.[4]

In 2018, the Australian government has two major inquiries investigating ways to protect freedoms of belief and religion. These are timely, as same-sex marriage (and transgender marriage) were made legal in 2017 (see Chapter 10). Several proposals suggest ways to protect the freedoms and rights, without detriment, for those who conscientiously believe in heterosexual marriage.

One proposal is to incorporate Article 18 of the ICCPR into Australian human rights law. Other suggestions are for a freedom of religion and belief anti-discrimination act, a religious freedom act, a bill of rights or a charter of rights.

These proposals aim at allowing beliefs of all parties – for marriage celebrants, wedding services providers, parents, school teachers, and so on – to be respected in disputes over the nature and definition of marriage. The areas of conflict that require solutions are identified in Table 1.1.

20.3 ALLEVIATING CONFLICTS BETWEEN THE BIOLOGICAL AND TRANSGENDER WORLD VIEWS

Whereas conflicts over the definition of marriage are between conflicted *beliefs* (religious, cultural or secular) about the nature of marriage, the conflicts over transgenderism are between a *belief* that people are defined by their fluid gender identity and the biological *fact* that sex is fixed, immutable.

What is *factual* and verifiable needs to be distinguished from what is a *belief* that does not have to be verifiable. Scientific observation tells us that the earth is round, but a democracy protects the right of a person to believe that it is flat.

The defining of gender identity in law has overridden laws that historically have recognised male or female as a self-evident *fact* of a person's biology. Being self-evident, it was usually considered unnecessary to define man and woman in law.

Indeed, both the *Universal Declaration of Human Rights* (UDHR) and the ICCPR treat the terms men and women as self-evident facts.

For example, the UDHR recognises the inherent

> dignity and worth of the human person and ... the equal rights of men and women ...[5].

The ICCPR calls on all

> States Parties ... [to the ICCPR to] undertake to ensure the equal right of men and women to the enjoyment of all civil and political rights ...[6].

It also calls for the death penalty never to be carried out on "pregnant women"[7]. Here, sex is recognised as self-evident, defined by reproductive function. Only a person who is biologically female can become pregnant.

From the recognition of biological sex flow many rights, protections, privileges and access to services. Sometimes these are recognised and protected in laws, regulations and government or public service policies but, often, they are informally recognised only in the culture.

For example, the recording of male or female on birth certificates is a requirement that is sometimes a specified requirement in births, deaths and marriages registration acts and/or regulations but, in most cases, it is taken as self-evident that a child is to be recorded as either male or female. Requirements for male and female restrooms are found mostly in building industry codes, not in state laws or regulations.

Table 1.1 sets out the conflicts between the biological and transgender world views, while Table 18.1 indicates that these conflicts have no easy resolution. This suggests that the two world views cannot be simultaneously recognised in law.

The key question is, do they both need to be recognised and protected in law, or can one be recognised in law and the other remain a liberty?

As the biological world view of man, woman and sex is based on science, it should take priority in law. The law should recognise biological sex, which is factual, scientifically verifiable, and from which inherent rights flow (see Chapter 3.2). Even transgenderism implicitly affirms biological sex. All definitions of gender identity define a person's gender identity against the reality of their birth sex (see Chapters 4.4, 6.2.6, 8.2.2).

Defining man, woman and sex does not proscribe, or in any way impede, belief in, and manifestation of, transgenderism. Transgenders are free to identify with any self-defined gender identity. What the law does not proscribe, people have the liberty to do.

At the same time, transgenderism is protected under Article 18 of the ICCPR, which protects all "beliefs".

20.4 CONCLUSION

A tolerant democracy aims to keep the peace by tolerating all views, beliefs, religions and ideologies. At the same time, a democracy should ensure the rights of most people are not overridden by the ideological claims of a minority.

To "keep the peace", laws should recognise the reality of biological man and woman and protect the inherent rights that flow from the fact of a person's sex.

This also avoids the state making transgenderism an established state belief, preserves a pluralist society and maintains diversity while, at the same time, it respects the transgender world view as a belief.

However, if governments give priority to the transgender world view over the biological world view in law, democracies risk becoming authoritarian states.

In the process, laws giving legal recognition and protections to a person by their self-chosen gender identity dissolve the meaning of sex, man, woman, feminism, gay, lesbian and heterosexual.

Diversity is replaced by uniformity. Everyone is treated same-same, as one shade of grey.

Endnotes

1. *International Covenant on Civil and Political Rights*, Section 18.
   https://www.ohchr.org/en/professionalinterest/pages/ccpr.aspx
2. Ibid.
3. Ibid.
4. *Sex Discrimination Act 1984,* as compiled on 1 July 2016, Section 5A.
   https://www.legislation.gov.au/Details/C2016C00880
5. *Universal Declaration of Human Rights*, Preamble.
   http://www.un.org/en/universal-declaration-human-rights/
6. *International Covenant on Civil and Political Rights*, Article 3.
7. Ibid, Article 6 (5).

CHAPTER 21

POSTSCRIPT

MICHEL FOUCAULT VERSUS THE UNIVERSAL DECLARATION OF HUMAN RIGHTS

Nothing in man – not even his body – is sufficiently stable to serve as the basis for self-recognition or for understanding other men.

Michel Foucault

If there is no common human nature, there are no universal human rights.

Patrick J Byrne

21.1 UNIVERSAL DECLARATION OF HUMAN RIGHTS

The 1948 *Universal Declaration of Human Rights* (UDHR) was a milestone in the history of human rights protecting human freedoms. Its Preamble explains how it was written in response to the "disregard and contempt for human rights ... [that] resulted in barbarous acts which ... outraged the conscience of mankind"[1] in World War II (1939-45).

It said the respect for universal (relating to all people)[2] human rights is essential "if man is not to be compelled to have recourse, as a last resort, to rebellion against tyranny and oppression"[3].

The Preamble establishes that the first rights to be respected, to ensure against "tyranny and oppression", are "freedom of speech and belief and freedom from fear and want"[4]. These are primary freedoms from which other freedoms flow. They are the guardians and guarantors of all other freedoms. They allow people to argue for and defend their freedoms and to speak and live according to their beliefs. They guarantee equality and diversity.

The UDHR Preamble insists that these rights are "equal" (being the same in quantity, size, degree or value)[5] for all people, "inalienable" (not subject to being taken away from or given away)[6] and "common" (universal) to all members of the human race.

These rights are "common" because they are based on the "inherent dignity" of all human beings. Inherent means "existing in something as a permanent, essential, or characteristic attribute"[7]. They can be described as intrinsic (belonging naturally; essential)[8] to our common human nature.

Our common human nature defines our common humanity. An essential characteristic of the human race is that it is made up of "men and women" who have "equal" human rights.[9]

The UDHR protects everyone, including all minorities

> without distinction of any kind, such as race, colour, sex, language, religion, political or other opinion, national or social origin, property, birth or other status …[10]

This is a broad protection that includes belief in transgenderism.

Hence, the title to this milestone in the history of human rights, the *Universal Declaration of Human Rights*.

Having nations sign up to the UDHR is not a panacea for stopping gross violations of human rights, barbarous acts or wars. However, as its Preamble suggests, the UDHR informs the conscience of society to respect the dignity of all people. It informs legislatures, encouraging them to find and develop the legal, economic and cultural means to ensure the dignity of all human beings is respected.

21.2   FOUCAULT DISSENTS

Michel Foucault (1926-1984) is regarded as the grandfather of transgender/queer theory. He asserted that "human nature" is only a cultural construction, and "man" must be recognised as the product of his social and cultural circumstances, a thing among things.[11]

Summarising his theory of human nature, *The Stanford Encyclopedia of Philosophy* (2018) says that Foucault's "critical philosophy" argued that

> the modern human sciences (biological, psychological, social) purported to offer universal scientific truths about human

> nature that are, in fact, often mere expressions of ethical and political commitments of a particular society.
>
> Foucault's "critical philosophy" undermines such claims by exhibiting how they are the outcome of contingent historical forces, not scientifically grounded truths.[12]

From this, Foucault (1971) theorised that there is nothing common to human beings to justify a common, inherent human nature. He claimed that

> nothing in man – not even his body – is sufficiently stable to serve as the basis for self-recognition or for understanding other men.[13]

Judith Butler (1989) described this statement as "Foucault's efforts to describe the mechanism by which bodies are constituted as cultural constructions …". She said that this "raises the question of whether there is in fact a body which is external to its construction, invariant in some of its structures …"[14]. Indeed, Foucault (1971) appears to confirm this interpretation when he says that human nature is a term that has been constructed "in terms borrowed from our society"[15].

If human nature is a construct formed by social, political, economic and other forms of power, then it does not signify any known common, innate, biological, metaphysical or spiritual essence among humans. It is not fixed but can change in response to changes in social, economic and other human power structures.

The subsequent development of transgender/queer theory (see Chapter 4.3) was based on Foucault's allusion to human nature as culturally constructed. This allows the theory to treat sex as fluid, not as a fixed, immutable, biological characteristic of the human person. It allows for the possibility of human sexual identity to be changed from a person's biological sex to a socially constructed gender identity.

Whereas the UDHR says that universal human rights are founded on human beings having an "inherent" human nature, Foucault implies that human nature is a cultural construct. What is socially constructed at one time in history can be culturally reconstructed at another time. If that is the case, there is no inherent, essential, common human nature.

If there is no common human nature, how can there be inherent, universal human rights? How can there be *equality* of rights for everyone if there is no inherent human *essence*, no common human nature from which to define equality?

21.3   RIGHTS: ONLY FOR THE MOST POWERFUL?

Underlying the idea of equal rights is the recognition that human beings possess a common essence/nature that dwarfs manifest differences between people. These include differences in race, skin colour, age, intellectual ability, beliefs and sex. The 20th-century movements for women's equality were based on the recognition of inherent equality between biological women and biological men.

From this common essence, the inherent human dignity of every human being is recognised. This is at the heart of what is meant by "equality for all", which a tolerant democracy recognises and first protects by guaranteeing basic freedoms of speech and belief.

However, when governments give priority to transgenderism over the recognition of an innate biological human essence, people can lose their employment, professional registration and face anti-discrimination tribunals for publicly manifesting their recognition of the biological world view. In such cases, the law is allocating superior rights to those holding the transgender world view.

Seventy years ago, the UDHR was a milestone against authoritarian governments, where those with superior rights dominated over those with inferior rights. Grading people by their class of rights is a pathway that can lead to oppression and tyranny. In the most extreme cases, tyranny is only overcome by rebellion.

In order to guarantee respect for the equal dignity of each and every person against oppression and tyranny, the UDHR called on governments around the world to recognise and respect the inherent (common to us all) human rights of all, including the rights of minorities. It aimed to unite the human race in solidarity (unity or agreement of feeling or action)[16] to respect universal human rights.

Respecting the primary rights to freedom of speech and belief requires both tolerance and generosity.

Under the UDHR prescription, protection of minorities, including transgenders, should be on the basis of the universal right of everyone to their freedom of speech and to hold and manifest their belief. By guaranteeing the rights of minorities, tolerant democracies guarantee people the liberty to socially adopt the gender identity of their choice.

In contrast, legislating for self-chosen gender identity provides grounds to prosecute for discrimination a person who recognises biological sex as fixed and inherent. This person is denied the right to live, speak and act in accordance with this biological world view.

21.4 CONCLUSION

The UDHR could only recognise, and advocate, equal rights for all if there is a common human nature that manifests the equal dignity of all human beings.

Foucault's claim that there is "nothing in man" to recognise things common to "other men" strongly implies that there is no universal, common human nature. So, how are rights to be determined?

Logically, rights are claimed and determined by those who are the strongest, the most politically and culturally powerful; in which case, the stronger can claim their rights at the expense of the weaker. This is a familiar path to an Orwellian society where some are less equal than others.

When laws prioritise the transgender world view, it is at the expense of the inherent rights of those who recognise the biological reality of male and female sex as inherent and immutable. As with other utopian ideologies, the universal rights to freedom of speech and belief are usually the first to be compromised.

Today, in the name of equality, transgender laws create inequalities and divisions. In the name of diversity, uniformity is imposed. Under the banner of protection from discrimination, authoritarian laws are imposed.

When an ideology like transgenderism is adopted in law, society is directed back towards historical times when states favoured established ideologies and religions.

This is a world astutely described in the *History of the Peloponnesian War* by the ancient Greek historian Thucydides (c. 460 BC – c. 400 BC) when he observed: "The strong do what they can and the weak suffer what they must"[17].

In the modern context, defining and protecting the newly created rights of one group over the universal, inherent rights of all risks society descending into a legal war of all against all.

Endnotes

1. *Universal Declaration of Human Rights*, Preamble. http://www.un.org/en/universal-declaration-human-rights/
2. "universal", *Oxford Living Dictionaries*. https://en.oxforddictionaries.com/definition/universal Accessed 20 June 2018.
3. Ibid.
4. *Universal Declaration of Human Rights*, Op, cit., Preamble.
5. "equal", *Oxford Living Dictionaries*. https://en.oxforddictionaries.com/definition/equal Accessed 20 June 2018.
6. "inalienable", *Oxford Living Dictionaries*. https://en.oxforddictionaries.com/definition/inalienable Accessed 20 June 2018.
7. "inherent", *Oxford Living Dictionaries*. https://en.oxforddictionaries.com/definition/inherent Accessed 20 June 2018.
8. "intrinsic", *Oxford Living Dictionaries*. https://en.oxforddictionaries.com/definition/intrinsic Accessed 20 June 2018.
9. *Universal Declaration of Human Rights*, Op. cit. Preamble. *International Covenant on Civil and Political Rights*, Article 3. http://www.ohchr.org/en/professionalinterest/pages/ccpr.aspx
10. *Universal Declaration of Human Rights*, Op, cit., Article 2.
11. "The Dead End of the Left? Augusto Del Noce's Critique of Modern Politics", Carlo Lancellotti, *Commonweal Magazine,* 6 April 2018. https://www.commonwealmagazine.org/dead-end-left
12. "Michel Foucault", *Stanford Encyclopedia of Philosophy*, First published Wednesday, 2 April 2003; substantive revision Tuesday, 22 May 2018. https://plato.stanford.edu/entries/foucault/?PHPSESSID=a67db9e6ad2d681797b094696328bf4a Accessed 23 July 2018.
13. "Michel Foucault", "Nietzsche, Genealogy, History", first appeared in *Hommage a Jean Hyppolite* (Paris: Presses Universitaires de France, 1971), pgs. 145-72. Sourced at https://noehernandezcortez.files.wordpress.com/2011/04/nietzsche-genealogy-history.pdf pg. 87. Accessed 17 June 2018.
14. "Foucault and the Paradox of Bodily Inscriptions", Judith Butler, *The Journal of Philosophy,* Vol. 86, No. 11, pgs. 601-607, November 1989. https://www.scribd.com/document/269154971/Butler-Foucault-s-Body
15. Review of *Noam Chomsky and Michel Foucault, Human Nature: Justice vs Power. The Chomsky-Foucault Debate [1971]*, edited by Fons Elders (London: Souvenir Press, 2011), ISBN: 978-1-595-58134-1, Asger Sørensen, *Foucault Studies*, No. 16, pgs. 201-207, September 2013, pg. 203. https://rauli.cbs.dk/index.php/foucault-studies/article/download/4132/4539 Accessed 17 June 2018.
16. "solidarity", *Oxford Living Dictionaries*. https://en.oxforddictionaries.com/definition/solidarity Accessed 20 June 2018.
17. Thucydides, *History of the Peloponnesian War,* Book V, 5.89-[1].

DEFINITIONS AND TERMS

THE TRANSGENDER WORLD VIEW VERSUS THE BIOLOGICAL WORLD VIEW

The biological and transgender world views have their own vocabulary. Many words common to both world views have different, or opposite, meanings depending on whether they are used in a biological or transgender context. Consequently, many words and terms are defined with two definitions, one for each world view.

For example, the word "gender" means binary male and female in the biological world context, but in the transgender context it means non-binary gender identity, that is, socially constructed terms, such as gender fluid, pangender, agender, etc. and cismale and cisfemale to describe men and women, effectively redefining male and female from biological terms to how a person "chooses" to self-identify.

Academics may (and do) use such technical language among themselves with justification, but its use extended to popular use and the law is an indication of just how far the suppositions and assertions hidden within transgender technical language stray from everyday experience.

Consequently, this dictionary is important to understanding the language of both world views.

* * * * * *

DICTIONARY OF BIOLOGICAL AND TRANSGENDER TERMS

AHRC: Australian Human Rights Commission.

BDMR: State and Territory Births, Deaths and Marriages Registration acts.

Binary: means relating to, composed of, or involving two things,[1] e.g. two biological sexes, male and female based on their complementary reproductive functions. Binary includes heterosexuals, gays, lesbians and medically transitioned transsexuals (opposite of non-binary).

Bisexual *(biological)*: means a person of one biological sex who is sexually attracted to members of both biological sexes.

Bisexual *(transgender)*: can mean a transgender person sexually attracted to two other transgender persons who may identify as being on a male-female spectrum, with a non-binary gender identity, or as genderless; or it can mean a person of one cisgender sexually attracted to other people of opposite cisgenders (see *transgender, cisgender*).

CAS: Court of Arbitration for Sport

Cisgender (cis male and cis female): means, in the transgender world view, a person choosing to *align* their gender identiy with their birth sex, in contrast to the biological world view that recognises sex as self-evident, fixed and immutable, not a matter of choice. *Cis* means "on same side as".

Child agency: Agency is the capacity of individuals to act independently and to make their own free choices.[2] Child agency means children having the power to act independently and being capable of making their own decisions.

Conversion/affirmation therapy *(biological world view)*: Conversion therapy refers to counselling a person with gender dysphoria to transition from their biological birth sex to a gender identity other than their birth sex. *Trans* means to shift fundamentally from one state to another. Conversely, *affirmation therapy* means affirming a person to identity with their sex at birth, to be comfortable with the body they are in.

Conversion/affirmation therapy *(transgender world view)*: Conversion therapy refers to counselling a transgender person to accept their birth sex in place of their gender identity; that is, to convert from transgender to their biological sex. Conversely, affirmation therapy means counselling a person to affirm their gender identity; that is, to affirm being transgender.

Disorder of Sexual Development (DSD): *See intersex.*

DSM-5: is the *Diagnostic and Statistical Manual of Mental Disorders* – 5 (2013), edited and published by the American Psychiatric Association as a standard reference manual for clinicians, researchers, psychiatric drug regulation agencies, health insurance companies, pharmaceutical companies, the legal system, and policy makers. It operates alongside the *ICD-10 Classification of Mental* *and Behavioural Disorders*, which is produced by the World Health Organisation.

Gay *(biological)*: means biological men who are attracted to men.

Gay *(transgender)*: means person A, who identifies as a man regardless of their birth sex, who is sexually attracted to person B, who identifies as a man regardless of their birth sex.

Consequently, two women can identify as men and be in a gay relationship (see *gender orientation*).

Gender *(biological)*: is from the Latin word *genus* which, in philosophy, means "a class of things that have common characteristics"[3]. The common characteristic of men is that they are members of the male sex. The common characteristic of women is that they are members of the female sex. Sex defines their biological "hardware".

Gender can also refer to characteristics associated with being a biological male or female, such as pregnancy, breast feeding, dress, hair styles, makeup and gestures, which can be considered part of a person's social "software".

Therefore, "gender" historically referred to men and women according to the biological sex (their hardware), or expressions of their sex-related characteristics (their software).

Gender identity *(transgender)*: refers to a person identifying by social characteristics only, with or without regard to their birth sex. The federal *Sex Discrimination Act 1984* says gender identity means the

> gender-related identity, appearance or mannerisms or other gender-related characteristics of a person (whether by way of medical intervention or not), with or without regard to the person's designated sex at birth.[4]

This allows for a person's gender identity to be on a spectrum, from complete maleness (one end) and complete femaleness (the other end), or anywhere in between. Or it can be non-binary and unrelated to sex (e.g. non-binary, gender diverse, androgynous, pangender, gender queer, inter gender, etc.).

Examples include a man socially identifying as a woman, or as agender, gender queer, androgynous, etc., or as genderless (see *gender orientation*).

Gender-fluid marriage: see *Transgender marriage.*

Gender dysphoria: occurs when a person experiences psychological distress caused by an incongruence between their biological sex and their self-defined gender identity and seeks psychological counselling (see also *DSM-5*).

Gender orientation: means orientation between persons identified by their *gender identities,* not by their biological sex. It could mean an androgynous person sexually attracted to a gender-diverse person, or a genderqueer person sexually attracted to an omnigender person.

Arguably, the federal *Sex Discrimination Act 1984* now recognises gender orientation.

In contrast, heterosexual, gay, lesbian and bisexual orientation are *sexual orientations* (see also *sexual orientation*).

Heterosexual *(biological)*: means a person of one biological sex sexually attracted to a person of the opposite biological sex; that is, sexual attractions between a biological man and biological woman.

Heterosexual *(transgender)*: can mean a cismale sexually attracted to a cisfemale and a cisfemale sexually attracted a cismale. Or, it can mean a biological man who identifies as a woman sexually attracted to a cismale; or a cisfemale sexually attracted to a biological woman who identifies as a man. Or, it can mean a biological woman who identifies as a man sexually attracted to a biological man who identifies as a woman (see also *gender orientation*).

Heteronormativity *(from essentialist feminist theory, based on recognition of biological male and female)*: concerns discrimination against biological women.

The feminist concept of heteronormativity says the binary, biological nature of men and women is fixed and unchangeable, but critiques laws, regulations and culture emphasising conditioned sex roles that promote the superiority of men over women, or the dominance of men over women. Usually, it also refers to laws and culture that promote heterosexuality as the preferred sexual orientation, over gay, lesbian or bisexual.

Discrimination is based on the imbalance of power between men and women, or an imbalance of power between the heterosexual versus the gay, lesbian and bisexual.

Heteronormativity *(transgender, non-binary)*: concerns claims of discrimination against people who identify as transgender, with a fluid gender identity.

It opposes laws that grant certain legal rights to men and women based on their biological birth sex, over those who identify with a self-defined gender identity (see Table 1.1).

Discrimination is said to be based on the dominance of those who recognise sex as biologically fixed over those who choose a self-defined gender identity other than their birth sex; that is, the dominance of the biological world view over the transgender world view.

As this heteronormative world view discriminates against transgenders, heteronormativity is regarded as intrinsically transphobic.

IAAF: International Association of Athletics Federations

Ideology: means a form of social or political philosophy in which practical elements are as prominent as theoretical ones; a system of ideas that aspires both to explain the world and to change it.[5]

Indeterminate sex: has three different meanings. Historically, in some jurisdictions, birth certificates allowed for "indeterminate sex" in cases where the sex of a stillborn child, or miscarried premature child, could not be determined.[6] More recently, "indeterminate" has referred to an intersex person.

Under the current *Australian Government Guidelines on the recognition of Sex and Gender* (2013), "indeterminate" covers a person's self-defined, fluid gender identity[7] (see *gender identity*).

Intersex: Means disorder of sexual development (DSD) or difference of sexual development.

IOC: International Olympic Committee

Lesbian *(biological)*: means biological women who are attracted to women.

Lesbian *(transgender)*: means person A, who identifies as a woman regardless of their birth sex, who is sexually attracted to person B, who identifies as a woman regardless of their birth sex.

Consequently, two men can identify as women and be in a lesbian relationship (see *gender orientation*).

LGBTIQ+: is the acronym for lesbian, gay, bisexual, transsexual, intersex, queer or questioning, plus more (see definitions of each of these terms in this Dictionary of Terms).

Man *(biological)*: means a member of the male biological sex, regardless of age (see also *sex (biological)*).

Man *(transgender)*: means either cismale or a woman who identifies as a man, with or without sex-change surgery (see also *sex (transgender)*).

Non-binary: means not based on two things; for example, a self-defined gender identity that is either on a spectrum of male-to-female, or unrelated to binary sex (e.g. gender diverse, androgynous, pangender, gender queer, inter gender etc.), or genderless (opposite of *binary*).

Normal, normality: means "that which functions according to its design"[8] and, in the context of this book, "normal" denotes the biological nature of humans as male and female (opposite to *queer, transgender, transnormativity*).

Queer theory, Q: "Queer is … *whatever* is at odds with the normal, the legitimate, the dominant."[9] A twin theory to transgender theory. Arguably, the two have morphed together (see *transgender*; opposite of *normal*).

Questioning, Q: A person exploring their sexuality, which is not fixed to their biology.

Same-sex marriage: means marriage between two biological men or two biological women (see *sex (biological)* and different to *transgender marriage*).

SDA: The *Sex Discrimination Act 1984*

Sex *(biological)*: means biological male and female, based on complementary reproductive functions where the male provides sperm and the female provides the ovum.

Sex *(transgender)*: in transgender language, and in Australian laws, *sex* and *gender identity* are now considered to be interchangeable. The *Australian Government Guidelines on the Recognition of Sex and Gender* (2015) says that, although *sex* and *gender identity* are "conceptually distinct, these terms are commonly used interchangeably, including in legislation"[10].

Sex identifier: refers to how a person's sex or gender identity is recorded on official forms. Historically, forms recorded Male or Female. Now, many forms record Male, Female, X (Indeterminate, Unspecified, Intersex); or Male, Female, X; or Male, Female, Other.

Sex recorded at birth *(biological)*: means self-evident, biological sex observed and recorded on a person's birth registration forms.

Sex assigned at birth *(transgender)*: refers to sex being assigned to a newborn, in the same way as a name is assigned as a matter of choice or preference. It implies that, although sex may be assigned at birth, it can also be reassigned later.

Sexual orientation *(biological)*: means heterosexual, gay, lesbian, bisexual; that is, sexual attractions between persons recognised by their biological sex.

Sexual orientation *(transgender)*: is better described as *gender* orientation (see *gender orientation*).

Definitions And Terms

SOGII: means sexual orientation, gender identity and intersex.

T, Transgender, trans: refers to persons being recognised by their socially constructed *gender identity* in place of their biological sex (see also *queer theory*; opposite is *sex (biological)*).

Transsexual, medically transitioned: means a person who undergoes sex-reassignment surgery and hormonal treatment to be reassigned as a member of the opposite sex to their sex recorded at birth. They are regarded as *binary* as they identify as the opposite of their sex at birth.

Transsexual, socially transitioned: means a person who socially identifies – by their gender-related identity, appearance or mannerisms or other gender-related characteristics – as a member of the opposite sex to their sex recorded at birth, without medical intervention. For the purposes of this book, the socially transitioned are considered *non-binary*, because they can also transition to another fluid *gender identity*.

Transgenderism, ideology of: means political advocacy for legal and cultural changes so that new laws and customs educate and encourage people, including children, to explore gender fluidity. It advocates that laws give protected attribute status to a person's self-defined gender identity and gender orientation (see *ideology*).

Transgender marriage: means "two people" are legally eligible to marry regardless of their gender identity or gender orientation. It is also known as *gender fluid marriage*. Following Australia's 2017 ABS survey on marriage, the amended federal *Marriage Act 1961* now recognises both transgender marriage and same-sex marriage.

Transnormativity: means political advocacy for wide-ranging changes to the law and culture to recognise all persons in transgender terms rather than as biological male and female (see *transgenderism*; opposite to *heteronormativity (transgender)*).

Unspecified sex: means a person who has no sex/gender identity, particularly with reference to a person in the process of reassignment from their biological sex to a different sex or gender identity.

Woman *(biological)*: means a member of the female biological sex, regardless of age (see also *sex (biological)*).

Woman *(transgender)*: means either cisfemale, or a man who identifies as a woman, with or without sex-change surgery (see also *sex (transgender)*).

"X" marker: means the X (Indeterminate, Unspecified, Intersex) identifier on official Australian government documents, including passports and marriage registration forms. A variation is found on Australian Capital Territory and South Australian birth registration forms (see *Indeterminate, Unspecified, Intersex*).

Yogyakarta Principles: a set of principles relating to sexual/ gender orientation and gender identity, intended to formulate international human rights principles for lesbian, gay, bisexual, transgender people and intersex people. It was developed at a meeting of the International Commission of Jurists, the International Service for Human Rights and human rights advocacy groups at Yogyakarta, Indonesia, in November 2006. Further LGBTIQ rights were added in September 2017.

Endnotes

1. "binary", *Oxford Living Dictionaries.*
   https://en.oxforddictionaries.com/definition/us/binary Accessed 16 June 2017.

2. Chris Barker, *Cultural Studies: Theory and Practice*, Sage, London, 2005; pg. 448.

3. "genus", *Oxford Living Dictionary.*
   https://en.oxforddictionaries.com/definition/genus Accessed 24 September 2017.

4. Federal *Sex Discrimination Act 1984,* Section 4, as compiled 1 July 2016.
   https://www.legislation.gov.au/Details/C2016C00880

5. "ideology", *Encyclopedia Britannica.*
   https://www.britannica.com/topic/ideology-society Accessed 17 June 2017.

6. *Sex Files: the legal recognition of sex in documents and government records,*
   Australian Human Rights Commission 2009, pg. 23.
   https://www.humanrights.gov.au/our-work/sexual-orientation-sex-gender-identity/publications/sex-files-legal-recognition-sex Accessed 5 June 2017.

7. *Australian Government Guidelines on the Recognition of Sex and Gender*
   (July 2013, Updated November 2015), pg. 9.
   https://www.ag.gov.au/Publications/Documents/AustralianGovernmentGuidelinesontheRecognitionofSexandGender/AustralianGovernmentGuidelinesontheRecognitionofSexandGender.PDF Accessed 19 June 2017.

8. CD King, "The meaning of normal", *Yale Journal of Biology and Medicine,*
   1945;18:493501, pgs. 493-494.
   https://www.ncbi.nlm.nih.gov/pmc/articles/PMC2601549/pdf/yjbm00493-0064.pdf Accessed 15 December 2017.

9. David M. Halperin, *Saint Foucault: Towards a Gay Hagiography,* New York: Oxford University Press, 1995, pg. 62.

10. *Australian Government Guidelines on the Recognition of Sex and Gender,*
    Attorney General's Department, Australian Government, (July 2013, Updated November 2015), Op. cit., pg. 4.